Engineering as a field of university study in India has grown by leaps and bounds in the past 25 years, most of it in private institutions and of highly varied quality, from the internationally renowned Indian Institutes of Technology to low-quality unaided private institutions. It is this huge and varied engineering education system which India depends on to make it a major player in the global economy. Professor Tilak's book—a detailed study of this complex subject based on extensive empirical data—is an essential reading for understanding whether the system as it now exists will be able to fill this role.
   –**Martin Carnoy**, *Vida Jacks Professor of Education and Economics & Lemann Foundation Professor, Stanford University*

Engineering education is one of the most important aspects of Indian higher education and central for India's future economy. It is also not well understood and significant parts of it are subpar. Dr. Tilak has provided a thoughtful data-driven and policy-relevant analysis.
   –**Philip G. Altbach**, *Research Professor and Distinguished Fellow, Center for International Higher Education, Boston College, USA*

This is possibly the first study to provide a systematifvc economic analysis of engineering education in India. Its juxtaposition of the macro-level with the micro-level makes it most valuable for research scholars and policy practitioners in India, while its recognition of the wider international context will interest readers in the outside world.
   –**Deepak Nayyar**, *Emeritus Professor of Economics, Jawaharlal Nehru University, New Delhi; former Vice Chancellor, University of Delhi*

A must reading for higher education policy makers in India, focusing on engineering by a prominent scholar in the field.
–**George Psacharopoulos**, *Adjunct Professor, Global Human Development, Georgetown University; Formerly with London School of Economics and the World Bank*

There are few in India who can match the expertise of Professor Jandhyala B G Tilak in the field of research in higher education especially the economics aspects of education at all levels. As Vice-Chancellor, National University of Educational Planning and Administration, his contributions to the promotion of higher education research are of historic significance. In the emerging decades, India will compete effectively with higher education in U.K. and U.S.A, largely because of valuable services of Prof. Tilak and a few others.

This book surveys the literature of world-renowned writers Robert Solow, Fritz Machlup, Theodoe W Schultz and others with the author's interpretations of their theories applicable to Indian higher engineering education. This book is a valuable addition to the study of higher education in India and aboard.
–**Vedagiri Shanmugasundaram**, *Founder Vice Chancellor, Monomaniam Sundaranar University; Former Director, Reserve Bank of India and IDBI; Senior Visiting Member, Linacre College, University of Oxford*

'Two great sectors are at the heart of higher education's many practical contributions to society through learning and research – engineering and health. In Economics of Engineering Education, Professor Tilak takes us inside engineering education and illuminates the role it plays in development. Get engineering education right, he shows us, and the nation is on track. The solid data and considered judgments in this book are making a crucial contribution to policy, the profession and the next generation that will build India'.
–**Simon Marginson**, *Professor of Higher Education, University of Oxford & Director ESRC/RE Centre for Global Higher Education*

I find this book very useful for evidence- based decisions and informed public policy regarding engineering education. The book illustrates emergence of private education and its impact on access, equity, quality, affordability and related issues currently faced in India. The systematic approach and methodology adopted in the study and credible data may help in framing right policies. Prof. Tilak's book will be useful to recalibrate the current approach to engineering education and offer policy pointers to regain the glory.
–**Bhushan Patwardhan**, *Chairman, National Assessment and Accreditation Council; Former Vice Chairman, University Grants Commission; Distinguished Professor, Interdisciplinary School of Health Sciences, Savitribai Phule Pune University*

Professor J.B.G. Tilak is one of India's best-known social science scholars and an international authority on the Economics of Higher Education. This most recent book is a timely contribution to academic and policy knowledge of engineering education in India. Engineering, with its many variants, civil, mechanical, electrical, and production is a key profession in any economy. As Prof. Tilak shows, engineering education in India has undergone a sea change over the past three decades. The implications of this need to be understood

Jandhyala B. G. Tilak is former Professor and Vice Chancellor, National University of Educational Planning and Administration, India and ICSSR National Fellow. He is an economist of education and is presently Distinguished Professor at the Council for Social Development, New Delhi, and Visiting Professor at Kautilya School of Public Policy, Hyderabad, India. He is also the recipient of the Pranavananda Saraswati award (UGC) for excellence in research in education, Dr Malcolm Adiseshiah award for distinguished contributions to development studies, Inspirational Teacher of the year award and the Devang Mehta award. His recent publication includes *Higher Education, Public Good and Markets* (2018), *Education and Development: Critical Issues in Public Policy and Development* (2018), *Education and Development* (Academic Foundation 2018), *Dilemmas in Reforming Higher Education in India* (2018) and *Trade in Higher Education* (2011).

Economics of Engineering Education in India

This volume focuses on the key trends and major developments in engineering education in India and reflects on the effects and challenges of its expansion on economic growth and development.

Analysing several dimensions relating to the status and growth of engineering education, this book:

— Highlights, in the overall policy environment, the rapid growth of engineering education, imbalances in the growth between different branches of engineering education, changing trends and patterns in their growth, quality of education, gender inequality, and inequality by caste, region and economic status and labour market conditions that influence the demand for engineering education.
— Reflects on the rapid growth of private sector in engineering education and its effects on equitable access, quality and other dimensions of higher education, and on overall development of the economy.
— Investigates the socio-economic characteristics of the students going to private colleges/universities, financing by the government vis-à-vis students/households, the unsteady growth in public financing of engineering education and educational loans as a method of financing.
— Explores the reasons behind the increasing demand of engineering education and the factors that have contributed to the rise of electronics engineering, computer science engineering and information technology-related areas of engineering as against some conventionally popular disciplines of engineering.

This volume will be of interest to students, teachers and researchers of education, higher education, engineering education, economics of education, sociology of education, and education and public policy. It will also be useful for policymakers and administrators in higher education, engineering/technical education in BRIC countries, and those interested in the study and growth of engineering education in advanced as well as emerging economies.

for development with deliberate expansion of the STEM fields in which Engineering plays an important role. By engaging theories and ideas about human capital development thorough empirical inquiry based on secondary and primary data, the author strengthens the merit of the book. Furthermore, by using a methodological approach beyond univariate account to engage in multivariate analysis that provides a rich and multidimensional analysis, the book informs the reader of the complexity of the interactions between the explanatory factors in the educational sector and entrenched socially significant determinants such as gender, caste, and region/state, as well as the dynamics of the public and private sectors of higher education and its financing. In addition to researchers and policymakers in the public and private sectors, this book will be an invaluable source to other education stakeholders including students, international agencies, and NGOs in their respective efforts to understand and effectively tackle the development of inclusive human resources.

–N'Dri Assié-Lumumba, *Professor, Cornell University & President, World Council of Comparative Education Societies* by both private and public institutions and, of course, students. This is the purpose of this excellent study.

–**W. John Morgan**, *Leverhulme Emeritus Fellow, Wales Institute of Social and Economic Research, Data, and Methods (WISERD), Cardiff University*

This commendable book presents a critical analysis of some of the major challenges in engineering education using valuable primary and secondary data. These challenges include: overzealous expansion and the resultant supply-demand mismatches which are reflected in high rates of unemployment, inequities in education by gender, caste/religion, and region, poor quality of education as revealed in lower employability of graduates besides, limited public financing and issues relating to affordability.

This rigorous research study systematically analyses some of these critical issues in engineering education in India with a futuristic perspective. I have no doubt that it will attract the attention of academia as well as administrators and policy makers. Given the paucity of systematically conducted research studies in this field, this study undoubtedly makes an invaluable reading on the subject of a great contemporary relevance.

–**Narendra Jadhav**, *Former Vice Chancellor, Savitribai Phule (Pune) University; Former Member, Planning Commission; Former Member of Indian Parliament, Rajya Sabha*

Economics of Engineering Education in India is an insightful new book by Jandhyala B G Tilak describing and analyzing in depth the remarkable growth, issues related to sources of funding, quality, employment of graduates, and policies for public and private engineering education in India. Professor Tilak is a well-known and respected scholar who recognizes the significance of highly skilled human capital in engineering fields to sustained per capita economic growth. This and more universal basic education are desperately needed for broader development in India. As this occurs, this book, which is likely to become the go-to source, can help make the provision of good quality engineering education's vital role more economically efficient.

–**Walter W. McMahon**, *Professor of Economics, and of Education, University of Illinois*

This is an impressive single-authored book on a timely topic painstakingly researched by an eminent scholar, authoritatively articulating ideas in the discourses on the emergence and quest for future direction of higher education

Economics of Engineering Education in India
Growing Challenges of Expansion, Excellence and Equity

Jandhyala B. G. Tilak

LONDON AND NEW YORK   ICSSR

First published 2024
by Routledge
4 Park Square, Milton Park, Abingdon, Oxon OX14 4RN

and by Routledge
605 Third Avenue, New York, NY 10158

Routledge is an imprint of the Taylor & Francis Group, an informa business

© 2024 Indian Council of Social Sciences Research (ICSSR) and Jandhyala B. G. Tilak

The right of Jandhyala B. G. Tilak to be identified as author of this work has been asserted in accordance with sections 77 and 78 of the Copyright, Designs and Patents Act 1988.

All rights reserved. No part of this book may be reprinted or reproduced or utilised in any form or by any electronic, mechanical, or other means, now known or hereafter invented, including photocopying and recording, or in any information storage or retrieval system, without permission in writing from the publishers.

Trademark notice: Product or corporate names may be trademarks or registered trademarks, and are used only for identification and explanation without intent to infringe.

British Library Cataloguing-in-Publication Data
A catalogue record for this book is available from the British Library

ISBN: 978-1-032-38572-3 (hbk)
ISBN: 978-1-032-55608-6 (pbk)
ISBN: 978-1-003-43022-3 (ebk)

DOI: 10.4324/9781003430223

Typeset in Sabon
by codeMantra

*With loving pranams at the Lotus Feet of
my beloved Swami*

Sri Sathya Sai Baba,

this book is dedicated to the memory of my
parents

Kunjali Lalita & Santisri Venkateswara Sastry

Contents

List of figures	*xiii*
List of tables	*xvii*
Acknowledgements	*xxi*

1 Introduction and Context — 1

PART I

2 Engineering Education in India: Challenges of Growth and Inequalities — 15

3 Emergent Challenges of Engineering Education in India: Quality, Finances and Employment — 63

PART II

4 Who Goes to Private Engineering Colleges and Why? — 117

5 Students' Choice of 'Modern' versus 'Traditional' Streams of Engineering Education — 147

6 Family Expenditure on Engineering Education and Its Determinants — 173

7 Funding of Engineering Education: Scholarships, Other Financial Assistance and Education Loans — 200

8 Students' Perceptions on Quality of Engineering Education — 217

9 Employability, Employment and Earnings of Engineering Graduates — 249

PART III

10 Summary, Conclusions and Policy Challenges 275

Appendix A (to Part I) *293*
Appendix B (to Part II) *307*
References *313*
Index *337*

Figures

2.1	Changing Distribution of Enrolments among Major Areas of Study in Higher Education (%)	29
2.2	Trends in Enrolments in Major Disciplines in Higher Education (%)	30
2.3	Declining Numbers of Registrants for Joint Entrance Examination for Admission in Engineering Studies, 2014–2020	32
2.4	Economic Growth and Number of Engineering Institutions (per One Million Population), 2018–19	35
2.5	Enrolment as a Percentage of Intake in Engineering Education by Region (2012–13 and 2018–19)	37
2.6	Enrolment as a Percentage of Intake in Engineering Education in India by States (2012–13 and 2018–19)	38
2.7	State-Wise Engineering Institutions per One Million Population in India (2018–19)	45
2.8	Regional Concentration of Institutions, Intake and Enrolment in Engineering Education, 2018–19 (%)	46
2.9	Ratio of Regional Concentration of Engineering Institutions	47
2.10	Distribution of Enrolments in Higher Education across Various Branches by Gender (2018–19)	49
2.11	Distribution of Enrolments in Engineering Education by Household Quintiles (%)	53
2.12	Popular Streams of Engineering and Technology, 2019–20 (Enrolment as a Percentage of Total Enrolments in Engineering Education)	54
2.13	Growth in Enrolments in Engineering Education by Major Categories of Sub-Streams (%)	56
2.14	Enrolment as Percentage of Intake in Major Categories of Sub-Streams of Engineering Education	58
2.15	Level-Wise Imbalance (Distribution of Enrolments) in Engineering Education, 2018–19 (%)	60
3.1	Faculty Vacancy as a Percentage of Total Sanctioned Strength in IITs, 2019	71

xiv *Economics of Engineering Education in India*

3.2	Faculty in Engineering and Technology Institutions	71
3.3	Growth in the Number of PhD Degrees Awarded in Universities	72
3.4	Rate of Growth in the Number of PhDs Awarded and Undergraduate Enrolments in Engineering and Technology (%)	73
3.5	Growth in the Number of PhDs Awarded in Relation to Undergraduate Outturn in Engineering and Technology in India	74
3.6	'Duplicate' Faculty in Engineering Colleges (%)	75
3.7	AICTE-Approved 'Progressive Closure' of Engineering and Technology Institutions	77
3.8	Number of Vacant Student Seats in Engineering and Technology Institutions	78
3.9	Expenditure on Technical Education as a Proportion of Total Expenditure on Education and GDP (%)	81
3.10	Public Expenditure on Technical Education as a Percentage of Total Expenditure on Education, 2015–16 and 2017–18	85
3.11	Public Expenditure on Engineering Education as a Percentage of Total Expenditure on Technical Education (States and Union Territories)	86
3.12	Household Expenditure on Higher Education per Student by Major Area of Study (₹ per Annum)	90
3.13	Household Expenditure on Fees and Other Items in Engineering Education by Household Consumption Quintiles	93
3.14	Fluctuating Rate of Hiring of Engineers (%)	96
3.15	Number of Placements as a Percentage of Enrolment in Engineering Education by Major Categories of Streams	97
3.16	Employability of Engineer Graduates (BE/BTech) (%)	98
3.17	Employability and the Number of Engineering Colleges in States	99
3.18	Job Role Preferences of Engineering Graduates	103
3.19	Engineering Graduates' Expectations on Salary (₹ in Lakhs per Annum)	104
3.20	Performance of the Engineering Education System in India	106
6.1	Public and Private (Household) Expenditure on Tertiary Education in OECD Countries, 2017	174
6.2	Family Expenditure (₹) on Engineering Education by Type of Educational Institutions	188
6.3	Family Expenditure (₹) on Engineering Education by Items and by Income Group	190
6.4	Average Tuition Fees by Students in Selected Engineering Education Institutions (₹ per annum)	196
7.1	Annual Average Amount of Financial Assistance Received by the Students by Annual Income of the Family (₹ in Thousands)	204
7.2	Percentage of Students Availing Educational Loans by Annual Income of the Family	207

8.1	Students' Opinion of Current Subject Knowledge Compared to When They Entered the Institution (Distribution of Frequency)	220
8.2	Students' Opinion on Confidence in Academic Abilities Compared to When They Entered the Institution (Distribution of Frequency)	220
8.3	Percentage of Students Reporting That Their Current Knowledge and Abilities are 'Stronger' or 'Much Stronger' than at the Time of Admission in the Institution	221
8.4	Students' Perceptions about the Quality of Their Education	224
8.5	Overall Confidence of Engineering Students (in All Branches in All Institutions)	226
8.6	How Many Students Have Taken Courses Outside Primary/Major? *(%)*	229
8.7	Students' Participation in Various Study-Related Activities	231
8.8	Participation of Students in Academic Activities (% of Students)	233
8.9	Time Use by the Engineering Students in India	234
8.10	'Used' and 'Never Used' Teaching Methods	236
8.11	'Frequently' Used Methods of Evaluation in Engineering Education, Response by Students (%)	237
9.1	Employability of Engineering (%) Graduates by Stream of Study, 2018 and 2022	257
9.2	Annual Earnings of Males in India by Educational Level, 2006 (₹)	258
9.3	Starting Average Annual Salaries of Engineering Graduates in India (₹ in Thousands)	259

Tables

1.1	Sample Size and Distribution of the Primary Survey	9
2.1	Growth of Engineering Institutions and Enrolment in India	27
2.2	Growth of Institutions and Intake in Engineering Education by Type of Institution	33
2.3	State-Wise Intake in Government and Private Engineering Institutions (2018–19)	34
2.4	Factors that influence Growth of Engineering Institutions	37
2.5	Number of Engineering Institutions in India by States, 2012–13 and 2018–19	39
2.6	Enrolments in Engineering Education per One Million Population, 2012–13 and 2018–19	40
2.7	State-Wise Concentration Ratio of Engineering Education Institutions	46
2.8	Regional Concentration of Engineering Education Institutions and Intakes by Management (2012–13 and 2018–19)	48
2.9	Women Enrolment in Total Higher and Engineering Education	50
2.10	Enrolment of Scheduled Castes and Scheduled Tribes in Engineering Education (% of Total Enrolment in Engineering & Technology)	51
2.11	Enrolments in the First Year of Engineering Degree Studies: Distribution by Social Category (2012–13 to 2018–19)	52
2.12	Region-Wise Pattern of the of Enrolments in the First Year of Engineering Studies in 2018–19 by Social Category	52
2.13	Enrolment in Engineering (First Degree) Programmes by Sub-Stream (%)	55
2.14	Stream-Wise Distribution of Enrolments in Engineering Education by Gender (%)	57
3.1	Top 15 Engineering Institutions in National Institute of Ranking Framework (NIRF), 2023	66
3.2	Indian Institutes in QS Rankings of World Universities, 2023	67
3.3	AICTE Projections: Programmed Requirement of Engineering Degree-Level Institutions and Admission Capacity	76

3.4	Union and States' Public Expenditure on Technical Education (₹ in Crores in 2011–12 Prices)	82
3.5	Union Government Expenditure on Select Institutions of Total Technical Education (Revenue Account) (₹ in Crores) in Constant Prices	83
3.6	Public Expenditure on Engineering and Technical Education (States and Union Territories) (₹ in Crores) in 2011–12 prices	84
3.7	Public Expenditure on Scholarships in Technical Education in Real Prices (States and Union Territories) (₹ in Crores at 2011–12 Prices)	87
3.8	Household Expenditure on Higher Education as Proportion of Total Household Consumption Expenditure across Major Areas (%)	90
3.9	Annual Household Expenditure on Engineering Education per Annum per Student (2017–18)	91
3.10	Annual Average Household Expenditure on Engineering Education by Select Socio-Economic Groups and Types of Institutions (₹)	92
3.11	Employability of Engineering Graduates by Sub-Stream (%)	99
4.1	Distribution of Engineering Students in Different Types of Institutions by Their Socio-Economic Profile	122
4.2	Determinants of Students' Choice in Favour of Private Engineering Institutions (against Public Institutions): Probit Estimates	130
5.1	Socio-Economic and Education Profile of Engineering Students: Distribution by the Type of Stream of Study	149
5.2	Probit Estimate of Students' Choice of Streams of Study in Engineering Education	167
6.1	Household Expenditure on Higher Education per Student by Major Area of Study (₹ per Annum)	175
6.2	Household Expenditure on Higher Education in India (₹ per Student/per Annum)	176
6.3	Family Expenditure on Engineering Education per Student, by Items of Expenditure (₹ per Annum)	187
6.4	Family Expenditure on Engineering Education per Student per Annum, by Gender, Caste and Type of Institution (₹ per Annum)	188
6.5	OLS Estimate of the Determinants of Family Expenditure on Engineering Education	195
6.6	Tuition Fees Paid by Students as a Function of Student Characteristics and Type of Institution	197
7.1	Percentage of Students Who Received Financial Assistance by Type of Institution and Department of Study	202
7.2	Average Amount of Financial Assistance Received by Students by Type of Institution and Department of Study (₹ per Annum)	203

7.3	Number of Students Who Received Educational Loan by Type of Institution and Department of Study	206
7.4	Who Gets Educational Loans? Logit Estimates of Determinants	209
7.5	Amount of Educational Loan Received by Students and by Type of Institution and Department of Study	211
7.6	OLS Estimates of the Determinants of Amount of Educational Loan Received by Students	213
8.1	Current Knowledge and Abilities Compared to the Time of Admission in Engineering Studies (Percentage of Students Who Reported 'Stronger' or 'Much Stronger')	222
8.2	Assessment of Quality of Their Graduates by Engineering Institutions and by Employers	224
8.3	Students' Perceptions about Quality of Their Education	225
8.4	Confidence of the Students on Their Preparedness for Future	226
8.5	Subjects Studied in Computer Science Engineering Course	227
8.6	Structure of Coursework and Student Study Patterns	228
8.7	How Many Students have Taken the following Types of Courses and How Many Courses?	230
8.8	Students' Participation in Internships and Other Programmes (% of All Students)	232
8.9	How Do Engineering Students Spend Their Time (Hours per Week)	234
8.10	Faculty with PhD Degrees in Selected Engineering Institutions in Three States	238
8.11	Faculty in Public versus Private Institutions (Proportion of Faculty)	239
8A.1	Current Knowledge, Abilities and Skills Compared to the Time of Entry into This Institution	242
8A.2	Participation of Students in Academic Activities	245
8A.3	Teaching Methods Used in Public versus Private Engineering Institutions	247
8A.4	Frequency in the Use of Methods of Evaluation	248
9.1	Private and Social Rates of Return to Higher Education by Gender in India, 2006 (%)	250
9.2	Estimates of Mincerian Rates of Return by Gender in India, 2006	250
9.3	Employment Profiles of Engineering Graduates (Engineering Students Who Have Got Job Offers in Campus Recruitment)	255
9.4	Logit Estimates of the Employment Probabilities of Engineering Graduates	263
9.5	OLS Estimate of the Annual Earnings of Engineering Graduates	269

Appendix A

A1	Indicators on Science and Technology (2010–18)	293
A2	Growth of Engineering Institutions in India	294
A3	AICTE Approved Institutions Offering Engineering Education 2020 (Degree and above Level)	294
A4	Enrolment as a Percentage of Intakes in Engineering Education in States (2012–13 and 2018–19)	295
A5	Distribution of Engineering Institutions and Population (Age Group 18–23) 2012–13 and 2018–19	296
A6	Government and Private Engineering Institutions and Intake: Distribution across States (%) 2018–19	297
A7	Enrolment in the First Year of Engineering in 2018–19 by Social Category (%)	299
A8	Regional Distribution of Institutions, Intake and Enrolment in Engineering Education, 2018–19 (%)	299
A9	Distribution of Enrolments in Higher Education across Various Branches by Gender (2018–19)	300
A10	Growth in Enrolments in Major Categories of Streams of Engineering	300
A11	Trends in Enrolments in Major Disciplines in Higher Education	301
A12	Number of Vacant/Unfilled Student Places in Engineering/Technology Institutions	302
A13	Enrolment as a Percentage of Intake in Major Categories of Engineering Streams	302
A14	Faculty Vacancies in IITs, 2019	302
A15	Faculty in Engineering/Technology Institutions	303
A16	Rate of Growth Rate in the Number of PhDs Awarded and Enrolment in Undergraduate Courses in Engineering and Technology (%)	303
A17	Number of PhDs Awarded in Engineering/Technology as a Proportion of Outturn of Undergraduate Programs (%)	303
A18	Number of Doctorate Degrees Produced in Universities	304
A19	Expenditure on Technical Education as a Share of Total Expenditure on Education (%)	305
A20	Public Expenditure on Engineering Education as a Percentage of Total Expenditure on Technical Education (States and Union Territories)	305
A21	India: Estimated Stock of Engineers, 1971–2003	306

Appendix B

B1	Definition and Notation of the Variables Used in the Statistical Analysis (in Chapters 4–8)	307
B2	Explanation on Some Terms/Variables	310
B3	Summary Statistics of the Variables Used in the Probit Analysis	311

Acknowledgements

In the course of the study, I have immensely benefitted from advice, comments, cooperation and support received from many scholars and institutions.

This book is an outcome of a research study financed by the Indian Council of Social Science Research, New Delhi, through its programme of National Fellows. I am grateful to the ICSSR for awarding the National Fellowship to me. ICSSR has also graciously granted permission to me to publish it. I am particularly grateful to Professor V.K. Malhotra, the then Member Secretary, ICSSR, for taking special interest in facilitating smooth process for publication.

The primary data that formed the basis for Part II of the study was collected in the context of a wider study financed by Stanford University and National University of Educational Planning and Administration. Their cooperation is highly appreciated. The encouragement and support extended by Professors Martin Carnoy, Prashant Lloyalka and Raffiq Dossani of Stanford University, who also participated in the collection of primary data from students and institutions in India, are highly appreciated. The support received from Professors Ved Prakash and R. Govinda, the then Vice Chancellors of National University of Educational Planning and Administration, is duly acknowledged. Thanks are also due to the students, heads and other authorities of various institutions surveyed for the study for their enthusiastic cooperation.

Mr Shibananda Nayak helped in processing the data, and Dr Pradeep Kumar Choudhury, Assistant Professor in Economics, Zakir Husian Centre for Educational Studies, Jawaharlal Nehru University, and Dr J. Viswanath, India EXIM Bank have provided valuable statistical and research assistance. Pradeep Choudhury has also co-authored Chapters 2 and 3 (Part I) jointly with me.

While the study was in progress, some of the results were published in a few professional journals. Acknowledgements to the respective journals are made separately. One paper was presented in the Seventeenth World Conference of the Comparative Education Societies, Cancún, Mexico. The valuable comments by the editors, the referees of the respective journals and others, particularly Professors Robert Arnove, Simon Marginson, Martin Carnoy, N'Dri T. Assié-Lumumba, Zehila Babaci-Wilhite, Baris Uslu, Süphan Nasir, Jürgen Rudolph, Iman Tohidian, M. Anandkrishnan, Seema Singh, A.

Mathew and others, are acknowledged with gratitude. The external reviewers of Routledge/Taylor & Francis have also offered valuable suggestions, which led to elaboration of details on a few aspects. I am also sincerely grateful to Professors H. Ramachandran, Yogindra K. Alagh and P.R. Panchamukhi for their encouragement and support and also to Professors R.S. Deshpande, Anil Sahasrabudhe, M.R. Narayana and K. Narayanan for their timely help in data collection. I also acknowledge with gratitude the generous observations on the book by Professors Martin Carnoy, Philip G. Altbach, Narendra Jadhav, Walter W. McMahon, Simon Marginson, William John Morgan, Deepak Nayyar, Bhushan Patwardhan, George Psacharopoulos, V. Shanmugasundaram and N'Dri Assié-Lumumba.

The Council for Social Development, New Delhi, has hosted me during the Fellowship. I am grateful to Professor Muchkund Dubey, President, CSD, for providing the affiliation and for showing keen interest in my work, and to all the faculty and staff for the cooperation and support extended to me. I am also thankful to Routledge for bringing out this book in the present attractive form.

Much of the draft of the study was finalised sitting at home during the COVID-19 crisis, which caused national lockdown and imposition of several kinds of restrictions. This affected the nature and kind of academic work in several ways. My wife Punya has been, as always, highly tolerant and immensely supportive of my working at home and outside. I simply say, my greatest appreciation is for her love, support and appreciation.

Jandhyala B. G. Tilak

The author and the publishers acknowledge with gratitude the gracious permission given by the editors/publishers of the following journals/books to use here in part or full the material published by the author in their respective journals/books:

Global Comparative Education: Journal of the World Council of Comparative Education Societies. Vol. 4 (2020) "Who Goes to Private Colleges in India and Why?"

Yükseköğretim Dergisi/Journal of Higher Education, Vol.10 (2020) "Determinants of Students' Choice of Engineering Disciplines in India"

Higher Education Governance and Policy Vol. 1 (2020) "Engineering Graduates in India: Determinants of Employment and Earnings"

Journal of Higher Education Policy and Leadership, Vol.1 (2020) "How do Students Finance their Higher Education in India?"

Journal of Governance and Public Policy, Vol. 11 (2021) "Family Expenditure on Engineering Education in India and its Determinants"

Journal of Applied Learning and Teaching (Kaplan Institute) Vol. 4 (2021) "Students' Perspectives on Quality of Engineering Education"

Journal of Contemporary Education Research Vol. 5 (2021) "Employment and Employability of Engineering Graduates in India"

Changing Higher Education in India, London: Bloomsbury Academic, 2022, "Engineering Education in India"

1 Introduction and Context

Engineering Education and Development

Investment in technical education makes a vital contribution to economic growth in terms of higher rates of growth of economy's productivity. This is regarded as crucial to the development of developing countries and to their ability to compete in the global economy. Higher technical education, specifically engineering education, is one of the most important components of human capital. This, in fact, is seen as 'specialised human capital'. The returns to such specialised human capital are estimated to be very high. Solow (1960) found that a mere one-eighth of the growth in the US was due to increase of inputs of labour and capital, and a major proportion of the unexplained productivity was due to 'technical progress', which is attributable mostly to investment in technical education. Nations have "no other field of investment that yields returns of this order" (Machlup, 1962, p. 189). In addition to direct returns, the externalities, including 'dynamic externalities', associated with investment in such specialised human capital are immense in any society (Abramovitz, 1989, pp. 40–41; Birdsall, 1996). As Schultz (1988) argued, increasing returns to total factor productivity were due to investment in specialised human capital formed through investment in higher technical and professional education, including engineering and technology; this kind of human capital checks the general pattern of diminishing returns and even contributes to increasing returns (see also Jorgenson & Griliches, 1967).

Recognising the potentially significant contribution of engineering education, the Government of India has laid special emphasis on the development of technical education. Though the first institute imparting engineering education was set up in India in 1842 in Guindy, Madras, and the first college in 1847 in Roorkee, it is only after independence that the development of engineering education picked up with the establishments of the Indian Institutes of Technology (IITs) in the 1950s. Compared to a steady slow growth during the first couple of decades after independence, there was a spurt in the growth of engineering colleges in the following decades – first with the growth of government and government-aided private colleges[1] and later with

DOI: 10.4324/9781003430223-1

the rapid growth of fee-dependent or self-financing private colleges and universities which are also generally known as unaided private institutions.

In all, during the post-independence period, there has been an impressive expansion of engineering education in the country that is regarded as without parallel anywhere else in the world. The achievement has been impressive from an almost zero professional education base to a large number of technological institutes of high standard – more than 20 IITs, 30 National Institutes of Technology (NITs), above 3,000 engineering colleges and 3,500 engineering polytechnics. These numbers do not include the vast network of about 320 science and technology institutions and laboratories of which 240 are major ones. All this is in addition to one of the biggest edifices in the world of higher education system – about 1,150 universities (including institutions deemed to be universities) and 43,000 colleges. All these institutions could contribute to rapid accumulation of specialised human capital. Accordingly, India could produce one of the largest reservoirs of scientific and technical manpower.

The economic returns to technical education in India are estimated to be fairly high. For example, in a growth accounting exercise, Mathur (1987) estimated the contribution of 'technological change' to economic growth in India to be quite significant. Estimates of rates of return (based on Mincerian earnings function) to scientific and technical education varied between 17.4 per cent (undergraduate Diploma) and 70.8 per cent (PhD degree). Similar high rates of return to scientific and technical education were also reported by Duraisamy and Duraisamy (1993) and Nalla-Gounden (1994). Recent estimates of rates of return for engineering education put the figure at 22 per cent for men in 2006 (Carnoy et al., 2012). Higher education contributes to technology achievement index (Tilak, 2003a); higher technical and professional education like engineering may be more significantly related to technology achievement index. Technical education is considered as a major instrument to fuel the engine for rapid and sustainable economic growth (Yadav & Yadav, 2010). Not only in terms of economic rates of return, the importance of higher education in overall development – income distribution, reduction in poverty and human development – is widely recognised (Tilak, 2003a).

Problem, Scope and Research Issues

India has entered the phase of rapid globalisation, and to be successful with globalisation policies, the country requires high-quality human capital. Accordingly, higher education, more specifically professional and technical education, in particular engineering education, has expanded rapidly over the years. The higher education scene is drastically changing in terms of demographics, economics, public policy and student preferences. Enrolments in engineering (and technology) experienced more than 100 times increase from 37,000 in 1960–61 to 38 lakh by 2019–20. As a proportion of total enrolments, students in engineering increased from about 5 per cent to nearly 16 per cent in 2015–16, which declined to 11 per cent, as described in detail in Chapter 2.

The rather unprecedented growth in engineering education in India has to be analysed in great detail, as it has serious implications for several aspects of development of higher education. The growth of engineering institutions, and private universities and colleges in particular, is an important feature of India's higher education expansion of the last two to three decades. Along with the growth in engineering education, inequalities by gender, social and economic characteristics of population in their participation in it also became sharp. Further, as the growth has been unplanned, it becomes unsustainable: in some states, the growth has already started experiencing decline. Further, the growth has been quite uneven across the states; growth in engineering education has been at the cost of other disciplines of study, and even within the area of engineering only a few disciplines – electronics engineering, computer engineering and related modern IT-related disciplines – experienced high demand, again at the cost of other areas of study. As the IT-related engineering education has become popular, other standard and important areas of engineering education have become less attractive. It will be interesting to examine the factors that explain the growth in the modern computer and related engineering and the low demand for other disciplines.

Further, the rapid growth in private engineering institutions seems to be displacing the public sector, as already private institutions form an alarming proportion of the total. Rather, much of the growth in higher education, including specifically engineering education, has taken place in the private sector. There is a significant change in the character of private partners in higher and technical education in India. People with some money in the 1950s and the 1960s used to donate to public institutions or set up philanthropy-based private schools and colleges; today, though, those with even a small fraction of that money prefer to set up private self-financing colleges or institutions deemed to be universities (Tilak, 2014, p. 35). Investment in higher education institutions is found to be the most rewarding and least risky one, yielding quick and very high pay-offs, with minimum risk of investment in all other sectors of the economy. Philanthropy and charity motives of investing in higher education have been replaced with profit motives and commercial interests. While the earlier involvement of different technical institutions in the country was with educational and cultural motives, the objective of recent establishment of private engineering institutions is strictly commercial. There is a phenomenal growth of profit-oriented commercial institutions in India after the 1990s compared to the philanthropy-based private institutions of the past. Many private institutions in technical and engineering education, though described *de jure* as charitable or not-for-profit institutions, are *de facto* profit-making institutions (Tilak, 2012). These institutions have largely contributed to vulgar forms of commercialisation in technical education in India.

The emergence of "a class of rich and well-to-do people consisting of politicians, top bureaucrats, business executives, small and big industrialists, traders, businessmen, technocrats, professionals in independent private practice a n d large land holders" and the nexus between all of them have helped in the spiralling growth of these private institutions (Kothari, 1986). It will be very valuable to analyse the growth of private engineering education in the country and its implications and the factors that contributed to such a rapid growth. The growth of private higher education has been remarkable in southern region of the country and not in other regions. There is also the phenomenon of 'excess demand' that may explain increase in the numbers of students going for private institutions. There may be several other social, economic and other factors. It is proposed to analyse some of these factors.

Rapid growth of private sector may have effects on quality and value/character-building of the students. The employability of graduate students has also become an important issue of concern: some describe our engineering, particularly the information technology (IT) graduates, as 'IT coolies' or 'cyber coolies'. In fact, the rapid growth is closely associated with the declining quality in education and graduate unemployment. The growth reached its peak around 2010–12 and then took a steep a downward trend. But in terms of quality, the sharply declining curve has taken no turn. These trends are not unique to India. In the pursuit of building a knowledge society, many countries have laid special emphasis on technical education, and within technical education, the engineering education has experienced similar trends. The issues of quality and employment are examined with the help of a variety of indicators.

Financing is a major policy instrument of the government, and it reflects the priorities accorded by the government and the society at large to a given activity. The importance attached to technical education in India by the government can be gauged by looking at the allocations to engineering education by the government. Even though investment in professional and technical education like engineering and technology is considered as a specialised human capital yielding high rates of return to the society with strong relationship with productivity and growth, it has not received as much attention as it should have been. During the last quarter century or more, increasing focus has been on private finances. Student fee and cost recovery measures have been on the rise, though the All India Council for Technical Education (AICTE) Committee (1994) has recommended that the government should make a firm commitment to the funding of higher technical education. It is proposed to briefly examine the trends in public finances and also the levels of fees in engineering education. Issues analysed in this regard include scholarships, loans and other issues related to financing of higher education. In this context, analysis of household expenditure on engineering education will provide further insights into the problem of financing higher education, which is examined in detail in the study.

Using secondary data available from multiple sources, this study aims at analysing some of these issues at macro level – the growth, the key challenges and prospects of engineering education in India.

Second, using primary data collected through a survey of students in engineering education, the study aims at analysing further in depth some of these issues such as growth of private education, demand for studies in electronics engineering and IT-related branches of engineering, quality of education, household costs of education, student loans and unemployment and related labour market conditions for graduate engineers.

The interest in the subject has spilled over from a larger inter-country study on higher education. With a view to analyse some of the important trends in higher education with a focus on engineering education, an international comparative study was conducted by Stanford University, concentrating on Brazil, Russia, India and China (BRIC). The global study was conducted with the participation of Martin Carnoy from Stanford University, Isak Frumin from the National Research University of Higher School of Economics in Moscow, Russia, Rong Wang from the Peking University, China, and Jandhyala Tilak from the National University of Educational Planning and Administration, India, with inputs on Brazil gathered from Jacques and Simon Schwartzman Centro de Estudos de Politicas Publicas e Educacao Superior at the Federal University of Minas Gerais, and it was published by the Stanford University Press (Carnoy et al., 2013). The study described in a comparative framework the higher education revolution that has taken place in the age of globalisation and the role of direct state financing, the centrality of the state, ideology of globalisation and the popular pressures on the state for expansion and the direction of expansion in higher education. But there are several issues that can be investigated further in depth with the help of data collected for the study. This is attempted here. In fact, this study examines those questions which did not figure prominently in the larger study; the treatment of data is also completely different. A huge amount of data collected on India (and in other countries) through questionnaires and interviews could not find adequate space in the synthesis study. The student survey provides data on several characteristics of students – their social, economic and academic background, their expenditure on education, their perceptions on the quality of engineering education and similar aspects. Information was also collected through questionnaire and interviews with academic faculty and institutional heads. Such data are rare and of immense value to unravel quite a few key dimensions of expansion of higher engineering education in India. This forms the database for the Part II of the study.

Structure of the Study

This study is organised as follows:

Part I, consisting of two chapters, presents a critical analysis of growth of engineering education in India, the current status, trends over time, inequalities in engineering education by gender, caste, regional, etc., quality of education, shortage of faculty, public and household financing of education, employability and other issues at macro level. All India data and state-wise data, until the most recent years, are used for this purpose. It gives the most up-to-date picture on the current status of engineering education and how it went through different transitions during the last seven decades. It identifies the problems, and critically looks at some of the reforms that have been attempted and some of the major recommendations made by several committees, yet to be implemented for the improvement of engineering education in India. We find sharp differences between public and private institutions in their functioning, performance and with respect to many other characteristics. In addition, we note differences in the growth patterns between various branches of engineering that we group them in this study into 'traditional' (like civil, mechanical, electrical and mechanical and automation) and 'modern' branches of engineering (like electronics, computer sciences, electronics and communications and IT-related engineering sciences). We focus on these two reference groups in the analysis based on primary data in Part II. In addition to the growth of private institutions, excess supply, vacant seats, closure of private institutions, regional imbalances and inequalities between different groups of population, the issues examined here include shortage of faculty, fake/duplicate faculty, production of doctorates, performance of the Indian institutions in global university ranks and national ranking framework, mismatches in the labour market, public and household financing, labour market preferences of engineering graduates and related issues.

With the help of primary data, some of the phenomena observed at macro level are examined in depth in Part II. It consists of six chapters, each devoted to a specific aspect. The questions examined are: students' choices of engineering colleges – public or private; students' choices of disciplines within engineering – modern subjects like electronics, computer engineering and IT-related subjects of engineering vis-à-vis conventional subjects like mechanical, civil or electrical; the extent and determinants of household expenditure on engineering education; student loans as a method of funding engineering education; and quality of engineering education and external efficiency of engineering education – labour market effects, viz. employment and earnings of engineering graduates.

Private education has grown very rapidly in India. How to explain the growing demand for private education? Chapter 4, apart from presenting a socio-economic profile of engineering students in India, examines the factors that explain who goes to private institutions. Within engineering education, all branches of education have not grown at the same pace. Compared to branches like mechanical, civil and electrical engineering education, which had been the crux of engineering education in India for decades, the preference of the students shifted drastically against these disciplines in favour of electronics, computer science and IT-related branches of engineering. Chapter 5 analyses the shift in demand in favour of such disciplines. An important question of wider concern is the increasing costs of higher education. In Chapter 6, an examination of household costs of engineering education is attempted, wherein we note that students spend heavy amounts on acquiring engineering education, both in public and private institutions. Student loans or educational loans have been an important source of financing of higher education. Introduced after restructuring in the early 1990s, educational loans have become popular, particularly for expensive professional and technical education. Loans are expected to help economically weaker sections of the society to improve their participation in higher education. But in practice, not only the poor but also the rich take educational loans. Chapter 7 analyses who gets educational loans and what are the factors that determine the receipt of loans by the students. The large expansion of engineering education seemed to have happened at the expense of quality of education. While many research studies focused on perspectives of the institutions, the policy makers, educational administrators, employer and policy makers, here the attempt in Chapter 8 has been to analyse students' perspectives on the quality of their education. Surprisingly, many students were found to be content and happy with the quality of their institution/education! But one of the most important dimensions of quality refers to employment of graduates. Chapter 9 looks at the students' preferences and labour market conditions faced by graduate engineers in terms of employment/unemployment and wages. A summary of the study, with a few major concluding observations and their policy implications, is given in the concluding Chapter 10 (Part III).

Database and Methodology

The analysis in Part I of the study is based essentially on secondary database. The sources of data used in the study include: All India Survey of Higher Education (AISHE) reports and the Analysis of Budget Expenditure on Education (ABEEE) (both published by the Ministry of Human Resource Development/ Education), AICTE annual reports and online data on its website and annual reports of the University Grants Commission (UGC). For information on labour market aspects, we rely on National Employability Reports (Aspiring Minds), India Skill reports, reports of the National Association of Software and Service Companies (NASSCOM), Federation of Indian Chambers of Commerce and Industry (FICCI), individual institutions' websites and also media reports and reports of several committees constituted by the AICTE. Besides these, we also used the disaggregated individual specific unit-level data available in the latest three education rounds in the National Sample Survey Organisation (NSSO) – the 75th round conducted in July 2017 to June 2018 (NSSO, 2018), the 71st round (NSSO, 2014) and the 64th round (NSSO, 2008).

Part II is based on the data collected through a sample survey of about 7,000 students studying in 48 engineering institutions in four major states in India, namely the National Capital Region of Delhi, Maharashtra, Karnataka and Tamil Nadu, where the growth of private engineering education has been phenomenal. In fact, Karnataka, Maharashtra and Tamil Nadu are the states which took the initial lead in setting up large numbers of institutions. Tamil Nadu and Karnataka are in south India, Maharashtra in the west and Delhi in the north. Andhra Pradesh, a state in the south, where private engineering education has grown very rapidly has not been considered here, as it was intended to have some regional balance in the sample. Engineering education has expanded very fast in the south and western parts of India, followed by a couple of states in north India. It has not expanded much in eastern India, nor in central parts of India. Its presence is rather minimum in central and eastern India. Thus, the sampled states represent the three major regions in the country where engineering education grew rapidly. In Delhi, besides private institutions, government and government-aided private institutions are also proportionately high compared to other states. These states, except Delhi (and along with Andhra Pradesh), are seniors in presaging and setting the tone and pace of engineering education and its privatisation and commercialisation in the country. The survey includes all varieties of engineering institutions of higher education in India, viz. IITs, NITs (known earlier as Regional Colleges of Engineering [RECs]), central and state universities, private universities, government colleges and private colleges – government-aided private, and private (fee-dependent/self-financing) institutions. IITs, NITs and central universities are governed and funded by the union (central) government, while others come under the jurisdiction of the state (provincial) governments. Private institutions are financed though fees, supplemented by other non-state sources, which are generally very small. Private institutions, of course, enjoy access to research and special funds provided by the state under different heads and the students in private institutions can access state-subsidised loans and fee reimbursement by the state. Most of the colleges offer only undergraduate study programmes, while universities, IITs and NITs enrol students for master's level engineering programmes and research programmes as well, in addition to undergraduate studies. But we considered only the students in the final year of first (bachelor's) degree studies in all the selected institutions. Some of the central institutions are known to be 'elite' institutions (IITs are ranked high in any ranking matrix) and many – particularly private ones – as non-elite or 'mass' institutions. The sample of institutions also includes some very old and some newly established ones. Thus, they together are somewhat fairly representative of the country in terms of high growth of engineering education, the geographical spread and the variety of institutions in terms of governance, funding, quality and other features prevalent in Indian higher education, though the numbers of sampled institutions and the students are small compared to the large network of institutions and vast student population. The relative distribution of the sample institutions and students also represents national distribution: the sample consists of one-third public and two-third private institutions; and similar is the distribution of students in the survey.

Some private institutions in Delhi, Tamil Nadu and Karnataka have, of course, refused permission to conduct the survey. So, finally the survey covered only 48 institutions, though we wanted to cover a few more. As a part of the survey, a few interviews and discussions with some students, institutional heads/deans/faculty, management and a few employers, and visits to classrooms and laboratories for observation were also conducted. The following are the details on the sample survey (Table 1.1).

The survey was conducted by the National University of Educational Planning and Administration in 2010–12 in the context of a larger international comparative study of BRIC countries (Carnoy et al., 2013), of which the author is a part. States and colleges were chosen based on purposive random sampling. Other considerations of the wider study determined the choice of institutions. Institutions were chosen based on purposive random sampling, essentially considering the availability of five major streams of engineering education – a few core/traditional – mechanical, civil, electrical, etc., and a few non-core/'modern' – electronics, IT, computer sciences and related disciplines of engineering education at first degree level, and all the students in the final (fourth) year enrolled in those departments formed the sample. While mechanical, civil and electrical engineering are traditionally highly popular branches of engineering, in recent years, electronics engineering, computer science engineering and IT engineering have become more popular. The reason for selecting the fourth (final) year students was their likely higher ability to give nearly comprehensive information about their studies, having completed more than three-fourths of their undergraduate study programme, the ability to decide about their future careers, further studies or employment, and having faced the labour market in the form of on-campus recruitment and the likelihood of already securing job offers in campus recruitment.

The larger study focused on examining the massive expansion of higher education – essentially technical – engineering, in the four BRIC countries. Through a pre-tested student questionnaire, a huge amount of quantitative data, apart from a small amount of qualitative data, were collected in India on a variety of dimensions of engineering education, including those relating to family background, educational and occupational background of parents,

Table 1.1 Sample Size and Distribution of the Primary Survey

State	Institutions			Students		
	Public	Private	Total	Public	Private	Total
Delhi	5	6	11	479	699	1,178
Karnataka	5	9	14	725	1,614	2,339
Maharashtra	4	12	16	750	1,766	2,516
Tamil Nadu	2	5	7	400	190	590
Total	16	32	48	2,354	4,269	6,623
Percentage Distribution	33.3	66.7	100	35.5	64.5	100

caste, religion, features of current education of students – public or private institution – the stream of engineering they are enrolled in, expenditure on engineering degree studies, job offers received and the starting salaries offered and students' perceptions on the quality education they received. The student survey has been extensively relied on in the context of all the chapters in Part II.

Apart from the survey of students through a questionnaire and a questionnaire administered on the institution heads, attempts were made to interview a few key responsible persons – heads, deans or faculty members, information on many key aspects, including on academic, financial and administrative aspects, from all the 48 institutions; but we could not have such interviews in all the 48 institutions. So, we used the information for selective purposes. For example, we used the information to analyse the institutions' perspective on the quality of education in Chapter 8. Our desire to compare and contrast information received from students with those of the institutions on aspects such as student fees, placements and quality of faculty remained unaccomplished. Since the entire Part II is based on a common sample survey of students and the issues examined in various chapters are closely related, one nevertheless finds a little bit repetition.

The descriptive and analytical study uses simple appropriate statistics in this study, including probit model and OLS (ordinary least squares) regression equation. While in Chapters 2 and 3 we largely use a descriptive analytical method, in several chapters in Part II statistical standard tools – probit or logistic regression model and OLS, the two standard and familiar econometric methods used extensively in the literature – are used using STATA software, apart from presenting descriptive statistics. More details on methodology and on the variables chosen are given in the relevant chapters.

Significance of the Study

With clear trends towards massification of higher education, India is on the verge of building a knowledge society. India's development goals include high and sustainable economic growth, production of globally competitive high-quality manpower and to become an economically advanced country, going beyond becoming a powerful Asian tiger economy. Realisation of these and related goals require a high level of human capital, both in quantity and quality. It has been realised that higher professional education – specifically engineering and technology education – has a vital role in boosting the economic growth of the nation.

While there are abundant numbers of studies on higher education in general, research on engineering education in India is rather limited. There are, of course, many valuable reports of committees and commissions on engineering education. Second, studies on higher education, and the reports of the committees on engineering education are largely based on official data collected from institutions, some are based on information collected from other stakeholders, very few studies are based on large surveys of students, with a view to relate their socio-economic background with their choices and behaviour in higher education, costs, employment and other such aspects.[2] But information on socio-economic background of students and their views, opinions and perspectives on education are too valuable to ignore in the context of sound policy making and efficient educational planning. This research study aims at filling this gap to some extent and to contribute to more informed policy making on issues such as planning the growth of engineering education, funding, student fees, loans, curriculum and other aspects. In the context of educational planning and also institutional planning in education, it is very important to know how students/parents decide on their options in higher education. By focusing on students, the study introduces readers to students' choice behaviour as a valuable base for more effective planning of higher education, engineering education in particular.

In the broad context of the National Education Policy 2020 (Government of India, 2020), the policy insights the study offers are quite significant, which are also described at the end of each chapter. It will help in making sound and informed policy with respect to several issues such as the desired levels of growth of engineering education, the effects of rapid growth of private education, improving equitable access to engineering education, public financing of education, including fees, scholarships, and loans, etc., and many other related issues in higher education in India.

Notes

1 'Government-aided private colleges' is a more appropriate term to refer to these colleges, which are familiarly known as private-aided colleges.
2 Some dated studies on higher education include V.K.R.V. Rao (1961) on the university of Delhi and Bose et al. (1983) in West Bengal, Singh (1993) on colleges of University of Delhi. National or state level studies are almost non-existent. A few studies examined socio-economic background of students using small sample surveys of a college or a town or so, for example, for limited purpose like examining women's participation and occupational preferences (Uplaonkar, 1983) or costs (Singh, 1993).

Part I

2 Engineering Education in India
Challenges of Growth and Inequalities

Engineering Education: Achievements, Aspirations and Concerns

It is well recognised that higher education plays a critical role in the development of nations by impacting a variety of dimensions of the society – social, cultural, economic, technological, political and human development (Tilak, 2003a). Higher education which includes technological and professional education, apart from general education, contributes to the dynamic economic growth with the production of 'specialised human capital' (Schultz, 1988), yielding direct economic benefits and playing an equally important role in producing a large multitude of externalities (McMahon, 2018). The valuable human capital and the socially conscious, civilised and enlightened citizens with critical thinking and noble values it produces contribute to the improvement in human well-being in its various facets. Further, in a competitive global knowledge economy that is experiencing rapid changes that are taking place in the global knowledge production in the twenty-first century, there is an increasing demand on higher education to produce ever-increasing quality and skilled human resources with creative minds and the higher education system contributes significantly in fulfilling these demands (Tilak & Choudhury, 2019). Also, the human capital produced by the higher education system by engaging itself in nation-building activities can fuel social, economic, technological, political and cultural transformation of the societies. For the same reason, individuals and nations invest in education, some very passionately. As a result, we find rapid growth of education, higher education in particular, in almost all countries of the world. World enrolments in higher education have increased 200-fold from roughly half a million in 1900 to about 100 million by 2000 (Schofer & Meyer, 2005, p. 898).

There has been an explosion in demand for higher education in the world during the last two decades of the present century – the number of students has more than doubled – going up from 100 million in 2000 to nearly 250 million in 2022 (UNESCO, 2022), and it continues to grow. By 2040, student enrolment in higher education is predicted to surpass 590 million (Martin & Godonoga, 2020). With the massive expansion of higher education across the globe, it has evolved over the years from transitioning itself

DOI: 10.4324/9781003430223-3

from the one providing education for a few elites to providing to the common masses (Trow, 2007). By widening access and producing more educated and skilled human capital, including specialised human capital, higher education promises a more prosperous planet.

In India too, higher education has experienced remarkable growth during the post-Independence period, and more impressively during the last three to four decades, in such a way that it became the second largest system in the world after China, pushing the US to the third place. The growing aspirations of young Indians, particularly in the critical phase of 'demographic dividend' that the country is passing through on the one hand and India's resolve to create a knowledge society on the other, have contributed to tendencies towards the massification of higher education. There were only 0.26 million students in higher education, enrolled in 750 colleges and 30 universities in India in 1950–51; the numbers increased to about 41.3 million students in 1,113 universities, 43,796 colleges and 11,296 'stand-alone institutions' in 2020–21 (MOE, 2022). The gross enrolment ratio as estimated by the Ministry of Education/Human Resource Development (MHRD), based on data collected from institutions of higher education through the All India Survey of Higher Education, has gone up by nearly 70 times – from 0.4 per cent in 1950–51 to 27.3 per cent in 2020–21 (UGC, 2015; MOE, 2022), though the current ratio is still far below the ratio in countries like China, many advanced countries and the world average (UIS, 2020). The *National Education Policy 2020* (GOI, 2020) aims at reaching a gross enrolment ratio of at least 50 per cent by 2035.

Within higher education, technical education and more specifically engineering education have registered an extraordinary high rate of growth. Engineering, science and technology have transformed the world we live in, contributing to significantly longer life expectancy and an enhanced quality of life for large numbers of the world's population (UNESCO, 2010). Given the increasing use of technology in human life, the critical role of engineering education in addressing the pressing challenges of our societies is well recognised worldwide, and accordingly, many countries of the world place engineering education and career engineering on a high pedestal as vital for economic growth; engineering has become an admired and aspirational profession (QEPEF, 2016). The importance of technical education, engineering education in particular, has been well acknowledged for a long period of time all over the world, including India.

The contributions of engineering education in India that started largely with building roads and bridges is currently addressing several new and emerging challenges, such as providing more equitable access to information for our populations, environmental protection and natural resource management, artificial intelligence, natural and man-made disaster mitigation and so on. Even today, a large number of engineering graduates from India have made an impact in the corporate world internationally. For instance, several

Indian engineering graduates are working in the Silicon Valley of the US and the survival and growth of IT (information technology) sector in this region is said to be largely dependent on them. In the expanding global knowledge economy, the impact of specialised human capital for rapid economic growth is being realised, and therefore, the demand for engineering education has gone up rapidly across the globe (Dubey et al., 2019).

There were only a handful of engineering institutions in India in the nineteenth century; but noticeable growth has taken place only after independence with the establishment of IITs, RECs and other institutions. Slow and steady growth took place during the first three decades after the launching of development planning in India in 1950. Growth has picked up since the beginning of the 1990s and a phenomenal expansion has taken place during the last three decades. But coinciding with the global trends (Altbach & Levy, 2005; Buckner, 2017), the expansion has been phenomenal in India too due to massive growth of private education, which has its own ramifications.

Among the various disciplines of study in higher education, the growth of engineering education during the last 50 years has been most impressive. In 2020–21, 13.9 per cent of all students enrolled in first degree courses in higher education are in engineering education (it was about 16 per cent in 2015–16, according to UGC [2018]), while this share was less than 5 per cent in 1990 and 7.2 per cent in 2005. Engineering and technology is the fourth major discipline (after arts, science and commerce) with an enrolment of 3.7 million students. In 2020–21, above one million students graduated in engineering and technology.

However, during the last three decades, engineering education in India has gone through, like the rest of higher education, several pertinent transitions. The profession has also experienced several internal and external shocks, the major ones being declining public investment, rapid privatisation, shortage of faculty and deteriorating quality. While the expansion of the higher education sector in India has helped the country to rapidly march fast towards a stage of massification, it is equally important to examine the trends and patterns of growth, as it is associated with several maladies. As a result, today, engineering education faces umpteen challenges, including critical shortage of teaching faculty, poor quality of education, extremely limited research output, rising student fees and overall costs of education, raising questions of affordability and inequalities in access, growing unemployment, low wages of engineering graduates and so on. Some of these problems are attributable to the unplanned and unbridled growth of the engineering education, a very rapid growth of the private sector and weak and ineffective governance mechanisms. A careful look at the expansion of the higher education system in India reveals that the expansion has been uneven on several fronts. Besides high levels of spatial/regional (inter-regional, interstate and intrastate) inequalities, with some regions/states growing fast and some lagging far behind others, a high degree of inequalities exist in access to higher education between several groups of population – social (caste and religion), economic and gender. These aspects have been highlighted by some scholars in the recent past (e.g. Tilak, 2015; Tilak & Choudhury, 2019). In addition, an important dimension that has not attracted much attention of many scholars refers to disciplinary imbalances in the growth of higher education. Higher technical education has experienced fast growth, particularly after the introduction of economic reforms in the early 1990s, which are widely felt to be irreversible. The high rate of expansion experienced, especially during the last three decades, has been propelled by the private sector. A high growth is clearly visible in cases of disciplines like engineering and technology, business management, financial management, hotel management, catering technology, architecture, town planning, pharmacy, etc., which are revenue-rewarding streams for private investors in education (Anandkrishnan, 2014) as well as to the students in terms of dividends in the labour market as compared to other disciplines like the humanities and social sciences, natural and physical sciences, apart from the arts and fine arts which are almost extinguished. It may not be wrong to perceive that the growth in technical education has taken place at the cost of these disciplines, creating enormous disciplinary imbalances in higher education.

Some of these problems are common to the entire field of higher education, but they have assumed more acute proportions in the case of engineering education. In addition, there are specific problems associated with engineering education, such as imbalanced development of engineering education – some sub-streams of engineering flourishing at the cost of other sub-streams, mismatches in the labour market reflected in gluts and shortages, rising fees and individual costs, predominant role of student loans and so on. However, except for several committee reports, very few studies have been devoted to systematically analysing the major challenges and issues that engineering education is facing. Particularly, the absence of studies examining socio-economic effects of the growth, including the nature of growth, is striking, which helps to understand how the new demand is created by the 'New Middle Class' (Fernandes, 2006). An important issue for examination is the inequality in the expansion of engineering education in India and the role of the private sector in this. It is worthwhile examining the changing trends and patterns in the growth of engineering education in the country, especially since the 1980s, and seeing whether the growth path was affected by economic slowdowns which brought a recession in the global economy and what have been the changing policy responses to these issues. The complexities found in the global engineering labour market have changed the discourse on engineering education. Understanding the engineering education market nowadays is becoming quite complex in India, particularly with the emergence of different kinds of players with different interests and a very large number of private-unaided institutions.

Among the very few studies on engineering education in India, Banerjee and Muley (2009) and Biswas et al. (2010) are important recent ones that provide a profile of the growth of engineering education in India. Banerjee and Muley (2009) document the trends in student intake, number of engineering graduates, postgraduates and PhDs. It also includes a comparison of a few select Indian institutions – an IIT, a NIT and a private engineering college. Biswas et al. (2010) go a little further and attempt to make a good assessment of the status of engineering education in the country in the light of national and global changes. These two studies serve as a precursor for our present study. Choudhury (2016), in a short paper, briefly examined the growth of engineering education in India in the post-economic reform period with a specific focus on expansion, enrolment pattern and public financing. During the last decade, that is after those major studies were conducted, there have been several changes in engineering education in India and global conditions. In fact, as Madheswari and Mageswari (2020, p. 215) observed, today "VUCA (volatile, uncertain, complex and ambiguous) characterise the engineering education scenario". All this necessitates a fresh study, which is attempted here. How volatile, uncertain, complex and ambiguous the system has become? We discuss the changing landscape of engineering education in India, using the data from several secondary sources and reports published by the Government of India with the hope of inspiring new studies and informed discussions. This chapter is an attempt to provide a comprehensive and up-to-date assessment of engineering education in India. It aims to identify and explore the major issues and new challenges faced by this sector in the contemporary times. We approach to examine the issues in engineering education in a different way from the few earlier research studies, as we integrate major issues in this field to get a comprehensive picture that would undoubtedly contribute to ongoing policy discourses and debates considerably and to further research. It must, however, be stated at the very outset that the analysis is limited with the availability of secondary data to several specific indicators on engineering education in India.

This and the following chapters present a critical, descriptive and analytical account of some of these challenges that engineering education in India faces and its prospects, using available data on engineering education and on conditions in the labour market for engineers and on the basis of a variety of alternative indicators. The analysis covers five major dimensions. First, the trends and patterns in the growth of engineering education in India and the major changes it has experienced over the years are discussed, particularly considering the expansion in terms of number of institutions and enrolments. Second, it also describes the emerging strong role of the private sector vis-à-vis the public sector in engineering education. In fact, since almost all the dimensions of growth in engineering education have an interface with the growing role of the private sector, we are not discussing the role of the private sector in a separate section. In fact, if one is speaking about engineering education in India, one would only be speaking about private education, as the public sector hardly accounts for 10–15 per cent of the total engineering education sector in the country. Third, concentrating on regional imbalances in the growth of engineering education, this study examines the region and state-specific growth of engineering education and inequalities in growth in engineering education, both at the regional and the state level. We also cover inequalities in access to engineering education by caste and gender. At the same time, we also recognise the caste, gender and region interacting with each other exacerbating inequalities. Fourth, we discuss quality concerns of engineering education in India. Fifth, using the data on public expenditure from Analysis of Budget Expenditure on Education (MHRD/MOE) and on household spending (collected from the National Sample Survey Office [NSSO]), some of the emerging concerns in financing of engineering education in the country are discussed. Sixth, changing labour market conditions that influence the demand for engineering education in India are analysed. The labour market conditions include employability, unemployment and wages associated with engineering graduate manpower. We also look at policy reforms that have been introduced at various points and the policy reforms that are being presently discussed. In a sense, we are narrowly concerned here with engineering education, though some aspects of technical education as a whole are also briefly examined, but on engineering education, the attempt has been to be comprehensive in the coverage of analysis of issues. The first three issues are analysed in this chapter and the others in Chapter 3.

An important contribution of the book is an analysis of the most recent data available in multiple sources of secondary data, policy documents and media reports on many aspects relating to engineering education. As the study is empirical in nature, the analysis mainly focuses on examining the issues using the latest data on standard indicators such as the number of engineering institutions, enrolments, sanctioned intake, attendance, faculty size, public (union and state governments) expenditure, household expenditure, employment and wages/salaries for engineering graduates. Reliable quantitative information is not adequately available to analyse aspects such as the labour market conditions and quality issues in engineering education, and therefore, some proxy variables are used. For example, information on the qualifications of the faculty appointed in engineering institutions and on their contributions to research, teaching and the third function – engagement with the society and community service – would have been better indicators of quality of teachers. We do not have information on these aspects.

At the outset, an important limitation of the study may be briefly noted. First, engineering education is offered in India in polytechnic institutes and colleges/universities and both are recognised by the AICTE, the apex body meant to regulate technical education in the country. Diploma-level programmes of three- to four-year duration are offered in polytechnics and degree (the first degree of four-year duration, postgraduate/master's level degree generally of two years duration or integrated degree programmes of five years and research – PhD studies of about four-year duration) programmes are offered in colleges, mostly in universities and university-level institutions only. As per the latest statistics (2021–22), there are 3,592 polytechnics with an enrolment of 3.8 lakhs and 3,011 degree (and post graduate degree) level institutions with an enrolment of 7.8 lakhs. Thus, in all, there are 1.2 million students in engineering education in the country in 5,908 institutions. Students who complete secondary education (grade 10) are eligible for admission in polytechnics, while students have to complete senior secondary level (grade 12) for admission in degree programmes. Diploma programmes are less expensive with lower levels of fees than degree programmes, and hence they are also accessible relatively more easily to the middle and lower socio-economic strata of the society. While both diploma and degree programmes are high in demand and are also valued in the labour market, a good number of secondary school graduates who complete diploma programmes also join degree programmes in the second year or third semester, given the social status accorded to degree programmes and additional advantages in wages associated with degree programmes. Though polytechnics form a sizeable part of engineering education, we focus here essentially on degree-level engineering studies which form a part of higher education, except for occasional reference to the pre-degree diploma studies.

The rest of this chapter is organised as follows: the next section gives a brief account of the major data sources used in the study. Section 'Growth of Engineering Education in India: Trends and Patterns' examines the changing trends and patterns of the growth of engineering education in terms of institutions and enrolment, particularly highlighting the changing growth pattern of this sector observed during the 1990s and later. Specifically, it reflects on the changes in the demand for engineering education in India during the last three decades, as this period has experienced dramatic global and national events – globalisation, emergence of global markets and global economic slowdown – which have had an enormous impact on the engineering education sector. In fact, along with economic reforms, the 1990s has also been associated with a social upsurge over the rights and privileges, including reservations in higher education and employment, of weaker sections in India. Inequalities in the growth in engineering education are discussed in Section 'Inequalities in Engineering Education' by examining variations in access of weaker sections of society identified by region, gender, social (caste) and economic groups to engineering education. Also, an attempt is made to compare and contrast the expansion of engineering education with the growth of other branches of technical education and other branches of higher education, including social sciences in this section.

Sources of Data

This and the next chapter are based essentially on secondary database. The sources of data used in the study include All India Survey of Higher Education (AISHE) reports that cover almost the entire higher education and the Analysis of Budget Expenditure on Education (both published by the MHRD/Ministry of Education), AICTE annual reports and online data on its website and annual reports of the University Grants Commission (UGC). Quite a bit of data compiled from AICTE website is also presented here (some in the Appendix A) for further use by researchers. For information on labour market aspects, we rely on National Employability Reports (Aspiring Minds), reports of the NASSCOM, FICCI and individual institutions' websites, reports of several committees constituted by the AICTE, UGC and other bodies and also media reports. Besides these, we use disaggregated individual-specific, unit-level data available in the latest three education rounds of the National Sample Surveys – the 75th round conducted in July 2017 to June 2018 (NSSO, 2018), the 71st round (Social Consumption: Education and Health) conducted in January to June 2014 (NSSO, 2014) and the 64th round conducted in July 2007 to June 2008 for data on household expenditure on education (NSSO, 2008). The 64th round (Participation and Expenditure in Education) covers a sample of 100,581 households (63,318 rural households and 37,263 urban households); the 71st round (Education in India) includes a sample of 65,926 households (36,479 rural households and 29,447 urban households) from all over India; and the 75th round (Household Social Consumption Expenditure on Education in India) collected data from 1.1 lakh households (64,500 in rural areas and 49,200 in urban areas). Unlike the more 'general' or 'normal' rounds, the focus of these three rounds of data was to collect information on three important issues related to education, in addition to many other household-level characteristics in detail: participation in education, family expenditure, often referred to as private expenditure, incurred by households on education, incentives provided by the government and the extent of educational wastage in terms of dropout and discontinuation along with the causes behind them. These surveys also provide data on the number of adults by the level of education attained, including higher education by discipline of study. Therefore, the NSSO data would help us to get some specific information about the engineering graduates that are not available from the MHRD, UGC, AICTE and other government organisations. Using NSSO data, we attempt to examine student attendance in engineering education by income quintiles. The variations in the household spending on higher education are shown by gender, location (rural-urban), household consumption expenditure quintile and type of institution. However, the findings from the NSSO data should be interpreted with caution as the sample size is small as we have restricted it to only engineering education, and that also varies from round to round. Our attempt to look at some issues at regional and state level from NSSO data ended up with too small sample size, and therefore it is omitted.

Growth of Engineering Education in India: Trends and Patterns

A modest beginning for the development of engineering education in India was made in the nineteenth century. The first engineering college was established for civil engineers in Roorkee (Roorkee College, earlier known by the official name of Thomson Engineering College) in Uttar Pradesh in 1847. India had a very little growth in engineering and technical education during the pre-independence period. However, increase in the demand for technical workers, particularly to execute public work plans such as roads, railway and bridges, led to the opening of a few engineering colleges in the mid-1850s and early 1900s. Some of the earliest engineering colleges established in the pre-independence period include Poona Civil Engineering College at Pune (1854), Bengal Engineering College at Shibpur (1856), Banaras Hindu University (1916), Visvesvaraya College of Engineering (1917) and Harcourt Butler Technological Institute, Kanpur (1920) (Bhatt, 2010). The training of all these colleges was primarily confined to the field of civil engineering. By Independence in 1947, there were only 44 engineering colleges in the country with an intake capacity of 3,200.

The importance of technical, especially engineering education, as an extremely critical factor for socio-economic development and technological advancement was well recognised in independent India. Just two years before independence, that is, in 1945, the Sarkar Committee was appointed to suggest options for advanced technical education in India. The Sarkar committee recommended the establishment of higher technical institutes based on the Massachusetts Institute of Technology in the four regions of India. In the opening address to the IIT at Kharagpur in 1951, the first Minister of Education of the Independent India Maulana Abul Kalam Azad stated:

> One of the first decisions I took on assuming charge as Minister was that we must improve the facilities for higher technical education in the country [and] that we would ourselves meet most of our needs... I look forward to the day when the facilities of technical education in India will be of such a high level that people from abroad will come to India for higher scientific and technical training.
> (Quoted in Kripal, 1990, p. 187)

Going by the recommendation of the Sarkar Committee, the Government of India established five IITs: Kharagpur (1950), Bombay (1958), Kanpur (1959), Madras (1960) and Delhi (1961) (Delhi was added on to the original four). The AICTE was set up in 1945 to oversee all technical education (diploma, degree and postgraduate) in the country. The Government of India expanded the base for engineering education extensively in the post-Independence period through successive five-year plans, particularly with the establishment of IITs, and RECs (later named as NITs). Many engineering colleges have been established after independence with the aim of making India a large industrialised country and that this would require far more engineers than those produced by older institutions. The first three decades witnessed setting up of a big network of engineering institutions consisting of engineering polytechnics, regional colleges, national institutes and universities in India. As Bhargava (2001, p. 77) rightly observed, after achieving independence, "the Indian leaders in the government and the planners immediately realised the importance of developing engineering education in the country to ultimately build its industry, roads, dams, communication system, power and drinking water facilities and other infrastructure in general".

Engineering education was considered as the foundation for improvement of overall quality of life of people and to raise the living standards of the people and the nation. The growth of technical education system in India is linked with the economic growth, and in the 1990s, it was considered essential for the expansion of knowledge economy. The report of the High Power Committee for Mobilisation of Additional Resources for Technical Education (AICTE, 1994) mentions: "Technical education is one of the most crucial components of Human Resource Development. It is a basic and essential input for national development and for strengthening our industry, economy and the quality of life of our people" (p. 2). The economic liberalisation launched in the 1990s gave impetus to the growth of Information Technology (IT) industry. As a result, starting from the 1990s demand for technical education in India rose significantly and engineering education became an attractive option to students as India started outsourcing IT and engineering services to the world, and employment opportunities in this field started growing exponentially (UNESCO, 2010; Dubey et al., 2019). Economic liberalisation and growth of service sector (relating to IT services) led to a high demand for engineering graduates in the country (Dubey et al., 2019). Rates of return to engineering education became very attractive. Based on NSSO data, Carnoy et al. (2010) has found that graduate engineers earn much higher than graduates in general higher education, and the rates of return are also high. According to these estimates, the private rates of return for graduate male engineers range from 20.4 per cent to 36.8 per cent under alternative assumptions in 2006. Social rate of return ranged between 16 per cent and 18.6 per cent. These are much higher than returns to graduates in general higher education. The high rates of return provide main explanation for the rapid growth in private demand for engineering education. Some experts point to what they call the 'engineering boom' that started in 1995 and peaked in the 2000s triggered by the IT phenomenon. Responding to the demands of the labour market, MHRD (2011b) recommended upgradation and expansion of engineering institutions in the country, and the government initiated a significant expansion of engineering institutions for the second time during the Eleventh Five Year Plan (2007–12), when eight new IITs, seven new Indian Institutes of Management (IIMs), ten new NITs, 20 Indian Institutes of Information Technology (IIITs), two new Schools of Planning and Architecture (SPAs), three Indian Institutes of Science Education and Research (IISERs) and many other technical institutes were set up in the country. With the increase in the requirement of more engineers, particularly in the IT sector during early 1990s, many new private engineering colleges in the self-financing mode were established. Government engineering colleges were not sufficient to feed the industry's appetite for engineering; therefore, many private engineering institutions came up, and this may be one of the reasons that IT as major subjects are offered in almost all private engineering colleges that were established in early the 1990s in India. Further, in the changing nature of work environment all over the world (World Bank, 2019), engineering skills in the area of ICT, artificial intelligence and other similar fields of engineering and technology gained big premium. With the expansion of Indian software service industry in the 1990s, there was a growing demand for engineering graduates in the national and global markets at an unprecedented level. Accordingly, there has been an exploding demand for engineering education.

During the last seven decades, engineering education in India has contributed immensely to growth and development specifically to the success of the industrial development of the country. The high growth of engineering education, particularly IT and related strands of engineering, has profoundly impacted every aspect of human life and contributed to "breaking old barriers and building new interconnections in emerging global village" (Kasturirangan, 2004, p. 74). It enabled India very significantly to strengthen its service sector, particularly IT-enabling or IT-dependent service sector (Dossani & Patibandla, 2012). India's exports of IT services, essentially software services, amounted to 40 per cent of total export of services. The surplus generated by these exports at USD 133.7 billion in 2020–21 could offset nearly half of the trade deficit in goods (RBI, 2021). Nowadays, the role of engineering and technical education is considered critical to India's aspirations of strengthening its reputation as a major competitor in the global knowledge economy (Blom & Cheong, 2010). Engineers are considered as "the backbone and form the core of a nation to enable it become a leading country in the world" (Bhargava, 2001, p. 77).

Thus, economic globalisation, emergence of knowledge markets associated with knowledge economies, changing payoffs to engineering graduates and changing overall pay structure of various professionals resulted in a large demand for engineering manpower by the IT industries and others and dramatically changed the technical education landscape of the country. In short, as a result of a multitude of factors, there has been a phenomenal expansion and the extremely narrow base of engineering education with which independent India started has emerged into a large network of 2,373 institutions with more than four million students in 2019–20. With such a growth:

> India has emerged as a major player in the world in the field of Engineering Education, and Indian engineers have contributed significantly to the economic and technological development of many foreign lands, not only in the Information Technology sector but also in general engineering services and in hi-tech research and development in solid state electronics, communications and embedded systems.
>
> (Biswas et al., 2010, p. ix)

Another important outcome has been that with rapid growth, the elite nature of engineering education slowly vanished to a great extent. The expansion of engineering education in India has attracted new waves of lower-income students to meet their aspirations for getting trained in technical fields (Loyalka et al., 2014). The social aspirations of the middle class and the opening up of economic opportunities due to globalisation on the one hand, the availability of student loans and the introduction of new policies such as fee reimbursement and financial assistance on the other have enabled huge numbers of students from the low- and middle-income classes to opt for studies in engineering education in India. An engineering degree is a preferred option for most senior secondary school graduates, and not just academically bright and economically well-off students. With the expectation of higher returns in Indian and global labour markets from engineering studies and also high returns in the marriage market in the form of dowries (Mishra, 2011), the demand for engineering education has become very diverse. An engineering degree is also viewed as a passport for entry into prosperous western labour markets. Access to engineering education is seen as an aspiration for social mobility and to reach a higher level of social status. Engineering education that was considered as an exclusive space for Indian elites till the 1990s has seen a turn by catering to the new ambitions of middle-class families. There was greater aspiration among new middle-class parents to send their offspring for engineering/technical studies, with the expectation that it would improve their own socio-economic status in the society. In fact, parental aspirations and resultant pressures were higher than the students' aspirations.

The net result was that overall access to engineering education improved dramatically. Enrolment in engineering and technology has increased from 96,000 in 1975–76 to 4.9 million in 2015–16, and then started declining, finally reaching 3.9 million by 2020–21. In 2012–13, enrolments in engineering and technology constituted the highest, 15.5 per cent 13 per cent of the total enrolments in higher education before declining rather steeply to 8.9 per cent by 2020–21. The corresponding figure was a little around 3 per cent in 1960–61, as shown in Table 2.1. The growth in enrolments has probably been faster than anywhere else in the world, and India is now regarded as having the second largest number of engineering students in the world, producing about nine lakh graduates a year (2017–18).

Around 25 per cent of the world's engineers are produced in India (Madheswari & Mageswari, 2020, p. 215). India is regarded as the world's number one country in producing engineering and science graduates (National Science Foundation, 2018). However, at the same time it is important to examine the nature of the growth of engineering education and its overall effects. The growing demand for technical education coupled with the inability of the state to invest further in technical education has led to the liberalisation of technical education (Mani & Arun, 2012), and resultantly the private sector seized the opportunity and almost invaded the engineering education sector. In 1947, there were only two private-unaided colleges of engineering in

Table 2.1 Growth of Engineering Institutions and Enrolment in India

Year	Institutions			Enrolments		
	Higher Education	Engineering Education	Share of Engineering in Higher Education (%)	Higher Education ('000)	Engineering Education ('000)	Share of Engineering in Higher Education (%)
1950–51	606	53	8.75	1,048.00	37.00	3.53
1960–61	1,864	100	5.36	1,728.77	85.60	4.95
1965–66	2,298	103	4.48	3,001.21	90.03	3.00
1970–71	3,299	107	3.24	2,426.11	96.06	3.06
1975–76	4,124	109	2.64	2,752.44	128.94	4.68
1980–81	4,396	149	3.38	3,605.02	176.54	4.90
1985–86	5,427	242	4.46	4,924.87	216.84	4.40
1990–91	6,323	277	4.38	6,574.00	315.72	4.80
1995–96	8,188	355	4.34	8,399.44	529.47	6.30
2000–01	11,568	678	5.86	12,043.05	795.12	6.60
2005–06	20,769	1,562	7.52	15,768.42	1,313.70	8.33
2008–09	25,951	2,237	8.62	21,501.15	3,333.16	15.50
2012–13	37,204	3,371	9.06	34,584.78	4,885.13	14.13
2015–16	42,188	3,364	7.97	37,399.39	4,076.28	10.90
2018–19	42,846	3,124	7.29	38,514.46	3,727.00	9.68
2019–20	55,165	3,723	6.75	41,380.71	3,685.62	8.91
2020–21	56,205	3,091	5.74			
Growth Rate*	6.69	6.02	–	5.39	6.79	–

Compound rate of growth per annum (%)
Source: UGC Annual Report (Various Years) and Annual Survey of Higher Education (various years).

India; the number could increase to 15 by 1980. But between 1980 and 1990, the number increased ten times, and the curve went on a steep rise thereafter.

Thus, starting from the late1980s, the private sector started slowly participating in engineering education and increased the pace very fast, as the government adopted a 'low public cost' strategy promoting private self-financing (unaided) engineering colleges and universities. This strategy immensely helped the government in expanding access to engineering education and at the same time building its political legitimacy, all with little public investment (Carnoy et al., 2010). Private engineering colleges and 'institutions deemed to be universities', known briefly as deemed universities, under the self-financing mode, have been established in big numbers in a very short period, and today the Indian engineering education system is characterised by the preponderance of private (self-financing) colleges and deemed universities. It is important to note that the growth of private sector in engineering education in India can be explained in terms of 'excess demand' and not 'differentiated demand' (Weisbrod, 1977; James 1987, 1993).

The private sector, which accounted for just 15 per cent of enrolments in 1960, by 2019 accounted for 86 per cent of admissions of all engineering institutions in India (Kapur & Mehta, 2004; AICTE, 2019). In states like Andhra Pradesh, Kerala, Karnataka, Tamil Nadu, Telangana and Maharashtra, the percentage of private engineering colleges in the total engineering colleges was more than 95 per cent in 2019. This meteoric growth of the private sector has been in response to the growing aspirations of the middle class coupled with the opening up of the Indian economy. As the government engineering institutions do not have the scope to accommodate the increasing demand, private actors played a dominant role, helped by an easy permissions system of state governments and an equally easy approval mechanism of the AICTE, the apex body for technical education in India. Private players include not only industrialists, religious trusts and politicians, but also liquor barons, sugar barons, real estate sharks and powerful caste organisations. These education overlords entered the scene, viewing professional and technical education simply as a means of increasing political power, making money or amassing land. Several private registered trusts and societies, including mainly those with commercial interests, also have contributed to this phenomenal growth of engineering education in the country. In a sense, the private sector has displaced the public sector in higher education, more specifically in engineering education, leaving no space for the public sector to function, not to speak of it to re-emerge as an important player in higher education in the country. Unlike philanthropy-based private institutions, these self-financing private institutions exploit the weaknesses of the system, including the ineffective governance and regulation by the state, imperfections in the market and attitudes of gullible parents, and function similar to the for-profit higher education sector that has grown in the US wherein students/families actually buy higher education services in the education bazaars

(Kirp, 2003; Levy, 2006; Kinser & Levy, 2007; Hodgman, 2018). The net result of all this is that this has strengthened social stratification world-wide (Marginson, 2016); and the basic intrinsic values of higher education such as its positive externalities, the social purpose and the nation-building role that higher education ought to serve and above all the public good nature of higher education have tended to disappear in favour of pecuniary values (Tilak, 2009a).

As discussed above, higher education in India has experienced a substantial growth in terms of the number of institutions and student enrolments during the last five decades. But all disciplines of higher education have not grown at the same pace. Data on discipline-wise distribution of enrolment in higher education reveals some interesting points: first, enrolment in the arts and humanities programmes is the highest among all disciplines in higher education, and this feature continued for the last five decades, but the relative share has declined from 45 per cent in 1973–74 to 38.6 per cent in 2018–19 (see Figure 2.1). Second, the enrolments in engineering and technology as a proportion of the total enrolments increased from 3.9 per cent to 12 per cent during the

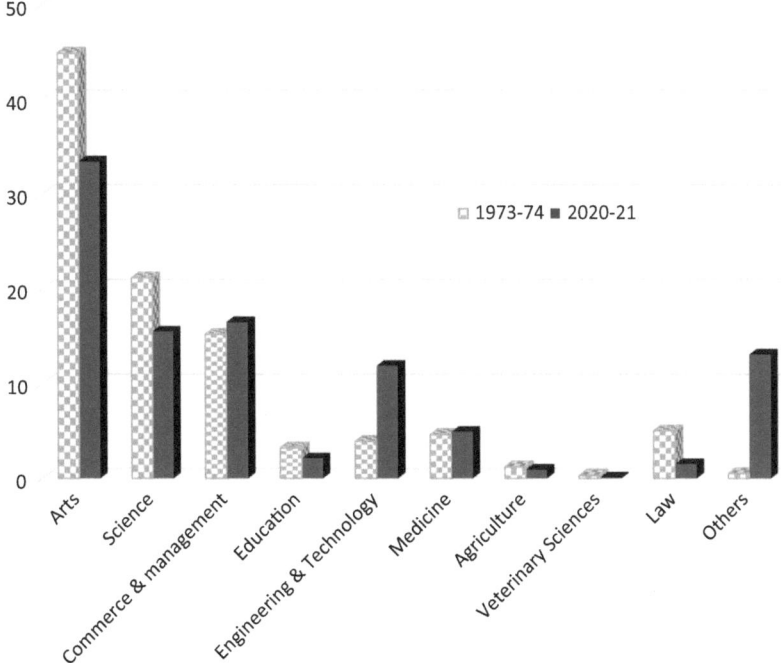

Figure 2.1 Changing Distribution of Enrolments among Major Areas of Study in Higher Education (%)

Source: UGC (1975–76) for data on 1973–74 and MOE (2022) for 2019–20.

same period. This is the discipline which has experienced the highest growth. Other disciplines such as commerce and management and education and law also registered a rise in respective shares over the period. But not only arts and humanities but also sciences, medicine, agriculture and veterinary sciences suffered during this period, experiencing declining shares in total enrolments.

The time series data presented in Figure 2.2 show that the trends were not smooth over the period. The decline in the relative share of arts began in the mid-1970s itself. After 2005–06, the fall was a little bit sharp. Commerce and management faculties enjoyed a good share, in fact, an increasing share, until 1990–91, and ever since then, a short phase of decline started which continued until 2005–06. Between 2005–06 and 2018–19, it experienced a phase of slow and steady growth. The trend line in the case of sciences was more or less static until 2001–01; the share marginally increased by 2005–06, but the rising trend could not continue later.

Of all the major disciplines, it is in the case of engineering and technology that we find five distinct phases during the period 1975–76 to 2019–20. During the first two decades, that is, 1975–76 to 1995–96, there was a very slow but steady growth; then, during the next decade, the slope changed to a marginally higher level. This phase was followed by a big surge between 2005–06 and 2010–11, when it reached its peak; it would maintain that level between 2010–11 and 2016–17. But in response to national and global economic problems, including employment, serious cracks affected the engineering education sector during the last three to four years when demand for engineering education began to decline and colleges were being closed. The relative share of engineering and technology

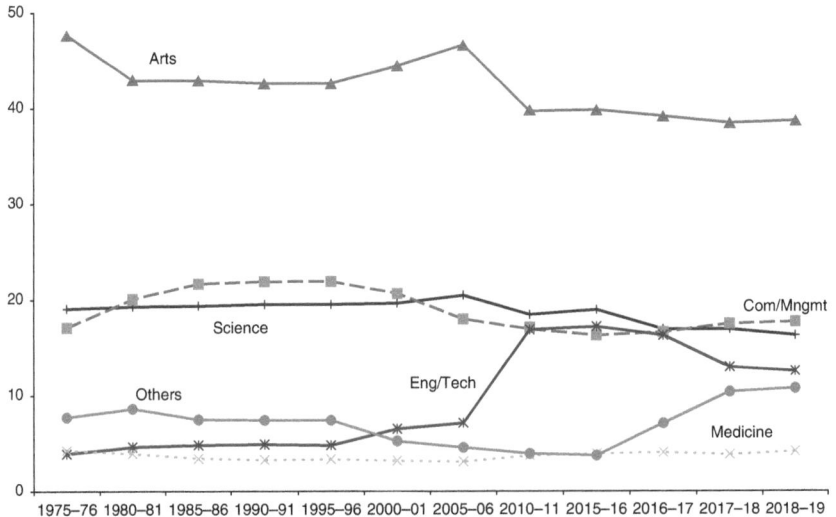

Figure 2.2 Trends in Enrolments in Major Disciplines in Higher Education (%)

Source: UGC Annual Reports and All India Survey of Higher Education (various years).

education fell sharply from nearly 16 per cent in 2015–16 to below 12 per cent in 2020–21. Will this downward trend be a short phase or a long one? It is difficult to make any predictions. But given the increasing importance of technology in national and global development, one can expect that the trends will be reversed; but it is difficult to predict how soon it will happen.

On the whole, engineering and technology education registered a very significant growth compared to other disciplines and higher education as a whole, as shown in Table 2.1. The number of engineering institutions increased from a meagre 53 (in 1950–51) to 3,124 in 2018–19, a growth by 59 times over the last 69 years (Table 2.1). Likewise, student enrolment in engineering studies has gone up from 37,000 to 4.1 million (an increase by 110 times) during 1960–61 and 2018–19.

The share of enrolments in engineering studies in overall higher education has also gone up from a little below 4 per cent (1960–61) to 12 per cent in 2020–21. The rate of growth of both institutions and enrolments in engineering education was quite high. However, recent years have seen a decline in the number of engineering institutions from 3,371 in 2012–13 to 3,124 in 2018–19. Similarly, the share of engineering in enrolments in higher education reached the highest proportion of 15.5 per cent in 2012–13 and declined afterwards. While higher education as a whole grew at a rate of growth of 6.4 per cent per annum between 1960–61 and 2018–19, the enrolments in engineering education increased at a rate of 8.4 per cent during this period of nearly two-and-a-half decades. Similarly, number of colleges and universities in overall higher education increased at the rate of 6.5 per cent as compared to 6.2 per cent in case of institutions of engineering education. The number of universities and colleges for engineering and technology has grown unchecked, particularly during the last three to four decades. As a result, there seem to be too many. It is widely being recognised that India has too many engineering institutions, and there is a need to control the growth of the institutions. While some have suggested closure of some of the institutions, some (MHRD, 2003; World Bank, 2013) suggested that the number needs to beat least kept constant and no new colleges be allowed to be opened.

More than enrolments, it is the number of registrants for entrance which may reflect the demand for engineering education more accurately. The decline in demand for engineering education after 2014 is abundantly clear from the decline in the numbers relating to the national-level common entrance examination, known as the Joint Entrance Examination (JEE) (Figure 2.3). The ranks obtained in the JEE are used not only by the IITs, NITs and other national institutes, but also often states and some specific institutions rely on JEE scores/ranks.

The massive expansion of engineering education in India is in general mainly due to the increased level of participation by the private sector. It is argued that the expansion of the private sector and the emergence of a new educational economy in India, particularly in engineering and technical education, have resulted in widening inequalities in educational opportunities.

In 2012–13, private institutions were 91.5 per cent of all the undergraduate-level engineering institutions in the country, with an enrolment share of 93.1 per cent (Table 2.2). There has been a marginal decline in engineering education in recent years. The share of the private sector in enrolments has come down to 86.7 per cent, with an intake capacity of 85.5 per cent of the total engineering intake in 2018–19. While the private sector obviously reacts to market signals, a detailed study is needed to understand the investment strategies of private players in higher education that would provide useful insights on the changing investment strategies in higher education in India.

The expansion of the private sector in engineering education varies widely across different states in India. For instance, in some states/union territories such as Andhra Pradesh, Telangana, Uttar Pradesh, Madhya Pradesh and Maharashtra, the share of private institutions to total engineering institutions is higher than the national average (see Table 2.3). Of the total 2,711 private engineering institutions in the country, more than 16 per cent are located in Tamil Nadu alone and the corresponding figure is 11.3 per cent each in Andhra Pradesh and Maharashtra. Similarly, with respect to intake in private engineering institutions, these states enjoy an advantage, with the intake rates being higher than national average. However, government engineering institutions in states like Delhi, Bihar, Assam, Jammu & Kashmir and Jharkhand have higher intake levels.

A majority of the economically better-off states (with per capita Net State Domestic Product higher than the national average) have a higher share of

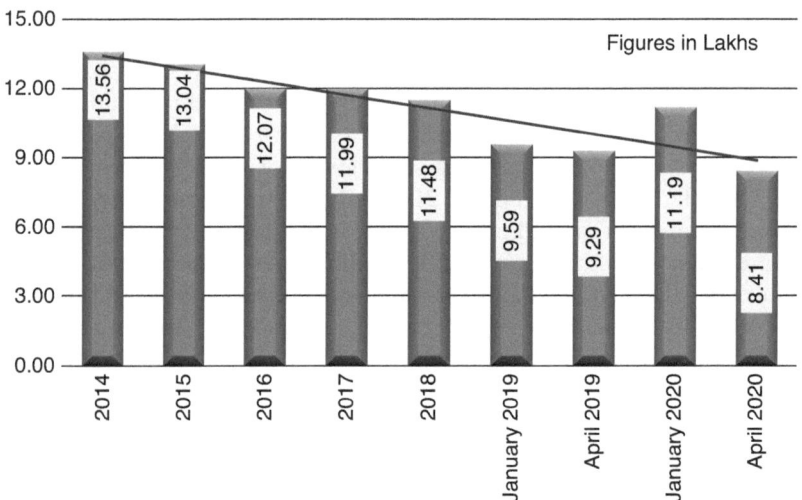

Figure 2.3 Declining Numbers of Registrants for Joint Entrance Examination for Admission in Engineering Studies, 2014–2020

Source: https://www.shiksha.com/b-tech/jee-main-exam.

Table 2.2 Growth of Institutions and Intake in Engineering Education by Type of Institution

Year	Institutions			Intake (in thousands)		
	Government	Private	Total	Government	Private	Total
2012–13	286	3,085	3,371	106.9	1,445.2	1,552.1
	(8.5)	(91.5)	(100)	(6.9)	(93.1)	(100)
2013–14	308	3,075	3,383	118.9	1,515.4	1,634.3
	(9.1)	(90.9)	(100)	(7.2)	(92.7)	(100)
2014–15	310	3,090	3,400	122.8	1,582.6	1,705.4
	(9.1)	(90.9)	(100)	(7.2)	(92.8)	(100)
2015–16	312	3,052	3,364	118.8	1,512.7	1,631.4
	(9.3)	(90.7)	(100)	(7.3)	(92.7)	(100)
2016–17	332	2,961	3,293	122.0	1,435.1	1,557.1
	(10.1)	(89.9)	(100)	(7.8)	(92.2)	(100)
2017–18	347	2,878	3,225	127.7	1,348.8	1,476.4
	(10.8)	(89.2)	(100)	(8.7)	(91.4)	(100)
2018–19	413	2,711	3,124	199.0	1,205.9	1,404.8
	(13.2)	(86.8)	(100)	(14.2)	(85.8)	(100)
Growth rate	6.32	−2.13	−1.26	10.91	−2.97	−1.65

Source: Compiled by the authors from AICTE Database.

private engineering institutions than their counterparts, that is, states with low per capita national state domestic product (NSDP) with very few exceptions. At the macro level, a direct relationship seems to exist between economic growth (NSDP per capita) and private participation in engineering education and also between the total number of engineering institutions (per one million population) and NSDP per capita, as the logarithmic trend lines in Figure 2.4 make it clear. The simple coefficient of correlation between NSDP per capita and all institutions is 0.69 and 0.47 between NSDP per capita and number of private institutions.

Apart from the level of economic development, is there any other factor that can explain the growth of the private sector? There may be several sociopolitical factors behind the growth or lack of growth of private sector in the states. The state policy also matters. Keeping these aside for a while, we wish to identify quantifiable factors, if any. First, we note that other variables like population of the age group of 18–23, which is the main pool from which demand for higher education emerges or government expenditure on engineering education, inadequacy of which will encourage the private sector to take advantage of the situation and open private institutions, are not found to be statistically significant factors in explaining the variations between several states in the growth of all engineering institutions. State income per capita is the most important factor that positively influences the growth of the number of institutions, in addition to industrial production (gross value

Table 2.3 State-Wise Intake in Government and Private Engineering Institutions (2018–19)

State and Union Territories	Institutions			Intake		
	Government	Private	Total	Government	Private	Total (in 000's)
Andhra Pradesh	16 (5.3)	289 (94.8)	305 (100)	9,790 (6.3)	146,376 (93.7)	156.2 (100)
Assam	11 (57.9)	8 (42.1)	19 (100)	2,415 (47.5)	2,670 (52.5)	5.1 (100)
Bihar	20 (52.6)	18 (47.4)	38 (100)	4,990 (45.3)	6,030 (54.7)	11.0 (100)
Chhattisgarh	7 (15.2)	39 (84.8)	46 (100)	1,930 (10.2)	17,052 (89.8)	19.0 (100)
Delhi	9 (52.9)	8 (47.1)	17 (100)	3,938 (43.3)	5,160 (56.7)	9.1 (100)
Gujarat	20 (15.9)	106 (84.1)	126 (100)	11,325 (18.4)	50,231 (81.6)	61.6 (100)
Haryana	18 (13.9)	112 (86.2)	130 (100)	6,181 (14.8)	35,692 (85.2)	41.9 (100)
Himachal Pradesh	4 (23.5)	13 (76.5)	17 (100)	900 (17.3)	4,293 (82.7)	5.2 (100)
Jammu & Kashmir	6 (54.6)	5 (45.5)	11 (100)	1,785 (45.3)	2,160 (54.8)	3.9 (100)
Jharkhand	8 (40.0)	12 (60.0)	20 (100)	2,750 (42.2)	3,771 (57.8)	6.5 (100)
Karnataka	24 (12.4)	169 (87.6)	193 (100)	14,720 (14.3)	88,179 (85.7)	102.9 (100)
Kerala	46 (28.8)	114 (71.3)	160 (100)	15,114 (27.1)	40,731 (72.9)	55.8 (100)
Madhya Pradesh	15 (8.1)	171 (91.9)	186 (100)	6,304 (8.0)	72,609 (92.0)	78.9 (100)
Maharashtra	30 (8.3)	333 (91.7)	363 (100)	9,515 (6.6)	134,546 (93.4)	144.1 (100)
Odisha	10 (10.6)	84 (89.4)	94 (100)	6,836 (16.9)	33,609 (83.1)	40.4 (100)
Puducherry	3 (17.7)	14 (82.4)	17 (100)	1,260 (15.9)	6,660 (84.1)	7.9 (100)
Punjab	10 (10.3)	87 (89.7)	97 (100)	6,175 (17.2)	29,739 (82.8)	35.9 (100)
Rajasthan	19 (16.2)	98 (83.8)	117 (100)	7,895 (17.2)	37,898 (82.8)	45.8 (100)
Tamil Nadu	56 (10.5)	477 (89.5)	533 (100)	58,975 (19.8)	238,525 (80.2)	297.5 (100)
Telangana	13 (5.4)	226 (94.6)	239 (100)	3,874 (3.3)	114,819 (96.7)	118.7 (100)
Uttar Pradesh	28 (11.1)	225 (88.9)	253 (100)	9,948 (9.6)	93,997 (90.4)	103.9 (100)
Uttarakhand	8 (27.6)	21 (72.4)	29 (100)	3,420 (32.5)	7,095 (67.5)	10.5 (100)
West Bengal	19 (20.4)	74 (79.6)	93 (100)	5,183 (14.1)	31,530 (85.9)	36.7 (100)
All India	413 (13.2)	2711 (86.8)	3124 (100)	198,928 (14.2)	1,205,892 (85.8)	1404.8 (100)

Source: AICTE Database.

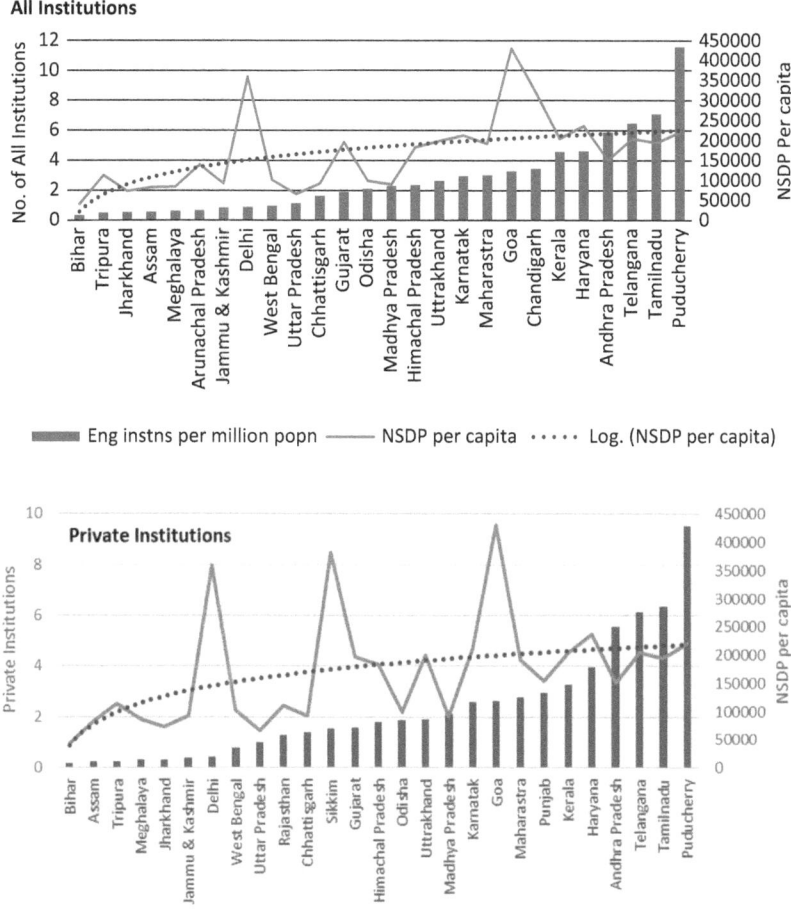

Figure 2.4 Economic Growth and Number of Engineering Institutions (per One Million Population), 2018–19

Source: Based on All India Survey of Higher Education 2018–19 and Census.

added as a percentage of gross state domestic product), which also influences positively the growth in the number of institutions (in 2012–13). But in another equation for 2018–19, we included rate of graduate unemployment, which is also found to be having a positive effect on the number of institutions. State income per capita is the most important factor that positively influences the growth of the number of institutions, in addition to industrial production (gross value added as a percentage of gross state domestic product), which also influences positively the growth in the number of institutions (in 2012–13). But in another equation for 2018–19, we included rate of graduate unemployment, which is also found to be having a positive effect on the number of institutions. That is, higher the graduate unemployment, the higher would be the demand for education. With the inclusion of unemployment in the equation, industrial production has turned out to be not statistically significant. Second, we get similar results for the equation that is used to explain interstate variations in private institutions (Table 2.4). After all, as the public sector institutions are generally small in number in every state, it is not surprising that the results are similar. However, in the case of private institutions, industrial production turned out to be important, both in 2012–13 and 2018–19. Further public expenditure is negatively related to growth in private institutions in 2012–13; the coefficient is statistically significant at 90 per cent level of confidence. As one expects, as the government expenditure on engineering education declines, private sector takes advantage and opens more and more institutions.

Many private institutions are not in a position to fully use their intake capacity. The admission rate as a proportion of sanctioned intake, which is also referred to as 'occupancy rate', has significantly gone down in the recent past – from 62.4 per cent in 2012–13 to 51.1 per cent in 2018–19. Thus, in 2018–19, around half of the sanctioned seats remained vacant. The percentage of vacant seats has come down marginally over the years – from 51 per cent in 2016–17 to 45 per cent in 2020–21. This is partly due to closure of many institutions.

We notice regional[1] variations in this too (Figures 2.5 and 2.6). As many as 61 per cent of the seats in the north-west region were vacant in 2018–19. In the country's western and southern regions, the enrolment of students in engineering courses is relatively better as the enrolments formed 59.7 per cent and 54.2 of the sanctioned intake, respectively. Regional imbalances in the growth of private higher education (in terms of both institutions and enrolments) continue to be a major issue, recognised as a serious concern long ago in the *National Policy on Education* in 1986.

Similarly, enrolments as a proportion of intake capacities also vary widely across different states. For instance, in some of the states/union territories such as Delhi, Chandigarh, Goa, Karnataka and Telangana, this share is higher than the national average of 51.1 per cent in 2018–19 (Figure 2.5). Unexpectedly, states like Tamil Nadu, Kerala and Punjab, which are much ahead of others in case of growth of technical and professional education, fare poorly with enrolment as a proportion of intake below the national average. This ratio is the lowest (around 30 per cent) in Himachal Pradesh, Haryana, Rajasthan and Chhattisgarh. This proportion has declined over the past six years in all the states except in Andhra Pradesh and Telangana, where it is around 60 per cent, as can be seen from Figure 2.5.

This decline in demand for engineering education is clear in the fall in the number of institutions and the enrolments, as shown in Tables 2.5 and 2.6. There is a 7 per cent fall in the number of institutions and 26 per cent decline in enrolments between 2012–13 and 2018–19. The decline has happened in

Table 2.4 Factors that influence Growth of Engineering Institutions

(Dependent Variable: *Ln* of Institutions per Million Population)

	All Institutions		Private Institutions	
	2012–13	2018–19	2012–13	2018–19
Ln net state domestic product per capita (NSDP)	1.2349*** (0.431)	0.9946*** (0.309)	1.1238*** (0.451)	1.0993*** (0.303)
Ln population (age group 18–23)	−2.1668 (−2.108)	−0.3686 (0.880)	−4.551* (2.90)	−1.4316 (2.424)
Ln gross value added from industry percentage of GSDP	0.4235** (0.209)	0.0222 (0.029)	0.656*** (0.241)	0.4745** (0.278)
Ln public expenditure on education as percentage of GSDP	−0.1783 (0.159)	−0.0032 (0.101)	−0.332* (0.173)	−0.1209 (0.122)
Ln graduate unemployment rate		0.8031** (0.416)		−0.6751 (0.537)
Intercept	−9.6964 (5.772)	−12.9716 (3.591)	−4.089 (7.236)	−12.6079 (7.315)
F-value	8.01	5.12	6.97	5.12
R-Square	0.531	0.553	0.525	0.552
Number of Observations	25	26	23	26

Figures in ( ) are robust standard errors. *** $p < 0.01$, ** $p < 0.05$, * $p < 0.10$.

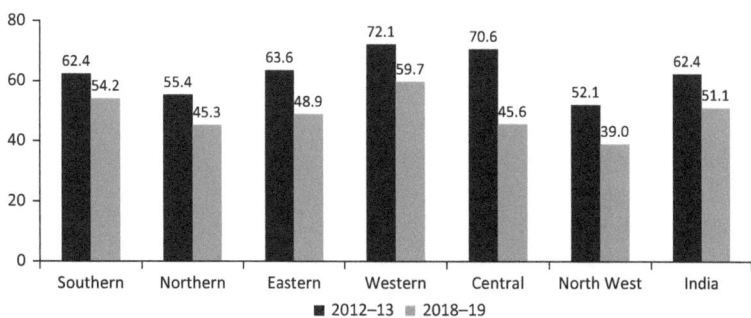

Figure 2.5 Enrolment as a Percentage of Intake in Engineering Education by Region (2012–13 and 2018–19)

Source: Based on AICTE Database.

both cases in almost all states and union territories, with very few exceptions. It is noticed that a large number of private engineering colleges in different regions are either closed or run the risk of being closed soon due to low enrolments. For instance, in 2019–20, AICTE has approved 22 degree-level

38 *Economics of Engineering Education in India*

private engineering colleges for 'progressive closure'[2] in the southern region. This figure was 24 in 2018–19. We refer to this further later.

The decline in the student enrolment is largely in private engineering institutions and not in public institutions. The private institutions did fairly well with rising student demand till 2010, but after the global economic slowdown in 2008, the impact of which was begun to be felt from 2010 onwards, clearly departing from early trends, there is a decline in the demand for

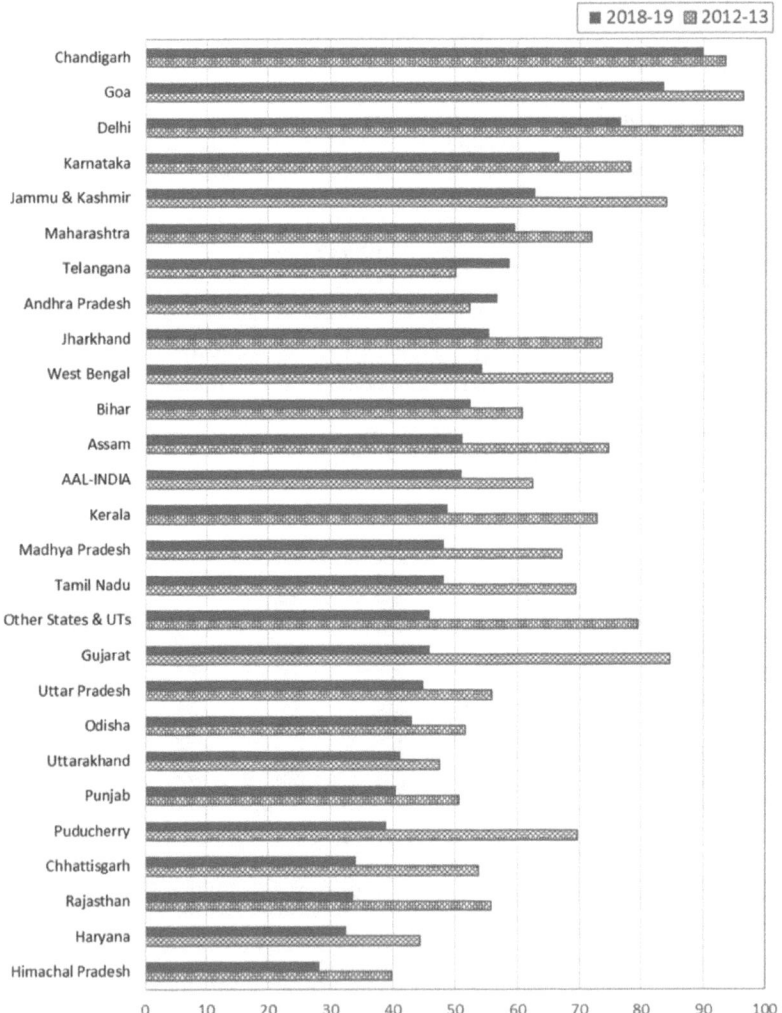

Figure 2.6 Enrolment as a Percentage of Intake in Engineering Education in India by States (2012–13 and 2018–19)

Source: AICTE Database.

Table 2.5 Number of Engineering Institutions in India by States, 2012–13 and 2018–19

	Institutions (Total)		Per one Lakh Population		Change (2012–13 minus 2018–19) in		Percent Change in the Number of Institutions
	2012–13	2018–19	2012–13	2018–19	No. of Institutions	Per One Lakh Population	
Andhra Pradesh	357	305	71.5	58.7	–52	–12.8	–14.57
Assam	14	19	4.4	5.6	5	1.2	35.71
Bihar	22	38	2.1	3.2	16	1.2	72.73
Chhattisgarh	50	46	19.3	16.2	–4	–3.0	–8.00
Delhi	18	17	10.5	8.7	–1	–1.7	–5.56
Gujarat	110	126	17.9	18.8	16	0.9	14.55
Haryana	159	130	61.7	46.0	–29	–15.7	–18.24
Himachal Pradesh	21	17	30.3	23.4	–4	–6.9	–19.05
Jammu & Kashmir	8	11	6.5	8.4	3	1.9	37.50
Jharkhand	14	20	4.2	5.4	6	1.3	42.86
Karnataka	192	193	31.1	29.6	1	–1.5	0.52
Kerala	153	160	45.5	45.8	7	0.3	4.58
Madhya Pradesh	226	186	30.6	22.9	–40	–7.7	–17.70
Maharashtra	369	363	32.5	30.0	–6	–2.5	–1.63
Odisha	98	94	23.1	21.0	–4	–2.1	–4.08
Puducherry	14	17	109.5	115.6	3	6.2	21.43
Punjab	103	97	36.8	32.7	–6	–4.0	–5.83
Rajasthan	137	117	19.7	15.3	–20	–4.3	–14.60
Tamil Nadu	513	533	70.6	70.7	20	0.1	3.90
Telangana	341	239	96.6	64.7	–102	–32.0	–29.91
Uttar Pradesh	320	253	15.8	11.4	–67	–4.4	–20.94
Uttarakhand	35	29	34.2	26.3	–6	–7.9	–17.14
West Bengal	83	93	9.0	9.7	10	0.6	12.05
All India	3,371	3,124	27.5	23.7	–247	–3.8	–7.33
Coef. of Variation			0.847	0.874			

Source: Based on All India Survey of Higher Education and Census of India.

engineering and other IT-related areas of study across the globe, a phenomenon which is quite significantly visible in India.

It was reported in the media that many private engineering colleges have shut their gates for new admissions, and the space is being used for running supermarkets, private schools and gymnasiums in recent years in states like Uttar Pradesh, Haryana, Andhra Pradesh and Telangana. In 2018–19, 105 engineering colleges were closed (AICTE, 2018). Additionally, 59

Table 2.6 Enrolments in Engineering Education per One Million Population, 2012–13 and 2018–19

	Total Enrolments		Per One Million Population		Change (2012–13 Minus 2018–19) in		Percentage Change in Enrolments
	2012–13	2018–19	2012–13	2018–19	Enrolments	Per One million population	
Andhra Pradesh	93,004	88,451	1,862	1,703	–4,553	–159	–4.9
Assam	3,190	2,605	101	77	–585	–24	–18.3
Bihar	4,732	5,783	45	49	1,051	5	22.2
Chhattisgarh	13,356	6,460	515	228	–6,896	–287	–51.6
Delhi	7,252	6,972	422	359	–280	–64	–3.9
Gujarat	45,998	28,213	749	421	–17,785	–328	–38.7
Haryana	29,254	13,621	1,135	482	–15,633	–653	–53.4
Himachal Pradesh	3,253	1,466	470	202	–1,787	–268	–54.9
Jammu & Kashmir	2,086	2,478	168	189	392	21	18.8
Jharkhand	4,311	3,611	128	98	–700	–31	–16.2
Karnataka	74,085	68,637	1,200	1,052	–5,448	–149	–7.4
Kerala	40,664	27,227	1,209	779	–13,437	–430	–33
Madhya Pradesh	66,865	38,012	905	469	–28,853	–436	–43.2
Maharashtra	11,2424	85,747	989	709	–26,677	–281	–23.7
Odisha	22,937	17,391	541	389	–5,546	–152	–24.2
Puducherry	4,682	3,087	3,661	2,100	–1,595	–1,561	–34.1
Punjab	22,184	14,552	792	491	–7,632	–300	–34.4
Rajasthan	34,756	15,429	499	202	–19,327	–296	–55.6
Tamil Nadu	178,493	14,3165	2,457	1,900	–35,328	–557	–19.8
Telangana	86,746	69,708	2,458	1,886	–17,038	–572	–19.6
Uttar Pradesh	81,553	46,686	402	210	–34,867	–191	–42.8
Uttarakhand	6,834	4,333	669	393	–2,501	–275	–36.6
West Bengal	25,625	19,906	278	207	–5,719	–72	–22.3
All India	967,829	717,617	789	544	–250,212	–245	–25.9
Coef. of Variation			0.931	0.986			

Source: Based on All India Survey of Higher Education and Census of India.

engineering colleges offering under graduate, postgraduate and diploma programmes are being closed in the current year (2020–21) by the AICTE. There are several private engineering colleges that are on AICTE's radar for low admissions, and they are running the risk of being closed at any time. According to AICTE data, of the 1.41 million BE/BTech student places available in 3,124 engineering colleges across the country, close to half (49 per cent) were not filled up in the academic year 2018–19; the corresponding figure was 53 per cent in case of private-unaided/self-financing engineering institutions.

The embarrassing reality is that thousands of student places in several self-financing engineering colleges have remained vacant over the years. Several engineering colleges in the country are tainted now as 'failed' institutions as they did not get enough revenues to survive. Several institutions have discontinued their programmes in specific branches of engineering due to low enrolment. A detailed survey (Chopra, 2018) conducted in 2017 reveals that the IT stream, which was the most favoured one earlier, has emerged as the least popular branch, with 770 institutes discontinuing the programme between 2012–13 and 2016–17. The second place goes to the branch of electrical and electronics engineering, which was discontinued in 635 colleges. Many other disciplines were also discontinued: computer science in 234 colleges, mechanical engineering in 185 colleges and civil engineering in 139 colleges. The maximum number of institutions that discontinued the programme in IT were in Telangana (157), followed by Andhra Pradesh (128) and Tamil Nadu (104). The closure of more IT departments in the country has been directly related to the global economic slowdown of 2008 that affected the IT sector the most. Several workers engaged in the IT sector lost their jobs and hardly any new recruitment has taken place in this field.

The oversupply of engineering manpower in the country has disturbed the entire ecosystem of engineering. Getting admission in engineering studies was socially prestigious for both students and parents in the early 2000s, but this has changed drastically within a decade. The massive expansion of engineering education, specifically self-financing engineering colleges, in the country has changed the higher education structure altogether. Engineering education which was being talked about only by a few educationists has now become the elephant in discussion rooms. The expansion in engineering education is reduced so drastically that the conduct of entrance examination for this field at the national as well as state and institutional level has become more or less a ritual with the number of students in the rank list practically matching the number of admission places available, except of course in prestigious public institutions such as the IITs and NITs. The overall imbalance or mismatch in the demand for admissions and availability of student places in engineering education is very high. Until recently, the demand used to be much above the supply, too many people chasing too few places, as students clearing their senior secondary (grade 12) board examination in mathematics and science streams used to aspire for an admission in engineering studies. But there has been a fall in the demand in recent years to such a level that supply now exceeds demand. AICTE data shows that in 2019–20, there are close to 1.3 million places for admission in undergraduate engineering studies in India, while only 0.9 million students took the national entrance examination of JEE.

Newly established self-financing engineering colleges find it difficult to run their institutions as their revenues are shrinking due to low enrolments. These colleges, which almost exclusively depend on student fees, are now adopting, apart from fair and unfair marketing communication tools like sponsored news items in print and electronic media, student fairs, advertisements in newspapers to taxis (Singh, 2016), many desperate measures – from offering fee concessions to diluting admission criteria; from paying middlemen to bring in students to hiring under-qualified faculty; to, in some cases as reported, letting out part of their campuses to corporate houses. With a decline in student enrolments, colleges increasingly depend on middlemen. However, due to the informal and unregulated nature of the phenomenon, it is difficult to map out the growth of middlemen engaged to get students into the engineering colleges and related aspects. But some media reports (Chopra, 2018; Sengupta, 2011) reveal that middlemen in some cases, fashionably known as consultants, make informal arrangements with schools and get the contact details of all their grade 12 pupils and reach them as soon as the board examinations are over. These middlemen spread their net to neighbouring states as well to 'hook' potential students. For example, for the student admissions in engineering education in Uttar Pradesh, middlemen began fanning out to Bihar in search of aspirants. For them, Bihar is currently the perfect hunting ground as there are a smaller number of engineering colleges there and students are happy to apply to colleges in Uttar Pradesh.

It has been reported extensively in the media that as a large number of student places in private engineering colleges remained vacant after the counselling processes were over, colleges have started providing direct admission to students who have not even appeared for any entrance examination, which is otherwise compulsory. The rank list in engineering education is prepared based on a ridiculously low pass percentage in the entrance examinations. As reported by M.T. Reju, the Commissioner of Entrance Examinations, Kerala (*The Hindu*, 09 July 2017), a student needs to score just 20 out of a total/maximum marks of 960 to make it to the rank list, which means that those who score a mere 2 per cent marks actually qualify to be admitted in engineering education! In this context, it is intriguing to analyse why and how an engineering degree that was considered quite prestigious till recently is now in the doldrums. The other important question that needs to be asked in this context is: what led to this situation? Among the more important factors that have been discussed to explain this situation in the literature and also in media reports is the role of self-financing colleges. Second, graduates coming out of the system are found to be lacking knowledge of the basics of engineering and therefore cannot be gainfully employed in the labour market, the blame going partly back to the institutions that offer poor quality education. Third, a poor and ineffective governance system is found to be responsible for the mess.

The proliferation and wholesale privatisation of engineering education in India has led to many more problems (Dubey et al., 2019). A few important ones include the inequality in accessing engineering education, the decline in the quality of engineering education and the failure of graduates to get gainful employment in the labour market. All these factors are related and discussed in detail in the following sections of the chapter.

Inequalities in Engineering Education

Despite significant improvement in demographic and social diversity in higher education, inequality still remains an important challenge. Inequality in education has several dimensions: regional, gender, social, economic and academic. Tilak (2015) has shown that inequalities in higher education by gender have narrowed in India over the years to minimum levels; inequalities by caste also improved at an impressive rate, though the situation is far from satisfactory; regional disparities were reduced, but the improvement is very modest. But Tilak (2015) also found that inequalities between the rich and the poor have been very high and they have actually widened over the years. We shall examine whether in case of engineering education the situation is similar or different. The issue of inequalities in the growth of engineering education in India is discussed here, focusing on four major dimensions in this section: regional/state, gender, caste and the discipline of study.

Geographic Disparities: Inter-Regional and Interstate

Regional imbalance continues to be a major issue despite the huge expansion of higher education in India in recent years, even though it was seriously taken up as a major issue in the National Policy on Education (Government of India, 1986, p. 6) when it stated that "steps will be taken to facilitate inter-regional mobility by providing equal access to every Indian of requisite merit, regardless, of his origins as [far as] the higher and technical education is concerned". With the initiatives taken by some states in the late 1980s and early 1990s, viz. Karnataka, Maharashtra, Tamil Nadu and Andhra Pradesh, to permit private institutions on self-financing basis, one witnesses a spate of new institutions coming up in these states. When the other states found that the initiatives of those states paid rich dividends in terms of funding and growth of institutions, many other states adopted similar approaches, and in no time the phenomenon of setting up self-financing engineering institutions (and other institutions of higher education) went viral all over the country. But the states that took the initiatives early continue to maintain the lead. By 2000–01, regional inequalities became very sharp, and the U.R. Rao Committee (AICTE, 2003) took note of it and strongly argued for measures for balanced regional development. But no special attention was given to the problem. Presently, around two-thirds of India's engineering institutions at undergraduate level are located in the states of Tamil Nadu, Karnataka, Andhra Pradesh and Maharashtra, even though they account for less than one-third of the total population of the country. The southern region has almost half of the of the total engineering institutons, whereas the eastern region has only a tiny number (Figure 2.5).

According to the latest statistics available from AICTE, there are around 1,447 degree-level engineering institutions (46.6 per cent of the total institutions in India) in 2018–19 in the southern region, which consist of five states and one union territory, namely Andhra Pradesh, Karnataka, Kerala, Puducherry, Tamil Nadu and Telangana, whereas there are only 226 institutions in the four major states of the eastern region that includes Assam, Jharkhand, Odisha and West Bengal (7.2 per cent of the total institutions in India). Interestingly, ten states and two union territories in the eastern and northern regions (Bihar, Jharkhand, Odisha, West Bengal, Haryana, Himachal Pradesh, Jammu & Kashmir, Punjab, Uttarakhand, Uttar Pradesh, Delhi and Chandigarh), accounting for 45.3 per cent of India's population, have only about 17.4 per cent of the total engineering institutions, with an intake capacity of 15 per cent. The eastern region is far behind the southern region and behind other regions in the country in terms of the number of engineering institutions.

In fact, if we look at the geographic concentration of engineering institutions, we note a very high degree of regional imbalance. As Figure 2.7 shows, Tamil Nadu, Telangana and Andhra Pradesh have the highest numbers of engineering institutions per one lakh population: 70 in Tamil Nadu, 64 in Telangana and 58 in Andhra Pradesh. On the other end, states like Bihar and Jharkhand have just three and five, respectively, per one lakh people! The figures relating to Assam and Jammu & Kashmir are also close to these states' numbers.

The region-wise students' intake for student admissions and actual enrolments also reveals more or less a similar pattern. Six southern states account for 49.3 per cent of the total intake (and 55.8 per cent of enrolment) in degree-level engineering institutions in 2018–19, while the eastern region has only about 6.5 per cent of the total intake (and 6.3 per cent of enrolments) in India. Ten out of the 28 states and eight union territories, namely Tamil Nadu, Andhra Pradesh, Maharashtra, Uttar Pradesh, Telangana, Karnataka, Madhya Pradesh, Gujarat, Kerala and Haryana, account for 80 per cent of the total student seats for admission in the country (Table 2.3).

The statistics clearly suggest that the glaring regional imbalance that exists in the field of engineering education in India leads to an oversupply in some regions and states and shortages in others (Rao, 2003; WENR, 2007). A careful look at the growth of institutions reveals that the regional imbalance is not only due to the establishment of a large number of private colleges in the southern region and lack of the same in other regions, but also due to imbalanced public supply of government engineering colleges.

The interstate inequalities in the distribution of the educational institutions can be analysed in the form of a concentration ratio, as given in Table 2.7, which also gives the extent of changes in the same during the recent period. The concentration ratio is the distribution of institutions in relation to the distribution of population.[3] If the value of the ratio equals one, the

Engineering Education in India 45

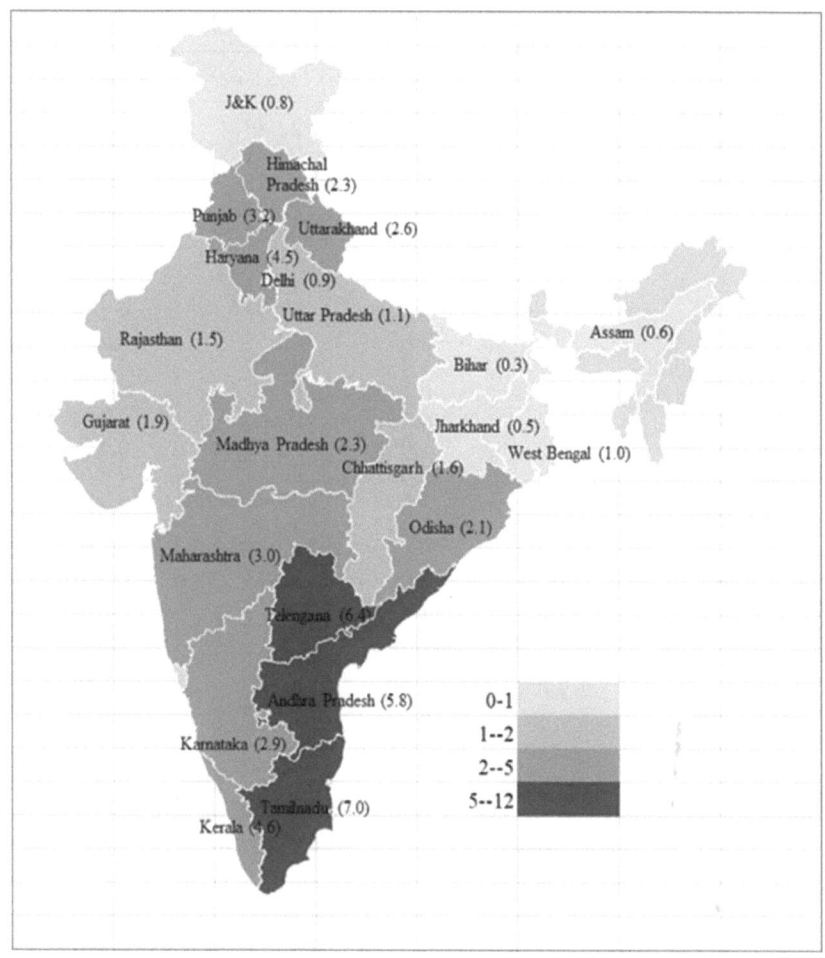

Figure 2.7 State-Wise Engineering Institutions per One Million Population in India (2018–19)

Source: Based on AICTE Database and Census of India.

distribution of institutions is proportionate to the distribution of population; if the ratio is above 1, it shows over-concentration, and if it is below 1, the state is underserved in relation to population. Such a ratio is estimated in 2012–13 and 2018–19, to note the concentration and the change therein (Table 2.7). The ratio ranges between 0.86 in Bihar and 4.31 in Puducherry in 2012–13. In 2018–19 also these two were at the two extreme ends in terms of concentration. There is a very high concentration in Puducherry, Telangana and Tamil Nadu with a ratio above 3. Tamil Nadu, which was the third in concentration ratio among the major states in 2012–13, rose to second in 2018–19. There are as many as 12 states with over-concentration and about

46 *Economics of Engineering Education in India*

Table 2.7 State-Wise Concentration Ratio of Engineering Education Institutions

	2012–13	2018–19	Change
Andhra Pradesh	2.583	2.549	−0.034
Assam	0.160	0.231	0.071
Bihar	0.086	0.146	0.060
Chandigarh	0.822	0.929	0.107
Chhattisgarh	0.691	0.664	−0.026
Delhi	0.349	0.332	−0.017
Goa	1.310	1.253	−0.057
Gujarat	0.643	0.792	0.149
Haryana	2.082	1.857	−0.225
Himachal Pradesh	1.134	1.077	−0.057
Jammu & Kashmir	0.237	0.392	0.155
Jharkhand	0.161	0.235	0.074
Karnataka	1.092	1.270	0.178
Kerala	2.032	2.456	0.424
Madhya Pradesh	1.095	0.944	−0.151
Maharashtra	1.145	1.248	0.103
Odisha	0.869	0.928	0.059
Puducherry	4.309	4.635	0.326
Punjab	1.271	1.414	0.142
Rajasthan	0.682	0.588	−0.094
Tamil Nadu	2.797	3.481	0.684
Telangana	3.407	2.758	−0.649
Uttar Pradesh	0.558	0.459	−0.099
Uttarakhand	1.176	1.102	−0.074
West Bengal	0.316	0.390	0.074
Other States and Union Territories	0.133	0.289	0.156

Concentration Ratio: See the text.
Source: Based on All India Survey of Higher Education and Census of India.

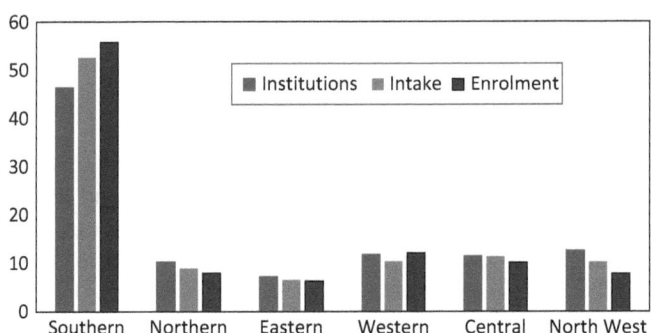

Figure 2.8 Regional Concentration of Institutions, Intake and Enrolment in Engineering Education, 2018–19 (%)
Source: Based on AICTE Database.

the same number with under-provision. Between 2012–13 and 2018–19, one does not find any significant change in concentration, implying that no special effective measures were taken to de-concentrate them so as to improve regional balanced development or the regional growth of engineering institutions in the country.

If we look at regional distribution across major regions in the country, we note that the southern region prospered well in terms of number of engineering institutions; and all other regions – northern, western, central, and north-west – lag far behind. Eastern region figures at the bottom. This is true with respect to number of institutions, intake and enrolment in engineering education, as shown in Figure 2.8.

Further, we note from Table 2.8 that it is in southern, northern and western regions where private sector dominates over the public institutions, while in eastern, central and north-western regions, the shares of the private sector are marginally lower than those of the public institutions; but in these regions, the overall numbers are also small. Between 2012–13 and 2018–19, the southern region had a steady share in institutions (46.6 per cent in 2011–12 and 46.3 per cent in 2018–19), but its share in intake increased from 49.3 per cent to 52.6 per cent. We also note that the regional concentration has got intensified between 2012–13 and 2018–19, with the ratio (Figure 2.9) increasing in case of southern and western regions. Though there is a small increase in case of the eastern region, it is too small; northern region and north-western region's disadvantage also increased. Table A6 in the Appendix A reveals some more interesting details across different states.

Regional and interstate disparities have thus been very sharp in the growth of engineering education. This would result in a lack of access to a majority of students in those states where institutions are few and in avoidable migration of students from those regions to the other regions where engineering education facilities are relatively easily available. Obviously, students who migrate

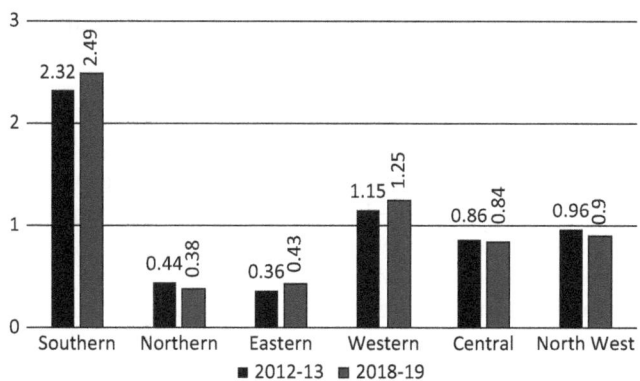

Figure 2.9 Ratio of Regional Concentration of Engineering Institutions

Source: Based on All India Survey of Higher Education 2012–13 and 2018–19.

Table 2.8 Regional Concentration of Engineering Education Institutions and Intakes by Management (2012–13 and 2018–19)

Regions	Institutions			Intake		
	Government	Private	Total	Government	Private	Total
2012–13						
Southern	35.3	47.6	46.6	37.4	50.2	49.3
Northern	10.5	11.3	11.2	9.3	10.9	10.8
Eastern	14.0	5.6	6.2	9.9	5.4	5.7
Western	8.0	11.4	11.1	7.2	10.4	10.2
Central	15.4	11.1	11.5	19.4	10.9	11.5
North-West	16.8	13.0	13.3	15.5	12.1	12.3
All India	100.0	100.0	100.0	100.0	100.0	100.0
	(286)	(3085)	(3371)	(106.9)	(1445.2)	(1552.1)
2018–19						
Southern	38.26	47.55	46.32	52.15	52.68	52.61
Northern	13.56	9.74	10.24	9.23	8.88	8.93
Eastern	13.56	6.57	7.23	8.64	5.94	6.32
Western	7.51	12.43	11.78	4.99	11.23	10.35
Central	10.17	11.66	11.46	9.83	11.60	11.35
North-West	16.95	11.91	12.58	14.34	9.53	10.21
All India	100.00	100.00	100.00	100.00	100.00	100.00
	(413)	(2711)	(3124)	(198.9)	(1205.9)	(1404.8)

Note: Figures in ( ) on intake for all India are in thousands.
Source: AICTE Database.

have to necessarily spend higher amounts on travel and engineering studies as a whole. Further location of the higher education institutions in some of these backward states will help in boosting economic and social development. Special efforts may be needed to correct the high degree of regional disparities and to ensure a regional balanced development in higher education.

Inequality by Gender

Over the decades, there has been a phenomenal growth in the enrolment of female students in higher education in India, and their share in total enrolment has reached 49 per cent in 2020–21, suggesting achievement of near gender parity (Table 2.9). Of the total enrolment of 40.2 million students in higher education in India, 20.1 million were women in 2020–21 (MHRD 2021). The gross enrolment ratio in higher education among girls is marginally higher than the ratio in the case of males (26.7 per cent among females and 27.9 per cent among males). But the picture is not the same with respect to all branches of higher education. In the arts, social sciences, basic sciences and medicine, the representation of females is higher than males, while in commerce, management and engineering and technology, female enrolment is less than males'

(Figure 2.10). For instance, out of the total student population in higher education, 18.7 per cent of males are pursuing engineering studies, while only 8 per cent of females do the same. Unlike in the case of 'soft' branches like humanities and sciences in which women constitute a higher proportion, in engineering education women constitute only 35 per cent of the enrolments in 2019–20. However, this marks a big increase from a meagre below 1 per cent in 1961–62 with an annual average growth rate of 15 per cent (Table 2.9). This rate of growth in women's enrolment in engineering education in the last four decades is higher than the growth in their enrolment in overall higher education, which is 8.1 per cent. However, the enrolment of females in engineering is still not at par with males.

Often, it is argued that engineering and technical education is a masculine domain and hence out of reach for women. Those who support this line of argument point to the perseverance of certain untenable social myths like 'women are emotional, while technology is strictly logical and hence, both do not go together'. There is also the view that men are good at mathematics and machines, while women have no clue about these areas (Rao, 2007, p. 187). But all this does not seem to be true, though quite a few studies have found that technical and professional education is, by and large, dominated by males more than general education, in which females constitute a larger proportion (Salim, 2008; Ghuman et al., 2009).

Nevertheless, the improvement in the participation of women in engineering education during the last four decades perhaps highlights the gradual rise of

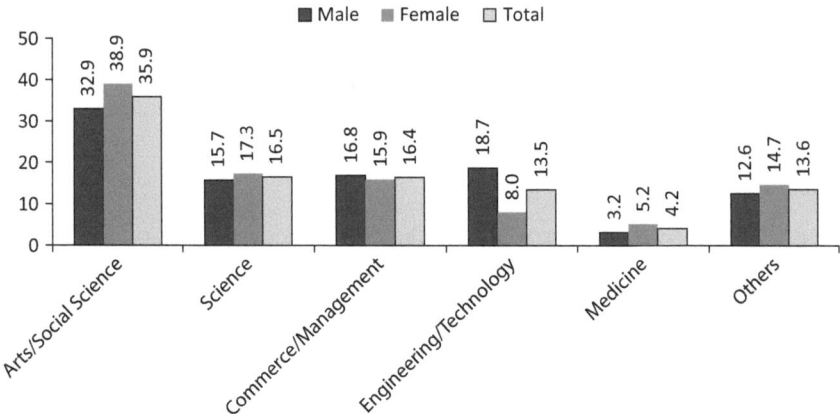

Figure 2.10 Distribution of Enrolments in Higher Education across Various Branches by Gender (2018–19)

Note: "Others" include education, law, agriculture, physical education, veterinary and animal sciences, hospitality and tourism, journalism and mass communication, library and information science and several other interdisciplinary areas of study.

Source: All India Survey of Higher Education 2018–19.

Table 2.9 Women Enrolment in Total Higher and Engineering Education

Year	Higher Education		Engineering Education	
	Total (in Lakhs)	Percentage Share	Total (in thousands)	Percentage Share
1961–62	1.9	17.8	0.3	0.8
1970–71	4.3	14.4	0.9	1.0
1975–76	6.0	24.5	2.1	2.2
1980–81	7.5	27.2	5.0	3.0
1985–86	10.7	29.6	12.2	6.9
1990–91	14.4	29.2	17.1	7.9
1995–96	21.9	33.3	26.4	8.4
2000–01	30.1	35.9	109.0	20.6
2005–06	44.7	37.1	186.0	23.4
2010–11	70.5	41.5	801.0	28.0
2015–16	134.7	47.3	1,360.0	27.8
2016–17	141.6	48.1	1,365.0	28.5
2017–18	174.4	47.6	1,234.0	29.0
2018–19	181.9	48.6	1,193.0	29.3
2019–20	188.9	49.0	1,126.0	35.4
2020–21	201.4	48.7	1,069.0	29.0
Growth Rate*	8.22	–	14.87	–

*Compound rate of growth per annum (%).
Source: Selected Educational Statistics (Various Years), UGC Annual Report (Various Years) and All India Survey of Higher Education (Various Years).

interest of women in this discipline of study. According to a study of the QEPEF (2016), in India, where women of the emerging middle class are increasingly fighting for equal rights, only 29 per cent of the population considers engineering as masculine, while an amazing 30 per cent consider it as feminine.

Inequality by Caste

Despite much overall improvement, caste is considered one of the important social barriers in accessing higher education, quality higher education in particular and quality engineering education more particularly. As a result, one finds wide variations in the access to higher education between different social groups in India. In 2018–19, the gross enrolment ratio in higher education was 23 per cent for scheduled castes (SCs) and 17.2 per cent for scheduled tribes (STs) as compared to the ratio of 26.3 per cent for all at the all India level (MHRD, 2019). Furthermore, it is generally felt that engineering and technical education in India has been highly selective in terms of providing access to the disadvantaged sections of the society such as SCs and STs (Rao, 2006), as it is relatively more expensive than other subjects and it also requires a strong academic background at the school level.

The percentage of enrolment of SCs in engineering education was 11 per cent in 2020–21, which was merely 3.8 per cent in 1985–86, registering an increase by three times. Similarly, the enrolment of STs in engineering education has increased from 1 per cent in the total enrolment to 3.1 per cent in a period of over 30 years (Table 2.10). Ghuman et al. (2009), using the data collected from a primary survey of 2,085 students in rural Punjab, found that as high as three-fourths of the total students coming from rural backgrounds, studying in different professional education programmes, belonged to the forward castes. It shows that while students from rural areas access professional education in large numbers, the socially backward groups lag far behind others.

The access to engineering education among females belonging to different disadvantaged social groups appeared to be far worse. Being women belonging to scheduled groups means a double disadvantage. Currently, of the total enroled in higher education, only 7.3 per cent of SC males and 0.9 per cent of ST females enrolled in higher education are in engineering education (Table 2.10). As Varma and Kapur (2010) found, a large number of students belonging to upper and middle castes/classes get admitted to the IITs in India. It was also pointed out that once admitted, students belonging to the upper and middle castes and classes are likely to have a much more positive experience and higher success rate than those belonging to lower castes and classes. IITs have been the most coveted institutions and are regarded as the exemplars of merit. In fact, they are said to be so meritocratic that some criticise them as 'upper caste institutions' (Subramanian, 2019), as education at the IITs has been for the privileged sections of Indian society, though the situation is gradually but slowly changing.

The enrolment of students in the first year of engineering education by different social groups shows that there has not been much improvement over the last seven years (2012–13 to 2018–19), for which data are available (Table 2.11). In 2012–13, 10.7 per cent students were enrolled in the first year of the undergraduate engineering programme; this number has increased marginally to 11.7 per cent in 2018–19. The respective figures for ST students are 2.5 and 2.7 per cent. The improvement seems to be very

Table 2.10 Enrolment of Scheduled Castes and Scheduled Tribes in Engineering Education (% of Total Enrolment in Engineering & Technology)

Year	Scheduled Castes			Scheduled Tribes		
	Male	Female	Total	Male	Female	Total
1985–86	3.61	0.22	3.83	0.99	0.04	1.03
1990–91	5.70	0.67	6.36	1.12	0.08	1.19
1995–96	3.91	0.46	4.37	1.61	0.18	1.79
2000–01	5.23	1.67	6.90	2.26	0.33	2.59
2005–06	15.06	5.38	20.44	5.31	1.88	7.19
2010–11	5.64	2.33	7.97	1.91	0.64	2.57
2015–16	7.26	2.85	10.11	1.89	0.62	2.51
2018–19	7.65	1.96	11.04	2.07	0.74	2.81
2019–20	7.41	3.42	10.85	2.05	0.77	2.82
2020–21	7.26	3.29	10.55	2.20	0.85	3.05

Source: Selected Educational Statistics (Various Years), UGC Annual Report (Various Years) and AISHE (Various Years).

small. Interestingly, the enrolment of students from the forward caste groups has declined from 44.1 per cent to 43.1 per cent during the same period. Minorities and STs too gained marginally.

If one looks at the regional distribution of the enrolment of students in the first year of engineering education, it is clear that the central and the northern regions fare poorly, with the lowest rates of enrolment of SCs (7.8 per cent in the central region) and STs (0.8 per cent in the northern region) (Table 2.12). Table A7 in Appendix A gives more details by states. In Goa, the proportion of SCs in the enrolments in engineering education is less than 1 per cent in 2018–19. Similarly, in the states like Uttar Pradesh and also in relatively better-off states like Haryana, Kerala, and Punjab the enrolment of STs in

Table 2.11 Enrolments in the First Year of Engineering Degree Studies: Distribution by Social Category (2012–13 to 2018–19)

Year	Scheduled Castes	Scheduled Tribes	Other Backward Classes	General/Open Category	Minorities	Total
2012–13	10.73	2.47	35.95	44.05	6.80	100 (9.67)
2013–14	11.73	2.61	35.91	42.85	6.91	100 (9.44)
2014–15	12.65	2.60	35.81	41.83	7.11	100 (8.75)
2015–16	12.71	2.85	36.10	40.99	7.34	100 (8.55)
2016–17	12.53	2.82	35.67	41.12	7.85	100 (7.86)
2017–18	13.04	2.78	36.23	40.47	7.47	100 (7.50)
2018–19	11.72	2.68	35.12	43.08	7.40	100 (7.17)

Figures in ( ) are absolute figures in lakhs.
Source: AICTE Database.

Table 2.12 Region-Wise Pattern of the of Enrolments in the First Year of Engineering Studies in 2018–19 by Social Category

Region	Scheduled Castes	Scheduled Tribes	Other Backward Classes	General/Open Category	Minorities	Total
Southern	12.02	2.09	42.83	34.45	8.60	100 (400.3) [55.8]
Northern	16.48	0.81	29.19	46.88	6.64	100 (56.8) [7.9]
Eastern	12.78	7.90	13.58	61.19	4.54	100 (45.0) [6.3]
Western	9.82	1.57	33.50	48.59	6.52	100 (86.9) [12.1]
Central	7.87	5.53	28.45	53.62	4.53	100 (72.7) [10.1]
North-West	11.79	2.62	14.55	64.09	6.94	100 (56.0) [7.8]
All INDIA	11.72	2.68	35.12	43.08	7.40	100 (717.6)

Figures in ( ) are absolute figures in thousands. Figures in [ ] are regional distribution in percentage.
Source: AICTE Database.

engineering education is less than 1 per cent. STs constitute a small proportion of the total population in some of these states; so is the case of SCs in Goa. In Puducherry and Tamil Nadu, OBCs account for the largest enrolment among all the states, and the general (or open) category students the least. The regional mapping of students in engineering education in India will provide clear insights to understand the specific dimensions of caste inequalities intersecting with regional disparities in accessing engineering education by various social groups.

To conclude, while there has been progress over the years in improving the participation of disadvantaged sections in engineering education, which can be attributed to the constitutionally guaranteed reservations for disadvantaged strata of the society,[4] the situation is not very satisfactory, even after 75 years of independence.

Unequal Participation by Economic Classes

NSSO provides data on the enrolment of students in various levels of education on average per capita monthly consumption expenditure of households. Considering household consumption expenditure as reflective of income levels of the households, we can analyse the enrolment pattern in engineering education by economic levels of households.

Figure 2.11 shows the extent of inequalities in enrolments in engineering education. About 80 per cent of the students belong to the top income quintile and about 7 per cent is accounted by the bottom 60 per cent of the population in 2007–08. The situation marginally improved by 2017–18: the share of the top quintile coming down to 68 per cent; the bottom two quintiles accounting for 7.1 per cent; and the third quintile accounting for another 10.3 per cent. Still, a high degree of inequality persists. After all, engineering

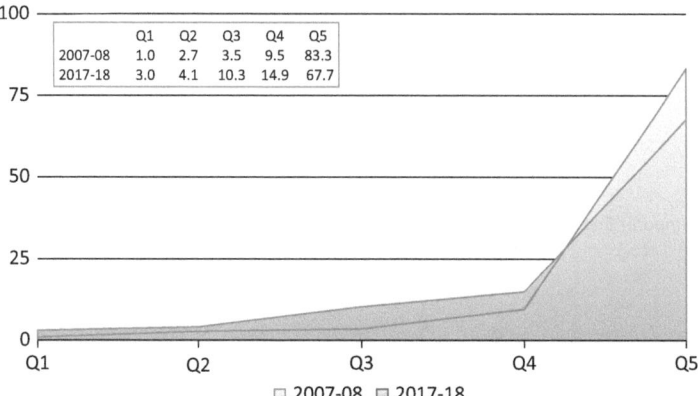

Figure 2.11 Distribution of Enrolments in Engineering Education by Household Quintiles (%)

Source: Based on NSSO data.

education is expensive and public support in the form of scholarships, reimbursement of fee schemes, fee waivers and loans is not effective enough to mitigate inequalities. As we see later, even the bottom expenditure quintiles have to spend considerable amounts to take up engineering studies.

Disciplinary Imbalance

We have already seen that the growth of higher education in India has been uneven, creating a more imbalanced system of higher education in terms of different branches of study. Within the broad stream of engineering also, we notice a high degree of imbalance between several sub-streams, as the growth of student enrolments in engineering education has varied significantly by different sub-disciplines. The engineering stream has 21 sub-streams like electronics engineering, computer engineering, mechanical engineering, electrical engineering and so on. It is clear from Figure 2.12 that the top five sub-streams in terms of enrolments in 2019–20 are computer engineering with 9.3 lakh students, mechanical engineering with 6.8 lakh students, electronics engineering with 6.1 lakh students, civil engineering with 4.8 lakh students and electrical engineering with 3.7 lakh students enrolled. In IT/computer application stream, there were 7.5 lakh students enrolled. These five streams account for more than 80 per cent of the total enrolments in engineering

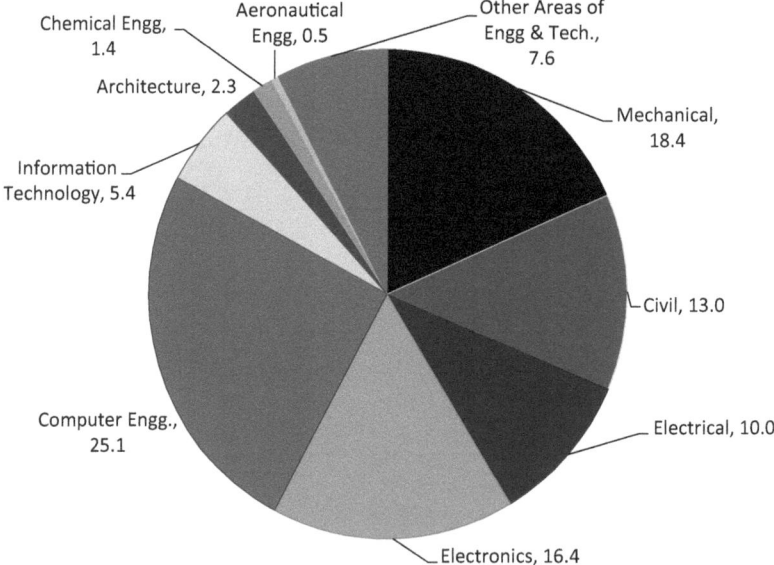

Figure 2.12 Popular Streams of Engineering and Technology, 2019–20 (Enrolment as a Percentage of Total Enrolments in Engineering Education)

Source: Based on All-India Survey of Higher Education 2019–20.

Table 2.13 Enrolment in Engineering (First Degree) Programmes by Sub-Stream (%)

	2010–11	2019–20	Change
Computer engineering	22.25	25.09	2.84
Mechanical engineering	16.64	18.38	1.73
Electronics engineering	25.34	16.40	–8.93
Civil engineering	8.65	12.99	4.34
Electrical engineering	13.46	10.02	–3.45
Information technology	11.45	5.38	–6.07
Architecture	...	2.50	...
Chemical engineering	1.36	1.40	–0.04
Agriculture engineering	0.215	0.608	0.39
Aeronautical engineering	...	0.502	...
Food technology	...	0.363	...
Metallurgical engineering	0.313	0.267	–0.05
Mining engineering	0.093	0.189	0.10
Marine engineering	0.189	0.143	–0.04
Dairy technology	0.066	0.089	0.03
Planning	...	0.027	...
Engineering and technology total	100.00	100.00	...
Total in millions	1.11	3.73	2.62

Totals include others not listed here.
Source: MHRD (2011a, 2020).

education. Distribution of enrolments across 17 sub-streams of engineering in 2010–11 and 2018–19 is given in Table 2.13.[5]

Economic liberalisation in the 1990s gave a major push to the Indian software services industry, which further boosted the demand for engineers trained in electronics and IT-related disciplines such as computer science and engineering, electronics and communications, and IT. With the 'IT craze' (Upadhyay, 2014), these streams emerged as the more popular branches among the students. Traditionally, popular branches such as electrical, civil and mechanical engineering have gone considerably down in student preferences. The boom in the IT sector in the early 1990s led to the opening up of several electronics and IT-related fields of study in newly established engineering colleges in India. Engineering colleges established after the introduction of policies of economic liberalisation started offering mainly electronics and IT-related streams. As Banerjee and Muley (2008) noted, the newly established engineering institutions concentrated on the disciplines related to the areas of computer engineering and IT-related areas. As a result, India has produced larger numbers of computer science and IT engineers more than in other disciplines. This was clearly linked with the labour market expectations of the engineering graduates as degrees in electronics and IT-related degree programmes helped them secure jobs relatively easily and quickly as compared to degrees in traditional subjects like civil and mechanical engineering.

56 *Economics of Engineering Education in India*

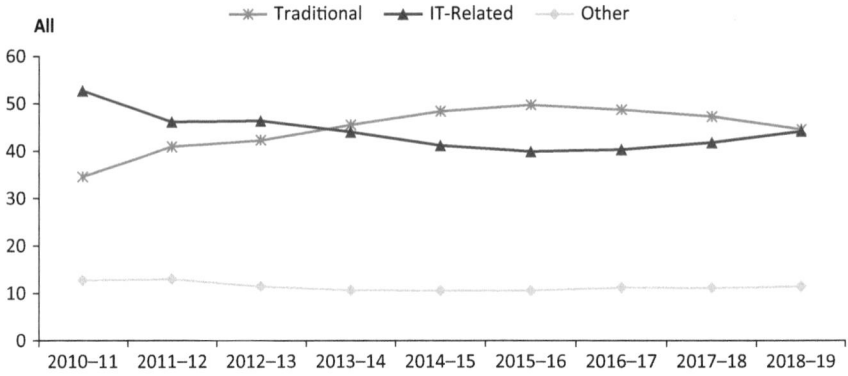

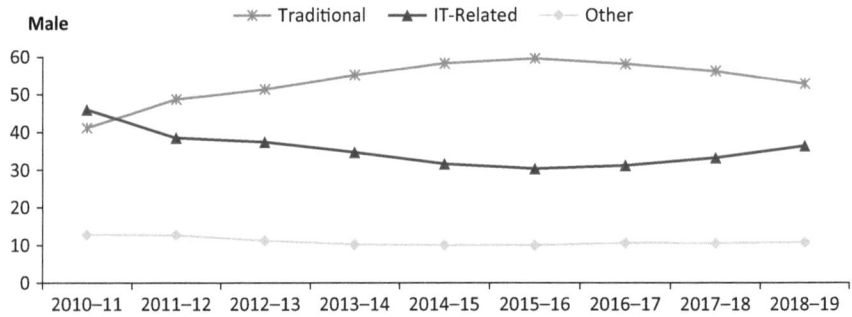

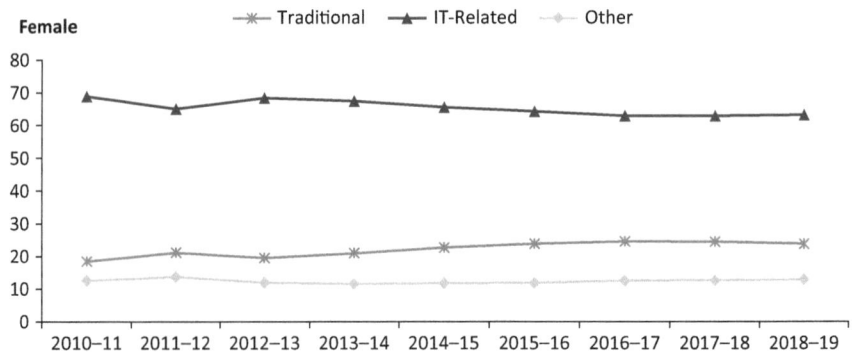

Figure 2.13 Growth in Enrolments in Engineering Education by Major Categories of Sub-Streams (%)

Source: Based on AICTE Database.

However, by 2010–11, the situation seems to have reached a peak, and the IT boom seems to have ended; after 2010, we notice a declining trend in the demand for these popular branches of engineering education. As per available data, after 2010–11, some new sub-streams were added to the stream of engineering and technology. By 2010–11, electronics engineering and computer engineering were at their peak in terms of enrolments, together accounting for 48 per cent of enrolments in all areas of engineering. IT accounted for 11 per cent of enrolments. But by 2018–19, the share of electronics engineering declined by 9 per cent points – from 25 per cent to 16 per cent – and the share of IT by 7 per cent points – from 11 per cent to below 5 per cent. Computer engineering did not register much change during this period. In contrast, civil engineering and mechanical engineering improved their relative positions (Table 2.14). On the whole, IT-craze has not vanished altogether.

The several sub-streams of engineering can be classified into three major groups: (a) 'traditional' streams that include mechanical, civil and electrical; (b) 'modern' (electronics and IT-related) streams that include electronics and communication, computer science and IT; and (c) other areas of engineering, which cover chemical, aeronautical, metallurgical, agriculture, food technology, mining, dairy technology and so on. A look at this pattern by gender gives us interesting insights into changing perceptions. As expected, more than half of the males in engineering education (51.5 per cent) were pursuing

Table 2.14 Stream-Wise Distribution of Enrolments in Engineering Education by Gender (%)

	2012–13			2018–19		
	Male	Female	Total	Male	Female	Total
Mechanical engineering	26.39	2.93	19.64	27.10	3.61	20.32
Civil engineering	12.51	6.91	10.90	15.33	10.47	13.93
Electrical engineering	12.47	9.77	11.69	10.43	9.75	10.23
Traditional total	51.37	19.61	42.23	52.86	23.84	44.48
Electronics engineering	18.55	29.57	21.72	13.09	24.52	16.39
Computer engineering	14.05	28.58	18.24	19.24	31.74	22.85
Information technology	4.80	10.31	6.38	4.04	6.94	4.88
Modern total	37.40	68.46	46.34	36.37	63.20	44.12
Other engineering and technology	7.69	7.82	7.72	5.87	6.18	5.96
Architecture	0.77	2.06	1.14	1.41	3.82	2.11
Chemical engineering	1.19	1.00	1.14	1.43	1.11	1.33
Aeronautical engineering	0.48	0.25	0.41	0.48	0.33	0.44
Agriculture engineering	0.27	0.36	0.30	0.51	0.66	0.55
Metallurgical engineering	0.25	0.18	0.23	0.27	0.20	0.25
Food technology	0.16	0.18	0.17	0.29	0.49	0.35
Mining engineering	0.17	0.01	0.13	0.27	0.02	0.20
Marine engineering	0.16	0.01	0.12	0.14	0.02	0.11
Dairy technology	0.05	0.05	0.05	0.07	0.09	0.08
Planning	0.01	0.02	0.02	0.02	0.04	0.02
Others total	11.22	11.93	11.43	10.76	12.96	11.40
Total (traditional + modern + others)	100.00	100.00	100.00	100.00	100.00	100.00

Source: AICTE Database.

studies in traditional areas of study such as mechanical, civil and electrical in 2018–19, while the corresponding figure was 23.8 per cent for females. Female enrolment in electronics and IT-related strands such as electronics, computer science and IT (63.2 per cent) is significantly higher than male enrolment in these streams (36.5 per cent). So women's demand for modern disciplines of engineering has not suffered much, as women tend to continue preferring IT-related subjects to traditional ones. Electronics and IT-related subjects are considered fashionable by many. Many view that only those who cannot get admission in modern IT-related subjects choose traditional branches. According to the 2018–19 data, among the traditional subjects, men prefer mechanical engineering to others, whereas women prefer civil engineering. But among the IT-related programmes, both men and women prefer computer science engineering.

The occupancy rate or the enrolment as a proportion of intake has decreased in almost all disciplines. The occupancy rate was 44 per cent in electronics engineering in 2017–18, 58 per cent in computer science engineering and 60 per cent in computer engineering. The rates for mechanical and civil engineering were 47 per cent and 48 per cent, respectively. It is higher in biomedical engineering, chemical engineering and agricultural engineering at above 60 per cent. In all, it was only 50 per cent.

It appears in those disciplines where the sanctioned intake is small, the occupancy rate is relatively high and vice versa. In Figure 2.14, we note the trends in occupancy rate across the three broad groups of streams between 2012–13 and 2016–17. But within these three groups of disciplines, there is

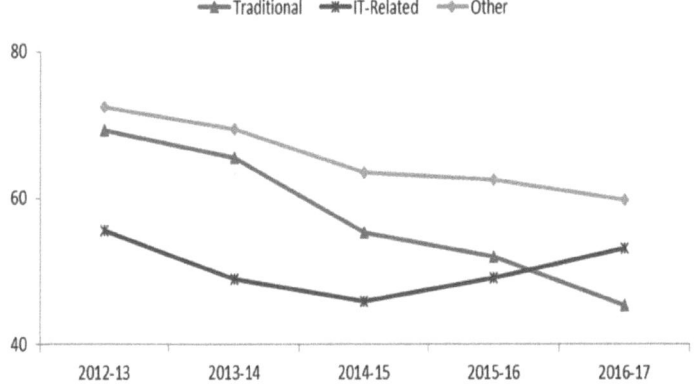

Figure 2.14 Enrolment as Percentage of Intake in Major Categories of Sub-Streams of Engineering Education

Source: Based on AICTE Database.

an increasing trend in the enrolment in modern strands after 2015–16. The share has increased from 49 per cent in 2015–16 to 53 per cent in 2016–17. It may be reflective of the revival of the IT sector in India which has brought new opportunities for the engineering graduates. According to AICTE data, the proportion of placements to enrolments in IT-related streams jumped from 12 per cent in 2012–13 to 47.9 per cent in 2016–17. This may also be partly due to the shutting down of several private engineering colleges across the country, as discussed earlier, due to the low demand for engineering education in India.

Level-Wise Imbalance

The other kind of imbalance that one notices is a very high proportion of students in first degree studies and almost nil in masters' and research programmes. This is similar to the pattern in the entire higher education sector, but the degree of imbalance is much higher in engineering education. In higher education, enrolments in undergraduate programmes form about 80 per cent, while enrolment in PhD programmes account for less than 0.5 per cent of the total, while the remaining nearly 20 per cent is accounted by students in master's level programmes (postgraduate and MPhil studies). But in the pyramid of engineering education, as high as 94.5 per cent of the students are enrolled in undergraduate programmes, 4.5 per cent in postgraduate and about 1 per cent in PhD programmes. MPhil programmes are rather rare in engineering studies (Figure 2.15). The PhD studies are of particular significance as most teaching and research positions require a PhD degree. Certainly, the number of graduate engineers who go on to masters' and doctoral studies in engineering in India is not keeping pace with the growing economy, and this needs to be stepped up significantly.

That very few students in engineering studies opt for postgraduate and research programmes has been highlighted by many as a major weakness that results in a restricted supply of teachers in engineering institutions and also limited research and development in critical and emerging areas of engineering and technology. The problem with respect to critical shortage of teachers in engineering subjects is already felt. There is a need to initiate special efforts to encourage first degree graduates to pursue master's and research programmes in engineering and technology. A committee appointed by MHRD (2009) recommended that all higher education institutions should become 'integrated' institutions necessarily offering undergraduate, postgraduate and research programmes, like the IITs. This might create and nurture research interests in young minds and enhance transition rates between the three levels, improving not only teaching in institutions, but also creating better environment for knowledge development and dissemination. A similar

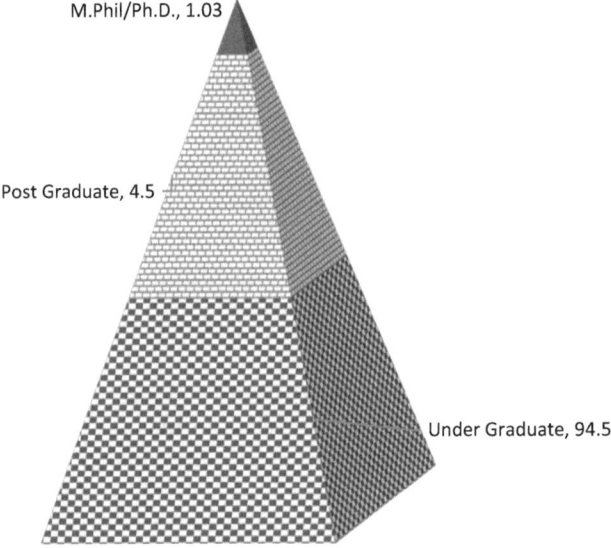

Figure 2.15 Level-Wise Imbalance (Distribution of Enrolments) in Engineering Education, 2018–19 (%)

Source: Based on AICTE Database.

recommendation has also been made by the Dr Kasturirangan committee (GOI, 2019) and this forms a provision in the National Education Policy 2020 (GOI, 2020).

Summary and Concluding Observations

India has registered a very impressive growth in its higher education during the post-Independence period and more impressively during the last three to four decades. Within higher education, there is a distinct pecking order, at the top of which are engineering and medicine and within engineering the IT-related 'modern' streams are at the top. Engineering education has experienced an enormous expansion, beyond experts' anticipations. The expansion of higher education and within higher education engineering education was necessitated firstly by changing increasing demographic composition in favour of the young, secondly by upward pressures with rapid growth in school (secondary and primary) education, thirdly by high economic growth, particularly in manufacturing and service sectors in India, increase in employment opportunities outside and fourthly, due to the familiar diploma disease.

There are several paradoxes and contradictions in the growth of engineering education, posing different kinds of challenges to the educational administrators, policymakers and rather the entire society. Based essentially on secondary data, an attempt has been made in this chapter to understand the changing face of engineering education in India during the last 50 years, focusing on expansion and inequalities in engineering education. Two major dimensions are discussed in this chapter, viz. (i) changing trends and patterns of the growth of engineering education and (ii) inequalities in growth in engineering education.

India has experienced massive expansion of engineering education during the last half century, which many experts regard as unsustainable. The explosion in numbers is propelled by the private sector. We find that engineering education, along with the rest of higher education in India, is heavily privatised, with about 90 per cent of the sector being in private hands. The private sector that is involved in engineering education today operates essentially on a commercial basis and less on a philanthropic basis. Mostly, private education is also financially not supported by the state. The dominance of the private sector in engineering education has resulted in several kinds of problems. The private sector has replaced the objective of private providers in education from social service by profit and displaced the public sector in the national space almost completely. The recent data on several aspects of engineering education show that it has created various kinds of distortions. The private sector invested only in those places where it was rewarding. This has led to a high degree of regional inequalities. The southern and western regions of India have experienced a very high growth of engineering institutions and enrolment as compared to the northern and eastern regions. This was also concentrated more in urban areas, widening rural-urban inequalities. The participation of the private sector also widened inequalities between social groups – caste, religion, gender and economic conditions of households. Inequality by gender has narrowed over the years. Further, the increasing presence of the private sector in engineering and other technical and professional education studies has led to disciplinary distortions, as the private providers are largely offering market-friendly and job-oriented programmes in those streams of engineering that help them expand enrolments, generate revenues through student fees, improve financial status and most importantly, increasing their profit margin. With their over-representation in decision-making bodies in public universities, they also influenced public policies, referring specifically to public institutions, and distorted them to their advantage. This also has led to deterioration in quality and standards in education, and thereby employability and employment of graduates. These, along with financing of engineering education, are analysed in Chapter 3, along with a discussion on policy actions required.

Notes

1 AICTE has classified all states into seven regions: central region consists of Madhya Pradesh, Chhattisgarh and Gujarat; the eastern region consists of Mizoram, Sikkim, Odisha, West Bengal, Tripura, Meghalaya, Arunachal Pradesh, Andaman & Nicobar islands, Assam, Manipur, Nagaland and Jharkhand; the northern region includes Bihar, Uttar Pradesh and Uttaranchal; the north-west region includes

Chandigarh, Haryana, Jammu & Kashmir, New Delhi, Punjab, Rajasthan and Himachal Pradesh; southern region includes Andhra Pradesh, Pondicherry and Tamil Nadu; the south-west region includes Karnataka and Kerala; and western region includes Maharashtra, Goa and Daman, Diu & Dadra Nagar Haveli. The southern and south-west regions together are considered as southern region here.

2 'Progressive closure' means an institute cannot admit the students for the first year during the academic year for a progressive closure has been ordered. However, the students (in the second year of studies onwards who are already on rolls) will continue their studies until they complete their four-year programme.

3 The concentration ratio is defined as the number of institutions in a state as a percentage of the total number of institutions in the country as a ratio of population in a state as a percentage of the total population in the country. See Varghese et al. (2018). This is similar to the coefficient of inequality defined by Naik (1971).

4 The *Constitution of India* provides for reservation of 15 per cent of employment in public sector for SCs, 7.5 per cent for STs and 27 per cent for OBCs. The proportions are based on the estimated shares of respective groups in the total population. The reservation for OBCs was added in 1993, and it is based on the criterion of social and educational backwardness with a creamy layer cap of ₹ 800,000 annual income of the household.

5 It will be valuable to examine the trends before 2010–11, but we do not have such detailed information by sub-streams for the earlier periods.

3 Emergent Challenges of Engineering Education in India

Quality, Finances and Employment

Issues and Challenges

There is widespread criticism of the quality of higher education in India, engineering education in particular, which has also impacted the employability of the graduates and their employment. Rather, graduate engineer unemployment is taken as reflective of poor quality of education provided in a vast majority of institutions, particularly the private ones. Continuing the analysis of a review of major trends attempted in Chapter 2, this chapter focuses on the concerns relating to the declining quality of engineering education, unstable public funding and labour market interface of engineering education. The next section 'Quality Concerns in Engineering Education' starts with discussing the teachers' position, their recruitment and their qualifications, as these are significantly related to the quality of faculty which will have an impact on their teaching and research. We also refer in this context to issues on regulation and accountability using National Board of Accreditation (NBA) reports and other policy documents of the AICTE (All India Council for Technical Education) and MHRD (Ministry of Human Resource Development) with an expectation that they may reveal relatively unknown factors, if any, behind the expansion of the private sector in engineering education and its impact on quality. This section also reviews some curriculum-related issues that are linked to the much debated industry-institute linkages. Also, we look at global university rankings and the National Institute of Ranking Framework (NIRF) data of MHRD that gives a comparative idea of quality of various engineering institutions in India. In Section 'Financing of Engineering Education in India', an attempt is made to unravel a few important dimensions of financing engineering education by the government and households. The analysis of data on public expenditure gives us an idea on the priority given by the state to technical education, specifically to engineering education, and how it has led to the expansion of the private sector. The National Sample Survey (NSS) data gives a few important details on household expenditure – expenses on fees and other items by students in different types of institutions and courses of study. These figures give an idea on the individual cost of engineering education in India. In this context, we also refer to data collected

DOI: 10.4324/9781003430223-4

from some selected institutions' websites on various types of fees (tuition and other fees) charged by some public and private institutions. Section 'Changing Labour Market Conditions and Engineering Education'focuses on labour market issues related to engineering education in India and how this field of higher education is influenced by the changing nature of work, both in the national and global markets. The issues discussed include employment/unemployment and employability of engineers, demand-supply mismatches in the labour market, outturn of graduates, placement (employment in campus recruitment), wages and differences by gender, type of institutions and discipline of study and finally, we look at some of the confusing signals one gets from the ever-dynamic labour markets. In the closing Section, a few major conclusions are drawn along with policy recommendations that emerge from the analysis of secondary data made in Chapter 2 and this chapter.

Quality Concerns in Engineering Education

We have noted that engineering education has expanded very rapidly during the last few decades. However, the observed growth in enrolment rates is not matched by comparable improvements in quality. As a result, of the multiple crises the higher education system in India suffers from, crisis of quality assumes serious proportions. Even though the quality of education has emerged as one of the most important concerns of policymakers in higher education in India, at the same time it is widely agreed that quality in education is difficult to precisely define and measure. We can only look at some proxy indicators that are related to quality. The quality of engineering education in India thus can be understood when we look at a few specific indicators.

First, at the top of the technical higher education pyramid is the small group of IITs (Indian Institutes of Technology), followed by NITs (National Institutes of Technology) and IIITs (Indian Institutes of Information Technology), which are funded by the union government; in the upper middle of the pyramid are central universities and a small number of select state universities; the lower middle consists of government colleges in engineering and technology and government-aided private colleges; and at the bottom are a very large number of private universities and colleges, which are funded substantially by the households and least by the state and are providing low quality education. The ones in the top of the pyramid are all considered 'elite', well-funded, highly selective and autonomous institutions designed to greatly increase the high end of the engineering and technical cadre in the country. The top and the middle clusters of the institutions are funded by the government and are supplemented by fee contributions from the students. Thus India has a few institutions of excellence at the top of the pyramid and a large number of colleges and deemed universities at the bottom of appalling quality, which are under the purview of the states, but more significantly in the private sector. Even though we have a large number of colleges offering engineering education, only 298 colleges are autonomous. Though whether autonomy delivers greater quality is questionable, it is widely perceived that the status of autonomy is partly reflective of the quality of an institution, as it is granted only if the college satisfies quite a few parameters relating to performance of the college, quality imparted in the college and overall capability of the college to function autonomously, apart from other factors such as infrastructure and the quality of teachers. Second, accreditation is indicative of some dimensions of quality of institution and the programmes they offer to some extent, as some standards are ensured. Out of all the AICTE-approved institutions of technical education, only 2,414 institutions offered NBA-accredited study programmes in 2020, as per the information available on the AICTE website. Referring to the quality of engineering institutions in the country, Subbarao (2013) observes that hardly 3 per cent of the engineering graduates are from 'good' institutes. He also observes that postgraduate programmes need special attention and that leadership, dedication and autonomy are essential to improve the quality of engineering education. Thus, with respect to obtaining autonomy, only a small number of institutions have been successful, and with respect to accreditation, a large number of institutions are yet to fulfil satisfactorily basic conditions.

Second, the government of India has recently launched National Institutional Ranking Framework, under which an institution is ranked based on a set of academic, extra academic and other parameters. The parameters considered include teaching and learning resources, research and professional practices, graduate outcomes, outreach and inclusivity and finally, perceptions of peer groups (academia and employers). The NIRF ranks higher education institutions in general and engineering institutions separately. Like any typical ranking system, the higher the rank of an institution, one would expect the institution to be of a higher quality and standards. There are 23 IITs, 31 NITs, 25 IIITs, a few technological universities and more than 4,000 institutions offering engineering education in the country. According to the NIRF 2023, as shown in Table 3.1, only the IITs, some NITs, and a few universities figure in the top 20 institutions of engineering. A large number of institutions are nowhere in the ranking system. As a Taskforce (VIF, 2015) highlighted, less than 2 per cent of the colleges secured 50 per cent of the marks in the NIRF. More recently, a new category of 'research institutions' has been introduced in the NIRF, according to which only those institutions would be considered that have at least 500 research publications indexed in the web of science or Scopus for a period of three years or 1,000 students enrolled for PhD programmes. It is yet to see how many institutions can qualify under this category.

Third, at the global level, the picture is more dismal. Not even one Indian institution figures in the top 100 institutions of higher education in the global rankings of universities. Eight IITs from India are placed in the top 1,000 global list of the Quacquarelli Symonds (QS) rankings 2023, with the IIT Bombay (IITB) in the top, with the world ranking of 172. A few IITs figure

Table 3.1 Top 15 Engineering Institutions in National Institute of Ranking Framework (NIRF), 2023

	Rank in Overall	Rank in Engineering
IIT Madras (Chennai)	1	1
Indian Institute of Sciences, Bengaluru	2	
IIT Delhi	3	2
IIT Bombay	4	3
IIT Kharagpur	7	6
IIT Kanpur	5	4
IIT Guwahati	9	7
Jawaharlal Nehru University, New Delhi	10	
IIT Roorkee	8	5
Benaras Hindu University, Varanasi	10	
Calcutta University	11	
Jadavpur University	13	10
Amrita Viswa Vidyapeetham	15	19
Manipal Academy of Higher Education	16	
IIT Hyderabad	14	8
IIT BHU	31	15
Anna University, Chennai	18	13
IIT Indore	23	14
NIT Tiruchirappalli	21	9
IIT Mines Dhanbad	42	17
NIT Surathkal	38	12
Vellore Institute of Technology	27	11

Source: MOE: NIRF, https://www.nirfindia.org/2023/OverallRanking.html, https://www.nirfindia.org/2023/EngineeringRanking.html

in the top 500 institutions, three of which figure below the rank of 200. While global ranking mechanisms have their own weaknesses, they nevertheless reflect some key dimensions of quality of universities, stressing the need for policy focus on raising quality and standards in Indian institutions (Tilak, 2016a). Table 3.2 gives an idea of where some of the well-known Indian institutions of technical education stand in world rankings. In the case of global ranking of institutions of engineering and technology, however, five IITs figure in the top 100, two of which, namely IIT Bombay and IIT Delhi, figure in the top 50. Many other institutions rank very poorly in the global rankings. Not only advanced countries, but also developing countries like China and small countries like Singapore perform better than India in these global as well as engineering- and technology-specific university rankings.

The problem is that the government seems to be focusing its efforts on raising quality of a limited group of institutions like the IITs and the NITs that produce actually a small proportion of graduate engineers.[1] IITs that produced 10 per cent of engineering graduates in the country in the 1970s and early 1980s accounted for only 0.5 per cent of graduates around 2011 (MHRD, 2011c). But even this strategy of focusing on IITs for improving

Table 3.2 Indian Institutes in QS Rankings of World Universities, 2023

	Rank among All 2023	Rank in Engineering and Technology Subjects 2023
IIT Bombay	172	47
Indian Institute of Sciences, Bangalore	155	106
IIT Delhi	174	48
IIT Madras (Chennai)	250	68
IIT Kharagpur	270	8
IIT Kanpur	264	856
IIT Roorkee	269	175
IIT Guwahati	384	222
University of Delhi	521–530	401–450
Anna University	551–560	289
Vellore Institute of Technology		240
Birla Institute of Technology & Science, Pilani	591–600	344
IIT Hyderabad	581–590	
Jadavpur University	701–750	
O P Jindal University	651–700	
Savitri Bai Phule Pune University	541–550	
University of Hyderabad	751–800	
Manipal Academy of Higher Education	751–800	
IIT Indore	396	...
IIT Bhubaneswar	802–850	...

Source: QS World University Rankings 2023. https://www.topuniversities.com/university-rankings/world-university-rankings/2023

excellence faces difficulties because of a faculty crunch and the limited public investments on research and development in these institutions (Carnoy et al., 2010).[2]

The fourth important indicator that reflects the quality of education is the employability of graduates. Several studies reveal that a majority of engineering graduates in India do not possess the required skills and are therefore not suitable for employment (Mani & Arun, 2012; Loyalka et al., 2014; Choudhury, 2019). The *Annual Employability Survey 2019* (Aspiring Minds, 2019) reveals that 80 per cent of Indian engineers are not fit for any job in the knowledge economy, and a similar observation was made by the NASSCOM (National Association of Software and Service Companies) and McKinsey study in 2005. The employability prospects of Indian engineering graduates have worsened in the past one-and-a-half decade, as a majority of them are not qualified enough for employment in engineering sector or in any sector.[3]

The overall pathetic situation is clear: less than 2 per cent of the colleges have scored above 50 per cent of marks in the NIRF; less than 5 per cent of the engineering graduates pass graduate attitude test in engineering (GATE); and less than 5 per cent of the engineering programmes are accredited by NBA with 'full accreditation' (VIF, 2019).

Why and how is engineering education so engulfed with unacceptable levels of poor quality teaching? Who is responsible for this? Is the expansion of engineering education leading towards a decline in its quality? What are the strategies being adopted by regulatory authorities (specifically by AICTE and NBA) to address this issue? What are the efforts made at the institutional level to improve the quality? These are some critical questions that need to be examined to understand quality-related issues.

It is widely noted that the exponential growth in engineering education in India has led to the supply of substandard graduates, and this issue has become quite serious in recent years (Dubey et al., 2019). India's engineering education system has a few bright spots of excellence engaged in both teaching and research like the IITs, NITs and IIITs, but is surrounded by a sea of substandard colleges that primarily aim at selling quickly poor quality degrees in the market. Such quality institutions exist both in the public and private sector, but predominantly in the public sector. The IITs figure, as already noted, in the global university rankings of the Times Higher Education (THE)/QS. The alumni of the IITs, for example, command national and global labour markets in science and technology. Likewise, India's second-tier engineering institutions like the NITs and several established government engineering colleges are also well regarded and have good faculty and student bodies.

On the whole, government or government-aided private colleges perform far better, imparting superior quality education than self-financing colleges. This is also clear from the students' preference for public versus private institutions. The meritorious students and talented teachers prefer public to private institutions (Loyalka et al., 2014). The quality of engineering education also depends on the institutional cultures that result in different experiences for students of similar educational and familial background (Malish & Ilavarasan, 2016), and in the Indian context, public engineering institutions are found to be successful in nurturing students better. The system of engineering education in the public sector in India has had very bright centres of excellence.

As Loyalka et al. (2014) noted, in India a minority of engineering students receive high-quality training in elite institutions while the majority of students receive low-quality training in non-elite institutions that are mostly managed by the private sector. It is also said that the problem of quality is largely with these engineering institutions run by the private sector and they are often established as family enterprises. Enrolment in many private technical and professional colleges is declining, partly due to the questionable quality (Varghese, 2015). It is widely acknowledged that the deterioration of the quality of engineering education in India is largely due to the unregulated and haphazard expansion of the private engineering colleges, as they tend to combine low quality with profiteering, shifting their attention in admissions from the student's academic ability to the parental ability and willingness to bear the expenses, and in their operations shifting their consideration from academic aspects to making profits. Only two private higher education institutions with a specific focus on engineering and technical education (Manipal Academy of Higher Education and Amrita Vishwa Vidyapeetham) from India have been included in the top 1,000 global list of 2020 QS World University ranking. Similarly, the NIRF 2020 for engineering and technology subjects finds that only two private institutions, viz. Vellore Institute of Technology and Amrita Vishwa Vidyapeetham, figure in the top 20, while all the others in the top 15 are public institutions.

With the massive expansion of engineering education, students with a much lower entrance examination score get admission in self-financing colleges, and therefore the entry level examination is not ensuring admission of only meritorious and quality students. An investigative status report in the *Times of India* (13 December 2017) reveals that there are 'middlemen' forming an integral part of the ecosystem created by an uneven growth in private engineering colleges. This phenomenon appeared over the last decade when a majority of the student places are lying vacant. With falling demand, with fewer and fewer students ready to take admission as degrees are getting steadily devalued, and with the rising threat of vacant seats (Gosavi, 2013), many self-financing colleges hire the services of middlemen to lure students, apart from several kinds of fair and unfair but aggressive marketing strategies (Singh, 2016; Singh & Singh, 2014). This is becoming a part of an unstated but widely prevalent admission mechanism. Engineering colleges, desperate for students, increasingly depend on these brokers for survival. Given the informal and unregulated nature of the sector, it is difficult to map the role and growth of the middlemen engaged in the engineering education, and also it is hard to obtain authentic official details on this interesting aspect. But the *Times of India* 2017 report in the context of Uttar Pradesh, where 65 per cent student seats were lying vacant, offers some interesting evidences. The commission charges paid to middlemen for getting students to some colleges ranges from ₹25,000 to ₹60,000 per student; and in some cases, colleges also offer a share of their annual revenue to them. The middlemen might also be charging students for their 'special' services. This appears to be a profitable activity for these agents, as each of them easily earns around ₹10 lakhs a year, and it is also beneficial for the academically weak students who have given up any hope of joining an engineering college. The presence of middlemen sourcing students for college admissions reflect a deplorable situation, resulting in the rapid and steep lowering of standards of engineering education in the country. The student's aptitude has little to do with his/her chances of getting into an engineering college, as anybody with 45 per cent marks in the senior secondary board examination – the minimum eligibility norm prescribed by AICTE for admission to undergraduate engineering studies – can be assured of admission if she/he is ready to pay fees to the college and a commission to an agent. In the *Times of India* (2017) survey, one middleman bluntly stated that meritorious students would never take admission 'through us'. It was economically rich students with ranks at the bottom who approached them. Since colleges are desperate, they even grant admission to students "who have barely any understanding of mathematics. I'm not sure if these students learn anything at all". The existing regulatory mechanism does not cover such issues and clearly tough guidelines of regulatory mechanism and their implementation are needed to tackle these and similar concerns. With such imperfect and corrupt practices, the so-called competitive entrance examination loses value, not being able to prevent a large number of low-quality students from entering into engineering education. Low-quality inputs in the form of such students obviously produce poor quality graduates. There is need to severely tighten the admissions and admission procedures in the institutions (see also Mehrotra, 2020).

In addition, we discuss below four important aspects relating to the quality of education: shortage of faculty, production of PhDs, recruitment of fake faculty and excess supply of engineering education.

Shortage of Faculty

The quality of education critically depends upon the teacher. After all, it is the teacher who is considered the pivot of the education system. Unfortunately, the entire higher education system in India suffers from an acute shortage of faculty. Functioning with very limited faculty, it falls far below the minimum requirements. The problem, which was evident for the past two to three decades, has got compounded over the years. It has been reported that in 2020, as many as 32,581 faculty posts in Indian universities were lying vacant in 2020, representing 18.4 per cent of the total sanctioned strength, according to the information provided by the Union Minister of Education in the Parliament. In the centrally funded higher education institutions, as many as 7,500 posts of teachers are lying vacant. The percentage of vacancy of teachers, it has been estimated, ranges between 30 and 50 per cent in the state universities. Even IITs suffer a severe degree of shortage of faculty (Figure 3.1). The 23 IITs together have a teacher vacancy of 38.2 per cent. The vacancy rate ranges from below 5 per cent in IIT Tirupati to above 60 per cent in IIT (ISM) Dhanbad. The problem is as grave in NITs and other national institutes as well as state institutes of engineering and technology.

According to the AICTE data, there has been a major decline in the size of faculty in the undergraduate-level engineering colleges by about 69,000 between 2017–18 and 2018–19 (Figure 3.2). As a result, in many colleges, even the first (bachelors) degree holders are engaged in teaching activities, while a doctoral degree is an essential condition. The World Bank (2013) found that hardly 20 per cent of the regular faculty in Andhra Pradesh hold PhD degrees. All this also poses problems in enhancing research capacity in engineering institutions. Not only we need teachers in good numbers with PhD degrees, but also there is need to set up extensive professional development programmes for the teachers in engineering colleges, as whether a teacher is having MTech/ME or PhD degree, she/he needs facilities for continuous upgradation of their knowledge and skills, as the AICTE committee (2002) suggested.

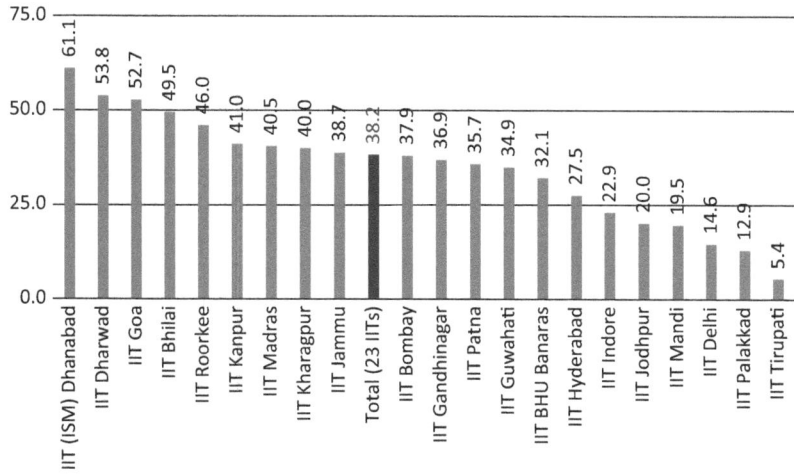

Figure 3.1 Faculty Vacancy as a Percentage of Total Sanctioned Strength in IITs, 2019
Source: Kalra (2019).

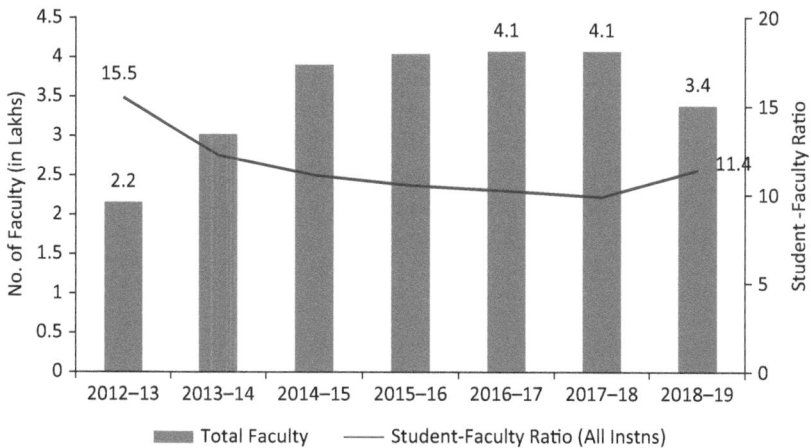

Figure 3.2 Faculty in Engineering and Technology Institutions
Source: AICTE Database.

Production of PhDs and Quality of Faculty

The faculty shortage is due to several factors: first, a limited supply of qualified graduates. The number of PhDs in a field like engineering and technology is very limited; very few bachelor degree holders go to master's level studies and fewer to research programmes, as already been noted. A research degree (PhD) is an essential qualification for a teaching position in higher education. Although having a doctoral degree does not necessarily imply that one will be a more competent teacher, there should be some connection between completion of a research degree and being able to teach a subject more competently than others. But many graduates are reluctant to enter the teaching profession, because of a poor academic environment on the one hand and better opportunities in job market for first degree holders on the other. In fact, faculty vacuum and poor qualifications of faculty stem from the low number of students pursuing PhD studies. So there is a big supply constraint. Public institutions have relatively a higher proportion of faculty with PhD degrees; they also produce a high proportion of PhDs and graduates of high quality compared with private institutions. Added to the overall shortage is the inability of institutions to recruit faculty due to bureaucratic and legal hurdles. Another reason is the reluctance of many institutions, particularly private ones, to hire faculty in general and faculty with doctoral degrees in particular, as they need to incur higher levels of expenditures on account of their salaries. These institutions try to do with a small number of teachers, less qualified ones and through different questionable practices. All this has increased the student-faculty ratio from 9.87 in 2017–18 to 11.39 in 2018–19 (Figure 3.2).

Availability of a small number of doctorate degree holders is considered as an important reason for the shortage of faculty. Only a small number of PhD degrees are awarded in engineering and technology, as shown in Figure 3.3. The corresponding number constitutes 18 per cent of the total number of PhDs awarded in India in 2018. This was below or around 5 per cent until 2005–06. It is only after 2006–07 onwards that there has been an upward trend. The growth picked up essentially during the last one decade, though the long term rate of growth (between 1950–51 and 2018) is also relatively impressive: 5.97 per cent per annum in the case of degrees in engineering and technology compared to 3.19 per cent in the case of doctoral degrees in all subjects.

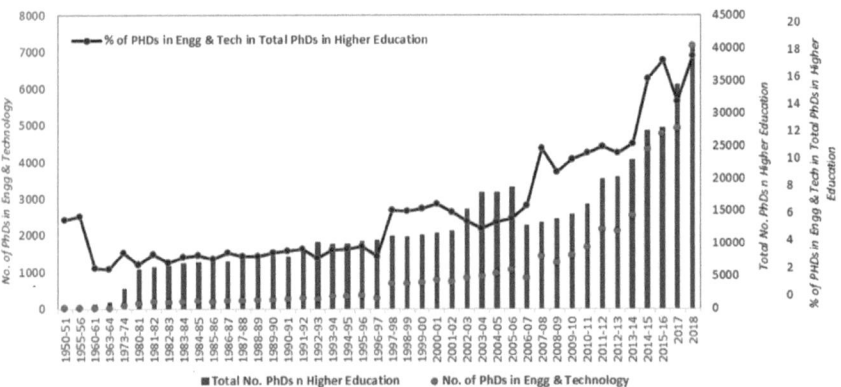

Figure 3.3 Growth in the Number of PhD Degrees Awarded in Universities

Source: Based on UGC *Annual Reports* (various years).

On the whole, while the total number of PhD degrees awarded in all subjects in India increased by about 222 times from 180 in 1980–81 to nearly 41,000 in 2018,[4] the number of PhDs in engineering increased by a whopping more than 700 times from a meagre ten to 7,160 during this period.

While enrolment in engineering studies at the undergraduate level has increased at a compound annual growth rate of 9.7 per cent between 1975–76 and 1990–91, it was only 4.4 per cent in case of the growth of PhD outturns.

A more or less similar trend is also observed between 1991–92 and 2010–11. However, a reverse trend has been observed during the last seven years (2011–12 to 2018–19), as shown in Figure 3.4. The rate of growth in PhD outturn is 18.6 per cent while it is 2.4 per cent in the case of undergraduate enrolment in engineering education in India during this period.

The number of PhD degrees awarded in the discipline of engineering and technology in 2018–19 in India was 7,160 (Figure 3.5). This shows an increase of about 46 per cent in the number of PhDs awarded from the previous academic year, that is, 2017–18. Still, the number of PhDs awarded as a proportion of total undergraduate outturn in India is less than 1 per cent (0.86 per cent), though it has gone up substantially in the recent years. This figure was merely 0.39 per cent in 2011–12.

The number of PhD degrees awarded in engineering and technology in 2018 – 7,160 – constitutes 18 per cent of the total number of PhDs awarded in India. This is a very significant growth. The sudden increase in the number of PhDs recently awarded may be due to the special efforts initiated by the government,[5] but more importantly due to the gloomy labour market conditions for engineering graduates completing undergraduate-level studies. As a result of the latter, instead of remaining idle, these graduates may be opting

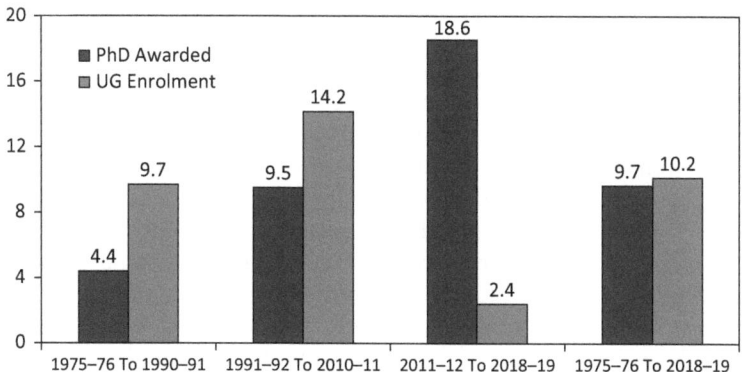

Figure 3.4 Rate of Growth in the Number of PhDs Awarded and Undergraduate Enrolments in Engineering and Technology (%)

Rate of growth: Compound annual rate of growth (%)
Source: Based on UGC *Annual Reports* (various years)

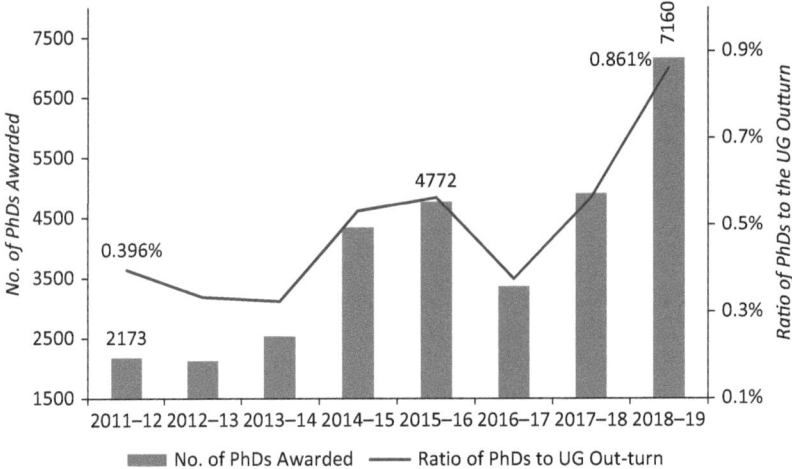

Figure 3.5 Growth in the Number of PhDs Awarded in Relation to Undergraduate Outturn in Engineering and Technology in India

Source: Based on All India Survey of Higher Education (various years).

for higher studies with/without an expectation of better jobs, a phenomenon generally described as the 'baby-sitting' role of higher education or 'diploma disease' (Dore, 1976). In this context, it is important to examine whether the increase in the PhD outturn will help in improving the existing faculty crunch in engineering education in India.

On the whole, there is still a lot to improve the situation with respect to doctoral research in India. Not only in number, but the quality of teachers is also crucial. A tiny number of faculty members in engineering institutions hold PhD degrees, and in many self-financing colleges, bachelor degree holders occupy teaching positions, formally or informally. Indian faculty in general, including faculty in engineering institutions, have very few research publications. The overall research productivity of faculty members in engineering education is quite low. Exceptions are very few. Part of the problem lies in the utter absence of a research environment. The poorly research-oriented teachers and students do not participate in research activities. Loyalka et al. (2014) observed that only about one-sixth of students in India participated in at least one faculty research project.[6] All students do not necessarily take up internships, and industry-institute collaborations are also limited. Students get motivated by inspiring high-quality teachers. A large number of private colleges have no qualified quality faculty in the numbers required, as the system itself is not producing them. Thus, India is experiencing a vicious circle in the supply of qualified faculty in the engineering education sector. A very good research environment in the institutions of higher education and a through grounding of the students in the subject at undergraduate level are essential to promote quality doctoral research (Gupta, 2010). In the case of both, a vast majority of institutions of engineering/technical education suffer from a huge deficit.

Recruitment of 'Fake Faculty'

Let's turn to the nature of faculty recruitment in private colleges. There is no authentic information recruitment of faculty in several engineering colleges. Very few attempts have been made by individual researchers to explore and examine this area. In one such attempt made by an open data campaigner Rakesh Reddy Dubbudu and his team using AICTE data reveals some serious anomalies (11 May 2015, *The Hindu*). Surprisingly, over 90 per cent of private engineering colleges in India have at least one teacher whose name also features on the rolls of another college, and there are at least 50,000 such 'duplicate' teachers. Colleges are expected to have their own full-time faculty and not supposed to share faculty, according to the AICTE guidelines. The state-wise picture on this is given in Figure 3.6. In Andhra Pradesh and Telangana, nearly a quarter of the total engineering faculty consisted of duplicate names, and about 90 per cent of the over 1,500 accredited engineering colleges in the states had at least one 'duplicate' teacher on their faculty. This is found to be alarming in Uttar Pradesh, as close to 60 per cent of faculty names consisted of duplications, while in Odisha it was 40 per cent. Almost every engineering college in these two states had at least one such case. Norms were being flagrantly violated by the engineering colleges in several states in the appointment of faculty and no action could be taken by the appropriate authorities, partly because of political support and economic power the managements of these colleges enjoy. After all, as Kapur and Mehta (2004) observed, the growth of private engineering colleges in the country is simply an artefact of politicians creating opportunities to collect rents.

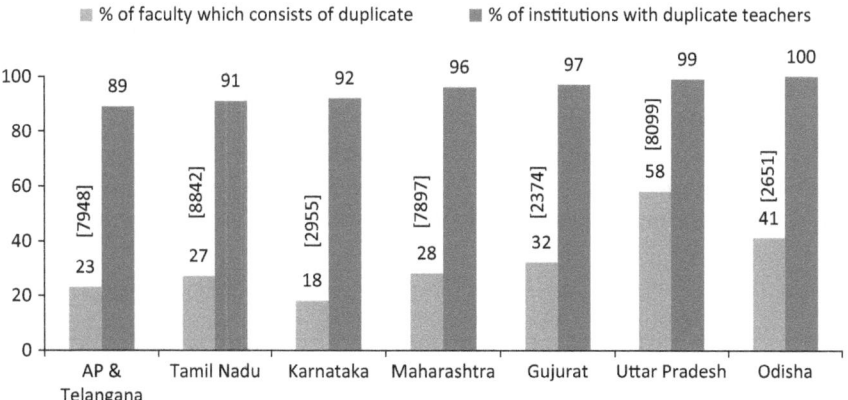

Figure 3.6 'Duplicate' Faculty in Engineering Colleges (%)
Source: Rukmini (2015) in *The Hindu*, 10 May 2015.

Excess Supply

Within engineering education, we have already noted excess supply: larger number of institutions than required and admissions much below the sanctioned intake levels. Now we look at the production of graduates in relation to the labour market requirements or absorption capacity of the labour market. We do not have detailed estimates of requirements of engineering manpower integrated with educational planning. But the high levels of unemployment of graduates imply that there is an excess supply of graduate engineers in India. We have also noted that every year, about 1.5 million graduates – higher than the numbers produced by the US and China together – are produced by the engineering education system in the country. This is regarded as one of the largest numbers in the world. But quite paradoxically, according to the World Economic Forum (2020), India ranks 32 among the countries in terms of the availability of engineers and scientists. Not only advanced nations like the US, Canada, the UK, Switzerland, and Japan are ahead of India, but also India is behind many developing countries, including Qatar which ranks 5, Malaysia (7), United Arab Emeritus (UAE) (3), Jordan (13), Chile (22), Ukraine (25), China (29), etc.[7] While these international comparisons are not necessarily perfect due to variations in definitions and methods, they nevertheless suggest that India is not necessarily overproducing engineer graduates, but producing large numbers of poor quality unemployable graduates. Some also believe that a rapidly growing economy like India would indeed require more and more engineer graduates. Further, while overall numbers may be high, there may be under-production of graduates in specific areas and overproduction in some other areas, creating gluts and shortages in the labour market.

While we do not have elaborate labour market information, some relevant information is available on the education system. There are some projections of requirements of colleges and number of graduates, but they do not seem to have been taken into account while allowing the growth of colleges and sanctioning of intake in those colleges. For example, AICTE has projected that the country would need 1,400 engineering colleges with an intake of 500,000 by 2014–15 (Table 3.3) (TEQIP, 2002). But in 2014–15, there were 3,364 colleges with an intake of 17.1 lakh students. We have far exceeded in practice the projections made by AICTE for 2000, 2005, 2010 and 2015.[8] Thus, there is a huge excess supply of institutions and thereby graduates.

Table 3.3 AICTE Projections: Programmed Requirement of Engineering Degree-Level Institutions and Admission Capacity

	2000	2005	2010	2015
No. of Institutions	838	1,000	1,200	1,400
Annual Intake	232,229	320,000	400,000	500,000

Source: TEQIP (2002).

Not exactly keeping such projections in mind, nor in response to the malpractices adopted by these colleges or the dubious quality of education they are offering, but essentially, as enrolments are falling, AICTE is ordering closure of colleges. Several engineering colleges in the country do not find takers for admission, a tough situation for the owners of these colleges to run their programmes as their revenues shrink. So, many colleges on their own might get closed. In a sense, the prevailing market forces compel such colleges, with excess capacity or underutilisation of the capacity (admissions being much below the intake capacity approved), to close down and the owners of these colleges project themselves as victims of circumstances. As Figure 3.7 shows, during the last eight years (2012–13 to 2019–20), AICTE has approved the progressive closure of 778 colleges across India. Still, in 2018–19, as against the total intake capacity at undergraduate level of 14 lakhs, the total enrolment was 7.2 lakhs, which is just around 51 per cent. Thus, close to half of the approved student seats (6.9 lakhs) have remained vacant without takers in several engineering colleges in the country in 2018–19.

In the context of declining demand, will the closure of institutes help imparting better quality engineering education? It is widely viewed that the oversupply of engineering colleges in the country is affecting quality, and hence, the closure of several colleges will help improve the situation. At the same time, it is necessary but not sufficient. The ever-widening gap between the supply and demand for engineering graduates in India raises several important issues that need special attention for academia and policy makers. One vital aspect may be to examine the changing parental aspirations in sending their children for an engineering education, given the gloomy labour market symptoms. Similarly, it would be edifying to listen to the owners who run private engineering colleges and who project themselves as victims of

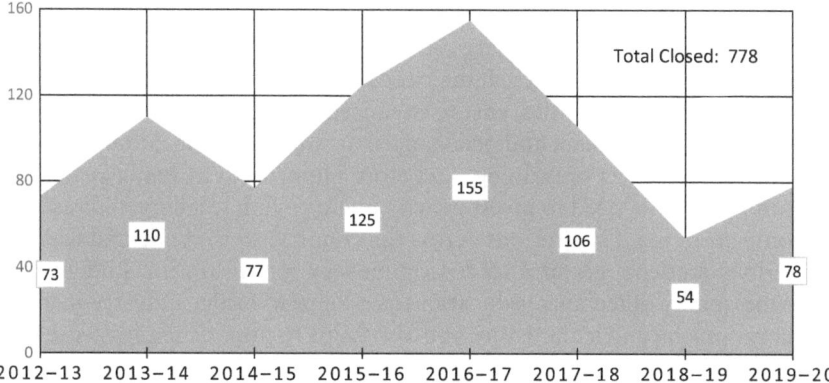

Figure 3.7 AICTE-Approved 'Progressive Closure' of Engineering and Technology Institutions

Source: AICTE Database.

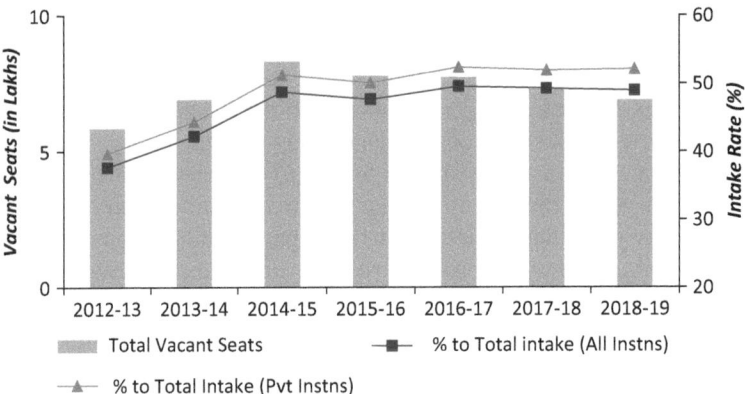

Figure 3.8 Number of Vacant Student Seats in Engineering and Technology Institutions
Source: AICTE Database.

circumstances. Some of these issues that are linked with the quality concerns of engineering education in the country call for alternative policy options.

The only major consensus that we have is "A serious situation has arisen in recent years because of the mushrooming of a large number of private technical institutions and polytechnics. Barring some exceptions, there is scant regard for maintenance of standards" (AICTE, 2003), and that we should take major initiatives to maintain standards and improve the quality. The change needed in our engineering education system is to make the transition from primarily teaching institutions to teaching and research institutions (Banerjee & Muley, 2009). The National Education Policy (GOI, 2020) also strongly pleads for having integrated university campuses where there are common facilities for undergraduate, postgraduate and research studies, so that close linkages between teaching and research are established. To improve the research ecosystem in engineering colleges, India needs to recruit qualified faculty, build advanced laboratory facilities, ensure enhanced societal and industry linkages along with better curricula and pedagogical arrangements (including compulsory internship as part of training) and more importantly, a better regulatory structure. There is a need to invest heavily in improving teaching and research environment in most institutions across the country, so that talented teachers and serious students get attracted. Compulsory internship for students can better the quality of technical education, as it helps to bridge industry-institute collaborations on curricular issues and also helps to provide ready-to-use professionals for the industry (Prabhu & Kudva, 2016).

While examining reasons for the low-quality engineering education imparted in India several studies highlighted inadequate public funds and glaring gaps in regulation, including alleged corruption.[9] India needs stronger regulatory measures to facilitate proper growth and expansion of engineering education and public policy needs to explore possibilities of evolving reliable and effective regulatory structures in India. Given the experience, ideas like 'self-regulation' or 'minimum regulation' that the National Education Policy 2020 proposed, may not work in Indian higher education with such a large network of private institutions. It is important to note that the kind of expansion that has taken place has led to a lack of accountability by private higher education providers.

Policy initiatives should aim at producing quality engineers with character and values who can be meaningfully employed in the labour market and contribute to the larger developmental goals of the country and society. Overall, engineering education in India fails to establish a robust technical ecosystem that can produce quality graduates.

Financing of Engineering Education in India

There has been a major shift in policies on financing of higher education in India during the last few decades. Declining public funding and advocating in favour of non-state funding of higher education, specifically passing the burden to households in terms of high fees and student loans, have been familiar trends. Higher education, which used to be heavily subsidised by the state (Tilak, 1993), is increasingly becoming dependent on the investment made by individual households (Tilak, 2003b),[10] with decline in general and specific public subsidies in higher education. Cost recovery measures, particularly student fees which have been used to generate more and more resources, have contributed to making higher education increasingly costlier for students, raising questions of the affordability of quality education. Student loans have not been significantly effective in mitigating the regressive effects of high fee levels. The problem of financing of technical education is also assuming different dimensions in quantum and nature since the beginning of the 1990s (Tilak, 1999). The increasing presence of the private sector in engineering education is raising questions on equitable access to quality higher education. Households belonging to the lower and middle socio-economic strata feel financially handicapped in sending their children to engineering studies. Further, it is expensive to maintain technical education at a high level of excellence. Keeping the increasing cost of technical education in mind, the report of the High-Power Committee for Mobilisation of Additional Resources for Technical Education (AICTE, 1994) has recommended that the tuition fee for government, and government-aided institutions should be revised to about 20 per cent of the recurring expenditure per student per year, which was only about 1–5 per cent when this recommendation was made, but few seemed to adhere to the recommendations, as many raised fee levels much beyond this proportion.

Against this background, we discuss here two important issues: (a) public financing of technical [11] and also specifically some aspects of public funding of engineering education and (b) household expenditure on engineering education.

Public Financing of Engineering and Technical Education

In the early 1960s, public funding and philanthropic contributions for higher education were a major part of the resource base of this sector in India and the funding from private sources in terms of fees and other payments from students were negligible. So were investments in education by the non-philanthropic (or profit-seeking) private sector. With the introduction of economic reform policies in the early 1990s, broadly known as structural adjustment programme, the trend shifted in a big way towards the private funding of higher education in general, and particularly in engineering education and almost all areas of technical education. Public support for higher education became weak in the decades following the economic reform era (Tilak, 2012, 2016b). It is argued that the beneficiaries of technical education are not only the students, but also the industry, the government and society at large, and therefore, the financial inputs to technical education system are to be viewed as a long-term investment in the national economy and the cost of such education has to be shared by all the three beneficiaries (AICTE, 1994). Of the three, the student is seen as the main beneficiary and has to bear a very high proportion of the cost. The increasing size of the private sector has further led to the strengthening of this view.

We analyse public support towards engineering and technical education in India with the help of secondary data obtained from Analysis of Budget Expenditure on Education (MHRD). Data on public expenditure on higher and technical education are available in this important source in two separate statements: (a) 'university and other higher' education and (b) technical education.[12] Public expenditure in engineering education is included as a sub-head in the statement on technical education. The data provided in this document that we use here on engineering education is partial in nature, as it only includes the expenditure made by governments in the states and union territories on 'engineering colleges and institutions' and does not include expenditures made by the union government on engineering education, including on the IITs and NITs. The IITs and NITs, along with central universities and other central institutions, are funded by the union government. This is briefly and separately described here.

The Education Commission (1966) recommended an allocation of 6 per cent of national income to education by 1986, and the CABE Committee (MHRD, 2005) reiterated the same and added that subject to fulfilment of this, at least 0.5 per cent of national income be allocated to technical education. It may not be proper to conclude that the share of technical education already exceeds the recommendation made by MHRD (2005), as the present share incudes expenditure on technical schools and polytechnics, which together account for above 35 per cent of the total, while the recommendation refers to technical education at higher level and the recommendation assumes a priori fulfilment of recommendation of allocation of 6 per cent of national income to education.

What is the relative priority accorded to technical education? In the gross domestic product (GDP), expenditure on technical accounted for a very small proportion. It was 0.3 per cent in 2005–06, which has increased to nearly 0.9 per cent in 2017–18 as per budget estimates.[13] In a sense, the priority given to technical education seems to be insignificant, but the education sector as a whole receives only about 4 per cent of the GDP.

Another indicator of relative priority given to a technical education can be understood when we look at the share of technical education in total expenditure on education. This proportion has increased from near 3.9 per cent in 2005–06 to 5.1 per cent in 2014–15 and then declined to 4.7 per cent in 2017–18 (see Figure 3.9).

Public expenditure on technical education in real terms[14] has increased, as shown in Table 3.4, from ₹14,685 crores in 2005–06 to ₹101,714 crores in 2017–18 (as per budget estimates). The actual expenditure was ₹72,764 crores in 2015–16. The increase at an annual growth rate of 17.5 per cent has been very impressive, as it is in constant prices. While the expenditure of the union government increased at a growth rate of 16.3 per cent, expenditure of states and union territories increased at 19.5 per cent. But the relative share of the union government has increased from about one-third to 50 per cent by 2009–10 and then declined to 41 per cent by 2017–18, while the relative share of the states and union territories in the expenditure has declined from 66 per cent to 59 per cent during this period. Note that this is the period

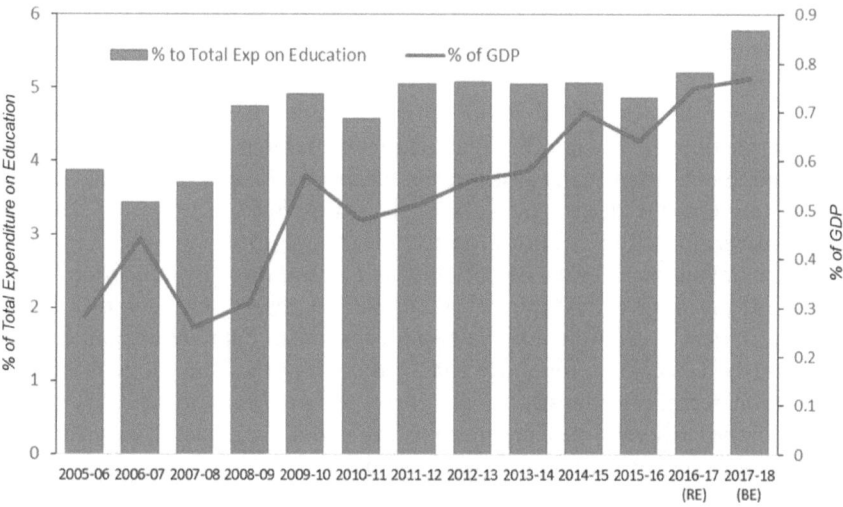

Figure 3.9 Expenditure on Technical Education as a Proportion of Total Expenditure on Education and GDP (%)

Source: Based on Analysis of Budget Expenditure on Education (Various Years), MHRD.

Table 3.4 Union and States' Public Expenditure on Technical Education (₹ in Crores in 2011–12 Prices)

	States and Union Territories	Union Government	Total	States and Union Territories	Union Government	Total
	₹ in crore			percentage		
2005–06	9,696	4,989	14,685	66.0	34.0	100
2006–07	14,947	9,793	24,740	60.4	39.6	100
2007–08	9,435	7,355	16,791	56.2	43.8	100
2008–09	11,271	10,125	21,397	52.7	47.3	100
2009–10	20,743	20,875	41,618	49.8	50.2	100
2010–11	18,928	19,219	38,147	49.6	50.4	100
2011–12	23,975	20,386	44,361	54.0	46.0	100
2012–13	30,604	20,652	51,256	59.7	40.3	100
2013–14	31,225	25,932	57,156	54.6	45.4	100
2014–15	39,726	33,487	73,214	54.3	45.7	100
2015–16	41,950	30,814	72,764	57.7	42.3	100
2016–17 (RE)	56,540	36,087	92,627	61.0	39.0	100
2017–18 (BE)	59,556	42,157	101,714	58.6	41.4	100
Rate of Growth (%)	16.33	19.46	17.50			

Note: RE: Revised estimates; BE: Budget estimates.
Rate of growth: Annual average compound rate of growth.
Source: Based on Analysis of Budget Expenditure on Education (various years).

during which several new technical institutions were set up by the union government.

It is generally observed that the centrally funded institutions are reasonably better funded, though the funds made available to them also fall short of requirements than many institutions funded by state governments or by others that come under the purview of the states. Such information like the union government's expenditure on technical institutions and other institutions was available in *Analysis of Budget Expenditure on Education* until 2013–14, but not for the later period. Table 3.5 gives a few such details on select technical institutions for the period, for which data are available. The IITs and NITs account for more than half of the total union government budget on technical education. The corresponding proportion used to be higher in the earlier years. The generous funding of these institutions can also be viewed as one of the main reasons for their better functioning and higher quality and standards. The funding pattern of IITs and NITs versus others strongly suggests that (a) quality education is costly and requires generous funding and (b) it is public institutions that can provide quality education compared to the others.

The expenditure of the states and union territories on technical education has increased from ₹1,799 crores in 1991–92 to ₹7,296 crores in 2015–16,

Emergent Challenges of Engineering Education   83

Table 3.5 Union Government Expenditure on Select Institutions of Total Technical Education (Revenue Account) (₹ in Crores) in Constant Prices

	1993–94	2000–01	2002–03	2003–04	2004–05	2005–06	2006–07	2007–08	2008–09	2009–10	2010–11	2011–12	2012–13 (RE)	2013–14 (BE)
IITs	142.1	505.0	657.7	649.6	638.6	709.6	730.4	894.0	1790.1	1777.7	1942.7	2322.9	2647.6	3850.1
Percentage in Total	35.1	45.7	47.6	46.4	44.3	46.6	41.6	42.9	40.9	32.6	32.5	29.1	31.0	40.9
RECs/NITs	72.5	134.5	190.0	216.7	273.6	280.5	221.8	**	1196.0	1431.9	1389.5	1588.3	1612.0	2109.1
Percentage in Total	17.9	12.2	13.8	15.5	19.0	18.4	12.6	**	27.4	26.3	23.3	19.9	18.9	22.4
AICTE	2.4	86.0	120.0	50.0	64.0	91.5	240.6	590.4	197.0	200.0	220.0	230.0	400.1	421.0
Percentage in Total	0.6	7.8	8.7	3.6	4.4	6.0	13.7	28.4	4.5	3.7	3.7	2.9	4.7	4.5
TEQIP		**	45.0	100.5	82.5	5.0	50.8	27.2	2.6	3.0	5.0	183.1	197.6	400.0
Percentage in Total		**	3.3	7.2	5.7	0.3	2.9	1.3	0.1	0.1	0.1	2.3	2.3	4.2
NITIE (M)		11.8	6.5	13.0	6.7	10.7	22.3	34.8	47.9	56.5	52.9	42.4	31.5	33.3
IIIT (A)		16.5	6.8	5.0	1.9	15.6	19.6	28.0	55.3	55.3	35.7	69.0	85.1	**
IIIT (J)		**	**	**	4.0	6.0	8.0	11.0	23.9	41.0	45.0	55.0	65.0	**
IIITDM(K)		**	**	**	**	**	1.0	2.0	2.0	5.0	20.0	75.0	80.0	**
Three New IIITs@		**	**	**	**	**	**	**	**	248.5	250.0	637.9	715.0	**
New NITs										14.8	25.0	80.0	140.0	**
Total Tech. Edn.*	405.2	1104.9	1380.6	1400.2	1441.7	1523.7	1757.2	2082.1	4371.5	5451.0	5970.4	7973.4	8545.3	9421.2

NITIE (M): NITIE Mumbai; IIIT (A): IIIT Allahabad; IIITM (G): IIIT and Management, Gwalior; IIIT (J): IIIT Jabalpur; IIIT D&M (K): IIIT Design and Management, Kanchipuram; *Totals include others not listed/or have been marked **; ** nil or included in *; @ yet to be set up.

Source: Analysis of Budget Expenditure on Education (Various Years), Ministry of Human Resource Development.

Table 3.6 Public Expenditure on Engineering and Technical Education (States and Union Territories) (₹ in Crores) in 2011–12 prices

Year	Total Expenditure on Technical Education	Total Expenditure on Engineering Education	Engineering Education in Technical Education (Percentage)
1991–92	1,799.8	394.4	21.91
1995–96	2,127.2	392.8	18.47
2000–01	2,877.9	557.0	19.36
2005–06	3,474.4	726.7	20.92
2009–10	4,659.1	711.4	15.27
2010–11	5,113.7	796.3	15.57
2011–12	5,691.6	856.6	15.05
2012–13	6,193.2	986.3	15.92
2013–14	6,666.0	1,100.6	16.51
2014–15	7,560.0	1,104.3	14.61
2015–16	7,296.0	1,393.0	19.10
2016–17 (RE)	8,671.0	1,338.0	15.40
2017–18 (BE)	10,622.0	2,774.0	25.80
Growth rate (%) (1991–92 to 2017–18)	7.07	7.75	

Growth rate: Average compound rate growth per annum.
Source: Based on Analysis of Budget Expenditure on Education (Various Years), Selected Educational Statistics (Various Years), UGC Annual Reports (Various Years).

that is, by about four times at the growth rate of 7.1 per cent, while on engineering education it has increased at the growth rate of 7.8 per cent during last two-and-a-half decades (Table 3.6). Interestingly, the share of public expenditure on 'engineering colleges and institutions' to total public expenditure on technical education in the states/union territories has declined from 21.9 per cent in 1991–92 to 19.1 per cent in 2015–16, which increased to 25 per cent in 2017–18, as per budget estimates.

However, expenditure on technical education as a share of total expenditure on education varies widely across different states in 2017–18. It ranges from a meagre 0.8 per cent (Rajasthan) to the highest level of 19.5 per cent in Chandigarh (Figure 3.10). What states like Andhra Pradesh, Karnataka, Bihar, Gujarat, Chhattisgarh, Madhya Pradesh, Uttar Pradesh, West Bengal, Tamil Nadu and the north-eastern states, including Assam, are spending on technical education is below the national average. In some of these states, it is the private sector that dominates.

The relative priority given to technical education in states varies very widely between states, as Figure 3.10 shows. It ranges from a meagre 1.1 per cent (Telangana) to the highest level of 76.7 per cent in Chandigarh in 2017–18. Chandigarh and Puducherry have been allocating above 10 per cent of the total expenditure on education to technical education. Then, in the second group of states, we find Kerala, Goa, Maharashtra and Jharkhand

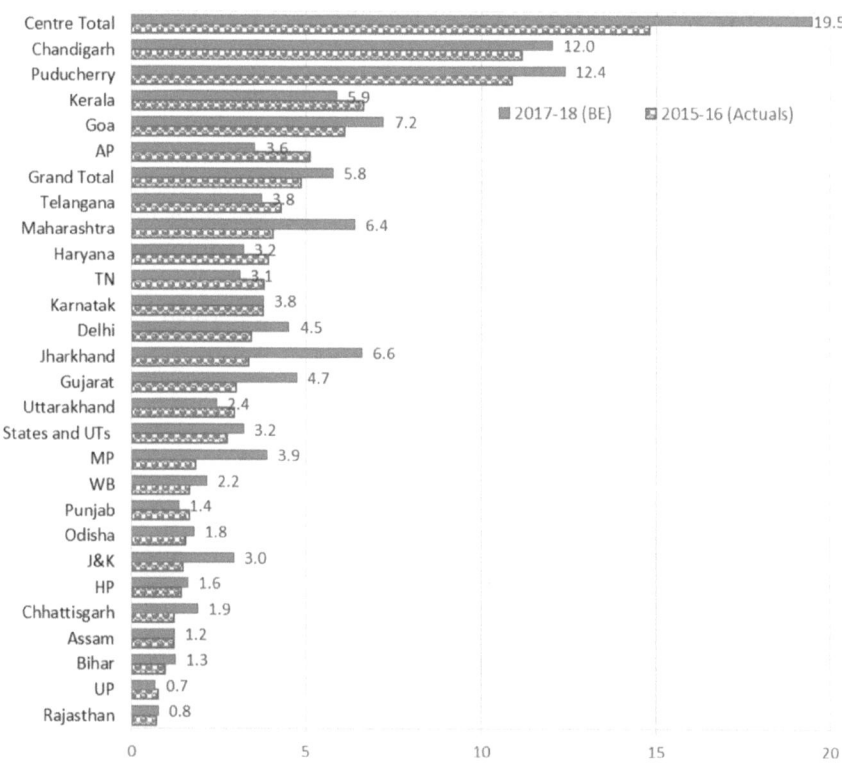

Figure 3.10 Public Expenditure on Technical Education as a Percentage of Total Expenditure on Education, 2015–16 and 2017–18

Source: Based on Analysis of Budget Expenditure on Education (2015–16 – 2017–18), MHRD.

that spend above 5 per cent but below 10 per cent. All others spend small amounts and also very small proportions of the total expenditure on education on technical education. Rajasthan and Uttar Pradesh spend less than 1 per cent. States like Karnataka, Maharashtra, Tamil Nadu and Haryana have spent below the all-state average on technical education. It is interesting to note that the states with lower public expenditure on engineering education have experienced a sharp increase in the private engineering colleges. For instance, in Telangana (with the lowest share in its public budget on engineering education allocated to technical education, i.e., 1.1 per cent), the share of private engineering institutions is 96.7 per cent with an intake capacity of similar level, as discussed in Section 'Financing of Engineering Education in India'.

In the budget on higher education, expenditures on scholarships and research have important implications. Expenditure on research promotes quality of education and expenditure on scholarships promotes merit as well as access of the weaker sections to higher education. We do not have

86 *Economics of Engineering Education in India*

detailed data on public expenditure on research in technical education. So let us examine the expenditure on scholarships.

Public expenditure on scholarships has also implications for household expenditure on education, which is an aspect that is examined here in the subsequent part of this section. In the budget on higher education, financial assistance in the form of scholarships to students is an important item that is meant to promote participation of the disadvantaged sections in higher education, and thereby to improve overall equity in higher education.

But scholarships form a very small part of the total expenditure on technical education: it was less than 1 per cent till 2005–06 which has increased

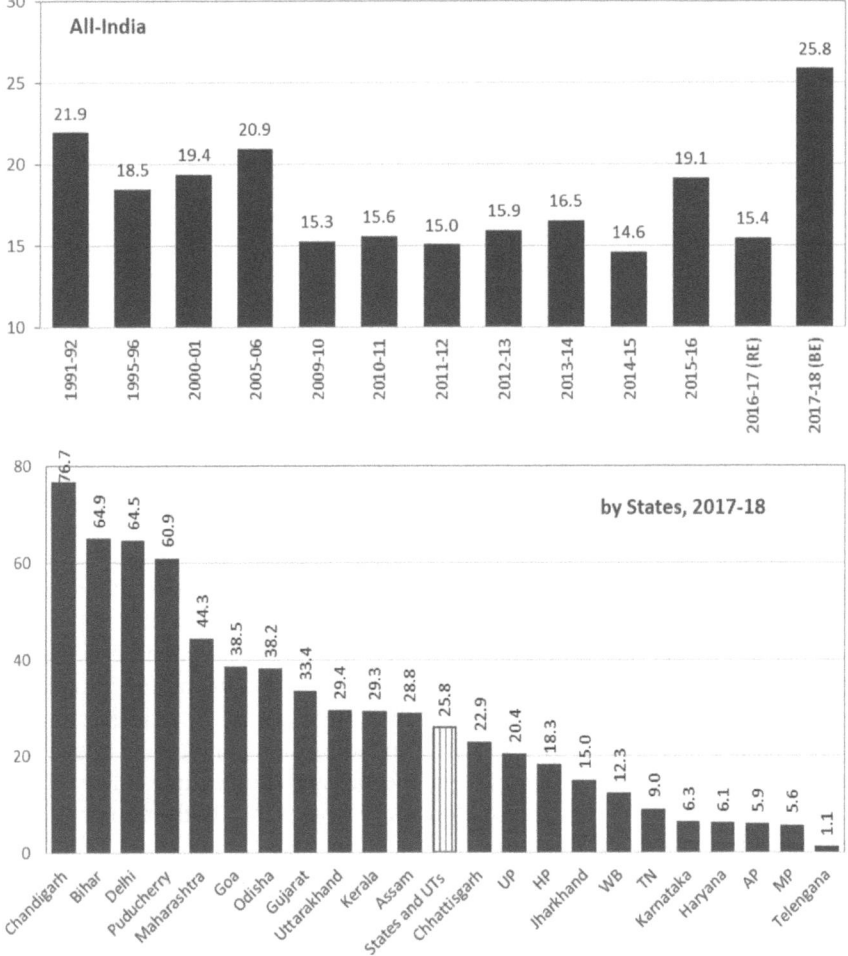

Figure 3.11 Public Expenditure on Engineering Education as a Percentage of Total Expenditure on Technical Education (States and Union Territories)

Source: Based on Analysis of Budget Expenditure on Education (Various Years), MHRD.

to 3.9 per cent in 2017–18 (budget estimate). It has been below 4 per cent, except in 2016–17, and as per the 'revised estimate', it was 8.7 per cent. The overall budget expenditure on scholarships in technical education has increased at a rate of growth of 16 per cent – from ₹9 crore in 1991–92 to about ₹400 crore in 2017–18 (Table 3.7).

Financial incentives in terms scholarships play an important role in improving access and retention of students, particularly those from marginalised backgrounds. Several studies, particularly in the international context, have found that the probability to enrol and continue in higher education increases with the availability of financial assistance to students (Schwartz, 1985; Moore et al., 1991; Monks, 2009; Glocker, 2011). Also, the National Policy on Education (1986) and National Knowledge Commission (2007) (Government of India, 2009) had recommended for a well-funded and extensive National Scholarship Scheme to improve access and retention of socially and economically underprivileged students in higher education. While scholarships and other measures of financial assistance to students have been used as an important measure of promoting equitable access to higher education for a long time, the allocation of public resources for scholarships has suffered a severe decline in India over the years (Tilak, 2004; Narayana, 2019). The need for higher financial assistance for students who take up studies in technical education is more rather than for those opting for general higher education. But public policy in India seems to favour a shift from scholarships

Table 3.7 Public Expenditure on Scholarships in Technical Education in Real Prices (States and Union Territories) (₹ in Crores at 2011–12 Prices)

Year	Expenditure on Technical Education	Expenditure on Scholarship in Technical Education	Expenditure on Scholarships in Total Expenditure on Technical Education (%)
1991–92	1,799.8	9.0	0.50
1995–96	2,127.2	4.9	0.23
2000–01	2,877.9	7.3	0.25
2005–06	3,474.3	13.7	0.39
2009–10	4,659.1	167.6	3.60
2010–11	5,113.7	173.6	3.39
2011–12	5,691.6	261.9	4.60
2012–13	6,193.2	240.3	3.88
2013–14	6,666.0	203.9	3.06
2014–15	7,560.0	290.7	3.85
2015–16	7,296.0	304.3	4.17
2016–17(RE)	8,671.0	748.6	8.63
2017–18(BE)	10,622.0	415.1	3.91
Growth rate (%)	9.6	15.9	

Source: *Analysis of Budget Expenditure on Education* (Various Years), *Selected Educational Statistics* (Various Years), UGC Annual Reports (Various Years).

to loans, considering the latter as a substitute to the former. This calls for an urgent discussion on the question of state support to engineering students in terms of scholarships, student loan and fee reimbursement policies for a nuanced understanding of this critical issue.

We do not have similar details for scholarships on engineering education, but we can look at the relative place given to engineering education in the total expenditure on technical education in the states and union territories. The expenditure on engineering education has increased at almost the same growth rate as expenditure on total technical education, which was around 7 per cent between 1991–92 and 2017–18. Engineering education accounts for about one-fifth of the expenditure on technical education. But the trend is not smooth; it had touched the lowest level of 15 per cent in 2011–12, when engineering education was at its peak in terms of demand and growth. As the private sector opened more and more institutions, the government perhaps did not feel the need to raise its expenditure significantly on engineering education. With respect to this proportion, we also find large variations across states. Chandigarh and surprisingly Bihar have spent about 65 per cent or more of the total education expenditure on engineering education, while on average, it was 25.8 per cent in 2017–18 among all the states and union territories. Again, states such as Andhra Pradesh, Madhya Pradesh and Telangana figure at the bottom. These states along with Tamil Nadu, Karnataka and Haryana spend below 10 per cent. Perhaps these states spend on other branches of technical education.

Funding, fees, regulation and many other aspects on which we note significant variations over time and between several states are clearly related to state-specific policies, which are conditioned by several factors such as socio-economic and political conditions and not the least on economic conditions, including state domestic product (SDP) per capita, fiscal resources, levels of industrialisation and levels of living of the people, though the effects of engineering education are not necessarily confined to the boundaries of the states. A detailed understanding of these aspects is important and requires state-specific studies.

On the whole, the picture on public funding on technical education does not give a satisfactory picture. The absolute levels of expenditure as well as relative priority accorded to technical education in national income and in education budgets are small, and there is a need to significantly step up when the country is aiming at taking advantage of the revolution in technology and at building a strong knowledge society. Several committees such as the AICTE (1994, 2003) made detailed suggestions on strengthening the resource base of technical education, which include:

a Raising public budgets both by the union government and state governments on technical education.
b Allocating sizeable proportion of resources for research and scholarships in technical education.

c Mobilising resources in the form of a technical education cess from the technical graduate employees and/or firms that employ technical graduates.
d Raising resources through the corporate social responsibility provisions of public acts.
e Developing a special fund or an educational development bank for funding technical education with public (union and states) and private funds.
f Efficient and effective utilisation of resources.
f Regulating student fees at about 20 per cent of the revenue expenditure of the institutions, besides pleading for combating the growing tendencies towards commercialisation of technical education.

Some of these recommendations partly figure in the initiatives taken later by the government, but no significant increase in the resource base of technical education could be seen.

Household Expenditure on Engineering Education

Due to the increasing presence of the private sector in engineering education (and also in other professional and technical education), families sending their children to engineering education need to spend a significant share of their incomes on their children's education. Inequalities in household expenditure on education reflect inequalities in society between different sections of the society. Using data collected in a few education-specific rounds of the NSS (64th in 2007–08, 71st in 2014–15 and 75th in 2017–18), we analyse a few aspects of household expenditure on higher education in India. The NSS figures do not include expenditure on private coaching that families incur to prepare their wards to appear in different competitive entrance examinations for admission in engineering education. With this note, let us examine household expenditure on engineering education in India.

According to the NSS data, the household expendiutre on higher education in India was around ₹26,400 per annum per student that accounts for 19.3 per cent of the household's annual income in 2017–18, and this was ₹14,500 a decade ago in 2007–08,[15] as shown in Figure 3.12. We observe significant variations in household's spending on different branches of study in higher education: the highest spending was made by families on their children's medical education (₹86,000), followed by engineering education (₹70,500) and then on 'other' disciplines (₹53,600) in 2017–18 – showing that medical education was the costliest discipline. Humanities at ₹11,161 figure at the other end of spectrum, commerce (at ₹18,478) and science (at ₹19,419) figure above humanities. So studies in medicine and engineering studies are 7.7 times and 6.3 times costlier, respectively, than humanities. This is apparent as even the tuition fees charged for professional studies are much higher than for general higher education studies, especially in private colleges and universities. Expenditures on other items are also normally higher in studies in engineering and medicine.

90 *Economics of Engineering Education in India*

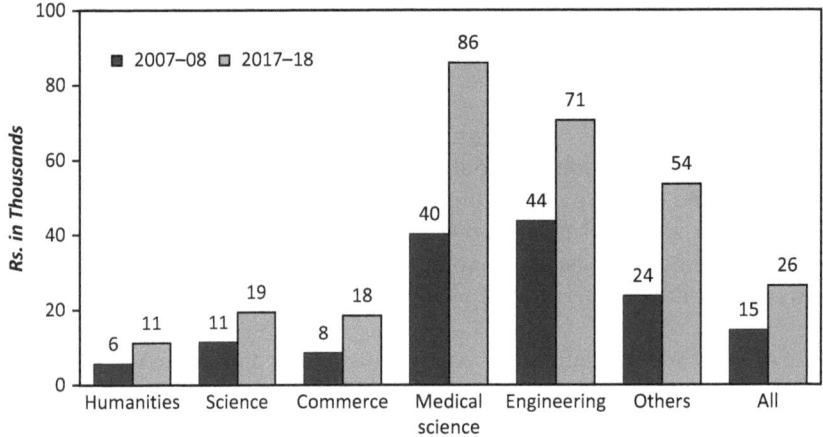

Figure 3.12 Household Expenditure on Higher Education per Student by Major Area of Study (₹ per Annum)

Source: Compiled by authors based on NSS 64th (2007–08) and 75th round (2017–18) data.

Table 3.8 Household Expenditure on Higher Education as Proportion of Total Household Consumption Expenditure across Major Areas (%)

Course	2007–08	2014–15	2017–18
Humanities	11.1	10.3	10.6
Science	18.3	17.8	17.2
Commerce	12.4	13.8	14.2
Medicine	58.7	58.8	50.5
Engineering	69.0	51.5	45.8
Others	33.1	35.3	31.4
All	23.0	22.0	19.3

Source: Compiled by authors based on NSS 64th (2007–08), 71st (2014–15) and 75th round (2017–18) data.

Notably, families sending their wards to pursue medical science have spent around half of their annual consumption expenditure, which is considered as a proxy of family income, towards their education in 2017–18; a decade earlier, this amount was 59 per cent. In the case of engineering education, families used to spend as high as 69 per cent in 2007–08, which came down to 46 per cent by 2017–18 (Table 3.8). The figures ranged between 10 per cent and 20 per cent in the case of humanities, sciences and commerce. In the last one decade, the share of total family income that went towards higher education came down in all disciplines in higher education and also for overall higher education as well. A detailed discussion on this would unpack trends better, but that is beyond the scope of this study. Still, it may be noted that it is not because higher education became necessarily cheaper, but that families'

Table 3.9 Annual Household Expenditure on Engineering Education per Annum per Student (2017–18)

Items of Expenditure	Expenditure per Student (₹)	Percentage of Total Spending on Engineering Education	Percentage of Total Household Consumption Expenditure
Fee	54,823	73.8	36.7
Non-Fee items			
Books, Stationery and Uniform	5,973	8.0	3.0
Transport	6,733	9.1	3.4
Private Tuition	3,005	4.0	1.5
Other items	3,793	5.1	1.9
Total Non-Fee	18,107	26.2	9.1
Total (Fee + Non-Fee)	70,575	100.0	45.8

Source: Authors' calculations based on 75th round unit-level data of NSSO (2017–18).

household economic status – overall expenditure/income levels – went up. We have noted in Table 3.8 that absolute levels of household expenditure on all disciplines increased over the years between 2007–08 and 2017–18.

The annual average household expenditure on undergraduate engineering education in India is reported to be around ₹70,600, which accounts for 45.8 per cent of the total annual family consumption expenditure (Table 3.9). Out of the total household expenditure spent on engineering education, ₹54,800 is incurred on fees (tuition fee, examination fee, library fee and other fees) and ₹18,100 on non-fee items such as expenditure on food, accommodation, textbooks, transport, private tuition, mobile, internet and others. Fees have accounted for 36.7 per cent and expenditure on non-fee items constituted 9.1 per cent of the annual consumption expenditure of the family. The share of expenditure on fee to total household expenditure on engineering education is 73.8 per cent, while it is 26.3 per cent on non-fee items. Households spend significantly higher amounts (and proportions) on fees as compared to non-fee items. This is mainly because of the higher levels of fees charged, particularly in private engineering institutions.

However, households also spend a significant share of their total budgets on non-fee items. Expenditures on food, accommodation, textbooks and other study materials and transportation take a major share (66 per cent) of the household expenditure on non-fee items and the remaining 34 per cent is spent on private tuition, mobile, internet and other items. Private institutions charge higher amounts on students' food and accommodation also than public institutions, where these items are also partly subsidised.

Levels of household spending on engineering education vary across socioeconomic groups and across types of institutions. Households spend ₹71,900 on the engineering education of their sons, more than their daughters which is around ₹67,100 (Table 3.10). While such a pattern is normally explained

Table 3.10 Annual Average Household Expenditure on Engineering Education by Select Socio-Economic Groups and Types of Institutions (₹)

Category		Fee	Non-Fee	Total
Gender	Female	51,770	21,456	67,190
	Male	56,050	17,016	71,939
	Inequality (M/F)	1.08	0.79	1.07
Location	Rural	41,731	17,020	55,453
	Urban	59,916	18,520	76,455
	Inequality(U/R)	1.44	1.09	1.38
Caste	SC/ST	40,241	15,799	53,781
	OBC	50,582	17,065	65,862
	General	65,752	19,477	82,999
	Inequality (General/SC-ST)	1.63	1.23	1.54
Institution	Government	37,174	15,659	50,235
	Government-Aided Private	55,071	19,832	70,955
	Private (unaided)	58,847	17,515	75,147
	Inequality (Private-Unaided/Government)	1.58	1.12	1.50
Income Quintile	Q1 (Poorest)	37,600	15,151	49,999
	Q2	46,071	18,286	60,502
	Q3	54,548	19,371	70,429
	Q4	62,343	19,708	80,755
	Q5 (Richest)	76,201	17,297	94,507
	Inequality (Q5/Q1)	2.03	1.14	1.89
TOTAL		54,823	18,107	70,575

Source: Authors' calculations based on 75th round unit-level data of NSSO (2017–18).

in terms of a gender bias (Tilak, 2002a; Kingdon, 2005; Azam & Kingdon, 2013; Saha, 2013; Kenayathulla, 2016; Wongmonta & Glewwe, 2016; Kumar, 2017; Kaul, 2018; Iddrisu et al., 2018; Datta & Kingdon, 2019), in the present case, this difference may be because of choice of college. It is possible that women are admitted in institutions that charge lower levels of fees, while men take admission in colleges that charge comparatively higher levels of fees. As high fee is perceived to be equivalent to a better quality of education, this may reflect a different kind of parental bias in favour of sons. Interestingly, spending on non-fee items is reported to be higher for women (₹21,400) as compared to men (₹17,000). As a result, the gender difference in the total expenditure on education gets marginally reduced.

Rural-urban disparities in household expenditures on education are significant. In 2017–18, urban households spent ₹76,400 towards engineering education of their wards, which is considerably higher than their rural counterparts (₹55,400), that is, there is a difference of 37.8 per cent between the two sectors in favour of urban areas. This gap in spending is largely attributed to the differences in tuition fees charged by higher education institutions (which is substantially high in urban areas); there are not many variations in spending on non-fee items. Similarly, variations in household spending are also prevalent across caste groups. As expected, the highest spending has been made on engineering education by students belonging to the general category (₹83,000) as compared to the scheduled groups (₹53,700) in 2017–18. This shows a spending gap of 1.5 times between general category students and scheduled students.

Household spending on education also varies by type of institution (government, government-aided private and private-unaided). This is as high as ₹75,200 in private (unaided) institutions in 2017–18, which is about 50 per cent higher than the expenditure in government institutions (₹50,200). This is apparent as tuition fee levels for engineering programmes are significantly high, especially in private institutions. The fee charged in private-unaided institutions was 60 per cent higher than the fee in public institutions.[16] Clearly, the directions of the fee regulatory commissions constituted in each state are rarely adhered to by these institutions. As Jadhav (2020, p. 79) observed, "There was absolutely no transparency whatsoever in the fees charged. Malpractices could not be controlled". In fact, malpractices are not confined to charging exorbitant fees from students.[17]

There is an elaborate structure of rules and regulations on most aspects of running an institution, so that these institutions do not adapt to malpractices and, inter alia, maintain proper standards, ensuring quality of education. But they are often flouted by private institutions.[18] Private investors influence and resist introduction of rules, regulations and norms regarding transparency in admissions, fee structure, scholarships, curriculum, recruitment of teachers

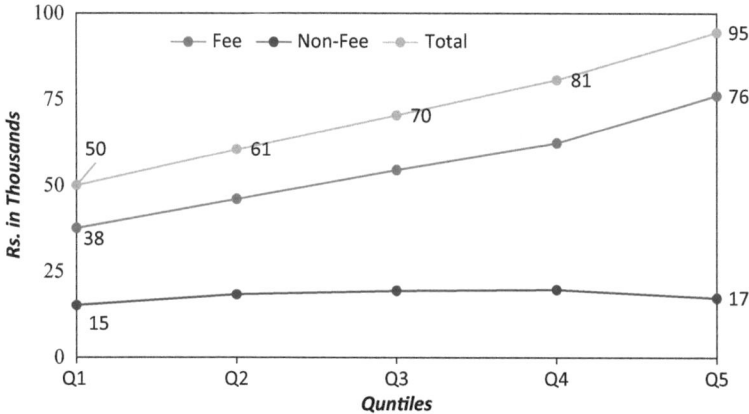

Figure 3.13 Household Expenditure on Fees and Other Items in Engineering Education by Household Consumption Quintiles

Source: Authors' calculations based on NSSO.

and their pay, etc. They even determine the public policies, with their vote power in public education bodies, and in state-level and national politics.

Household spending varies most with the economic status of the households which is measured in terms of monthly consumption expenditure in the present analysis. Household expenditure per student increases with each successive consumption expenditure quintiles. It ranges from ₹49,900 for the lowest quintile to ₹94,500 for the highest quintile in 2017–18 (Figure 3.13). The rich-poor gap in the spending on engineering education is estimated to be 89 per cent in 2017–18. The richest households spend almost double the expenditure of the poorest quintile. Interestingly, not only the total expenditure, but the fee paid by top quintile is also twice the fee paid by the bottom quintile. Rich students might prefer to opt for costly institutions which charge high fees under the assumption that the higher the cost, the better the quality of education, though the relationship between the two is yet to be proven.

Changing Labour Market Conditions and Engineering Education

The discussion on growth of engineering education in India remains incomplete, without a discussion on employment and related issues of engineering graduates. This is particularly important in the context of rapidly changing demand for engineering manpower and other conditions in the labour market in India and abroad. Technology is advancing at an unprecedented space across the world and has transformed the global labour market. The adoption of exponential technologies is disrupting industries by creating new markets and transforming existing markets through product or business innovations. In the new age of automation and unprecedented technological advances, the nature of the job market in several economies is changing rapidly. Modern technology is changing the skills that employers seek, and therefore, the training imparted in the educational institutions needs to be revisited. In fact, today, graduates are not sure about the use of knowledge and skills they have obtained during their studies in the dynamically changing labour markets. In the labour market, job roles are being drastically modified, redefined and changed altogether, and certain types of jobs are becoming redundant and new occupations with new roles are created. We are riding a new wave of uncertainty as the pace of innovation continues to accelerate and technology influences extensively the very basic characteristics of the labour market (WDR, 2019).

Engineering being a technical field that produces specific human capital is most severely affected by the rapid technological progress. As a result, the nature and composition of skills that are required for an engineering graduate is going through a huge transformation. Globally, engineering education is experiencing an increasing pressure on graduate employability, particularly in the context of the changing environment in the labour market. The complexities found in the global engineering labour market have changed the discourse in the discipline. It is important to analyse what it means to be an engineer in the twenty-first century and how the skills and training imparted in institutions might better prepare engineers of the future (Winberg et al., 2020).

With fluctuating labour market conditions and unplanned growth of engineering education, mismatches have arisen between supply and demand for engineering manpower. The mismatch in India can be divided into two broad categories. First, there is the skill deficit or skill gap, where a worker's skill is not up to the requirements of the job. Second, there is skill underutilisation (over-education or over-skilling), which arises when the level of education and skill exceed those required by the job. The latter causes 'bumping down' – low-skilled jobs being offered to high-skilled workers. But a more familiar mismatch refers to the numbers of graduates produced and hired. Sengupta (2017) has estimated proportional mismatches with respect to educated manpower at all levels, using the data from several rounds of NSS. In 1993–94 and 2004–05, there were actually shortages in engineering manpower (degree level), but the quantum of shortages was very small. By 2011–12, the situation began to change, and there was a negative mismatch, the supply exceeding demand, but again by a very small proportion. We do not have such estimates for the period after 2011–12. But it is quite possible that the supply exceeds demand by increasingly larger proportions, as the available evidence on employment and unemployment trends suggest.

The data from the NSSs show that unemployment among the educated in India has been consistently rising over the years. Among the general graduates and above, the rate of unemployment increased from 16.1 per cent in 1983 to 35.9 per cent in 2017–18. While the rate of unemployment is rising among the youth with almost any level of education, the rate of growth is the highest in the case of those with technical education. It was 37.9 per cent in 2017–18, a sharp increase from 17.3 per cent in 1983 and 19.8 per cent in 1999–2000 (Khare & Arora, 2023).

We do not have similar comparable data for engineering graduates. We have data on employability of graduates, hiring rates and placement records available from institutions of engineering education, which are analysed here.

Employment and Employability of Engineer Graduates

Having noted that 'employability' and 'employment' are not the same: workers can be employable, but not necessarily employed; and the converse might also happen when labour markets are imperfect: workers might be employed, though they are not employable, we analyse a few aspects relating to employability and employment of engineering graduates in this section. The rate of hiring of engineers has declined from 28 per cent in 2014 to 22 per cent in 2018, as shown in Figure 3.14. After a small increase in the following year to 23 per cent, it rose by eight points to 31 per cent in 2020. According to this, nearly 70 per cent of engineers are unemployed in 2020; the figure was nearly 80 per cent in 2018.

Data on placement records also do not indicate any better situation. In 2017–18, out of the total number of engineering graduates of 7.93 lakhs, only 45 per cent were selected for employment in campus placement processes

96 *Economics of Engineering Education in India*

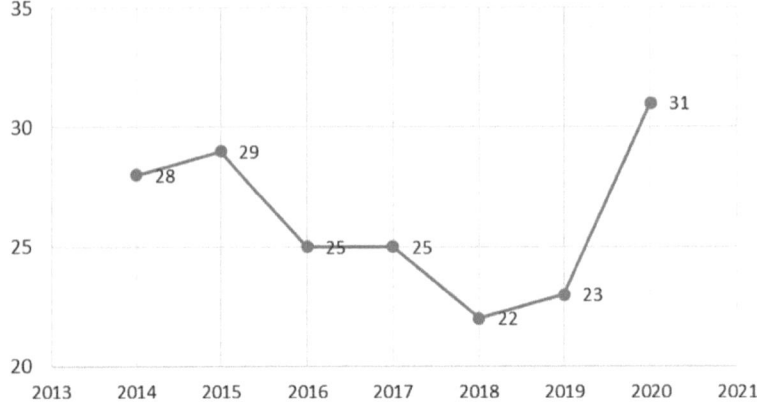

Figure 3.14 Fluctuating Rate of Hiring of Engineers (%)
Source: Statista Research Department, https://www.statista.com/statistics/1043283/india-hiring-rate-engineers/

in AICTE-approved institutions. Of course, the corresponding rate is much higher in IITs, NITs and IIITs, where it was reported to be 77 per cent in 2018–19 (Nigam, 2020).[19]

It may be necessary to analyse the placement records by looking at the sub-stream of engineering, as different streams performed differently. AICTE data on placements enables us to do this.[20] Technological obsolescence in the labour market seems to have suddenly resulted in a declining demand for graduates in electronics and IT-related engineering. The number of placements as a proportion of enrolments of engineering graduates trained in electronics and IT fields has gone down from 53 per cent in 2014–15 to 47.9 per cent in 2016–17. With the IT boom in the preceding period, this figure went up by more than four times from 12 per cent in 2012–13 to 53 per cent in 2014–15. Employment conditions for graduates in traditional areas of engineering improved from 19.8 per cent in 2013–14 to 37.8 per cent in 2016–17, as graduates in the modern (IT-related) areas and other areas suffered (Figure 3.15). In several cases, engineering graduates in India are employed in non-engineering occupations that offers them a substantially lower salary.

How does one explain the high rate of unemployment among the engineer graduates in India? As the U.R. Rao Committee (AICTE, 2003, p. 162) stated:

> The rising unemployment of scientists and engineers in the country is primarily due to (i) poor quality of our graduates coming out of our technical institutions (ii) lack of entrepreneurship, partly due to the limited availability of venture capital but mostly due to the inability of our students to venture and (iii) poor growth in the industrial sector.

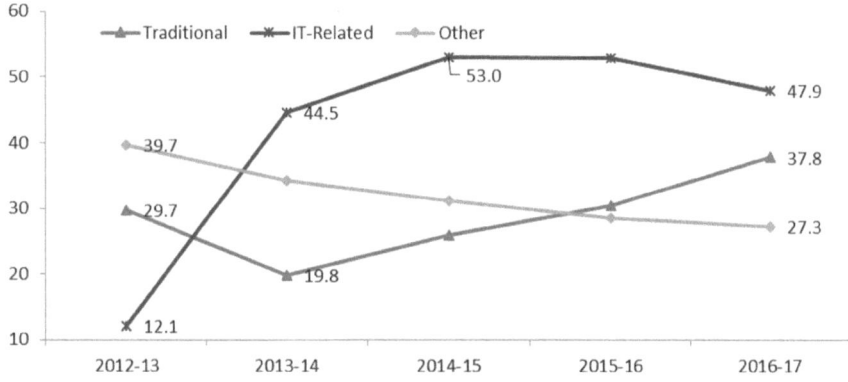

Figure 3.15 Number of Placements as a Percentage of Enrolment in Engineering Education by Major Categories of Streams
Source: AICTE database.

First, the issues of employment and unemployment of engineering graduates are coupled with the slowdown in the overall employment visible in the Indian economy. The unemployment rate in India has increased significantly over the last decade: 6.1 per cent in 2017–18 (PLFS, 2019), while graduate unemployment is 16.3 per cent in 2019 (Statista Research Department, 2020). In an interview to the *Indian Express* (13 December 2017), NITI Aayog Vice Chairperson Rajiv Kumar sees the decline in the demand for engineering graduates in the labour market as a sectoral shift that might be happening in the Indian economy – a shift from traditional factory manufacturing jobs to emerging sectors like e-commerce. Second, and more importantly, there are also problems with the type and nature of graduates who pass out and the engineering education they receive.

Due to weak labour market signals, many graduates still go for engineering education and end up in unemployment – open or disguised. Graduates who are managing to get jobs are either mal-employed or employed on very low wages. As it is often argued, the prevailing labour market indications – low employability of engineering graduates coupled with an abysmal record of job placement – reflect the poor quality of engineering education in the country. Looking at the quality of graduates being produced by a large number of colleges in India, experts (e.g. MHRD, 2003) have described them as 'IT coolies' or 'techno coolies' or 'cyber coolies'. The quality attributes in terms of, inter alia, skills and knowledge, with which the graduates come out of the colleges determine the employability of graduates.

Many employers in the labour market do not find engineering graduates worth employing. A few high-paying firms of high repute are able to recruit the few high-quality graduates produced by the best institutions, and generally like what they get, but a large number of medium and small firms are generally dissatisfied with the quality of the pool of graduates available to them. According to NASSCOM and McKinsey (2005), only 25 per cent of the engineering graduates are employable in India. Likewise, as per the latest Annual Employability Survey 2019 (Aspiring Minds, 2019), 80 per cent of Indian engineers are not fit for any job in a knowledge economy.

According to the India Skills Report (Wheebox, 2020), the employability of engineer graduates has remained static at around 50 per cent, with marginal fluctuations between 2014 and 2018. In fact, there has been no change in the employability prospects of Indian engineering graduates in the past nine years! Then suddenly it improved to 57 per cent in 2019, after which there was a steep fall to below 50 per cent (Figure 3.16). These fluctuating trends should indeed be a matter of serious concern, as they make any forecasting and planning difficult. The rate of employability of graduates also differs by sub-streams of engineering. Graduates in electronics and communications engineering and in IT (information technology) are most employable, with a rate of above 60 per cent, and the employability is the least in case of civil and mechanical engineering, with a rate of below 40 per cent. The year-wise variations are also wide, as shown in Table 3.11. Employability has improved in almost all disciplines, but still variations exist, except in 2021, when COVID-19 affected all sectors.

Aspiring Minds Team (2019) made an interesting analysis that shows that employability of graduates (in IT services) is low in those states where there are too many colleges like Tamil Nadu, Andhra Pradesh, Maharashtra and Karnataka and reasonably high in those states which have fewer colleges like Delhi, Bihar, Jharkhand and Uttarakhand. Note that the former group of states also has a larger number of IT companies than the others. In fact, Aspiring Minds Team (2019) found a clear inverse relationship between the number of engineering colleges in a state and the employability of graduates, as shown in Figure 3.17. A large number of colleges in the states where employability is low are also private colleges. This makes it clear that

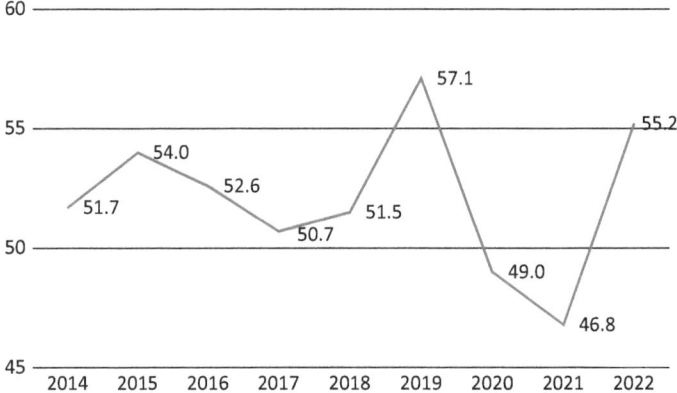

Figure 3.16 Employability of Engineer Graduates (BE/BTech) (%)
Source: Based on Aspiring Minds (2019, 2020, 2021, and 2022).

Table 3.11 Employability of Engineering Graduates by Sub-Stream (%)

	2018	2019	2021	2022
Civil engineering	44	50	26.5	35.4
Mechanical engineering	43	53	34.2	38.2
Computer science engineering	44	58	38.3	60.7
Information technology	52	60	48.3	63.5
Electrical engineering	50	60	47.4	64.8
Electronics and communications	58	61	39.9	68.7
All engineering branches	52	57	46.8	55.2

Source: India Skills Report, 2020, 2021 and 2022.

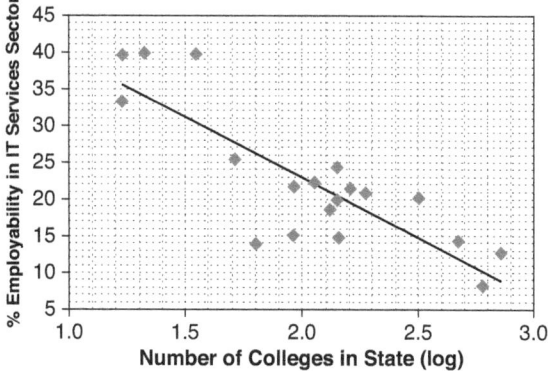

Figure 3.17 Employability and the Number of Engineering Colleges in States
Source: Aspiring Minds Team (2019). (Reproduced with permission.)

expansion has taken place at the cost of quality measured in terms of employment, and private colleges have not cared much for quality.

What steps should be taken for improving the poor employability of engineering graduates in India? Apart from economy and structural factors, it emerges that the quality of engineering education one receives is an important factor that explains employment/unemployment and wages in the competitive labour market.

Several studies and reports provide compelling reasons why undergraduate engineering education is in need of change to respond to the complex challenges in the labour market (Badran, 2007; Sahin, 2010; Adams et al., 2011; Winberg et al., 2020). For instance, literature on employability of engineering graduates emphasises curricular and pedagogical arrangements to prepare graduates for work and also to address several other risks and uncertainties they are going to face in the changing labour market. Therefore, higher education institutions must keep pace with the rapidly evolving technology to enable individuals to be future ready and reduce their rate of obsolescence (Ernst & Young, 2017).

The nature of engineering skills that a graduate needs to get employment in labour market is going through a big change in India. In addition to the foundational skills gained from mathematics, physics and engineering sciences, graduates should also learn key professional skills such as communication, collaboration, teamwork, project management, professional ethics and the broader environmental and societal issues. In fact, graduate engineers are expected to have (a) soft or core employability skills, which cover generic attitudinal and affective skills, such as reliability and teamwork, (b) communication skills, such as written and verbal communication skills in English, and (c) professional skills, which generally cover cognitive skills related to the engineering professions, such as the ability to apply engineering knowledge, as well as design and conduct experiments and related data analyses and interpretation.[21] But as Blom and Saeki (2011) found in the case of soft skills, such as reliability and self-motivation, there are huge skill gaps. Employers in India seem to be more interested in this type of skills. They rated professional skills the lowest on average among the three factor skills. This may be partly because employers think that engineering-related skills can be partly acquired during in-house training even after graduation while core employability skills would require longer time frame to be acquired. The *National Employability Report* further finds that only a handful of engineering graduates possess the next generation technical skills, which give them better employment prospects, while a majority seems to have difficulty finding suitable employment. Only 2.5 per cent of Indian engineers possess the skills in artificial intelligence (i.e. machine learning and data science), important skills required in the changing labour market; 1.5 per cent to 4.5 per cent of engineers possess the necessary skills in data engineering; and only 2.8 per cent to 5.3 per cent are qualified in wireless technologies that industry requires (Aspiring Minds, 2019). According to the Aspiring Minds (2019), only 40 per cent of engineering students in India get opportunities for internships and only 36 per cent undertake projects outside their assigned coursework. Even today, the engineering discipline in India is very theoretical, and students learn primarily through the lecture method. Similarly, the report also highlights that engineering students in India have very little industry exposure, as they are trapped in a college bubble all the time. Only 47 per cent of students attend industry talks, and more importantly, 60 per cent of the faculty do not discuss how engineering concepts apply to industry. Most talks that students attend are intra-departmental rather than seminars, workshops, conferences or webinars that typically feature outside experts and scholars who present complementary or alternative perspectives.

Providing on-the-job training to engineering graduates is seen as being costly and risky for many employers, and therefore, not a viable option. In fact, industries generally do not seem to be willing to spend much on the training of their employees. They keep subtle pressure on the academics to produce ready-made employees. One forgets that educational institutions are better suited to provide training of mind rather than for the job market that is continuously changing, which even the best of industry experts cannot forecast (Ananthasayanam, 2009). It is also argued that after getting a good professional on-the-job training, employees bargain for higher wages, which if not conceded means they might leave the company to join another. Also, providing adequate training for the job market needs a threshold level of learning, normally absorbed at the undergraduate stage, which is missing among a majority of the engineering graduates. Therefore, it is important to see whether ta four-year course in engineering after a senior secondary education actually adds any valuable employable skills in the graduates. Students need to be better equipped with employability-enhancement skills such as critical thinking, problem-solving, teamwork, decision-making and adaptability, among others.

Engineering institutions should aim to develop twenty-first-century skills (beyond core academic subjects) among young graduates. Engineering institutions should lead in preparing professionals in cutting-edge areas such as artificial intelligence, 3D (three-dimensional) machining, big data analysis, machine learning, robotic process automation, cloud computing, data engineering and data science that will create a huge wave of transformation across industries in the coming decade. But, even today, the curricula and pedagogies in a majority of engineering institutions focus on imparting traditional technical knowledge, ignoring the new skills that are in demand in the changing labour market situations; thus, the engineers fail to possess hard skills in a soft context.

Additionally, an emphasis needs to be given to strengthen the interdependent relationship between engineering knowledge and professional skills among engineering graduates to improve their employability. It is argued that in the changing labour market situations, apart from having a good conceptual understanding of basic science and mathematics, engineering students also need to develop generic skills, such as creative and critical thinking, problem-solving abilities, decision-making and so on (Badran, 2007; VIF, 2019). The new engineers need to know how to work in teams, given the importance of social skills in the workplace (Sahin, 2010). Also, in the changing labour market situations, there is a need for engineers to acquire soft skills like co-operative working, communication and presentation skills, business ethics, interpersonal relationships and skills to handle contemporary societal changes (Jha, 2005; Adams et al., 2011). Accruing these skills (in addition to gaining technical knowledge) would prepare graduates better to compete in the new world economy and in finding gainful employment in the labour market.

As has been constantly argued, there is a need for strategic policy interventions to strengthen the industry-academia interactions to improve linkages between engineering education and labour market in India. However, the latest AICTE-CII survey (CII, 2018) has revealed that 78 per cent of the total institutes have some linkages with industry, while 22 per cent have no linkages at all. Only about 7.4 per cent of the engineering institutions (710 out of

9,581) have received some funds from industry for setting up a department, cell or a laboratory. Out of the 710 institutions that have received funds, about 419 (60 per cent of the total) have received up to ₹5 lakhs, while only 46 institutes have received ₹1 crore and above. Strong linkages with industry might not only help in mobilising more financial resources, but also human resources in the form of experienced industrialists and more importantly, help in modernising the curriculum and content of engineering education. This may help in better planning of the growth of engineering education in the country. To minimise the gap between the demand and supply of engineering graduates, India should develop a mechanism that can better anticipate demand for different skills and vocation in the labour market and give that feedback to the technical education sector. This may be difficult in a fast-changing dynamic environment. But some important signals can as well be drawn from such an exercise. With the policy inputs, engineering education should prepare youths to participate in the future labour market, where they will work together to address global challenges using their technical expertise and social skills. The aspirations of a twenty-first-century engineering education require new thinking and new ways of doing, and those require engineering graduates to get advanced knowledge and skills in technical and professional areas. With globalisation, the technical education in India faces twin challenges: it has to be extremely useful for the domestic economy and at the same time made internationally relevant (Subramanian, 2015, p. 118).

Preferences and Aspirations

Now, let us briefly review the changing labour market aspirations of the graduates produced from the higher education system. Students' preferences and aspirations for and from different jobs also play an important role in explaining the phenomenon of unemployment. These are not static and they are also rapidly getting altered over the years. Aspiring Minds (National Employability Reports for Engineers, 2014, 2016 and 2019) has surveyed students' preferences towards the kind of job roles, classified as software development, core engineering jobs (such as mechanical, electrical, electronic or civil engineer) and management-related jobs. Interestingly, a majority of engineering graduates seem to have a strong preference either for software jobs or core engineering jobs, which is found to be true in all three points of time with small variations (Figure 3.18).

It is noteworthy to mention that despite the mushrooming of job opportunities in managerial roles like technical sales, marketing and content development, engineers do not seem to prefer these jobs as yet, even though quite a few of them end up there. It is widely viewed that engineering graduates take up non-engineering jobs in the labour market as they, with a few exceptions, simply don't get suitable jobs in engineering, and their skills are considered not good enough for good jobs in the engineering sector.[22] As a result, engineering graduates are often employed in non-engineering jobs that offer them a substantially lower salary.

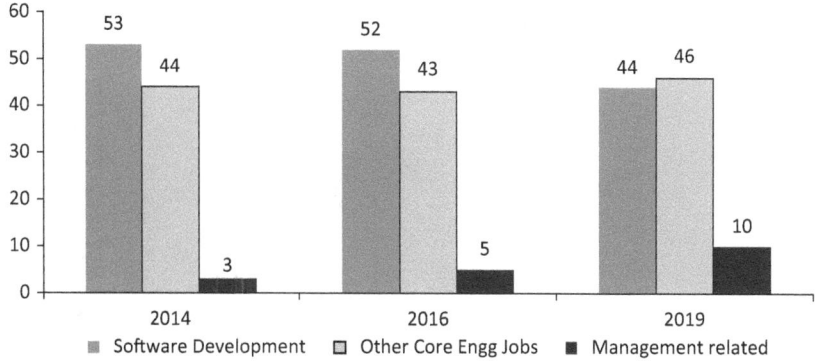

Figure 3.18 Job Role Preferences of Engineering Graduates
Source: National Employability Report – Engineers 2014, 2016 and 2019.

The reports by Aspiring Minds have also detailed the graduates' job aspirations by their branch of study, gender, tier of college they have studied in (ranks of the colleges based on the employability of their students)[23] and by tier of city. There are visible variations between them. For instance, graduates with a computer/IT background are mostly interested in software jobs, while students with core engineering branches prefer equally software and core engineering jobs. Surprisingly, for management-related roles, students from tier one colleges (colleges with higher rates of employability of students) show a maximum inclination. Similarly, women in large numbers aspire to work in managerial positions as compared to men.

Obviously, students while choosing to go for engineering education, consider labour market returns. Engineering being a privileged profession associated with high salaries, fresh graduates normally expect good salaries. The National Employability Reports for Engineers (Aspiring Minds) for the last three years have collected information of expectations of engineering graduates regarding their salaries in the job market. There are variations in the expected salary predicated by branch of study, by the quality of college and by gender (Figure 3.19). Graduates of mechanical engineering and civil engineering aspire for higher salaries, followed by computer science and IT-related branches and then circuit branches (electronics engineering, electrical engineering and instrumentation engineering). However, this is not in line with general perceptions, according to which graduates in computer/IT-related subjects of engineering command the highest pay due to their increasing demand in the labour market. Probably because of a recent fall in demand for IT graduates in the labour market, they tend to limit their monetary aspirations.

The salary expectations also vary according to the level of college one has attended and by gender. As expected, graduates from tier one colleges (proxy of better quality) aspire for much higher salaries in comparison to

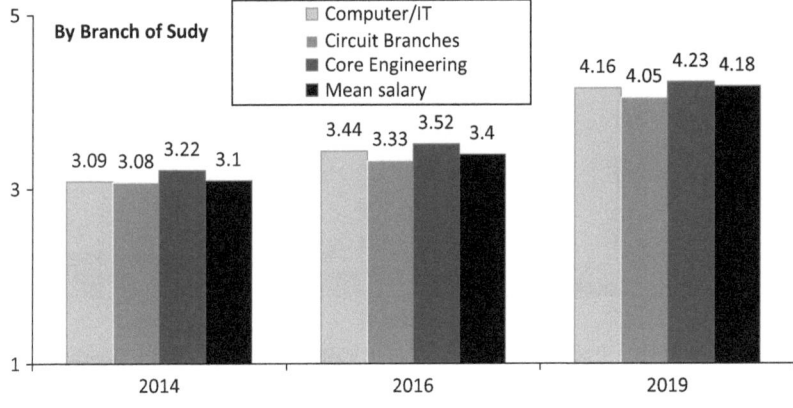
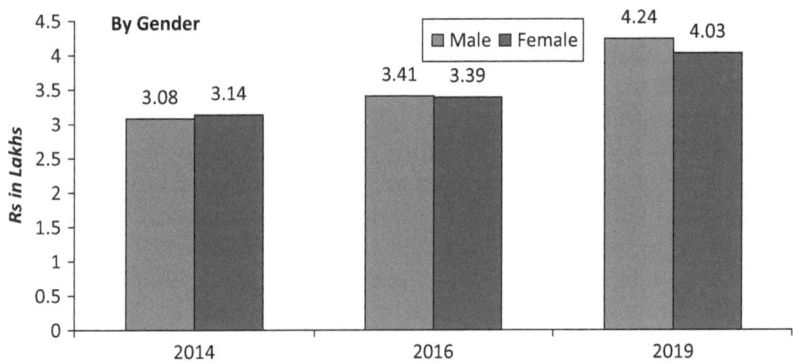
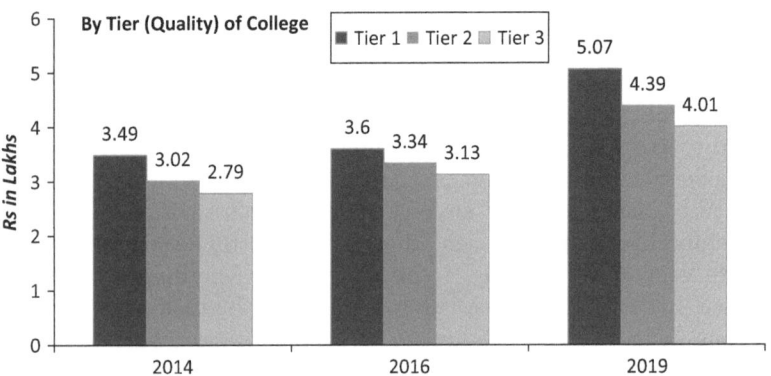

Figure 3.19 Engineering Graduates' Expectations on Salary (₹ in Lakhs per Annum)
Source: Aspiring Minds' National Employability Report – Engineers 2014, 2016 and 2019.

tier two and tier three college graduates. While the difference between the mean aspired salary of engineers from tier one colleges and tier two colleges is ₹68,000, the difference between those from tier one and tier three is ₹1.1 lakhs in 2019. Students from poor quality engineering colleges do not get a placement in large companies; also in some cases, major employers in the job market do not even participate in the placement exercises of these institutions. Therefore, graduates from these colleges limit their salary aspirations likewise and do not even aspire for high pay.

On average, women seem to aspire for a slightly lower level of salaries than male engineering graduates in 2016 and 2019, while in 2014 the salary expectations among women were higher than the expectations of men. It is also observed that women students often access tier two or tier three colleges, and accordingly, they get offers with low salaries. On average, the salary expectations of engineering graduates are not high: around ₹4 lakhs per annum.

The variations in aspired salaries between colleges, or between branches of study or by gender are small in a given year. They were around ₹3 lakhs in 2014, which increased to about ₹4 lakhs in 2019. Only in 2019 do we find marginally higher differences between students of three tiers of colleges. In 2019, graduates from tier one colleges expected high salaries (₹5.1 lakhs); this is the maximum figure we find in Figure 3.19. In the same year, those from tier three colleges expected ₹4 lakhs as their salary on average. Perhaps by 2019, the quality differences in the graduates (identified by colleges) are being clearly noticed by employers.

The choices of students in choosing engineering studies and the sub-stream therein and their labour market aspirations critically depend upon labour market information. Hence, regular manpower surveys and labour market surveys are needed that provide detailed information, which will be helpful not only to students/graduates, but also public authorities in planning engineering education for the future.

Such information will also be immensely useful for institutional planning. Though manpower planning per se is no more found to be meaningful, manpower analyses and labour market analyses that were a part of manpower planning would be extremely useful (Tilak, 1995), particularly for specialised human capital categories like engineering manpower. Noting the absence of a satisfactory system of manpower planning, the AICTE (2015) recommended bringing out an annual report on demand and supply of technical manpower in India.

The overall performance of engineering education in the country can be summed up in the form of a diagram (Figure 3.20). Only about half the available student places get filled in; of those who take admission, two-thirds to three-fourths graduate; and among those who graduate, not even half get employment. The problems lie at every stage – from policy and planning of opening engineering institutions, their functioning, and the process of

106 *Economics of Engineering Education in India*

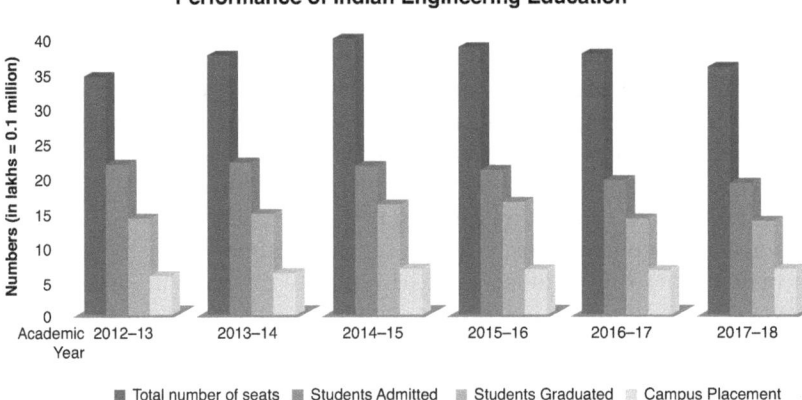

Figure 3.20 Performance of the Engineering Education System in India
Source: https://engineering.eckovation.com/engineering-education-performance-report-engineering-colleges-india/ (Reproduced with permission).

delivery of education to the utilisation of graduate manpower. The system requires a multi-pronged major reform.

Concluding Remarks and Policy Implications

Engineering education in India faces several formidable challenges, some of which are caused by unbridled expansion, as discussed in Chapter 2. Three major challenges are identified in this chapter: (i) quality of engineering education, (ii) financing of engineering education by the government and households and (iii) changing labour market conditions that influence the demand for engineering education. The system is found to suffer from a very severe degree of staggering paucity of well-qualified teachers and the resultant, viz. the quality of engineering education has been very unsatisfactory. This will pull down the contribution of engineering education to economic growth. Second, public funding for engineering education has been very inadequate, necessitating increase in the burden on households, and thereby raising issues of affordability of the low and lower middle strata of the society. Third, labour market information system on engineering manpower and its utilisation, both are very limited, resulting in imbalances reflected in gluts and shortages.

The large-scale expansion has not been accompanied by sustained quality, let alone improved quality; in fact, it is plausible to argue that the expansion has taken place at the cost of quality of education. The quality-quantity trade-off has become clear; and democratic pressures coupled with economic constraints have made the latter preferable to the former. It appears that the union government had concentrated on quality improvement by focusing, in the pursuit of excellence, on a few high-quality institutions like the IITs, leaving quantitative expansion to the states, which, given their fiscal constraints, have left the task to the private sector, which cared little for quality. But it is important to realise, as the AICTE (2003, p. 162) observed, "The future of the country depends on the quality of technical education we impart in our institutions and the type of practical training we provide to enable the future generation of engineers to become competent innovators, designers and product manufacturers".

With the massive expansion of poor quality engineering education, the employability of graduates has been greatly questioned in the labour market. Several surveys have come out with the fact that only about one-fourth of the graduates are actually employable as the rest do not possess the required skills that the labour market needs. It is argued that the majority of the engineering graduates in India receive low-quality training in non-elite institutions while very few get high-quality training in elite institutions. Also, little is understood about the contours of the changing labour market in the country and its influence on the demand and supply of engineering education. The labour market is currently witnessing the new age of automation and is also being driven by unprecedented technological advances that require a new set of skills among the engineering graduates. How far are the engineering institutions in India fulfilling such needs? Our understanding of the issues is that there is not much emphasis on the curricular and pedagogical arrangements to prepare graduates well for work in the changing contexts. The poor academia-industry inter-linkage is another grey area in the engineering education sector in India. Additionally, most engineering colleges in the country (including many government institutions) are facing an acute faculty crunch, not to talk of the lack of physical infrastructure and laboratories to impart quality education and training. On the whole, the problem of quality assumed high proportions due to (a) shortages of quality faculty, (b) unbridled growth of private education, (c) weak and ineffective governance, including limited coverage of the accreditation system, (d) inadequate and skewed public funding and (e) scanty attention to curricular reforms.

All these issues discussed in the study are strongly linked with the financing of engineering education in India. Recent data shows wavering and even declining trends in public expenditure and increasing trends in household expenditures on engineering and technical education over the years. But the increase in the latter cannot compensate for the shrinkage of the former. An increasing involvement of the for-profit private sector in engineering education has placed a clear emphasis on household investment. However, with the decline in enrolments in recent years, the earnings of the private engineering colleges are shrinking, compelling institutions to compromise further with quality by recruiting fewer numbers of qualified teachers, not providing minimum physical infrastructure, laboratories and other facilities, fuelled by a failure to provide adequate industry and corporate exposure. At this juncture, the role of the government is critical to reform/renew the engineering education in India. In addition to investing more on this, the government should also look at the possibility of rethinking on the role of the private sector in technical education and to re-establish the dominant role of the state.

Overall, as discussed here, engineering education in the country has undergone a sea change over the last three decades, particularly with the increasing presence of the private sector. The nature of changes in Indian higher education is very much nuanced and amassed over time, but is also multi-woven with policy paradigms at the global and national levels in the macro politico-economic and education sectors. An expansion of the private sector has benefitted greedy private investors in education; expansion of technical – engineering in particular – has helped the IT sector in India and not less importantly internationally; the 'new middle class' and upper classes began to view expansion of higher education offering new opportunities to them in India and abroad and significant private benefits from all this; the imperfect markets, including imperfect education markets, emerged and flourished; and overall expansion has benefitted the state politically and economically. The economic reform policies, which were originally instigated by the World Bank and western players, are being widely welcomed. The nexus between politicians, bureaucracy and businessmen involving political parties and caste groups and not the least the new middle class (and upper classes) worked well with the tacit support of the state through its explicit policies and even absence of policies. In fact, several state governments openly promoted the idea of self-financed engineering institutions by openly welcoming private players through policy deregulation. As Fernandes (2006) described, the democratic politics in the era of economic reforms is highly influenced by the new middle class and other factors. Many of these changes are not unique to India; many developing countries seem to undergo similar experiences. These issues are important, but the focus of this study is somewhat so narrowly confined as not to include these aspects and rather confine to some specific aspects.

All these suggest the need for a major restructuring of the engineering education sector, specifically with a better understanding of emerging market dynamics. Leaving the market to operate freely in engineering education (as has continued for the last three decades) may lead to a great distortion in the sector, which started with the devaluation of the engineering degree. Therefore, there is an urgent need to focus and discuss the changes that the engineering education sector has experienced (and continue to be experiencing) in the recent years. These may include understanding the changing aspirations of parents for engineering education, revisiting the role of the private sector, searching for new strategies to cope up with the declining demand and above all, an effective intervention of the state to regulate and restructure the engineering education sector to address the recent changes. The massive expansion of engineering education emphasises the need to ensure that the system and institutions are effectively and efficiently governed and managed to meet the needs of industry and society. We are conscious that this study has left out many important issues like faculty recruitment policy, students' choice for institutions and study programmes and a nuanced understanding of the students' experiences in and outside the classroom that have serious policy implications. Lack of data is one of the important reasons for not addressing several of these concerns, and therefore, we argue for building a strong comprehensive database that covers historical as well as current data on a large set of dimensions of engineering education that would contribute to quality research, informed and effective policy making and planning of technical higher education in the country. This certainly calls for some urgent action.

Besides setting up an institutional structure that would build such a robust and comprehensive database, the study highlights a few important policy implications. First, there is a need to effectively regulate the growth of engineering education in the country. Permissions and approvals to open new institutions – public or private – and to offer new programmes need to be based on reliable and transparent and scientific data on the need for such institutions and programmes rather than being influenced by political and economic considerations. Leaving this to market forces result in different kinds of imbalances and chaos, as we have already seen. As the AICTE (2018) committee has recommended, no new college may be allowed to be started. Permissions may be deferred for opening of new colleges for a few years. In the meanwhile, the government may have to take up on a large scale weeding out the substandard institutions and consolidation of the engineering education system, adopting closures and mergers of institutions. It is not only those where enrolments are less than intake that they need to be closed, but also in case of the institutions in those states where the intake is higher than the national average, as argued by the U.R. Rao committee (AICTE, 2003). As it is mandatory that all institutions and all the programmes they offer need to be subject to a national assessment, the mechanisms of assessment and accreditation need to be made robust, scientific and transparent, leaving no chance for manipulation. Several loopholes in granting permissions to open and in assessment and accreditation of the institutions, apart from shortfall in accreditation, are highlighted often in the media. The process of approval by the AICTE for opening new institutions or new degree programmes is based on a set of criteria, including the credibility of the management, teachers, assurance of compliance to AICTE norms and standards, approval by the state government and market relevance of the curriculum. In addition, there is a further process of accreditation by the NBA, which was set up by ACITE to assess the qualitative competence of the various programmes offered by the professional/technical institutions. NBA is regarded as having higher standards and strict criteria relating to the capability of the institutions, teachers and the quality of the programmes. But these mechanisms have been proven to be insufficient and ineffective, as many institutions are often reported to be flouting these criteria and still functioning. Several loopholes in granting permissions to open and in assessment and accreditation of the institutions are highlighted often in the media, stressing the need for very effective regulatory mechanisms and quality assurance systems.

Second, a clear focus has to be laid on improving the quality and standards in higher education. Besides consolidating existing institutions and regulating the future growth, special attention has to be given to the recruitment of quality faculty and the provision of a good learning environment that includes good infrastructure consisting of libraries, classrooms, laboratories and modern equipment, which will be conducive for good teaching and learning and also for research. The Technical Education Quality Improvement Project (TEQIP) project (www.teqip.in), launched by the government of India with the assistance of the World Bank in 2003 as a 10–12-year project for improving the quality of engineering institutions, partly addresses some of the quality concerns in government and government-aided private institutions, and in phase II and III, in addition, the self-financing private institutions. But it is felt that "due to shortage of academic and non-academic staff and other factors, the scheme has not been able to achieve its targets as desired" (Patel, 2016). Educational institutions – either public or private – cannot be left with such high rates of vacancies as we have found. The overall research environment needs massive improvement in majority of the institutions. The need for major curricular reforms needs no emphasis. The curricula may have to include knowledge and skills in the core domain, but it also needs to add many other individual traits and social, cultural, and human values. The aim in all this should be not just to improve the employability of the graduates, but also to produce holistic personalities who will be able to serve society better. Vertical linkages between high-quality institutions like IITs on the one end and the undergraduate institutions on the other, as envisaged under TEQIP, and horizontal linkages between several institutions of the same level may go a long way in enhancing the standards of education in the system as a whole. Otherwise, we may continue to have a few pockets of excellence amidst a myriad of institutions characterised by mediocrity.

Third, private investors find investment in setting up engineering and technical education institutions yielding high and quick returns, as the existing fee regulatory mechanisms are weak, and there is scope for making money out of fee reimbursement systems floated by some state governments like Andhra Pradesh (Reddy & Reddy, 2019). These mechanisms, which are actually meant to help students, seem to help the private management more. Both need to be examined and made efficient in such a way that they do not become sources of profit-making. In one of the reports, it was found that in some states, a good number of institutions generate fees in such a way that more than 50 per cent excess revenues are generated. Philanthropy needs to be insisted as an essential major component of the activities of private investors in education.

Fourth, higher education, including technical education, has to be necessarily inclusive in nature. Major initiatives are necessary to ensure that no academically deserving student is prevented from entering engineering institutions for lack of economic resources. Along with general subsidies, specific public subsidies targeted to help the disadvantaged sections have to be strengthened in the form of scholarships and other financial assistance. The limitations, in fact, the ill effects of the cost recovery measures like student fees and loans need to be taken note of in making public policies on financing higher education.

Finally, there is a need for special attention to be focussed on private institutions. As many of the ills in engineering education are associated with private institutions, we need a strong and effective regulatory mechanism that oversees almost every activity of the institution, without at the same time becoming a hindrance to its proper development. In this context, the proposal of the National Education Policy 2020, to have a common uniform approach for the regulation of public and private institutions, may be counterproductive or the proposal to have a 'little but tight' regulation may not work. Given the size of the private sector in technical education and given various other features that distinguish the private institutions from public institutions, a clear robust system of regulation of private institutions is necessary.

In independent India, there have been several commissions and committees that examined the problems of technical education, engineering education in particular, in recent years and made valuable recommendations, some of which have been acted upon and many not. Non-reflection of the policy recommendations of the commissions, committees, expert groups and task forces in the actions of the government and the institutions and continuation of the deficiencies have been familiar features of the education scene in the country. Most recently, the Government of India (2020) proposed a new National Education Policy which promises a set of sweeping reforms, successful implementation of which might transform the whole education sector, including specifically technical and more specifically engineering education. The policy purposes, inter alia, developing holistic and multidisciplinary higher education institutions, whereby all mono discipline institutions like engineering colleges, technical universities and IITs will be transformed into multidisciplinary institutions offering more subjects outside the core discipline, like arts, liberal arts, humanities and social sciences, emphasising the core content values as well as human traits like human values. As the Delors Commission (1996) opined, "valid responses to the problems of mismatch between supply and demand on the labour market can come from a more flexible system that allows greater curricular diversity and builds bridges between different types of education". The Policy does attempt at exactly the same. The multidisciplinary institutions will also provide undergraduate, graduate and research programmes, focusing on all the three functions of higher education, namely teaching, research and community engagement. They may also offer integrated programmes covering undergraduate and graduate studies. Some of these proposals may promote interests in studies at master's level and research programmes, which would result in better knowledge production and dissemination, besides increasing the supply of qualified faculty.

The policy also promises the granting of graded autonomy by developing a stage-wise mechanism to all institutions in such a way that finally all institutions will be independent with no affiliation to any university. Besides setting up a National Research Foundation to promote research in all areas, the policy proposes revamping of regulatory structure. All institutions will be governed and regulated by a board of governors at the institutional level and by a Higher Education Council of India at the national level. The AICTE will become a professional standard-setting body. While some of these proposed reforms aim at improving the overall quality of education substantially, they seem to be inadequate to address one particular problem that we have highlighted, namely the growth of commercially oriented self-financing colleges. Though the policy promises to curb all tendencies towards commercialisation of education, it is not clear how that will be done. It also promises, as already noted, 'little but tight regulation'. Given the experience, one may be sceptical on how reduction in regulation will improve the system; curb a multitude of malpractices associated with private institutions and even some public institutions; and how many institutions will be able to be governed better by internally constituted boards of governors with much reduced state control. The promised 'little but tight' regulation may actually allow further mushrooming growth of such commercially oriented, poor quality institutions, leading to further aggravation of problems.

Presenting a critical analytical descriptive account on the status and prospects of engineering education in India in a comprehensive way in this and the previous chapter, the analytical account given here may help to bring a new understanding on a variety of complex issues in engineering education contributing to richer discussions in academic as well as policy forums, we do note that there is much scope for further research. Our findings offer clear directions for further research. First, our analysis focuses on the issues and challenges of engineering education at the national level and we see great value in similar studies at the state/regional levels. This would help to address some region-/state-specific issues in engineering education which are not covered in this study. For instance, why do the patterns in the growth of engineering education in southern states differ from northern states? How does the changing demand for engineering education in the country vary across states? Is it linked with the state-specific policies on engineering and technical education? Second, we discuss the issues in engineering education exclusively at the undergraduate level only. We have not examined issues relating to postgraduate and PhD levels of education in the field of engineering, except making a few occasional references, which needs a separate study. Third, as this study is limited to engineering education only, similar attempts should be made covering other disciplines of higher and professional/technical education in India. What is happening to arts, humanities and social sciences is also important to analyse. This would also help to provide a comparative picture of engineering education with other disciplines of study in higher education. Fourth, in the changing nature of labour market, it is important to take stock of the production of professional graduates in different disciplines and comparing that with their demand in the job market. Manpower analyses are important, as they throw light on a variety of dimensions that will have implications for educational planning as well as economic planning, including for market interventions. Such analyses would help in reducing mismatches, even though manpower planning per se lost its charm over the years in the rapidly changing world. Last, further research is required on the cost recovery measures such as student fee and student loans (both of which have become very popular methods) adopted by the state to fund costly disciplines such as engineering education and their effects on the growth of higher education and their implications for labour market and the society at large.

Notes

1 The IITs and NITs together account for just 3 per cent of enrolments, but get 50 per cent of government funds (Sharma, 2018).
2 In general, the investment in science and technology in India is very low compared to many other developing and developed countries. In terms of the resultant indicators also, India fares very poorly.
3 Some issues relating to labour market and engineering education are discussed in the next section.
4 India ranks fairly high among countries of the world in terms of number of PhD graduates. In 2014 US which was on the top produced 67,449 doctoral graduates. About 40 per cent of new doctorates awarded in the OECD area are in science, technology, engineering and mathematics (STEM) (OECD, 2016).
5 In the recent years, the Government of India announced the Prime Minister's Research Fellowship Scheme for 1,000 BTech/BE graduates for pursuing doctoral studies in IITs and the Indian Institute of Science. Such measures are important, but still inadequate.
6 More detailed evidence on this is given in Chapter 8.
7 According to UIS statistics, countries like Russia, the US, Iran, Japan, South Korea, Indonesia, Ukraine, Mexico, France and Vietnam are regarded as the top ten countries in terms of production of engineers (Interesting Engineering, 2016). It appears that data on India and China were not considered in these calculations.
8 Details on the basis and method of these projections are not available.
9 Issues relating to public funding are discussed in the following Section.
10 Private sector investments are not referred here, mainly because most of those investments are gradually recovered from students in the form of student fees.
11 Technical education in India covers programmes in engineering and technology, management, architecture, town planning, pharmacy, applied arts and crafts, and hotel management and catering technology. As we note here, engineering education constitutes only a small part only, accounting for about 15 per cent of the total expenditure on technical education in the states/union territories (2014–15).
12 Expenditure on engineering and other departments of technical education in comprehensive universities, particularly on non-allocable overall heads, also gets included in the university and higher and not in technical education. However, under technical education, we also find small amounts of 'assistance to universities'.
13 We have data until 2015–16 on actual expenditure, 'revised estimates' (RE) for 2016–17 and 'budget estimates' (BE) for 2017–18. It may be noted that generally, budget estimates turn out to be much higher than actual expenditure, while the revised estimates are found to be close to but still are marginally higher than actual expenditure.

14 Public expenditure in real terms/constant prices is estimated by using the GDP deflators, considering 2011–12 as base year, data on which are collected from the *Handbook of Statistics on Indian Economy* (2019–20), Reserve Bank of India (RBI, 2020b).
15 The amounts of expenditure reported here are at constant prices, unless otherwise mentioned.
16 Fee varies among the public institutions and also among private institutions. For example, even among the IITs, it ranges from ₹1.11 lakhs per student per semester in IIT Goa and ₹1.52 lakhs in IIT Jodhpur (in 2020). In each state, fees are prescribed in government and private institutions by a fee regulating committee. But they also vary between and within a state(s). The fee regulation committees prescribe fees for each specific private institution within a state, and hence, very wide variations exist between different private institutions even within a state. For example, 'reported' fee levels varied between ₹32,500 and ₹77,500 among 23 sampled self-financing engineering colleges in Tamil Nadu in 2008 (Rani, 2010).
17 A few years ago, the Government of India attempted unsuccessfully to enact a legislation, "Prohibition of Unfair Practices in Technical Educational Institutions, Medical Educational Institutions and Universities Bill 2010" to curb some of the familiar practices being followed by private institutions in India. See Tilak (2010a) for details. A few other legislations for reforming higher education also could not go through. See Tilak (2010b).
18 But surprisingly, in an interview to media, the then Chairperson of AICTE, the apex body that regulates technical education in India, Anil Sahasrabudhe said that currently it would be impossible to run an institute without compromising on quality when there are so many unfilled seats. Reported in *Indian Express* (2 February 2018). https://indianexpress.com/article/education/impossible-to-run-an-institute-without-compromising-on-quality-when-there-are-so-many-unfilled-seats-says-regulator-anil-sahasrabudhe-aicte-chairman-4978567/
19 Out of the total number of graduates – 23,928 – as many as 17,946 secured employment in campus recruitment process.
20 It is important to note that data on placements provided by AICTE or individual institutions do not normally include data on those who secure employment later, after leaving the college.
21 Many engineering institutions concentrate on only the professional engineering skills. The NBA identified the following as the attributes of engineer graduates: engineering knowledge, problem analysis, design and development, conduct investigation of complex problems, modern tool usage, engineer and society, environment and sustainability, ethics, individual and team work, communications, project management and finance and life-long learning.
22 In the same context, it may be noted that very few engineer graduates take up jobs in the research and development sector, again as they do not possess necessary skills for such jobs (Borah et al., 2019).
23 All colleges included in the Aspiring Minds' survey were ranked based on the employability of their students. Those in the top 33 percentile were considered as tier 1 colleges; those in mid-33 percentile range were considered as tier 2 colleges; and those in the bottom 33 percentile set were taken as tier 3 colleges.

Part II

4 Who Goes to Private Engineering Colleges and Why?

Introduction

As noted in Chapter 2, within higher education, it is private education that expanded at an alarming growth. Even though a good number of private colleges of engineering are getting closed during the last few years and enrolments in private colleges are declining, private sector still accounts for a major share both in the number of institutions and in student enrolments in technical education as well as in general higher education. Engineering education, like other branches of higher education, including general higher education, is offered in India in public institutions – central and state government institutions and government-funded (aided) private institutions and private institutions (also known as unaided or self-financing institutions, which are almost exclusively dependent on student tuition). Secondary school graduates today are confronted with a choice problem, between public and private institutions; faced with an increase in choice, it is natural for school graduates to be anxious on how to make efficient choices. In practice, graduates of higher secondary education wishing to pursue studies in engineering education seek admission in many or all of these institutions and finally the successful graduates end up in taking admission in one institution.

Demand for private education has been explained in the literature in terms of 'excess demand' (demand for education exceeding supply of public education) (Weisbrod, 1977) and 'differentiated demand' (demand for private education for quality or for any other kind of education different from the one provided in public institutions) (James, 1987). It is generally felt that in the case of higher education in India, it is the phenomenon of excess demand and not much the differentiated demand that explains the growth of private education.[1] Students may opt to go to private universities or colleges for a variety of reasons, primarily because of inadequate supply of public education, and second due to higher perceived quality offered by the private institutions, inability to get, particularly those with low qualifying scores, admission in government institutions, availability of residential/hostel facilities, physical distance of the institution and several other factors.

Demand for higher education has long been analysed by researchers in many countries using human capital theory (e.g. Cohn & Morgan, 1977–78; Clotfelter & Rothschild, 1993; Chowdry et al., 2008). In India also there are quite a few studies (e.g. Chakrabarti, 2009; Basant & Sen, 2013; Choudhury, 2012, for a survey). They concentrated on overall demand for higher education, but not separately for private education vis-à-vis public education, and highlighted the importance of family economic and social background, apart from fees and other aspects, and at macro level growth in population in explaining demand for education. For example, Krishna (2014) focused on engineering education as a whole, and finds that a student's decision to get enrolled in an engineering college depends on the foundational education from an urban set-up. Receiving of education from a rural area lessens the chances of a student to attend an engineering college; the chances further goes down if one is poor and is a member of scheduled caste (SC). Quite a few scholars have examined the issue of university choice and the factors that influence the same (see Muniswamy et al., 2014, for a survey). What is less analysed is the factors that determine the choice of a type of institution for higher education – public or private. While the literature on school choice focusing on public-private distinction is somewhat abundant, it is dominated by studies on school-level education (e.g., see Russo & Ranieri, 2017); very few studies have focused on higher education, higher engineering education in particular. By examining the question, why do students choose to go to private colleges or universities or public institutions for engineering education in India, this study adds to the limited literature.

Several studies (e.g. Sandy, 1989; Bifulco et al., 2009; Gross, 2018) that examined the issue of school choice universally found that a student's academic ability, family income and parental education are each significantly correlated with the decision to attend private or a public school. James (1987) and Cheechi and Jappelli (2005) argued that quality plays the most important role in the parental choice of the schools. Many of these studies conducted on US education also found that race is an important factor, with white students being much more likely to enrol in private schools and black students in public schools. Hu and Hossler (2000) examined correlates of student preference for private institutions over public institutions in their senior year in high school and found that in addition to student and family background and student's academic characteristics, students' responses to tuition costs and availability of financial aid have a substantial linkage with student preference for a given type of institutions – private or public. These studies, particularly focusing on private school students, provide only limited analysis on how school choices work in higher education. Many scholars, including Manski and Wise (1983) and Sá et al. (2011), who focused on higher education, have not looked at private versus public choice. Sá et al. (2011) estimated a bivariate probit model to examine higher education choices in Portugal – type of higher education institution (university versus polytechnic) and the decision regarding leaving home for higher education.

Concentrating on competition for students between several universities in general, Aydın (2015) analysed university choice process with the help of economic models, sociological models, combined models and the marketing approach, and investigated factors such as reputation and attributes of universities, personal factors, location, job prospects, university fees, financial aid/scholarship, reference groups, families and other information sources that impact the choices of students. Of all the factors, reputation of the institution, distance from home and location turned out to be significant factors in student choice in Scotland (Briggs, 2007). Jackson (1982) argues that provision of scholarships or subsidies is the best mechanism of influencing student choices. In fact, of all, public image or reputation of the institution seems to be one of the most important factors influencing student choices. Nguyen and Taylor (2003) used a multi-nominal logit model to investigate the destination of high school graduates in the US, destination being defined as two-year public higher education, two-year private education, four-year public higher education and four-year private higher education institutions. In a study on Malaysia (Muniswamy et al., 2014), career prospects and reputation of the university and its programmes were found to be the most important factors in the students' decision of a place to pursue further studies. Using factor analysis and chi-square statistical formulation on the data collected from 261 students in Thailand, Agrey and Lampadan (2014) found that support system in the university (availability of a bookstore, guidance/counselling office, scholarships, credit transferability and spiritual programming), learning environment (modern learning environment and facilities), reputation (beautiful campus, library and computer lab) and job, health care services, residential accommodation, extracurricular activities and safe and friendly environment as the most important ones that impact students' choice of an institution. In a similar study of choice of management institutions in Punjab, India, Gill and Malhotra (2019) found academic, social and personal factors, placement, financial incentives and faculty and staff to be very important. In a study on higher education in India, Dhaliwal et al. (2019) found public image, employability, promotion rate, fee structure and quality of academic programmes as important influencing factors to making the institutional choice by the students/households. In a study on University of Beira Interior in Portugal, Raposo and Alves (2007) concluded that institutional reputation and other characteristics relating to the institution's do not explain much; they, however, have not considered many important individual factors. Panda (2006) made an attempt on engineering education in Odisha and Choudhury (2012) the same in Delhi. But for these few studies, many seemed to have focused on university choices without focusing clearly on public-private distinction.

The question between private versus public education is receiving increasing attention; but very little is known about the factors that guide students' or parents' choice between private and public institutions. The choice of a type of higher education institution is indeed a complex process involving a wide variety of factors. As Sá et al. (2011, p. 690) noted, "choices comprise a set of expectations, aspirations, desires and representations of the future as well. Nevertheless, those complexities involved in the choice process are not easily dealt with in applied work". In this chapter, the attempt is to unravel some of these complexities.

Complexities could be more in the case of higher education in India, characterised by imperfect markets and asymmetry of information, along with misleading advertisements and aggressive marketing practices. In higher education, especially in higher professional/technical education in India, the general perception is: government institutions provide better quality education than private ones; the latter are also associated with several questionable practices and methods of operation (Tilak, 2009a). Exceptions on both sides do exist, but they are very few. Accordingly, it is widely acknowledged that in India, the meritorious students with high scores in senior secondary-level examination and with higher ranks in the national/state-level common entrance examinations prefer government engineering institutions such as the Indian Institutes of Technology (IITs), National Institutes of Technology (NITs) and state government engineering colleges, the preference being almost in the same order, whereas less meritorious students (with lower ranks in the entrance examinations) are left with no choice except going to private institutions, which are widely recognised as low-quality institutions but where admissions are relatively easily available as they have excess capacity – supply being more than demand, of course, if high fees can be afforded. However, this does not seem to be the case always. In some cases, students prefer private to government institutions and in some other instances, students qualified to be admitted in government institutions may not be able to take admission in those institutions due to a number of socio-economic and other reasons. For example, students who do not get their preferred branch of study in government institutions may opt for private institutions, if they are offered the branch of study of their choice; or they may opt for a private college because of its proximity to their residence; or because of some other factors, including fees and other related costs. Examining students' choice of engineering colleges in Orissa, Panda (2006) has found two important reasons for students not joining prestigious government institutions like IITs and NITs, even if they got selected: (a) not being able to get selected in their preferred branch of study and (b) hesitation of parents to send their daughters or even sons to places far away from home, either for financial or for other reasons.

Thus, the choice of students for government and private institutions seems to be complex in nature and is influenced by a set of socio-economic, institutional and other related factors.[2] It is not only complex, but also can be far from efficient, given the asymmetry of information, imperfections in labour market as well as in education markets and a interplay of many factors. Hence, there is need to study the dynamics involved in the students' choice of government versus private engineering institutions in India. It is important to note at the very outset that students in India do not necessarily have unlimited choice between private and government institutions because of the supply constraint (of admissions in government institutions) and the counselling system followed in the admission process. Students usually indicate in their application for admission their first preference in favour of government as against private institutions. Due to the excess demand for government institutions, many students do not necessarily get admission in these institutions (even if they have a strong preference) and hence get compelled finally to go to private institutions. So, in practice, students do not have much choice between government and private engineering institutions, mainly due to limited supply, and even among several private institutions for various reasons; therefore, a typical choice function for the engineering students in the Indian context may not exist. But there is still a rationale to look at what makes students prefer to go to private or government engineering institutions, as in some cases students prefer private to government institutions and in some other instances, students opt to go to private institutions, even if they get admission in government institutions, as described earlier.

A Profile of the Students

Based on the primary survey of students in the four states described in Chapter 1, one can derive a socio-economic profile of students in engineering education. Table 4.1 provides a detailed profile of the sampled engineering students in India. A few important features are as follows:

- Engineering education is still male centric: 71.4 per cent of the engineering students are men.
- A little less than 30 per cent of the students belonged to socially backward sections – Scheduled Tribes (SCs, STs) and Other Backward Classes (OBCs) of the society.
- A majority of the students come from families with parents having higher education and also with fathers who are engaged in professional occupations.
- As high as 70–90 per cent of the students in engineering had their schooling in private institutions in urban areas with English as medium of instruction.
- Nearly half the students took private coaching as preparation for competitive entrance examination. It means that about half – actually a little more than half – the students who got admission into engineering education did not take coaching. So coaching is not that essential as people feel to enter engineering education.
- Majority of the students wish to pursue modern streams of engineering like computer science engineering, electronics engineering, telecommunications and information and technology.

- More than one-third of the students go outside their native state for engineering education.
- A majority of the students (58 per cent) belong to lower income strata (with an annual family income below ₹5 lakhs).

Table 4.1 Distribution of Engineering Students in Different Types of Institutions by Their Socio-Economic Profile

	(a) Gender			(b) Residential Status		
	Male	Female	Total	Outside the State	Within the State	Total
Government	24.77	18.89	23.09	20.13	17.88	18.71
Private						
Government-Aided	9.29	14.99	10.92	13.06	11.35	11.98
Private	65.95	66.12	66.00	66.80	70.77	69.30
Total	100.00	100.00	100.00	100.00	100.00	100.00
	(4,728)	(1,895)	(6,623)			
Distribution	71.40	28.60	100.00	37.00	63.00	100.00

(c) Social Category

	SC	ST	OBC	General	Total
Government	36.4	48.39	29.34	19.34	23.09
Private					
Government-Aided	17.18	21.77	13.23	9.35	10.92
Private	46.42	29.84	57.43	71.30	66.00
Total	100.00	100.00	100.00	100.00	100.00
Distribution by Social Category	7.40	1.90	19.40	71.30	100.00

(d) Family Income

	< ₹100,000	₹100,000 to ₹500,000	₹500,000 to ₹1 million	> ₹1 million	Total
Government	20.22	24.54	22.69	31.74	23.58
Private					
Government-Aided	19.12	8.37	6.30	4.1	10.65
Private	60.66	67.10	71.01	64.16	65.77
Total	100.00	100.00	100.00	100.00	100.00
Distribution by Family Income	17.60	40.80	7.80	33.70	100.00

(*Continued*)

Table 4.1 (Continued)

(e) Parents' Occupation

	Professional Workers	Service Workers	Unskilled Workers	Businessmen/ Women	Others	Total
Father's Occupation						
Government	24.63	29.27	25.98	13.16	29.03	23.05
Private						
Government-Aided	9.40	16.06	17.82	8.43	15.44	10.62
Private	65.98	54.67	56.19	78.41	55.53	66.33
Total	100.00	100.00	100.00	100.00	100.00	100.00
Distribution	57.60	7.80	5.30	19.90	6.90	100.00
Mother's Occupation						
Government	21.75	22.44	26.73	57.66	20.78	24.41
Private						
Government-Aided	9.55	10.67	16.83	4.07	9.44	9.28
Private	68.70	66.89	56.44	38.28	69.78	66.31
Total	100.00	100.00	100.00	100.00	100.00	100.00
Distribution	25.20	9.10	2.00	8.40	55.20	100.00

(f) Parents' Education

	Illiterate	Primary	Secondary	Higher General	Professional	Total
Father's Education						
Government	23.08	33.66	24.81	22.23	23.6	23.20
Private						
Government-Aided	7.69	14.85	13.54	9.4	11.08	10.61
Private	69.23	51.49	61.65	68.37	65.32	66.19
Total	100.00	100.00	100.00	100.00	100.00	100.00
Distribution	0.20	1.60	16.80	55.80	25.60	100.00
Mother's Education						
Government	31.15	25.10	25.81	21.62	26.24	23.55
Private						
Government-Aided	14.75	15.06	13.56	8.16	9.30	10.31
Private	54.10	59.85	60.64	70.22	64.46	66.13
Total	100.00	100.00	100.00	100.00	100.00	100.00
Distribution	1.00	4.30	31.50	55.20	8.00	100.00

(*Continued*)

Table 4.1 (Continued)

(g) Academic Background of the Student

	Type of School			Location of the School		
	Government	Private	Total	Urban	Rural	Total
Government	23.25	24.10	23.86	19.55	27.54	20.46
Private						
Government-Aided	11.18	10.94	11.01	8.32	8.13	8.3
Private	65.58	64.96	65.13	72.13	64.33	71.24
Total	100.00	100.00	100.00	100.00	100.00	100.00
Distribution	28.00	72.00	100.00	88.60	11.40	100.00

	Medium of instruction			Education Board			
	English	Others	Total	CBSE	ICSE	State Board	Total
Government	22.93	28.06	23.69	25.83	17.92	22.67	23.45
Private							
Government-Aided	10.56	13.03	10.92	4.77	6.25	14.48	11.20
Private	66.51	58.91	65.39	69.40	75.83	62.86	65.35
Total	100.00	100.00	100.00	100.00	100.00	100.00	100.00
Distribution	85.20	14.80	100.00	30.50	3.80	65.60	100.00

	(h) Average Percentage of Marks Secured by the Students in Senior Secondary Examination by Board				(i) Percentage of Students Who Took Pre-Admission Coaching		
	CBSE	ICSE	State Boards	Total	Yes	No	Total
Government	81.83	87.36	86.76	85.01	25.58	15.51	20.28
Private							
Government-Aided	72.89	80.28	76.13	75.72	4.41	11.35	8.06
Private	76.19	80.90	77.51	77.19	70.01	73.15	71.66
Total	77.46	82.01	79.39	78.84	100.00	100.00	100.00
Distribution					47.40	52.50	100.00

	(j) Percentage of Students Who Appeared in Entrance Examination for More than Once			(k) Percentage of Students Who Got the Admission in the Branch of First Choice		
	Yes	No	Total	Yes	No	Total
Government	58.23	20.78	23.13	21.39	30.79	23.70
Private						
Government-Aided	1.01	11.95	11.27	10.87	11.91	11.13
Private	40.76	67.26	65.60	67.74	57.30	65.17
Total	100.00	100.00	100.00	100.00	100.00	100.00
Distribution	6.30	93.70	100.00	75.40	24.60	100.00

(*Continued*)

Table 4.1 (Continued)

(l) First Choice of the Brach of Engineering

	Electrical and Electronics	Computer	Information Technology (IT)	Telecommunication	Electrical
Government	17.80	25.58	17.57	30.01	44.65
Private Government-Aided	10.56	12.23	2.72	9.80	13.65
Private	71.64	62.18	79.71	60.19	41.70
Total	100.00	100.00	100.00	100.00	100.00
Distribution	11.60	33.30	8.10	27.90	4.60

	Civil	Mechanical	Instrumentation	Management	Others	Total
Government	7.41	9.35	12.5	0	8.02	23.68
Private Government-Aided	69.14	3.96	1.39	0	15.33	11.12
Private	23.46	86.69	86.11	100.00	76.65	65.19
Total	100.00	100.00	100.00	100.00	100.00	100.00
Distribution	1.40	4.70	1.20	0.10	7.10	100.00

- A higher proportion of students with higher percentage marks in senior secondary education examination are in government institutions rather than in private ones. Government institutions seem to attract more meritorious students. In either case, the average minimum level of marks is as high as 75 per cent. Students securing below 75 per cent marks in their examinations perhaps cannot dream of entering engineering education.
- Further, as per the survey, a majority of students who appeared only once in the entrance examination get into private institutions, while a majority of those who tried more than once in entrance examination get admission in government institutions, meaning that it is indeed tough to get admission in government institutions, which are considered qualitatively superior but limited in supply.
- Among those who go to public institutions, electrical engineering is the first choice, followed by telecommunications and computer science engineering, while information technology (IT) is the first choice followed by electrical and electronics engineering and computer science engineering are the major choices for those who enter private institutions.
- In terms of distribution by every characteristic feature – gender, caste, household income, etc., – a larger proportion of students are enrolled in private institutions than in public institutions because of the very limited number of public institutions and relative over-supply of private colleges and universities.

The Methodology

Whenever the dependent variable is a dichotomous or a binary variable, that is, it can have only two possible outcomes, yes or no, and takes alternative discrete values of zero and one, of the kind we have – whether the student is enrolled in private institution or not, the appropriate statistical tool to analyse the determinants is the probit regression model, also known as the 'normit' model (Gujarati, p. 608), which is extensively used in applied economics and econometrics. This is also considered as more appropriate than linear regression and other regression models. The probit model helps to estimate the probability of the dependent variable to happen, given the value of the predictor or the independent variable (Aldrich & Nelson, 1984; Liao, 1994). The probit analysis provides statistically significant findings on which predictors or the explanatory variables increase or decrease the probability of the dependent variable falling into category one or the other. The most common form of the probit regression equation, when there are multiple regressors, is as follows:

$$\Pr(Y = 1 | X_i) = \varphi(\beta_o + \beta_i X_i)$$

where Pr refers to probability (of Y becoming equal to 1), Y is the dependent variable, X_i are the predictors or the regressors, β_i are parameters to be estimated that show the likelihood or probability or odds of change in dependent variable versus independent variables and ϕ denotes non-liner cumulative distribution function of the standard normal distribution.

Marginal effect denotes how much the (conditional) probability of the outcome variable, that is, the dependent variable changes from 0 to 1, when the value of the particular regressor changes, holding all other variables constant. Marginal effect shows the magnitude of impact of an explanatory variable on dependent variable. Thus the estimates of marginal effects provide insights into how the explanatory variables shift the probability of happening of the outcome (dependent) variable. Using the econometric software STATA, the probit regression model is estimated here to analyse the predictors of students' choice in favour of a private engineering institution against a public institution in India. The dependent variable in the model is defined as follows:

ENG_INST_TYPE = 1, if the student is enrolled in a private institution;
= 0, otherwise, that is, if the student is enrolled in a government or government-aided private institution.

The function estimated[3] is:

$$\text{ENG\_INST\_TYPE} = \alpha + \beta_i X_i + \varepsilon$$

where X_i are the regressors, β_i are the coefficients of the explanatory variables, α the intercept and ε the random disturbance term capturing unobserved characteristics or simply known as error term.

Explanatory Variables

The choice between government and private engineering institutions is indeed not a simple and clear process, as it involves mutually interacting factors, including individual characteristics, household factors and academic background of the students. We concentrate on the choice of the type of institution and link it with a set of probable factors, which are chosen based on the review of literature, other information and knowledge of the system. The final selection of the variables is also constrained by the availability of data. The following are considered as possible determinants for the empirical analysis here.

Individual Characteristics: Gender and caste are considered here as the two most important individual characteristics that may have influence on the students' choice of institutions.

Household Factors: Among the household factors, family income, as a measure of economic status of the households, parents 'occupation, parents' education, household demographic burden measured in terms of the number of siblings in the family and residential status of students, whether they migrated from other states or whether they were natives of the same state where the institution is located, are considered here.

Students' Academic Background: As the educational background of the students influences their choices, six major aspects relating to the higher secondary schooling and related characteristics of the students are considered here, namely, academic achievement at school level, that is, percentage of marks secured in the higher secondary-level end examination, medium of instruction followed in the higher secondary school, type of board of higher secondary examination, type of the higher secondary school, location of the higher secondary school and whether students have taken pre-admission coaching to appear in the entrance examination.

Current Education of the Students: We have also considered a few major factors related to the current education of the students, such as the branch/stream of engineering, household expenditure on engineering education (as a proxy for household costs), receipt of any financial assistance like scholarship or educational loan for the current studies and whether student is engaged in any part-time work during studies.

Employment and Educational Aspirations: Finally, future plans of the students that include employment potential and educational aspirations are taken into account to examine whether they have any influence on students' choice of the type of institutions.

Some of the explanatory variables used in the analysis are continuous and some are used in the dummy form. A few details on variables, including their notation, definition, explanation and summary statistics, are given in Appendix B.

Empirical Results and Discussion

The probit estimates are given in Table 4.2. The pseudo R-square of 0.26 indicates joint significance of all coefficients of regressors. Based on these estimates, we make the following observations:

Effect of Individual Characteristics

Gender and caste are two individual characteristics that are widely acknowledged to be important in determining participation in higher education and also in the choice of institutions by the parents. Gender plays an important role in demand for higher education, more particularly in the case of demand for expensive engineering education (Rao, 2007). It is generally perceived that the parents in India hesitate to send their daughters to far-off places (to other states or to different cities within the same state) for their higher education in comparison to their sons (Panda, 2006), even though the situation is changing as parents tend to send their children even abroad for further studies and employment. In some cases, an institution is basically preferred by girls if it is situated close to their locality or having a hostel facility, whether it is public or private. Female students might prefer enroling in private to government institutions, if accessibility – particularly in terms of distance – to the private institution is better than the latter one. Distance is not considered as a big issue for many male students. Second, caste dominates almost every development aspect in Indian society. Caste of the student can also be an important determinant in explaining demand for higher education in government versus private institutions. Generally, it is observed that students from lower social background (e.g. SCs, STs and OBCs) are more likely to prefer public to private institutions.

Gender: Results show that both the individual characteristics (gender and social category) are statistically significant in determining students' choice of institutions. About 67 per cent of the total female students have taken admission in private institutions as against 65 per cent among male students (Table 4.1). The difference is small; but the marginal effect associated with 'gender' shows that a female student has 4 percentage points more likely to attend private institutions than a male student. The less probability of female students seeking admission in government institutions may be due to the fact that a significant proportion of male students takes pre-admission coaching to prepare them for the entrance examination and they might get into government institutions.

Caste: The presumption that students from lower social category (SCs, STs and OBCs) are less likely to enrol in private institutions than the students from the general category, as private education is costly and as, more importantly, the state reservation policy may not be strictly followed in these institutions (see, e.g., Sengupta, 2020) also holds true in this study. The degree of implementation of reservation policies, differences in costs of higher education, availability of scholarships[4] and availability of special development programmes for disadvantaged students may also be responsible for the students belonging to lower strata to choose government institutions.

The probability of enrolling in private institutions is less for the students belonging to SCs, STs and OBCs than general category students. The estimates of the two dummy variables (SCs and STs) on the probability of enrolling in private institutions compared to government institutions show this clearly. Furthermore, as revealed by the corresponding marginal effects, between the SCs and STs, the probability of attending private as against government institutions is less among the former than among the scheduled tribes. Besides the reservation policy, the reason may be attributed to the relatively low socio-economic background of SCs, STs and OBCs students, and as a result, they may also feel more 'comfortable' and be able to 'adjust' better in government institutions, which have better policies such as anti-ragging, provision of remedial and bridge courses and where discrimination by caste is very much less if not nil than in private institutions.

Effect of Household Characteristics

Family Income: Economic status of the households is widely recognised as an important factor in explaining the demand for higher education (Tilak, 2015; Tilak & Choudhury, 2019). Given the relatively high subsidies and low costs of higher education in public institutions, one can hypothesise that students from low-income strata would prefer government institutions to private institutions for their higher education. In fact, very low-income families may not go for higher education, if they do not secure admission in public institutions. But high costs of private higher education might not prevent high-income families to opt for private institutions, if admission is available. Thus, one can expect a positive relationship between the economic capacity and the probability of attending private engineering institutions. But given the high quality and even the reputation and brand of public institutions in engineering education, students from high-income strata families would also prefer admission in public institutions. Thus the effect of economic status of the family (measured in terms of annual income) on the students' decision to take admission in government versus private institutions is generally expected to be high. So, we have attempted to empirically estimate the effect of economic status on the admission of students in government versus private engineering institutions.[5]

The probit results in Table 4.2 indicate that the probability of taking admission in private institutions is positively related with the annual income of the family, that is, the students from higher-income families are more likely to take admission in the private as against government institutions. This supports the common presumption that the students from well-off families opt for the high-cost private engineering institutions, whereas the students belonging to low- and middle-income families enrol themselves in

Table 4.2 Determinants of Students' Choice in Favour of Private Engineering Institutions (against Public Institutions): Probit Estimates

Variables	Coefficient	Standard Error	Marginal Effect (dy/dx)#
Individual Characteristics			
Gender	0.189**	0.093	0.052
SC	-0.626***	0.153	-0.214
ST	-1.852***	0.365	-0.644
OBC	-0.287***	0.113	-0.088
General	Reference		
Household factors			
lnHHY	0.027	0.048	0.008
Fathocp_Prof	-0.157*	0.096	-0.052
Fathocp_bus	0.111	0.102	0.031
Fathocp_other	Reference		
Mothocp_Prof	0.304*	0.113	0.078
Mothocp_bus	-0.077	0.171	-0.023
Mothocp_other	Reference		
Father_ED	0.003	0.015	0.0009
Mother_ED	-0.016***	0.013	-0.005
Siblings	-0.158***	0.044	-0.045
Nativity	0.336***	0.087	0.099
Student's Academic Background			
SEC_marks	-0.038***	0.005	-0.110
SEC_medium	-0.604***	0.117	-0.199
SEC_board	0.401***	0.095	0.118
SEC_SCH_type	0.155*	0.087	0.045
SEC_SCH_location	0.085	0.137	0.024
PRE_coaching	0.094	0.076	0.027
Students' Current Education Status			
STREAM_study	0.734***	0.084	0.236
lnHHEXPR	0.566***	0.059	0.162
Scholarship	-0.299***	0.100	-0.093
Loan	-0.004	0.119	-0.001
Part_time	-0.102	0.115	-0.030
Employment and Educational Aspirations			
Employment	0.341***	0.083	0.103
ED_ASP	-0.049	0.081	-0.014
Constant	0.318	0.759	
Log Pseudo Likelihood	-721.797		
Pseudo R^2	0.263		
Number of Observations	1,693		

Note: Level of Significance: *** $p < 0.01$; ** $p < 0.05$; and * $p < 0.1$.

low cost government institutions. But the coefficient is statistically not significant. About 60 per cent of the students from lower-income households have attended private institutions as against 65 per cent from upper middle-income households (Table 4.1).

Parents' Occupation: It is widely held that occupation of the parents has an orientation towards sending their children to government or private institutions. High status occupation of the parents gives an opportunity to their children to take admission in good quality engineering institutions. Students belonging to these families are able to take rigorous pre-admission coaching, which helps them secure a good rank in the entrance examination conducted for the admission into different institutions. Further, parents working in professional occupations may have better access to information and may be able to help their children in choosing appropriate institutions to pursue degree-level engineering studies, besides family income enabling the child to opt for a good quality institution, even if they are very costly.[6] There may also be different effects of occupation of father and mother on the household's choice of institutions. Parental occupation is included here as it might capture the effects of the family's some kind of non-financial (social capital) resources.

The regression results confirm that a student whose father is a professional/technical worker is less likely to enrol in private institutions than the students whose fathers belonged to other occupations such as clerical and related occupations (service workers, farmers, fishermen and related workers, skilled workers, unskilled workers and retired persons). However, a mother as a professional worker is more likely to send her children to a private institution as against a government institution than the student whose mother is engaged in other occupations; the coefficient is statistically significant at 1 per cent level. The difference in influence of the parents' occupation (between father and mother) on students' choice of institutions needs to be probed further in detail.

Parents' Education: Another important variable considered for analysis is the educational level of the parents of the students.[7] It is expected that higher educated parents, that is, parents with higher levels of education, may be more concerned about the quality of education and may be more aware of the nature, quality and other aspects relating to various institutions, and hence, they would like to enrol their children in good quality government or private institutions than parents with less or no education. The main measure of educational attainment used in the literature is the highest level of education completed by the head of the household. Education level can be measured in terms of years of completed education or as an ordinal variable with the obvious ordering of education from the lowest to the highest level of education.[8] To analyse whether mother's education has more (or less) effect than father's education on sending their children to government or private institutions, years of schooling of both father and mother are considered as two separate independent variables. However, the results are not clearly conclusive. The coefficient associated with father's years of schooling turns out to be positive but is found to be statistically not significant, whereas the coefficient of mother's years of schooling is negative and statistically significant. Hence, the presumption that the educated fathers send their children to government institutions or vice versa does not hold good as per these estimates, while mother's education influences positively in increasing the probability of the student going to a government institution. The difference in the effects of parents' education – between fathers and mothers – is interesting but difficult to easily explain.

Size of the Household: Number of siblings in the family[9] is taken as an indicator of 'demographic burden' the households face. It is generally believed that the households with a large number of siblings may not be able to spend higher amounts of money on education, as demand for resources for alternative purposes would be higher in these families. In many cases, parents fail to afford the study expenses of other children if one or two children are already in the education system, and it is more so if in technical/professional higher education in India or abroad. The issue becomes more complicated if the child is a girl and her sibling(s) (particularly any brother) is already attending higher education. Hence, it is expected that number of siblings in the family will have a significant impact on students' demand for engineering education in government or private institutions. A household with larger number of siblings might be associated with lower levels of participation in engineering education, especially in private engineering education as this is more expensive than in government institutions. So, due to the high cost of education in private institutions, one can expect a negative relationship between the number of siblings in the family and the students' admission in private institutions. Households with more children need extra money for their maintenance-related expenses and therefore spend less on education, particularly higher and professional education. Such a presumption is found to be true here. The results presented in Table 4.2 indicate that, as one can expect, the presence of more siblings in the family reduces the probability of attending private as against government institutions. The marginal effect of the coefficient shows that an increase in one sibling in the family reduces the probability of attending private institutions by 1 percentage point.

Residential Status: Residence of the students is also believed to be an important factor in influencing demand for private versus public higher education. In the literature, residence of the respondent is generally defined in terms of rural and urban. However, in the present case, location refers to the state of domicile of the students – whether the student belongs to the same state where the institution is located or whether she/he came from some other state in India for higher education. This also gives some idea of the extent of interstate migration of students for higher education. The survey includes students from almost all the states (including the Union Territory of Chandigarh and Andaman and Nicobar Islands) in India in the sample. To make a meaningful comparison and also due to less frequency for each state, state of domicile of the student is categorised as: (a) 'the state in which the institution is located' and (b) 'other states'.[10]

Generally, one may expect that students coming from other states are supposed to take admission in government institutions (especially in central government institutions). Students may not go to another state to take admission in the private institutions, as access to similar and expensive private institutions might as well be available to the students in their own states. Such a view is also confirmed to be true in the present analysis. The probit estimates in Table 4.2 suggest that the students coming from the states in which the institution is located were more likely to attend private institutions than the students belonging to the category of other states. Around 70 per cent of the students who had come from their own states had taken admission in private institutions, whereas the share was 65 per cent among students who had come from other states.

Effect of Educational Background of the Students

Students' Academic Background: Academic background exercises considerable influence on students' choices. The background factors considered here include academic performance in examinations, type of school attended, the medium of instruction, location of the school, etc.

Academic Record: Earlier studies suggest that academic attainment is a very important factor in influencing demand for higher education. This, namely academic performance of the students measured here in terms of percentage of marks scored in senior secondary-level final examination, may be considered as a significant factor in determining students' decision to take admission in government or private engineering institutions. Generally, it is felt that the students scoring well in senior secondary examinations have higher chances to perform better in the highly competitive entrance examination,[11] which finally matters most and thus more likely to secure admission in government institutions. Percentage of marks scored in the senior secondary examination is used as a continuous variable in the probit model applied to estimate the students' choice function of engineering institutions.

Controlling for all other factors, the percentage of marks secured by the students in the higher secondary examination is negatively related with the probability of taking admission in private institutions. Stated differently, the percentage of marks scored in senior secondary examination is positively related with the enrolment in government institutions. The marginal effect indicates that 1 per cent increase in the marks reduces the probability of enrolment in private institutions by 1 percentage points (column 4 of Table 4.2). Though the percentage of marks does not have a direct role in the admission of government or private institutions, it reflects the cognitive merit of the students which helps them in securing a higher rank in the entrance examination and hence to take admission in a better quality institution (especially in government institutions). Simply stated, students with better academic background go for government institutions and vice versa.

Medium of Instruction: Classroom teaching in most of the private senior secondary schools takes place in English medium, whereas the government schools teach students in the regional language(s); only in central (government) schools and in exceptional cases in some state schools, the medium of instruction used is English. The medium of instruction matters much, as the national entrance examinations and later the engineering degree studies are mostly conducted/offered in English (and to a lesser extent in Hindi) only. So it is expected that students from English medium schools have a higher advantage generally in the entrance examination and finally in getting into quality government institutions – national or state level – than students from schools with the medium of instruction other than English. This variable is used in the probit model as an explanatory variable to see if there is any relationship between the students' medium of instruction in the senior secondary level and their choice of government institutions versus private institutions.

The probit results given in Table 4.2 show that students who had completed their senior secondary schooling in English medium are more likely to go to private institutions than the students who had completed their schooling in local/regional language (non-English medium). Around 67 per cent of the students who had completed their senior secondary schooling with English as medium of instruction enrolled themselves in private institutions as against 59 per cent among the students studied in a regional language (Table 4.1). Though it needs to be further examined, it may be noted that English medium does not necessarily help the students in securing high ranks and accordingly admission in quality government institutions. Further, students who go to English medium schools (majority of which are also private), may come from better-off sections of the society.

Type of School: Along with the medium of instruction, the effect of the type of school the student graduated at secondary level – from public (government including government-aided) or private – is of significance. At school level, the general perception is private schools offer better quality education than government schools (e.g. Kingdon, 1996), though the evidence is not conclusive. It is argued that private schools offer better quality education than government schools and the demand for private education may also mean to some extent the demand for quality education (Tilak & Sudarshan, 2001, p. 6). Growth of private schools in India, mainly attributed to the breakdown in the functioning and quality of government schools, is well documented in the literature (e.g. Tilak, 1992b, 1994; Tilak & Sudarshan, 2001; Kingdon, 2017; Kumar & Choudhury, 2021). Hence, private schools are favoured in India mainly on quality grounds, besides a few other theoretical and empirical aspects like excess and differentiated demand, government failure, efficiency, accountability, job market relevance, quick response to market signals, etc. Taking these into consideration, it can be rationally expected that the students graduating from private senior secondary schools would seek admission in government institutions for higher education and vice versa. But surprisingly, the probit estimates reveal a contradictory picture. The students who complete their senior secondary schooling from private schools are more likely to end up in private institutions. The difference in favour of private institutions is by 7 percentage points. So one may be tempted to infer from these results that the English medium and even private school system do not necessarily provide high-quality education, if our presumptions that high-quality students prefer government institutions in higher engineering education and government engineering institutions offer better quality than private colleges are necessarily correct. But as we noted, there are several factors and they also interplay in the choice of the type of higher education institution.

Location of the School: Rural-urban differences are generally very wide in most aspects of higher education. Urban schools tend to have better infrastructure and are perceived to be better quality institutions. So the rural-urban differences can also be expected to influence students' choice of the type of higher education institution. It is generally presumed that students in urban higher secondary schools receive better quality education than the students of rural schools. Schools belonging to rural areas in India are mainly maintained by the government and lack in adequate quantum basic physical and human infrastructure needed for providing quality education (Bhatty, 1998; Drèze & Kingdon, 2001). However, a large number of higher secondary schools in urban India are privately managed and provide quality teaching to the students which help them performing better in their careers. Instead of considering rural-urban differences based on the student's/family's original place of living, the location of the senior secondary school from which the student graduated is considered here. While it is expected that students from urban higher secondary schools seek admission in government institutions, the regression coefficients presented in Table 4.2 reveal that students graduating from urban higher secondary schools are more likely to take admission in private institutions than students of rural schools. About 71 per cent of the students from urban senior secondary schools have taken admission in private institutions, whereas the share is 56 per cent among students who graduated from rural schools.

Education Board: Among the variables on academic background, the board of education matters. All secondary schools in the country are necessarily affiliated to central (all India) boards or state (government) boards of examinations. Prominent boards are: Central Board of School Education (CBSE) and the Council for the Indian School Certificate Examination, a private body that conducts Indian Certificate of Secondary Education Examination (ICSE) at all India level, hence known as central boards and various state (government) boards. In all, there are 34 boards of secondary and senior secondary education in India, and more than 95 per cent of the schools are affiliated to state boards. Given the variations in quality in curriculum offered by different boards, students come out with varying capabilities, which will have an impact on their choices. Generally, CBSE curriculum is regarded to be of higher standard than others. It is generally believed that the schools managed by CBSE and other central boards provide good quality education (mainly the curriculum and syllabi are written in the contemporary context and revised periodically as per the need of the students), which helps to develop the cognitive skills of the students in a better way. However, the syllabi followed in the state boards, with some probable exceptions, are not up to the mark for the intellectual development of the students. Besides syllabus, students studying in schools managed by the central boards are taught by trained and qualified teachers. According to a National Achievement Survey of grade ten students that was conducted by the National Council of Educational Research and Training (NCERT, 2018), students from CBSE and ICSE schools fared better than those from various state boards in all disciplines across India.[12] Hence, examination board of the senior secondary schooling – central or state – is considered here for our analysis.[13] As expected, the empirical results show that students studying in the schools affiliated to central boards are more likely to take admission in government institutions than the students who graduated under state boards.

Coaching for Entrance Examination: Due to excess demand (i.e. demand being greater than supply of engineering education), admission into engineering colleges has always been a tough proposition, with an ever-increasing number of students seeking entry on the one hand and limited availability of quality institutions such as IITs and NITs on the other. The competition is very tough among the students for admission in different institutions, and it is more so in government institutions. The common entrance examinations conducted for admission to professional courses in India are highly competitive and demand elaborate preparation and special coaching to secure high ranks (Sivasankaran & Babu, 2008, p. 90). Hence, preparatory coaching, which is also quite expensive, is widely perceived as an essential pre-requisite for securing high ranks in entrance examination and then in obtaining admission in any good engineering education institutions in India, though a good number of students who do not undertake such coaching also get high ranks and admission in good quality institutions. In general, it is held that students taking pre-admission preparatory coaching to secure good ranks in the entrance examination prefer to enrol in government institutions as against private institutions. The results here indicate that it is true: students who have attended pre-admission coaching have higher probability preferring admission in government institutions to private institutions.

Effect of Factors Related to Students' Current Education Status

Stream of Engineering: Based on the prevalence of major streams of engineering education in undergraduate education in India, students enrolled in five major streams (majors) of engineering, viz. electrical engineering, mechanical engineering, computer science engineering, electronics and communication engineering and IT were chosen to constitute the main sample of the survey. As mentioned in Chapter 1, these majors are broadly categorised into two groups, namely traditional and modern/IT-related streams of engineering. Traditional streams include electrical engineering and mechanical engineering, whereas modern areas include computer science engineering, electronics engineering, electronics and communication engineering and IT. Government institutions seem to lay more emphasis on traditional/standard disciplines such as mechanical engineering, civil engineering and electrical engineering, while private colleges and universities respond to market-influenced demands of students and open highly demanded and more revenue-generating, IT-related/modern disciplines like computer science engineering, electronics and communication engineering and IT. Of course, in some cases, the rigid structures of government institutions do not allow them to be flexible in offering new disciplines and programmes of study. Further, the traditional streams of engineering like mechanical and electrical require heavy infrastructure in the form of laboratories and workshops and huge investments, which the private institutions might be reluctant to make. Similarly, some engineering colleges are famous for specific disciplines of study.

Demand for modern branches of engineering education is very high compared to traditional areas, which used to be the main chunk of engineering education in India for a long time. In general, the preference of the student for a given area of study is so strong that often students do not mind compromising on their choice of an institution.[14] Hence the STREAM_STUDY may have a significant effect on the students' choice of government vis-à-vis private institutions. Students preferring modern streams have higher preferences for private institutions, as many private institutions offer such courses compared to government institutions, whereas students preferring traditional areas of engineering may opt for government institutions. Some government institutions are also known more for some of the traditional streams of engineering. So students prefer a particular institution to others, given their preference for a stream of engineering.

Given the above, one can expect that the students willing to study traditional disciplines may have higher chances to enrol in government institutions, whereas students interested in enrolling in modern/IT-related streams go for private institutions. It is confirmed here that students keen on modern streams of engineering are 73 per cent more likely to prefer private institutions than government universities or colleges. The choice of a stream of study seems to play a strong role in the choice of the type of institution. In fact, if there is a choice between type of institution and the choice of stream of engineering, it appears the latter is more dominant.

Household Cost: Compared to general higher education, households have to spend a lot on professional education like the engineering education in India. The fee and other household cost of education is generally considered as one of the important factors determining students' choice of government versus private higher education institutions, as the higher educational cost that the students have to incur discourages the students from low- and middle-income families to opt for the same. Generally, the fees and other expenditures are higher in private institutions than in government institutions. Total household expenditure on engineering education is used as a proxy of household cost of education in the probit regression here in logarithmic form. This, the household cost, as described later in this chapter in detail, includes the household expenditure on fees (library fees, examination fees and fees on games and sports), non-fee items (dormitory or housing, food, transport, textbooks and other classroom materials) and other related expenses (improving communictions in English language, purchase of computers, internet, phones, entertainment and other necessay expenses). As per the survey data, the total household expenditure per student was ₹110,000 in government institutions and ₹166,000 in private institutions. However, these figures do not include the opportunity cost of education. Difference in the household expenditure on government and private institutions is mainly due to the difference in the fees, though in the case of other items also one finds a big difference. Students in private institutions pay fees which is two times more than in government institutions.[15]

Here, it is hypothesised that the students' choice in government versus private institutions is considerably influenced by the costs of education. Household expenditure on education is taken as proxy of household cost of education. The estimated probit coefficient of household cost (lnHHEXPR) shows that it is positively related with enrolment in private institutions. Household costs also reflect the ability of the households to spend on education of their wards. So, households with higher ability to spend opt for private institutions, as we have already seen.

Financial Support: The availability of scholarship, loan and part-time work might reduce the financial burden and may stimulate more demand for admission in those institutions where these are available.

Scholarship: Scholarships and stipends reduce household costs of education. Availability of scholarships or any other financial assistance in an institution can be expected to influence students' choice of an institution. Hence, students may prefer those universities/colleges where there is a high probability of getting such financial assistance than others. This may be very important, particularly in the case of students coming from low- and middle-income families, as it will have implications for the financial burden of the households considerably. The probability of getting financial assistance[16] is comparatively higher in government than in private institutions. This increases the students' preference in favour of government compared to private institutions. We find the same in the present analysis: students with higher probability of getting scholarship are less likely to take admission in private than in government institutions. After all, government institutions have separate budgets for scholarships, especially for the students coming from disadvantaged sections of the society such as SCs, STs, OBCs, physically challenged (handicapped) and students from poor economic backgrounds, whereas private institutions hardly provide any good number and decent amounts of scholarships.

Student Loans: Also related to the household costs is the availability of education loans. Engineering education being a costlier discipline of study, many students would like to avail educational loan facility to cover the costs of education. The probability of getting educational loan varies among students enrolled in government and private engineering institutions, as banks tend to discriminate between the institutions and also between programmes and students, as we see in Chapter 7. Further, some institutions – government or private – have arrangements with banks and other lending institutions, if any, to arrange for quick loans to the students admitted in their institutions. It is generally observed that students enrolled in government institutions have higher chances of getting educational loans from commercial banks than students enrolled in private institutions. So it can be expected that the students seeking admission in engineering education may prefer those institutions where the probability of getting a loan is higher. Availing of an educational loan by the student from commercial banks for study is considered as an explanatory variable.

Results in Table 4.2 indicate that the students who are keen on educational loan are less likely to take admission in private institutions by 98 percentage points than government institutions. This shows that the scope of getting educational loan from commercial banks by a student is higher if she/he takes admission in government institutions than in private institutions. Commercial banks may feel more assured, to a great extent, regarding the repayment of their loan amount by the graduates of government institutions. These students might get jobs in the labour market soon after the completion of their study and also with decent salary.

Part-Time Work: Engineering students belonging to lower- and middle-income groups and not necessarily receiving any financial support (scholarship or educational loans) may look for opportunities to engage themselves in part-time jobs to cover at least a part of their cost of education. Accordingly, students choose government or private institutions which will provide them scope to work outside during their study. But such opportunities are not evenly available in all institutions; availability of such opportunities obviously influences students' choice of institutions. Hence, the part-time work engagement of student is included as one of the explanatory variables in the probit analysis. In this study, we find that two-thirds of students have taken part-time jobs. The results show that the students who wish to get involved in part-time jobs during their study are more likely to enrol in the private as compared to government institutions. This may be due to the fact that in some cases, private institutions provide better opportunities of working part-time on campus compared to government institutions. Further, it is also reported that many private institutions may not be very strict in insisting on regular attendance of students in classroom activities and may instead allow them to appear in the final examinations even without having the required minimum percentage of attendance in the classes. This may not be the case in government institutions; they may insist on full and regular attendance in classes/laboratories/workshops/seminars and so on, which will not allow much time for part-time work. So, students who would like to work part-time may prefer private institutions.

Effect of Employment Prospects and Educational Aspirations

Employment Prospects: Employment is normally an important consideration for anyone pursuing higher education, particularly expensive engineering education. Hence, it needs to be considered in every analysis of demand for higher education. Ideally, measures of labour market conditions, such as employment or unemployment rate and earnings associated with graduates of private versus public engineering institutions of higher education, should be used to examine the effects of labour market conditions on students' choice of the type of institution. Unfortunately, our survey does not cover employment or earnings of engineering graduates, as it was conducted on students currently studying in the final (fourth) year (seventh or eighth semester) of engineering degree programme, who were yet to complete the programme. However, we tried to capture employment potential of the programmes/institutions by looking at placement profiles. On-campus recruitment of students before they complete their studies is common in many engineering institutions of higher education in India. Only a very few institutions do not allow this practice in their campus, as this dilutes the pedagogical objective of the institutions and the students as well. Prospective employers visit the institutions and conduct on-campus recruitment process and make offer of jobs to the suitable students, who will take up the employment after completion of their studies. So we collected information on 'whether the student has got any job offer through on-campus recruitment', which can be considered as a proxy of employment capacity of various engineering degree programmes and the institutions. It is important to note that the employers do not necessarily visit all institutions; they visit only those institutions that have a high brand and/or proven record of producing quality graduates. So on-campus recruitment is also viewed as employers' recognition of the institution. Out of nearly eight lakh engineering graduates, only less than half of them get jobs through campus placement, according to the All India Council for Technical Education (AICTE) data, as noted in Chapter 3. In other words, students' decision to take admission in government or private institutions also largely depends on the extent of campus recruitment opportunities the institutions provide to their graduates or simply on 'placement' records of the institutions. In this sample, only 26 per cent of the total engineering students have got employment offers through on-campus recruitment.[17] Of the 26 per cent of the engineering students who got job offers, 65 per cent are enrolled in government institutions and 35 per cent in private institutions. Thus, performance of the public and private institutions varies widely in placement records. Hence students may consider on-campus recruitment records of the institutions while making a choice to take admission in government versus private institutions; this variable is considered a dummy variable in the students' choice equation. The probit results reveal that the students caring for employment assurance are less likely to go to private as against public institutions. This may be due to the reputation of the government institutions where the students will be getting employment in the on-campus recruitment process relatively more easily than graduates from private institutions.

Educational Aspirations: In recent years, engineering graduates usually enter into the job market after completion of their undergraduate studies, and very few of them go for higher studies, that is, to pursue master and PhD-level programmes. Particularly, only those who are interested in academic careers may prefer to go for further studies. Such opportunities are relatively more available in government institutions than in private ones. So the students who have ambitions to go for further studies might choose government institutions. Quite interestingly, in our sample, around 40 per cent of the students have expressed intention to go for further studies (Master or PhD-level programmes), the share being higher in private institutions than in government institutions (43 per cent and 36 per cent, respectively), though public institutions in general offer better opportunities for further studies. What is the impact of students' ambitions to go for further studies on their choice in favour of government versus private institutions for their undergraduate studies?

The probit estimates show that students who intend to study further are less likely to enrol in private institutions by 54 percentage points as compared to government institutions. This may be due to the existence of larger avenues and facilities in public institutions for higher studies and research in engineering disciplines compared to private institutions. Many private institutions offer only first degree programmes and only a very few offer master's and PhD degree programmes.

Recap and Conclusions

In this chapter, we modelled the determinants of the choice of senior secondary school graduates with respect to private versus public institutions for higher education in engineering in India. In fact, there are three phases in students' decision-making relating to their higher education: first, students decide whether or not they wish to go for higher education; in the second phase, they decide which discipline of higher education they would like to pursue – medical, or engineering, or management, or social sciences, or basic sciences or more; in the third phase, they have to choose the institution they would like to apply for. Hossler and Gallagher (1987) refer to these three as predisposition, search and choice. We are concerned here with the third phase of choice-making. Here also we are confined to the choice between public versus private institutions.

Descriptive analysis and the probit equation estimated to examine the factors explaining students' choice of the institutions lead us to sum up a few important findings as follows:

- The presumption that for many reasons, students belonging to socially backward strata (SCs, STs and OBCs) are more likely to prefer government institutions and are less likely to enrol in private institutions holds true in this study. Similarly, from a gender point of view, a female student has 4 percentage points more likely to attend private institution than on average a male student.
- The probit results indicate that the presence of a larger number of siblings in the family reduces the probability of attending private institutions as against government institutions. The other two statistically significant and important household factors determining students' choice for institutions are the parents' occupation and state of domicile of the students. Surprisingly, income of the family is found to be statistically not significant. While mother's education has a positive influence in the student's preference towards government institutions, father's education has no statistically significant effect.
- As expected, a student graduating from a secondary school which is under a central (government) board is more likely to enrol in public institutions of engineering education than a student graduating from a school managed by a state board.
- The probability estimates relating to medium of instruction followed in the senior secondary school and the percentage of marks scored in the entrance examination yield results in somewhat expected directions. Students who completed their secondary education in English medium are more likely to go to private institutions, while those who score high marks in the school end examinations are less likely to enrol in private institutions. Obviously, students with better academic background (marks) and with English medium can compete for better quality institutions, which are in the state sector.
- It is also shown here that pre-coaching is not essential to get admission into undergraduate studies in engineering. Among those who joined engineering institutions, more than half did not have pre-coaching to prepare for entrance examination.
- Students' choice of an institution is significantly determined by the employment prospects, or more specifically, employment assurance that can be indirectly derived from the performance of the institution in terms of campus recruitment and offers of placement in jobs made to the students. Offer of employment of students through on-campus recruitment is considered as a positive indicator of employment-providing capacity of the institutions. As government institutions are able to offer better opportunities for

employment through on-campus recruitment by reputed companies, they become a preferred choice of the students seeking admission than private institutions. The probit estimates confirm the same. Obviously, due to the reputation or brand name of the government institutions, graduates will be able to secure good employment easily than in those graduating from private institutions.
- The other factors determining students' choice for institutions include the availability of scholarships, cost of engineering education and the streams of engineering that students intend to choose. Students who could secure scholarships mostly from the government do not prefer private institutions. Students in private institutions afford the higher costs (of private institutions) and spend more than those in government institutions. Last, students interested in modern (IT-related) branches of study seem to be getting more into private institutions than government institutions. This is because government institutions focus more on and offer traditional streams, though they also offer modern streams of engineering sciences to a lesser extent, while private institutions, responding to the market demand, tend to offer more admissions in IT-related and other modern areas and less or almost nil in other traditional but important programmes.

To sum up, among the statistically significant factors, after caste, the most important ones that explain the choice for admission in private institutions are preference for modern streams of engineering, secondary schooling in non-English medium schools and the high cost of education. The next three important factors are secondary schooling in a school affiliated to state board, the location of the school (in rural areas) and mother's education. While mother's education has a negative effect on the probability of student preferring a private institution, all others among the above predictors positively influence the choice in favour of a private institution. Some of them require in-depth probing of many related aspects, which is not attempted here. Some of the results are in conformity with the general presumptions and findings of other research studies; but there are some that also question the widely held general presumptions. They require further investigation.

Singling out different factors that explain students' choice is important, but is indeed difficult. The results also indicate the strong interplay of several factors, making explanation difficult. We find here that a multitude of factors explain why students choose public or private institutions for engineering education in India. We may note that quite a few considerations that we outlined in the very beginning limit generalised conclusions we can draw from these findings. The imperfect education market in a developing country like India, characterised by large-scale growth of private education and diminution of public sector, asymmetry of information – there are no strict regulations requiring institutions to share basic information that empowers students to make more informed choices, the limited supply of engineering education facilities of quality, the admission procedures and uneven economic abilities

144 *Economics of Engineering Education in India*

of the households – does not mean the existence of a genuine free choice in a typical market framework for the parents or students in selecting a type of engineering institution. Also parental pressures and preferences are so strong that students feel severely constrained to exercise their own choice (Rao, 2019). So it is important to note that we have used the choice function in this study in a restricted sense.

Notes

1 According to NSSO (2016), 29 per cent of students reported joining private institutions at graduate and above level because of non-availability of government institutions nearby and another 27.5 per cent for not getting admission in government institutions, though they have tried.
2 The choice framework of demand for higher education in UK using *luck egalitarianism* theory is discussed in detail by Voigt (2007).
3 Before a full elaborate equation is estimated, a preliminary exercise was attempted with estimating an equation of enrolment in public institution with variables of gender, entrance score, mother with higher education, log family income and type of secondary school attended. The odds of choosing a public institution rise if the student is a female. The odds also increase with score in entrance examination and log family income. These are statistically significant at 99 per cent level. The estimated probit-odds ratios are: GENDER (0.807), RANK (score in entrance examination) (1.038), $lnHHY$ (0.889), SEC_SCH_TYPE (public) (–1.205) and MOTHER_HIGHER (0.941). Encouraged by these results, an elaborate equation is estimated considering a few other variables.
4 Some of these are considered as additional variables in the probit analysis. We have not found much multi-collinearity between several independent variables chosen. The sample is also large enough in size to mitigate the problem, if any.
5 The economic status/capacity of the household is measured here and in other chapters in Part II in terms of annual income of the family. Information on actual income collected in the survey was grouped into four income brackets: (i) less than ₹100,000; (ii) ₹100,000 to ₹500,000; (iii) ₹500,000 to ₹1 million; and (iv) above ₹1 million. While we use these income categories in presenting the descriptive characteristics given in Table 4.1, in the probit analysis, mid-values of each income bracket are used in measuring the income variable as if it is a continuous variable, and for smoothness, the logarithmic value has been used in the probit model. For the open-ended last income category, the upper limit is taken as ₹2 million (see Appendix B).
6 Information on occupation of the parents was collected in the survey on 16 occupational categories, which are regrouped here into three: (a) professional or technical workers; (b) businessmen/women; and (c) others. The reclassification was found necessary due to small numbers of observations in many of the occupation categories such as clerical and related workers, service workers, farmers, fishermen and related workers, skilled workers (foreman, craftsman etc.), unskilled workers (ordinary labourer), retired and workers not classified by occupation (athlete, actor, musician, unemployed, partially unemployed). All these occupations are included in the category of 'others'. The 'professional or technical workers' include both junior and senior professional workers like doctors, professors, lawyers, architects, engineers, nurses, teachers, editors, photographers and bank employees. In the case of mother's occupation, it is important to note that

housewives (homemakers) constitute about 23 per cent of the total number of mothers in our sample, which was included in the 'others' category. See Appendix B for further explanation on variables. The broad occupational classification we adopted does not necessarily correlate with the economic classes, as, for example, some in 'others' might earn higher than those in (a) or (b), or those in (b) might earn higher than (a) or lower than those in (b).

7   The educational qualifications of all members of the family may matter in the choice of different institutions, but this is not considered here, as we could not attempt at developing any aggregate measure of educational level of all the members of the household, as we do not have the data on all the members; moreover, in nature it can be problematic, and both methodologically and conceptually it may not be free from errors.

8   Students were asked to mention in the survey the highest level of education attained separately by both their parents. Table 4.1 gives details of educational levels of parents. For the regression analysis, the actual levels of education are converted to years of schooling, as the latter is considered a better indicator and has been extensively used in the literature than the level of education.

9   Several studies have examined the impact of total family size on demand for education. However, due to the non-availability data on total family size, the impact of the number of siblings in the family is considered here.

10 The survey does not include information on the students by their geographical location, that is, whether they belong to rural or urban region. However, it gives data on the location of senior secondary schools (rural or urban) in which the students completed their secondary education, which is considered here as another explanatory variable, as described later.

11 Rank order scores of students secured in the competitive common entrance examinations may be more important in the choice. But as the examinations are conducted by a central government body and also by various states and in some cases, by the institutions themselves, it is problematic to use the ranks without standardising them, which is not attempted here. And hence, ranks are not used in our analysis.

12 https://www.hindustantimes.com/education/survey-finds-class-10-students-of-cbse-icse-perform-better-than-their-state-boards-peers/story-OURp2u3oiMn6VATbemZpKJ.html

13 About 90 per cent of students in our sample have come from CBSE board and 8 per cent from schools affiliated to different state boards. As only 25 students (2 per cent of the total students covered in the study) had completed their senior secondary examination through ICSE board, which is also a central board, CBSE and ICSE are grouped into one category as 'central board'. Due to the small sample size of each of the state boards, it has not been attempted to analyse the impact on students' choice of institutions by each state board separately. Even if such data are available, it would be difficult to use, as they need to be standardised using somewhat arbitrary weights. The different state boards vary widely in their quality, standards, evaluation and other procedures.

14 Chapter 5 is concerned with the determinants of choice of sub-streams within engineering.

15 It would have been better to take the *net* household expenditure, that is, the total household expenditure on engineering education minus the amount of scholarship or any other financial assistance received. However, we do not have the required details on the amount of scholarship or financial assistance received by students during their programme of study. But we have information on whether a student has received scholarship or not, which is taken as an independent binary variable in the estimation of students' choice for government versus private institutions.

16 In the survey, we collected information on whether a student has received any scholarship or not during their programme of study, and the variable SCHOLARSHIP is defined to take the value 1 if she/he received any scholarship and 0 otherwise.
17 As the students covered in the study are from the fourth (final) year of their studies, they are expected to get a job offer before they graduate with the help of the placement cells of their respective engineering institutions. The figures do not include those who secure employment directly in the labour market after completing their studies. A few more details on this subject based on our survey are given in Chapter 9.

5 Students' Choice of 'Modern' versus 'Traditional' Streams of Engineering Education

Introduction

Among the many branches of higher education, engineering education has grown relatively very fast in India. As described in Chapter 2, while branches like mechanical, civil and electrical engineering have enjoyed huge popularity for a long period, in recent years areas like computer science engineering, electronics and communication engineering, information technology (IT) and telecommunication engineering have gained more popularity. In fact, some of these popular ones have been introduced in Indian institutes of engineering education only during the last quarter century, coinciding with the revolution in information and communications technology. The job market in these evolving areas is also expanding fast compared to job market in standard traditional areas, where the market is either stagnant or growing at a very slow rate. But even with respect to the modern branches, job market is experiencing fluctuating trends.

Senior secondary school graduates interested in Bachelor's (or first or undergraduate) four-year degree studies in engineering education in India indeed face a choice problem. They need to choose the stream, unlike in some western universities, at the very time of applying for admission into the first year of the four-year degree programme in engineering studies. The dilemma for the students to choose a branch of engineering among as many as 21 branches of engineering presently being offered in engineering institutions in India begins immediately after completing senior secondary school education. It appears that a large number of students are not clear about what they want to choose; only a small section may have some clarity on what discipline or major they would like to pursue. But it is commonly perceived that the students with better academic record at school level and higher ranks in the competitive entrance examinations (held at national or state level and/or in a few cases at institutional level) wish, on a seemingly 'free choice/option' basis, to enrol in the streams such as computer science engineering, electronics and communication engineering, IT or telecommunication engineering, which are perceived to carry high premium in the labour market – higher probability of getting employment in the country or outside

DOI: 10.4324/9781003430223-7

and higher wages, and also in social status and prestige, as against standard traditional streams such as civil engineering, mechanical engineering and electrical engineering. But the choice is indeed a complex process, as it is influenced by a variety of factors, availability of the streams of study in the institutions, which is a major supply constraint, reputation of the institute, fees charged and other expenditure associated with different streams, peer effects, physical proximity of the institution where a given stream is available, etc. In addition to students' aptitudes, attitudes and interests, the choice may also be influenced by individual cognitive factors, characteristics like gender and caste, quite importantly by household's socio-economic and educational conditions and many other factors. In some cases it is not just the reputation of the institution, but the image of the department that matters in choosing 'majors' or specific streams (Korfmann et al., 2021). The choice might also get influenced by fair and unfair marketing strategies adopted by the engineering institutions, particularly private colleges and universities, in developing countries like India (Singh & Singh 2015). The final selection is also guided, rather almost decided, by the student counselling processes offered by public bodies at the time of admission. In short, students' choice of a particular stream of engineering studies (or for that matter any area of study – minor or major) cannot be adequately accounted for by any one single factor. It is influenced by a multitude of factors, which often interplay. In fact, students may not have a genuine 'free' choice, as there are severe supply constraints and market imperfections, including asymmetry of information which plays an important role in making the choices (Simões & Soares, 2010). So, given all this, the question is: what are the factors that influence students' choice of streams in engineering studies at first degree level in India? A modest attempt is made in this chapter to answer this question by examining the possible determinants of students' choice of streams of engineering education in India.

How do students choose between the traditional and modern streams of engineering? Before this question is answered, let us quickly note a few salient features of the profile of the engineering students in India.

A Short Profile of the Engineering Students in India

Drawing from the survey, a short profile of students in engineering education classified under the two groups of streams – traditional streams (mechanical, civil, electrical, mechanical and automation engineering) and modern streams (electronics engineering, electronics and communications, computer science engineering and IT-related areas of engineering) – is given in Table 5.1.

A few striking features of the profile may be noted as follows:

- According to our survey, nearly 70 per cent of the students are enrolled in modern streams of engineering, while about 30 per cent goes to traditional

Students' Choice of 'Modern' versus 'Traditional' Streams 149

disciplines. These figures coincide with the pattern of distribution at national level, as given by the AICTE (All India Council for Technical Education) quoted earlier in Chapter 2. Gender differences are minor in this respect, though they are marked in enrolments in engineering education as a whole vis-à-vis the rest of higher education.
- Interestingly, we find no big difference in this pattern between different social groups, viz. scheduled castes (SCs), scheduled tribes (STs), other backward classes (OBCs) and general population. While 60 per cent of the students among STs chose modern areas, in the general population the corresponding proportion is 70 per cent.
- In every income bracket, a majority of the students opt for modern disciplines. So is the case of students classified by parental occupation or parents' education. In other words, whatever be the economic status of the household or the educational level and/or occupation of the parents, students' first preference seems to be modern disciplines over the traditional ones.
- Students migrate to other states more for admission in modern disciplines than in traditional branches of engineering. Those who prefer traditional branches take admission in the institutions in their own states.
- A majority of secondary school graduates from both public and private schools are enrolled in modern disciplines.

Table 5.1 Socio-Economic and Education Profile of Engineering Students: Distribution by the Type of Stream of Study

(a) By Gender

	Distribution by Column			Distribution by Row			
	Male	*Female*	*Total*	*Male*	*Female*	*Total*	*Number*
Traditional	32.4	27.7	31.0	74.5	25.5	100.0	2056
Modern	67.6	72.3	69.0	70.0	30.0	100.0	4567
Total	100.0	100.0	100.0	71.4	28.6	100.0	6623
Number	4,728	1,895	6,623				

(b) By Nativity

	Distribution by Column			Distribution by Row		
	Outsiders (Outside the State)	*Natives (Within the State)*	*Total*	*Outsiders (Outside the State)*	*Natives (Within the State)*	*Total*
Traditional	26.0	36.4	32.5	27.0	70.4	100.0
Modern	74.0	63.6	67.5	40.6	59.4	100.0
Total	100.0	100.0	100.0	37.1	63.0	100.0

(Continued)

Table 5.1 (Continued)

(c) By Social Category

	SCs	STs	OBCs	General	Total
	Distribution by Column				
Traditional	36.4	40.3	33.3	29.6	31.0
Modern	63.6	59.7	66.7	70.4	69.0
Total	100.0	100.0	100.0	100.0	100.0
	Distribution by Row				
Traditional	8.7	2.4	20.8	68.1	100.0
Modern	6.8	1.6	18.8	72.8	100.0
Total	7.4	1.9	19.4	71.3	100.0

(d) By Family Income

	< ₹100,000	₹100,000–500,000	₹500,000–1,000,000	> ₹1,000,000	Total
	Distribution by Column				
Traditional	40.1	27.7	24.3	26.3	30.4
Modern	59.9	72.3	75.7	73.7	69.6
Total	100.0	100.0	100.0	100.0	100.0
	Distribution by Row				
Traditional	33.4	53.5	9.0	4.2	100.0
Modern	21.8	60.9	12.2	5.1	100.0
Total	25.3	58.6	11.2	4.8	100.0

(e) By Parents' Occupation

	Professional	Service	Unskilled	Businessmen	Others	Total
	Distribution by Column					
By Father's Occupation						
Traditional	28.4	37.4	44.1	29.1	30.4	30.2
Modern	71.6	62.6	55.9	71.0	69.6	69.8
Total	100.0	100.0	100.0	100.0	100.0	100.0
	Distribution by Row					
Traditional	55.5	9.9	7.9	19.6	7.1	100.0
Modern	60.7	7.2	4.3	20.7	7.1	100.0
Total	59.1	8.0	3.4	20.4	7.1	100.0
By Mother's Occupation						
	Distribution by Column					
Traditional	28.3	30.9	47.5	15.3	28.1	27.8
Modern	71.7	69.1	52.5	84.7	71.9	72.3
Total	100.0	100.0	100.0	100.0	100.0	100.0

(*Continued*)

Students' Choice of 'Modern' versus 'Traditional' Streams

Table 5.1 (Continued)

	Distribution by Row					
Traditional	22.4	8.4	2.2	20.0	47.0	100.0
Modern	25.9	10.5	3.7	3.7	56.2	100.0
Total	26.1	9.2	1.7	4.9	58.1	100.0

(f) By Parents' Education

	Illiterate	Primary	Secondary	Higher General	Professional	Total
By Father's Education						
	Distribution by column					
Traditional	23.1	37.6	36.9	29.0	28.7	30.4
Modern	76.9	62.4	63.1	71.0	71.3	69.6
Total	100.0	100.0	100.0	100.0	100.0	100.0
	Distribution by Row					
Traditional	0.2	2.0	20.5	53.2	24.2	100.0
Modern	0.2	1.4	15.2	56.9	26.2	100.0
Total	0.2	1.4	16.8	55.8	25.6	100.0
By Mother's Education						
	Distribution by Column					
Traditional	32.8	43.6	31.8	27.7	28.5	29.8
Modern	67.2	56.4	68.3	72.3	71.5	70.2
Total	100.0	100.0	100.0	100.0	100.0	100.0
	Distribution by Row					
Traditional	1.3	4.5	34.6	50.7	8.9	100.0
Modern	1.4	6.2	41.5	43.7	7.2	100.0
Total	0.8	3.9	28.9	58.6	7.8	100.0

(g) By Academic Background of Students

	(i) Type of School			(ii) Location of School		
	Government	Private	Total	Urban	Rural	Total
Distribution by Column						
Traditional	34.3	28.6	30.2	28.9	44.2	30.6
Modern	65.7	71.5	69.8	71.2	55.8	69.4
Total	100.0	100.0	100.0	100.0	100.0	100.0
Distribution by Row						
Traditional	31.8	68.2	100.0	83.5	16.5	100.0
Modern	26.3	73.7	100.0	90.8	9.2	100.0
Total	28.0	72.0	100.0	88.6	11.4	100.0

(*Continued*)

152 *Economics of Engineering Education in India*

Table 5.1 (Continued)

	(iii) Medium of Instruction			(iv) Board of Examination			
	English	Non-English	Total	CBSE	ICSE	State Board	Total
Distribution by Column							
Traditional	27.7	42.4	29.8	26.1	27.5	32.6	30.4
Modern	72.3	57.6	70.2	73.9	72.5	67.5	69.6
Total	100.0	100.0	100.0	100.0	100.0	100.0	100.0
Distribution by Row							
Traditional	79.0	21.0	100.0	33.7	2.9	63.4	100.0
Modern	87.9	12.1	100.0	13.0	2.1	84.8	100.0
Total	85.2	14.8	100.0	32.5	4.4	63.1	100.0

(v) By Academic Performance: Average Percentage of Marks Secured by the Students in Senior Secondary Examination by Board of Examination

	CBSE	ICSE	State Boards	Total
Traditional	75.3	77.5	74.8	75.0
Modern	78.2	83.7	81.5	80.5
Total	77.5	82.0	79.4	78.8

	(vi) Students Who Took Pre-Admission Coaching			(vii) Students Who Appeared for Entrance Examination		
	Took Coaching	No Coaching	Total	More than Once	Once Only	Total
Distribution by Column						
Traditional	30.0	32.8	31.4	35.2	30.2	30.5
Modern	70.1	67.2	68.6	64.8	69.8	69.5
Total	100.0	100.0	100.0	100.0	100.0	100.0
Distribution by Row						
Traditional	45.2	54.8	100.0	7.2	92.8	100.0
Modern	48.4	51.6	100.0	5.8	94.2	100.0
Total	47.4	52.6	100.0	6.3	93.7	100.0

(viii) Students Who Got Admission in the First Choice of Stream

	In the First Attempt	Not in the First Attempt	Total
Traditional	25.8	36.2	28.3
Modern	74.2	63.8	71.7
Total	100.0	100.0	100.0

(*Continued*)

Table 5.1 (Continued)

(ix) By 'Discipline of First Choice' of the Student

Enrolled in	First Choice										
	Civil	*Computer engineering*	*Electrical*	*Electrical and electronics*	*Telecommunication*	*Information technology*	*Mechanical*	*Instrumentation*	*Management*	*Others*	*Total*
Traditional	82.7	13.5	93.4	15.9	18.2	10.9	88.5	84.7	42.9	74.1	28.2
Modern	17.3	86.5	6.6	84.1	81.8	89.1	11.5	15.3	57.1	25.9	71.8
Total	100.0	100.0	100.0	100.0	100.0	100.0	100.0	100.0	100.0	100.0	100.0
Total (row distribution)	1.4	33.3	4.6	11.7	27.9	8.1	4.7	1.2	0.1	7.2	100.0

- While students with marginally better academic background (higher percentage of marks at senior secondary level) are enrolled in modern subjects, the difference between traditional and modern streams is only marginal, that is, students with nearly equally good academic background chose traditional areas.
- In the case of both traditional and modern branches, more than half the students did not take pre-coaching.
- A majority of the students get admission in the discipline (or group of disciplines – modern or traditional) of their first choice.
- Among the various streams of first choice, computer science engineering tops the list, followed by telecommunications and electrical and electronics engineering. Among the major streams, civil engineering is the least preferred one.

Determinants of Students' Choice

What Does the Literature Suggest?

The student's choice for engineering education is positioned in the literature in the broader theoretical framework of 'luck egalitarianism' (Arneson, 2000). Luck egalitarianism[1] uses the familiar distinction between 'choice' and 'circumstances' to draw the line between *just* and *unjust* inequalities; inequalities resulting from circumstances beyond an agent's control are unjust and must be rectified, while inequalities resulting from individuals' choices are justified. Accordingly, it can be argued that inequalities arising from self-selection of the disciplines (traditional or modern) are not morally problematic as they are based on individuals' choices. However, it is also argued that this impression is mistaken. Luck egalitarians might take seriously the idea that 'brute luck' affects the choices people make, and these effects are particularly obvious when we look at the decision-making process of engineering students of different socio-economic backgrounds. Qualitative research studies on this aspect reveals a significant impact of unequal background conditions of students on the choice of different streams of study, making it less likely that economically weaker students apply for admission in those branches, which are associated with high levels of fees and related expenditure. Hence, though the students' decision to enrol in different streams of study refers to their individual choices, these choices are not sufficient to legitimise further consequences emanating from them.

There are quite a few studies on the students' choice of university/institution, as described in Chapter 4, but not many can be found on the choice between disciplines of engineering in India. Hofstein et al. (1977) found that the selection of physical science streams in Israel's post-secondary education was significantly related to the socio-economic background. Elchardus and Spruyt (2009) have found that students' selection of academic streams and sociopolitical attitudes of students are related. The selection is highly influenced by socialisation and sociopolitical attitudes. In a cross-country study on students' interest in science and technology studies, OECD (2006) concluded that students' choices of disciplines in higher education are mostly determined by their images of the professions associated with the studies, the content and curricula and the quality of teaching. According to Goyette and Mullen (2006), gender and race explain the pattern of students' choice in the universities between vocational and arts and science courses of study in the US. It was further found that financial reward attached with a programme influences the choices of Asian Americans in their study programmes. In an interesting study on the UK, Rimfeld et al. (2016) found that in the choice of subjects by students, there was substantial genetic influence. Examining the students of the Southampton University, Maringe (2006) concluded that students seem to be adopting a consumerist approach in their decision-making in higher education. The importance attached to the labour market motives in terms of employment and career prospects significantly outweigh those related to pursuing higher education on the basis of subject interest and a love for the subject. Students consider programme and price-related issues as more important than many other aspects. Wiswall and Zafar (2015) show that the choice of college major, strongly reinforced by the choice of occupation, is affected by expected labour market earnings, perceived ability and heterogeneous tastes of students. Students self-assess themselves on their comparative advantage in certain subjects and their preference for particular occupations leads them to select the respective fields of study in higher education (Altonji et al., 2016; Kirkeboen et al., 2016).

In a study on analysis of choice of youth in Indian higher education, Chakrabarti (2009) notes a significant influence of gender on the selection of disciplines: females have higher odds of selecting arts/humanities subjects compared to males; and gender bias against females is pronounced in science, commerce, medicine, engineering and other professional disciplines. According to Panda (2006), the three most important reasons behind selecting IT-related streams in engineering education as against standard areas of study by the women engineering students in Odisha are: (a) education level of the parents, (b) occupation of the parents and (c) job market perspectives (see also Choudhury, 2012). Thus we note from the literature review that a wide set of factors influences students' choices of subjects in higher education.

The Method

Under this theoretical and empirical setting, let us examine the factors determining students' choice of streams in engineering education in India. How do students resolve the choice problem between traditional and modern disciplines of engineering? What are the factors that explain the choice of the students? Or what are the determinants of demand for various streams in engineering education? A probit model is used here in an attempt to answer these questions, which are relatively less examined in the literature, while demand for higher education in India in general and to a lesser extent the demand for engineering education received attention of many scholars.

Empirical Estimation

Students' choice between traditional and modern streams of engineering studies is influenced by a variety of factors such as individual characteristics, household factors, academic background of the students, factors related to current education of the students and factors relating to employment and intentions of the students to go for further higher education. It is indeed a complex process, involving mutually interacting factors. Determinants of students' choice of streams is analysed here using probit model, linking the choice of the discipline with a set of factors. The same methodology that was used in Chapter 4 is adopted here. The dependent variable in the model here – the stream of study the student is enrolled in – is a binary variable and is defined as follows: STREAM_STUDY = 1, if the student has enrolled in modern streams; = 0, otherwise, that is, if the student has enrolled in traditional streams. The probit equation is estimated here as follows:

$$STREAM\_STUDY = \alpha + \beta_i X_i + \varepsilon$$

where X_i are a set of explanatory variables, β_i are coefficients of the explanatory variables, α the constant and ε the error term.

Determining Factors

The choice between traditional and modern streams of engineering studies is influenced by a multitude of factors and processes, and it is indeed a multifarious process with several factors mutually interacting with each other (Aydin, 2015). Drawing from the literature general knowledge and based on our survey, a few important variables on individual characteristics, household background, student's academic background, student's current educational status, employment prospects and educational aspirations of students are considered here as possible determinants. The selection of factors is partly constrained by the availability of data in the survey that formed the basis of the study. Rationale for the inclusion of different predictors in the probit model is elucidated below.

Individual Attributes

Gender: Gender is an important factor in determining participation in higher education and also in the choice of disciplines. It is commonly observed that women students prefer modern areas to traditional branches. This may be due to two important reasons: (a) traditional streams of study like mechanical and electrical engineering are highly laboratory-intensive and hence are generally not liked by women; and (b) graduates in traditional branches usually get jobs in labour-intensive activities like manufacturing or related organisations which may not be preferred by women graduates. Instead, women may like, if there is a choice, to take white-collar, soft skill-oriented 'desk jobs' by graduating in modern subjects such as computer science engineering, electronics and communication engineering and IT. So gender, defined as a binary variable GENDER (1 for men and 0 for women), has been introduced to study the male-female differences on the choice of streams between modern and traditional ones.

Caste: The social category of the students (CASTE) may be an important individual characteristic feature in determining not only demand for higher education, but also the choice of disciplines in engineering education. Modern streams are nowadays associated with higher social status, and students of all strata may prefer choosing modern branches of engineering. However, one may hypothesise that the students belonging to general category have higher preference to enrol in modern engineering streams (over traditional areas) than the students from lower social background (e.g. SCs, STs and OBCs) who are more likely to prefer traditional branches. It may be due to the fact that modern subjects like IT and computer engineering require modern new skills like impressive communication skills, sophisticated knowledge of English and more, which many students belonging to lower social background may not necessarily possess at the same level as general category students. Hence, it may become difficult for the socially backward category students to get admission in the IT-related departments like computer science engineering, electronics and communication engineering and IT. Thus, caste of the students can be an important factor in explaining demand for engineering education in modern versus traditional areas. Caste is used here in the form of four different dummy variables, namely SCs, STs, OBCs and

GENERAL. The regression coefficients of SCs, STs and OBCs are interpreted in relation to GENERAL, which is used as the reference category.

Household Characteristics

Among the household characteristics, four factors can be identified to represent household economic status, household income, education and occupation of the parents and the residence of the household, respectively.

Household Income: Economic status of the households is widely recognised as an important factor in explaining demand for higher education (Tilak, 2015; Tilak & Choudhury, 2019). We feel that it might influence the choice of disciplines as well, as low-income families may not be able to afford those areas, like say modern IT-related branches, as these branches may be associated with higher levels of fees and other related charges. Obviously, parents with lower economic capacity choose the areas that fit their budget and may not favour those streams which necessitate higher expenditure. It is also plausible to argue that the low-income households do not prefer to take risks in the labour market (in terms of unemployment and low wages) associated with the lesser-known, newly emerging areas compared to the branches of engineering about which some historical knowledge exists. Hence, household income has been used in the regression equation to represent economic status of the households. Household income is introduced in the equation as a continuous variable.

Parents' education and occupation may reflect parents' many characteristics, including genetics. Parents' education and occupation might capture the effects of the family's non-financial resources and some kind of 'social and cultural capital', in addition to genetical factors.

Parents' Occupation: It is generally observed that students choose certain courses over others which match their parents' education and occupation. Students whose parents are IT professionals may wish to enrol themselves in IT-related or similar disciplines instead of traditional or some other disciplines. Contrary to this, there may be another possibility that students opt for certain branches that are greatly in demand irrespective of their parental occupation. Thus, parental occupation may have different effects upon the students' choice of streams and it may be difficult to predict the direction. The experience of parents from a particular occupation may influence choice of disciplines of study of their wards. So father's and mother's occupations are included in the equation here in the form of six binary variables – three relating to father's occupation and three to mother's occupation.

Parents' Education: Similarly, one can expect parents' education to have a significant effect on student's choice of streams, as students in many cases tend to choose the subjects of study which may match with the educational level of their parents or with parents' interests. Parents with higher level of education can generally be considered better informed about the benefits associated with studying a particular discipline than the parents with lower level of education. Higher educated parents may be also more concerned about the quality of education and may be more aware of institutions and various disciplines and even sub-disciplines of study, and hence they would advise their children to make a proper choice. Highly educated parents in India tend to send their children to IT-related streams compared to less or uneducated parents. This may be due to the fact that educated parents may know the employment potential of traditional and IT-related disciplines more clearly than uneducated or less educated parents. The general impression is that IT-related/modern streams lead us to white-collar jobs, whereas traditional streams such as mechanical, civil and electrical engineering give blue-collar jobs. This is well understood by educated parents compared to uneducated/less educated parents. Educated and better placed parents may also be more knowledgeable about the advantages of studying particular disciplines, such as the higher salary packages, possibilities to get employment abroad and so forth, relatively more clearly than less educated parents who may not necessarily be aware of the differential labour market rewards associated with different streams. Rather, the latter may at best be concerned with the choice between the engineering and non-engineering courses of higher education and may not necessarily bother about choice within engineering. It is possible that the uneducated/less educated parents also might want their children to go to modern branches with/without any such knowledge. So parents' education, measured in the form of years of schooling, is considered here in the regression equation to examine the effect of parents' education. To analyse whether mother's education has more (or less) effect than father's education, the education of both are considered as two separate variables.

A measure of educational attainment used extensively in the literature is the highest level of education completed by the head of the household. Some have considered the education of every member of the household or total education of the entire household in such contexts.[2] While in Table 5.1, we referred to the levels of education, in the regression analysis the years of schooling corresponding to each level is considered as a better indicator, which is also more extensively used in the literature than the level of education.

Nativity: Students go to far-off places to get admission in the stream of their choice, if admission in those streams is not available in institutions near their home or in their home state. Students who do not wish to go outside their state may end up joining those areas which are available within the state. As shown in Table 5.1, about 73 per cent of students belonging to other states have taken admission in IT-related branches, while it is 63 per cent for students who are from the same given state where the institution is located. To examine whether nativity of a student has any effect on the choice of the majors, we include a variable on nativity, measured in a binary form – those from the same state in which the current engineering institution is located versus those from other states – in the equation.[3] Students from almost all the states (including Union Territories of Chandigarh and Andaman and Nicobar Islands) in India are represented in the sample.

Students' Educational Background

One can expect previous educational background of the students to considerably influence the students' preference for a stream in higher education, specifically modern or traditional streams. Students from different educational backgrounds get different exposure to build their future career. For example, at the very beginning of higher secondary education (i.e. in Grade XI itself in India), students' future education path is decided, as the students have to opt for humanities, arts and commerce versus sciences and mathematics; and within the latter group, between biological sciences and physical sciences. Only those who take physical sciences at higher secondary level can proceed to higher studies in engineering and technology.[4] In some cases, institutions give weightage to students' performance in their qualifying examination while giving admission in different streams. Students with good academic background have higher chances to perform well in the selection process and are able to secure admission in the branch of their choice. On the other hand, students from poor academic backgrounds may not perform well in the entrance examination, which ultimately minimises their choice.

With respect to previous educational background of students, six major dimensions are identified, namely: (i)Academic achievement at school level, that is, *percentage of marks* secured in the higher secondary school end examination; (ii) *Medium of instruction* followed in the classroom teaching at the higher secondary level (English or other languages); (iii) The *board of higher secondary examination* – central board or state (provincial) board that the school was affiliated to; (iv) The *type of management of higher secondary school* (government/government-aided or private); (v) *Location* of the higher secondary school (rural or urban).

Among the above, while the first one, namely percentage of marks, is considered here as a continuous variable, the other ones are binary variables. These aspects related to higher secondary schooling and related characteristics of the students should give a fairly good idea of the students' academic background. By including them in the probit equation, we examine its influence on the probability of students' choice of a given stream or a category of streams of study.

Pre-Admission Coaching: Competition for admission in engineering studies is very tough, so students take preparatory coaching for the entrance examination. Given that such coaching is very expensive and that competition for modern disciplines is generally very high, students wishing to seek admission in these areas may necessarily take the preparatory coaching, though it is not essential. Hence, we have also considered whether a student has taken pre-admission coaching to prepare for the entrance examination or not as a binary variable. It is hypothesised that students taking pre-admission coaching to secure a good rank in the entrance examination and thereby get preferential treatment from institutions in granting admission in the streams of their choice may opt for modern streams.

Factors Relating to Current Education

Some of the factors relating to current education status of the students itself might influence the choice of streams. For example, students wishing to pursue studies in modern subjects might join private institutions, as more private institutions than public institutions offer more and more admissions in such areas. Or the cost of education might influence the choice of disciplines. These two dimensions are taken into consideration; accordingly, the following predictors are chosen on current education: type of institution, cost of education, availability of scholarships, educational loans and opportunities for part-time work on campus as probable determinants of students' choice.

Type of Institution: The type of institution the students have enrolled themselves in may have a significant effect on their choice of IT-related versus traditional disciplines. This is mainly because there seems to exist a trade-off between the choice of institutions and streams of study in engineering education. More clearly, students preferring modern disciplines seek admission in private institutions, whereas students enrolled in government institutions might prefer taking a traditional areas. This is primarily due to the fact that students may compromise on the discipline of study if they get admission in government institutions; similarly, they may compromise on the institutions if they are able to secure admission in modern streams (see Chapter 4). However, the students securing a good rank in the entrance examination need not compromise either on the type institution or the discipline of study, that is, they may get admission in their preferred institution as well as in the discipline of their choice. It is also important to note that some public or private institutions are famous for certain disciplines, modern or traditional. After all, all branches or subjects are not necessarily delivered at the same level even in a good university or a college. Hence students may get confused whether to opt for a good institution or a good stream. Students preferring modern branches go to private institutions, as many private institutions offer such streams compared to government institutions, whereas students preferring traditional branches may opt for government institutions. Rather, the choice of discipline and the choice of type of institution seem to be closely related.

Household Cost: The fee and other related costs of education associated with each branch of study can be one of the most important factors determining students' choice of disciplines, as the high cost of a programme may discourage the students from low-income families to opt for the same. Generally, the fees and other expenditures are believed to be higher in modern, highly demanded programmes compared to others. Total household expenditure on engineering education incurred by each student/parents is used as a proxy of household cost of education in the probit regression in logarithmic form. This includes the household expenditure on fees (library fees, examination fees, fees on games and sports), non-fee items (dormitory or housing, food, transport, textbooks and other class materials) and other related expenses (improving comunications in English, purchase of computers, internet, phones, entertainment and other necessay expenses) (see Chapter 6). Household cost is used as a continuous variable in logarithmic form in the estimation of logistic regression.

Further, net household costs get considerably reduced by the availability of scholarships. Some costs can also be covered through student loans and engagement in part-time on-campus work. So it would have been more appropriate to take in our analysis the *net* household expenditure, that is, the total household expenditure on engineering education minus the amount of scholarship or stipend or any other financial assistance received. However, we do not have the required details on the amount of scholarship or financial assistance received by students during their programme of study. The HH_COST also does not include opportunity cost of education. Thus, we considered three additional variables along with *gross* household costs, viz. scholarship, student loan and engagement in on-campus part-time work.

Scholarship: Availability of scholarship or any other financial assistance in an institution can be expected to play an important role in the students' choices of disciplines, as more scholarships may be available in some disciplines and less in case of others. This may be very important, particularly of students belonging to low- and middle-income strata who may be interested in degree studies in engineering, but may not mind the stream of engineering. Students might choose those subjects where they have higher chances of receiving scholarships. Students were asked in the survey to report whether they have received any scholarship or not during their programme of study. This information has been used to generate a binary variable.

Educational Loans: Like scholarships, educational loans reduce the current financial burden of education on the households. Engineering education being a costlier discipline of the study, many students opt for educational loans to cover the costs of their education. But loans may not be evenly available across all branches of study. Banks might also discriminate formally or informally the students in different branches of engineering. While engineering students have higher chances of getting loans than say students in natural and physical sciences or humanities and social sciences, among the engineering students those who are enrolled in modern branches of engineering which are in high demand in the labour market may have higher probability of getting loans than the students who join traditional departments. So the availability of loans may be expected to impact students' choices of various streams of study, if students are keen on availing educational loans offered by commercial banks. Some institutions may also have formal arrangements with banks to provide loans to their students. The survey provides information on whether a student has received any educational loan for her/his studies from commercial banks during the programme of study or not, which is used as a binary variable in the equation.

Part-Time Work Opportunity: Engineering students belonging to low- and middle-income groups and not receiving any financial support (scholarship or educational loans) or otherwise usually go for part-time jobs to continue their study. But the scope to do part-time job differs from department to department in an engineering institution. Availability of such opportunities obviously influences students' choice of departments or branches of engineering. Hence, engagement of student in part-time work is included as one of the explanatory variables in the probit analysis.

Job Prospects and Educational Aspirations

What does the student want to do after a bachelor's degree in engineering – employment or further studies – and what are the important factors that may influence one's selection of the subjects at bachelor's level? Hence we identified two important factors in this regard: employment prospects and plans for further studies.

Employment Prospects: Generally, career prospects i.e. prospects of getting a good job are an obvious factor that influences students' choices regarding the branch of study in higher education and in the choice of sub-streams of engineering.[5] Hence, labour market conditions such as probability of getting employment and decent wages after graduation are important variables that need to be considered in any analysis of the present kind. But the survey does not cover information on employment or earnings of graduates. Employed engineering graduates did not form the respondents in the survey. However, we tried to capture employment potential of the programmes by looking at placement profiles. On-campus recruitment of students before they complete their studies is common in many engineering institutions of higher education in India. Prospective employers visit the institutions, conduct on-campus recruitment process and make offer of jobs to the suitable students, who will take up the employment after completion of their studies. It is important to note that employers visit only those institutions that have a high brand and/or proven record of producing quality graduates and recruit from only those areas that they are interested in or the institution is known for. So on-campus recruitment is also viewed as employer recognition of the programme and the institution. Securing job offer on-campus recruitment is considered here as a dummy variable to reflect employment prospects associated with a given discipline.[6]

Educational Aspirations: It is generally felt that some disciplines offer much scope for higher studies (master's and doctoral programmes), and hence those who wish to go for further studies for whatever may be the reason (e.g. to take up academic and research career or to further the chances of better employment) may opt for certain streams and not others. To test the impact of students' aspirations to go for further studies on their enrolment in traditional versus modern/IT-related branches of engineering, it is also included as a dummy variable in the probit model. It is a dummy variable and takes the value of 1 if the student has expressed a desire or plan to go for further studies and 0 otherwise, that is, if the student does not have the willingness to go for further studies. Based on the current labour market conditions, one can hypothesise that the students intending to go for further studies after completion of their graduation might prefer enrolling themselves in traditional branches than the students who do not have any intention or plan for further studies.

In the empirical model estimated, some of the explanatory variables used in the analysis are continuous and some are used in the dummy form. Appendix to Part II gives notation, definition and measurement of variables and a few summary statistics on these variables. More details on the way the variables are generated are also given in Chapter 4 and the results in Table 5.2.

Results and Discussion

The choice between traditional and IT-related branches of engineering is influenced by individual characteristics, household factors, academic background of the students and factors related to current education of the students.

Individual Characteristics

As expected, the individual characteristics of the students, viz. GENDER and CASTE, have considerable impact on the choice of students between IT-related versus traditional branches of engineering. As noted earlier (Table 5.1), among the total women students, 72 per cent have taken admission in IT-related departments as against 67 per cent among male students. The study by Panda (2006) reveals a similar pattern in women students in Odisha; around 80 per cent wished to join in the IT-related streams like instrumentation and electronics engineering, computer science engineering, whereas the least preferred streams are mechanical and civil engineering. Gender turns out to be a statistically significant factor in the present analysis as well. Women students seem to prefer soft areas like electronics and other IT-related disciplines to hard manual branches like mechanical and civil engineering. The results in Table 5.2 show that compared to male students, women students are more likely to study in modern branches, as expected. Women are 21 per cent more likely than men to opt for modern streams as against traditional ones.

With respect to social background, is caste an important factor in influencing the student choice of streams? More than 70 per cent of the total students from general category have taken admission in IT-related streams as against 59 per cent among the students belonging to STs and 63 per cent among SCs (Table 5.1). But the probit results are not so robust. The econometric results in Table 5.2 do suggest however that the probability of seeking admission to IT-related departments was significantly higher for the students belonging to general category than the students belonging to SCs and STs. More clearly, the estimates show that being a SC reduces the probability of admission in IT-related departments by 1 percentage point and being ST by 3 percentage points. Surprisingly, belonging to the OBC group increases the probability of attending IT-related subjects by 5 percentage points as compared to the general category students. OBCs are, after all, not as backward as SCs and STs. Many of them are economically as advanced as middle and upper strata of the society. However, out of these, only the coefficient associated with OBC is statistically significant at 10 per cent level of significance.

Role of Household Characteristics

Among the household factors, we expected household income to be a significant determinant of students' choice. As noted from Table 5.1, with increase in household income, the proportion of students attending modern branches increases. About three-fourths of the students from middle- and higher-income strata go for modern/IT-related subjects, while the corresponding figure is less than 60 per cent for the students belonging to low-income families. Thus, one can expect a positive relationship between the economic capacity of the households and the probability of choosing modern streams. But statistically, household income turns out to be not significant in the choice function estimated here. In every income group, modern branches attract larger numbers of students than traditional areas of study.

Occupation of the parents is expected to matter significantly in the students' choice between modern versus traditional disciplines of engineering. Probit estimates reveal that students whose fathers work as professionals or technical workers are more likely to enrol in IT-related disciplines than the students whose parents belong to 'other occupations' like clerical and related work, service work, farming, fishermen and related workers and retired persons. Same is the case for students whose parents are involved in business activities. The probability of enrolment of students in IT-related studies increases by 3 percentage points if the occupational category of the father is professional or technical or business. Interestingly, however, mothers' occupation has an opposite effect: the coefficient associated with occupation of the mother is negative in value. Mothers who are professional workers or businesswomen might prefer their children opting for standard traditional streams. This may be because of the generally perceived relative stability in labour market conditions with respect to jobs for the graduates of traditional disciplines compared to those jobs that are related to modern branches. Mothers may be more cautious in guiding their children in their choice of streams of study. They might feel that traditional disciplines offer more stable and secure jobs. The differential effects of parents' education, however, need further probing.

Similarly, the probit estimates also show that parents' education has also a positive effect on increasing the probability of their children enrolling in modern branches, though the coefficients are small in value and statistically not significant. Higher educated parents might view the modern streams highly promising in the near future and advise their children accordingly. There is not much difference between effect of the father's education and mother's education on student's choice.

The results further show that among the household factors, NATIVITY is statistically significant in determining the students' choice of the stream of engineering they wish to pursue. Students belonging to the state where the institution is located are less likely to take modern/IT-related streams than the students of other states. The marginal effect suggests that students belonging to the state where the institution is located are less likely by 9 percentage points taking admission in IT-related branches. After all, students migrate to other states when they do not get admission in their own state in the disciplines of their choice, which are largely the IT-related branches in this case.

Effect of Educational Background of the Students

Earlier studies suggest that academic attainment is a very important factor in influencing demand for higher education. Students scoring well in the senior secondary examination have higher chances to perform better in the entrance examination and thus are more likely to enrol in the disciplines of their choice, more commonly in the highly demanded disciplines like the modern disciplines. But it is important to note that more than the academic scores in the school end examination, it is the rank in the competitive entrance examination that matters in securing admission in the areas of one's choice. Examination scores in the school end examination and ranks in the common entrance examination are not necessarily always positively correlated. But in view of the complications involved in using ranks awarded by different boards, unless standardised, only examination scores are used.

The results show that among the six factors considered on academic background of the students, the percentage of marks secured in the higher secondary examination turns out to be an important and statistically significant factor: the higher the percentage of marks scored in higher secondary examination, the higher is the probability of taking admission in modern branches than traditional branches. One per cent increase in the marks in higher secondary end examination increases the probability of opting for modern subjects by 7 percentage points. This is in conformity with the general belief that the students scoring high percentage of marks in their senior secondary examination may perform better in the entrance examination as well and would opt for IT-related branches of engineering.

Among the six factors on academic background, the other important one relates to the board of examination. Students who studied in schools affiliated to state (provincial) boards are found less likely to enrol in IT-related streams than the students who graduated from schools affiliated to a central board. Generally, CBSE curriculum is regarded to be of higher standard than others. The standard of curricula and quality of education are believed to be better in schools affiliated to central board, and hence, students graduating from central boards may tend to go for modern branches. The econometric results show the same: students graduating from state (provincial) board are 26 per cent less likely to get admission in modern discipline than those who studied under central (government) board. The medium of instruction, defined in a binary form – English or others – is found here to be not a statistically significant factor in influencing students' choices of streams, meaning that the students' choice is not much influenced by the medium of instruction at the school level, contrary to popular beliefs.

Other important variables relating to student academic background considered here include type of school – public (central or State government/government-aided) or private, location of the school – rural or urban, and whether a student took coaching in preparation for entrance examinations.

An important factor that influences students' many decisions, including their choices of higher education, relates to the type of school they graduated from: public or private. It is expected that the students graduating from private senior secondary schools would seek admission in branches of high demand or disciplines which are regarded as of high brand and status. But probit estimates show that students who had studied in private senior secondary schools were less likely to take admission in modern disciplines. This is contrary to the general though unfounded impression that private schools provide effective teaching environment with quality teachers, well-developed curricula and competitive student atmosphere which helps them to be better informed about their options and might influence students to take admission in modern branches. But this is not the case: private schools might not necessarily provide that competitive advantage. However, the coefficient is statistically not significant.

Rural-urban differences are generally very wide in most aspects of higher education. They may be believed to be influencing students' choice of stream of engineering as well. Students studying in urban schools have locational advantages in the form of better information, apart from better quality schooling. Hence, students who graduated from urban schools may make better or wiser choices than those graduating from rural schools. The former may have higher chances to prefer modern streams than the students from rural schools. Thus one can expect that students' choice of disciplines differs with the location of the senior secondary school they have studied in. The results confirm this. Students who graduated from senior secondary schools located in rural areas have less probability of taking admission in modern departments than the students from rural senior secondary schools, as revealed by the probit estimates. Around 70 per cent of the students who have completed their senior secondary schooling from urban areas have taken admission in IT-related departments, whereas the corresponding figure is 55 per cent for the students who graduated from rural senior secondary schools (Table 5.1).

Table 5.2 Probit Estimate of Students' Choice of Streams of Study in Engineering Education

Variables	Coefficient	Standard Error	Marginal Effect (dy/dx)#
Individual characteristics			
Gender	0.215***	0.083	0.065
SCs	−0.029	0.149	−0.009
STs	−0.106	0.280	−0.034
OBCs	0.176*	0.101	0.053
General	Reference category		
Household factors			
*ln*HHY	0.051	0.044	0.016
Fathocp_prof	0.085	0.089	0.026
Fathocp_bus	0.108	0.091	0.033
Fathocp_others	Reference category		
Mothocp_prof	−0.068	0.103	−0.022
Mothocp_bus	−0.031	0.155	−0.010
Mothocp_others	Reference category		
Father_ED	0.009	0.013	0.003
Mother_ED	0.002	0.011	0.0006
Nativity	−0.293***	0.079	−0.090
Student's academic background (at secondary school level)			
SEC_marks	0.023***	0.004	0.007
SEC_medium	−0.025	0.106	−0.008
SEC_board	−0.257***	0.084	−0.079
SEC_SCH_type	−0.068	0.078	−0.021
SEC_SCH_location	−0.084	0.119	−0.027
PRE_coaching	0.0009	0.070	0.002
Students' current education status			
ENGG_INST_type	0.758***	0.086	0.260
*ln*HHEXPR	−0.004	0.044	−0.001
Scholarship	0.002	0.096	0.0006
Loan	0.091	0.109	0.028
Part_time_work	−0.001	0.11	−0.0003
Employment prospects and educational aspirations			
Employment	−0.166**	0.081	−0.051
ED_ASP	−0.039	0.071	−0.012
Constant	−2.088	0.629	
Log likelihood	−890.356		
Pseudo R^2	0.097		
Number of observations	1,706		

Notes: (a) Statistically significant level: *** $p < 0.01$, ** $p < 0.05$, * $p < 0.10$.
(b) (#) Marginal effect, dy/dx, is for discrete change of dummy variable from 0 to 1. This shows the magnitude of impact of an explanatory variable on dependent variable.

While many students aspiring to go to engineering studies take coaching to prepare well for the entrance examination, a good number of students do not take coaching and yet obtain high ranks. Since there is higher competition for modern streams like computer science engineering, electronics and communication engineering and IT, students aspiring to get admission in such disciplines might more probably take pre-admission coaching than others. This is also confirmed by our results: those who go for coaching prefer and finally get admission in IT-related modern branches of engineering, though the coefficient is statistically not significant and very small in value. Interestingly, in both groups of streams, a majority of students were those who had not taken pre-coaching, as shown in Table 5.1.

Effect of Factors Related to Current Education of the Students

Among different factors related to current education of the students included in this category, the type of institution the students have taken admission (ENGG_TYPE) has a significant relationship, whereas other factors like whether the students have received educational loan or not (LOAN), whether the students have received scholarship or not (SCHOLARSHIP), facilities for part-time work (PART_TIME_WORK) and household cost of education (lnHHEXPR) are statistically not significant.

The results throw some light on the existing trade-off between type of institution and branch of study. The results show that students studying in private institutions are 76 per cent more likely to have opted for modern branches than the students studying in government institutions. This is largely because many private engineering institutions were established offering mainly IT-related streams. Provision of branches like mechanical and electrical engineering requires huge investment in laboratories and infrastructure, which the private institutions might not be interested to make. In contrast, most government institutions focus relatively more on providing strong traditional disciplines. The choice in the case of the type of institution and discipline of study are closely and intricately related, as we noted in Chapter 4.

Contrary to normal expectations, cost does not seem to matter much. The household cost, measured in the form of household expenditure and included as a continuous variable in logarithmic form in the estimation of logistic regression, turns out to be not as a significant variable. The coefficient is, however, negative in value, suggesting that higher cost dissuades the student to opt for modern disciplines. Student preference for a stream is not influenced by household expenditure. As per the survey data, the total household expenditure per student was ₹150,000 per year, which constitutes 47 per cent of the annual average income of the family, which is high, but it appears the difference in household expenditure between the disciplines is not high, as we shall see in Chapter 6.

Scholarship, educational loans and engagement in part-time work reduce the current financial burden of education on the households. They are also expected to influence the students' choice of streams. As per the estimated values of marginal effects in Table 5.2, variables on loans and scholarships, like total household expenditure, do have a positive effect on student's choices for IT-related areas, but the coefficients are not statistically significant. Part-time work opportunities have negative influence on students' preference for modern disciplines, though the coefficient is statistically not significant. As we have noted, the number of students receiving scholarship or loan or engaged in part-time work constitutes a small proportion of the total number of students.

Effect of Employment Prospects and Educational Aspirations

In recent years, engineering graduates usually enter the job market after completion of the undergraduate studies, and hence very few of them go for higher studies (i.e. to pursue masters and PhD-level programmes). But there are some who wish to go for further higher education, either in engineering or in some areas of higher education. Particularly those who are interested in academic careers may prefer to go for further studies. Management programmes are very popular among the engineering graduates in India. But students may also go for masters (and research) programmes in engineering and technology. So, depending upon their interests, students will chose those disciplines that offer better employment opportunities (in the country or outside) or those that facilitate progress to further higher studies.

Though the coefficient is not statistically significant, the results in Table 5.2 indicate that such a hypothesis is likely to be valid, and that students who desire to go for further study (to masters and doctorate level) are less likely to enrol in IT-related departments than the students who are not interested in further studies. Two plausible reasons for this are: (a) the available scope to do higher studies might be higher in traditional departments of engineering education than in IT-related studies; and (b) the relatively easy availability of jobs for the graduates of IT-related studies, that is, the students from IT-related disciplines possess higher opportunity cost of going for further studies than the students from traditional disciplines.

More importantly, as expected, the probability of getting employment after graduation (EMPLOYMENT) has a statistically significant influence on choice of a stream of study. It is found that job offer from on-campus recruitment is positively associated with increasing the probability of attending IT-related branches by 2 percentage points higher than a stream with lower employment probabilities – the traditional disciplines. Students taking admission in IT-related branches have higher chances of getting jobs in the labour market than the students enrolled in traditional departments. Thus, students seem to consider on-campus recruitment records of various disciplines and institutions while making a choice between admission in alternative disciplines and institutions. However, it is also argued that students not only take expected economic returns into account when choosing a stream, but also they consider their chances of academic success.

Summary of Findings

Engineering education has expanded fast in India in the last three decades. However, all branches of engineering education have not grown at the same pace. While the standard traditional branches like mechanical, civil and electrical engineering had been popular for a long time, in recent years areas like electronics engineering, computer science engineering and IT-related engineering have evolved fast. Senior secondary school graduates face a dilemma of making a rational choice in selecting the disciplines of their study. An attempt has been made in this chapter to examine the factors that influence students in their decision-making, relating to choice of main streams in engineering education at undergraduate level, by estimating probit regression equation. We identified a few major factors – individual, household, academic background of the students, current educational practices, future employment prospects and educational aspirations – as possible determinants in this context and the results are discussed in detail in the previous pages. A few key signals are clear from the analysis:

- The probability of seeking admission in modern/IT-related departments is significantly higher among the students belonging to general (caste) category than the students belonging to SCs and STs. Surprisingly, belonging to the group of OBCs increases the probability of enrolling in IT-related disciplines as compared to general category students. Perhaps OBCs are as good as the general category, if not better, with respect to their socio-economic background. Similarly, the other individual characteristics that determine the probability of attending IT-related courses include gender. Compared to male students, female students are more likely to choose IT-related branches, though gender differences are not very marked.
- Native place of the students is found to be statistically significant in explaining the students' choice. Students migrate to other states to take admission in modern disciplines, while a majority of those who do not migrate get enrolled in traditional streams. However, many other household characteristics are found to be statistically not significant but the coefficients give expected results.
- In the case of academic background of students, performance in the higher secondary-level examination turns out to be a statistically significant factor in the students' choice of streams. Higher the percentage of marks scored in higher secondary examination, the higher is the probability of taking admission in IT-related departments than in traditional branches of engineering. This confirms the general belief that meritorious students score high percentage of marks in their senior secondary examination and also perform better in the competitive common entrance examination and finally opt for modern branches. Similarly, students who graduated from schools affiliated to state (provincial) board are less likely to enrol in such stream as against traditional departments. Generally, the quality is believed to be better in schools affiliated to central boards, and hence better students seem to opt for modern courses in engineering.

- The results also show strong positive relationship between enrolment in modern branches and enrolment in private institutions. After all, many private engineering institutions offer admissions more in modern/IT-related disciplines than in traditional areas, while many government institutions concentrate on providing education relatively more in traditional areas. Note that the traditional branches require higher investment in relatively more expensive laboratories and instruments, which many private institutions may not be forthcoming to make.
- As expected, employment potential and enrolment in streams are also related. Students taking admission in IT-related courses visualise higher chances of getting better or faster employment in the labour market than the students enrolled in other areas.

Some of the results are in conformity with general understanding and some not. This study provides empirical evidence and unravels some of the issues involved in the students' choice of engineering streams at undergraduate level.

An important limitation of the study is that we assume free choice for the students to select the discipline of their like. But in practice this is not the case. There is a severe supply constraint, in addition to several kinds of market imperfections, including asymmetry of information that do not allow true free choice principle to operate. Second, there may be several important factors that we could not consider in our quantitative analysis, constrained essentially by the survey data that formed the basis of this study. Many important related aspects could not be captured in the survey. For example, dowry, an important feature in Indian society, may have a very dominating effect on the students' choice of branches in engineering. Engineering graduates in IT-related disciplines carry higher dowry. Women also tend to prefer such graduates for marriage. Further, scope for emigration to the western world for higher studies or for employment also does influence students' choices. There may be several other quantifiable or intangible factors that could not be brought into this quantitative exercise here. So the results need to be interpreted subject to these limitations.

It has been found here that almost everyone prefers to choose modern streams as against traditional branches of engineering. Indian economy is already experiencing a situation of a glut in the labour market with 'IT' engineers. The quality of these IT graduates is also on the decline. Their labour market returns are experiencing a downward trend. But more importantly, engineering education scene is getting imbalanced, with more and more low-quality private institutions concentrating on modern disciplines at the cost of standard traditional disciplines. Due to the asymmetry of information, students' preference for engineering education is still high, and more specifically, the demand in favour of IT-related disciplines is growing. But traditional areas are also important for the rapidly growing economy. Low turnout of graduates from traditional departments in years to come may pose a serious bottleneck in the rapidly industrialising and fast modernising economy. Public attention is required on how to boost demand for standard disciplines of engineering in order to have a balanced development of all disciplines of engineering and how to check the growth and functioning of low-quality private institutions, which are actually fragmenting engineering education, by focusing on some disciplines at the cost of some basic and standard subjects. The trends observed here on engineering graduates in India, dominated by market forces, are not unique. Many other countries are experiencing similar trends. Higher education, particularly engineering/technical education, is growing very fast in many developing and advanced countries like China, Brazil and Russia, to mention a few. Quite a few countries are also experiencing unbalanced growth of several branches in engineering education of the kind noted here; and they are also experiencing frequent labour market imbalances. Hence the analysis attempted and the results arrived at here could be of policy relevance for many other countries.

Notes

1 According to luck egalitarianism, distributions should reflect the choices that it is reasonable to hold agents responsible for, while the differential effects of 'brute luck' must be compensated for. It is associated with the theorists such as Arneson (1989, 1990), Cohen (1989) and Dworkin (1981, 2002, 2003).
2 But this is not considered here due to unavailability of data. Even if available, aggregation of education at household level may be subject to methodological problems and errors.
3 In a few states in India, places in engineering institutions are reserved for natives (residents of the state) and a small proportion (around 15 per cent) for outsiders (outside the state).
4 They are not eligible for admission in medicine and so on, though they can opt for general (arts, humanities, sciences etc.) subjects.
5 Contrary evidence also exists: students do not only take expected economic returns into account when choosing a discipline, but also their chances of academic success. Rochat and Demeulemeester (2001) provide a detailed analysis on this aspect in the context of Belgium higher education.
6 The same variable is also used in Chapter 9 to analyse the employment and earnings of engineering graduates.

6 Family Expenditure on Engineering Education and Its Determinants

Introduction

Expenditure on education is incurred in two major domains: public and household. Both are crucial for the social investment in education to be optimum (Majumdar, 1983). Normally, there are important complementarities between the two; but often the two either complement each other or in some contexts substitute each other (Tilak, 1991; Wolf & Zohlnhöfer, 2009; OECD, 2020b). In either case, both are critical for education process, as in the absence of either of them, optimal investment does not take place. Both public and family expenditures[1] on education are of crucial importance for children's development and learning. As Lunn and Kornrich (2018, p. 159) observed, "current family spending patterns may have significant consequences for future generations' well-being".

How much should parents spend on their children's education? This is an important question for reasons of distributive justice and economic efficiency, as it is generally not desirable in either case to base human capital investments in children on the parents and their incomes (Hoxby, 1998, p. 309). While there are no precise answers to this question, a few considerations are widely recognised as important when discussing this issue. First, education, including higher education, is a public good, benefiting all in the society. Second, promotion of equal access to education is an important objective of every modern welfare state. Third, ability to pay of the families or individual choices should not determine the policies on financing of education, including the decisions by the families to enrol their children in education and their financing.

What are the current patterns of family financing of education? Available statistics show that in many countries, households meet a sizeable part of total investment in education; further, families in many developing countries spend far higher amounts on education than those in developed countries. Even among the poorest countries, household expenditures on education are sizeable. This is true, as shown in Figure 6.1, even in the case of higher education. With families meeting sizeable parts of the costs of education, they are

DOI: 10.4324/9781003430223-8

174 *Economics of Engineering Education in India*

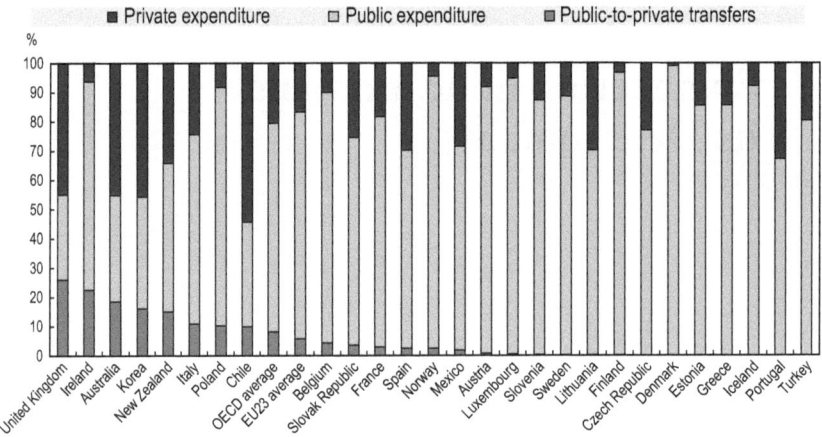

Figure 6.1 Public and Private (Household) Expenditure on Tertiary Education in OECD Countries, 2017

Note: International expenditure is aggregated with public expenditure.

Source: OECD/UIS/Eurostat (2020a)

increasingly recognised as 'hidden funders' of education (Huebler & Lega, 2017).

For a long time, it was believed that families in India do not spend much on education, and that education, including higher education, is provided by the state nearly free to everyone or it is highly subsidised. Such a presumption remained unchallenged for a long time, as evidence on family expenditures on education in India has been scarce. It has remained for a long time as an unexplored terrain. The only source of data on family expenditure on education available for a long time has been the *National Accounts Statistics* (Government of India) that provides data on 'private final consumption expenditure' on education (earlier combined with recreation etc.). Until the National Sample Survey Organisation (NSSO) launched the 42nd round in 1986–87, which provided for the first time detailed data on household expenditure on education, the few studies conducted (e.g. Tilak, 1985, 1991, 1995, 2000, 2002c; Motkuri & Revathi, 2020) were based only on National Accounts Statistics. But since only an aggregate gross figure – for all levels of education together, and with no details by items – is available in this source, analyses have been restricted, though some useful insights came out, such as the size of expenditure incurred by households on education relative to total private (household) expenditure in comparison with government expenditure on education or as a proportion of national income, estimates of coefficients of elasticity and determinants of household expenditures. Factors considered for examination of determinants included household characteristics, individual characteristics, parental occupation, parental education and a few supply-side factors. Though the NSS initiated the education survey in

1986–87, it was the 52nd round conducted in 1995–96 which was the first survey extensively used by scholars expanding the framework of examining determinants of household expenditure on education. While the NSSO continues to conduct education surveys regularly, a few others such as the India Human Development Surveys (by the National Council of Applied Economic Research) and the National Family and Health Surveys (by the Indian Institute of Population Studies) have also been conducted in recent years, covering some aspects of education. The National Sample Surveys conducted from 1986 to 1987 (42nd round) onwards have provided valuable evidence to show that families do spend considerable amounts on education – on 'free' primary (Tilak, 1996) to higher education.[2] The evidence also shows that family expenditures incurred by students and/or their families on higher education had grown fast by 82 per cent in about a decade between 2007–08 and 2017–18, as shown in Table 6.1. The expenditure varies by the areas of study, with engineering and medicine costing much higher than other streams of study. Households also have to spend higher amounts in the case of studies in private institutions than in government-aided or government institutions. In Table 6.2, we further notice that not only professional/technical education costs much higher than general higher education, but also that there are sharp differences between urban and rural households and also between males and females. While gender differences are not high in general higher education, these are marked in professional and technical education. Interestingly, on average, households spend higher amounts on first degree (graduate level) studies than postgraduate studies. Postgraduate studies are generally more subsidised. The high level of expenditure may be beyond the economic capacity of many of the families in India (Nair, 2004).

The high level of expenditure and the trend of increasing household expenses on education might imply growing inequity in education, which is a serious concern of a welfare state. After all, the high burden that the families face with high and increasing levels of family expenditures on higher education creates a situation in which higher education would be unaffordable for most people in the low- and middle-income groups and at the same time widening further the inequalities in education.

Table 6.1 Household Expenditure on Higher Education per Student Across Major Areas of Study (₹ per Annum)

	2007–08	2017–18	Increase (%)
Humanities	5,596	11,161	99.45
Science	11,350	19,419	71.09
Commerce	8,420	18,478	119.45
Medical science	40,160	85,972	114.07
Engineering	43,654	70,575	61.67
Others	23,698	53,606	126.20
All	14,519	26,423	81.99

Source: Compiled by the author based on NSS 64th (2007–08) and 75th round (2017–18) data.

Table 6.2 Household Expenditure on Higher Education in India (₹ per Student/per Annum)

	All	Rural	Urban	Male	Female
General Higher Education					
2014					
Graduate	13,478	11,527	16,771	13,324	13,649
Postgraduate and above	15,999	14,604	17,744	15,417	16,641
2007–08					
Above higher secondary	7,360	6,327	8,466	7,386	7,324
2014					
Professional and Technical Education					
Graduate	73,342	60,832	80,414	74,341	71,683
Postgraduate	71,431	52,358	82,181	68,152	75,891
Engineering Education					
Government	42,401	40,832	43,418	43,710	38,367
Government-aided Private	69,996	61,516	74,291	70,248	67,873
Private (Unaided)	78,227	68,439	83,443	78,449	77,995

Source: Based on NSSO (2016).

Research on the determinants of family expenditure on higher education is very valuable for public policy making, but it is virtually non-existent in India; many studies concentrated on primary or elementary or school education. But the significance of studies on higher education is increasingly recognised, particularly in the context of dwindling public budgets and in the context of formulation of alternative public policies on financing of higher education, more specifically on the cost recovery measures in higher education. Public policies are being formulated based on feeble research evidence.

Why do families invest in education of their children? Some pose the same question: how much people are willing to invest in their children's education? But this may not be right, as families may feel compelled to invest in and may not be voluntarily 'willing' to spend on education. Typically, families invest in education as they have high expectations from spending on education. Family investment in higher education is influenced by a wide variety of factors. Household investments in education exhibit characteristics of instrumental rationality as well as emotional expressions (Lin, 2019). Keeping the emotional expressions such as love, respect and treating it as a noble responsibility or an essential mechanisms of strengthening of family relationships through parental investments on children's education aside, however important they are, the decision-making process of households regarding investment in education can be understood at least partly in terms of economic factors, as per the human capital theory (Becker, 1975). Mostly, families invest in education, anticipating significant lifetime benefits from education – economic and non-economic. The net economic benefits of education are measured familiarly in terms of earnings and internal rates of return. Despite several limitations that the estimates of rates of return are associated with, they are found to be useful in educational planning, including in the investment of decision-making process, both in the public and household domains. According to available evidence, rates of return to higher education are high, both to the individual and to the society at large (Tilak, 1987; Duraisamy & Duraisamy, 1993; Carnoy et al., 2012). In the life cycle model of household decisions at the micro economic level, if returns to education are high, families may choose to invest in education in order to increase the earnings capacity and other benefits in the future, even by refraining from present consumption. But if the income of the household is low, effective demand for higher education can be low, and there can be serious under-investment in education, resulting in a loss to the individual and society at large. Families may or may not be willing to borrow money for education, as education is 'risky'; moreover, the credit market for higher education is generally imperfect and yet to be developed in many developing countries (Tilak, 1997). Thus, it is mostly felt that the levels of investment of the households in education are related to household income levels. A general finding is that families with high income levels spend higher than families with low income levels on education. If the expected private rates of return – monetary and/or non-monetary – are attractive, households may not necessarily be spending on education constrained by ability to pay and also by other economic, social and cultural factors, which are the principal focus of examination here.

It is also possible that families feel compelled to spend on education if public efforts are inadequate, which reflected in the limited number of public institutions and unsatisfactory quality of physical and human infrastructure available in those educational institutions. As a result, even poor households might spend on education out of compulsion. So one can say that the lower the quantum of public institutions and quality of infrastructure and other facilities in public institutions, *ceteris pari bus*, higher could be the level of household expenditure on education and vice versa. Hence, household expenditure on education can be relatively higher in developing countries where public investment is low than in rich countries. If the public provision of education is reasonably good, families may not feel the need for spending on their own, particularly on private education. Therefore, it can be argued that household expenditure substitutes public investments in education, as they fill the gap in investments, caused by shortages in public investments in developing countries. On the other hand, it is also argued that if government spends well on education and provides good quality education, households might feel enthusiastic and willingly contribute to education, and thus supplement pubic efforts. Thus household and government investments in education are related, either substituting or complementing each other. Supply-related factors, thus, might be an important set of factors that determine the extent of household investments in education (Tilak, 2002a).

Due to various social, cultural and personal reasons, families may have strong preference to spend on the education of their children or vice versa. In fact, several characteristics of the families, such as religion, caste, household size, educational and occupational levels of the parents and so forth, which could be called social, cultural, economic, demographic, educational, occupational and other factors, might also influence the nature and quantum of expenditure that the households spend on education of their children. This chapter examines the pattern of family[3] expenditure on engineering education in India and the determinants of the same.

Review of Literature

There is a vast amount of literature on household expenditure on education in many countries. Apart from measuring the extent of household expenditure on education and analysing growth, rural-urban, and male-female differences in it, by drawing from Engel's law (curve) of family expenditure in economics (Lewbel & Houthakker, 2008) which describes how household expenditure in absolute real terms or as a proportion of the household budget on a particular good or service varies with household income, and Working's (1943) statistical laws of family expenditure which state that distribution of household expenditure is influenced by a variety of factors such as family customs and standards and the goods and services that the family have to choose, to mention a few; many scholars have examined the relationship between household income and household expenditure on education and estimated coefficients of elasticity. Since household expenditure has been found to vary by many other macro growth (e.g. economic) and household, including individual characteristics (e.g. gender, race, region and caste), researchers have examined varying patterns of household expenditures on education. Some have also attempted to examine various probable factors, including household income, that influence household expenditure on education.

Some researchers have compared household and public expenditure on education and examined the relationship between the two (Williams, 1983 in Australia; Tilak, 2002a; Sarkar, 2017a; Motkuri & Revathi, 2020, in India) and have highlighted the complementary or substituting roles of each other. Income elasticities of educational expenditure have been estimated by several scholars in many countries (Hashimoto & Health, 1995 in Japan; Psacharopoulos et al., 1997 in Bolivia; Tilak, 2002a, in India; Psacharopoulos & Papakonstantinou, 2005, in Greece; Tansel & Bircan, 2006, in Turkey; Omori, 2010, in the US; Qian & Smyth, 2011, in China). Based on coefficients of income elasticity, Tilak (1991) has concluded that households do not necessarily respond more promptly than government to educational needs in India, contrary to what Schultz (1981) has argued.

When determinants of household expenditure on education are examined, family income or economic level measured by proxy variables has been found to be having significant incremental effect on household expenditure on education. Donkoh and Amikuzuno (2011) analysed several factors that determine the household spending on education in Ghana and found that though female headed households tend to spend less than male headed households, it was concluded that the difference is mainly because female headed households' affordability to spend on education is much less than those of male headed households. A positive relationship between household income and investment in education (in absolute values) has been found in many studies, the probability of spending on education increasing with household income (expenditure) level (e.g. Tan, 1985; Psacharopoulos et al., 1997; Kanellopoulos & Psacharopoulos, 1997; King, 1998; Acevedo & Salinas, 2000; Psacharopoulos & Mattson, 2000; Tilak, 2000, 2002a; Urwick, 2002; Tansel & Bircan, 2006; Omori, 2010; Qian & Smyth, 2011; Shafiq, 2011; Rizk & Owusu-Afriyie, 2014; Acar et al., 2016; Acerenza & Gandelman, 2017; Asankha & Ajantha, 2020; Demiroglari & Gürler, 2020). But the economic burden of expenditure is higher on families with lower incomes (Duraisamy & Duraisamy, 2016; Lakshmanasamy, 2017), as poorer households tend to spend a higher proportion of their budgets on education than richer households. In other words, as income levels rise, families tend to spend proportionately a lower proportion of their income on education. Like in many other countries, in Greece poorer families were found to be spending a higher share of their income on the education of their children (Psacharopoulos & Papakonstantinou, 2005). In a few other studies, the patterns have turned out to be the other way. For example, Kanellopoulos and Psacharopoulos (1997) found that households in Greece belonging to the bottom 20 per cent of the expenditure distribution spent only 6.5 per cent of their annual income on education, whereas it was 55.8 per cent in case of households belonging to the upper 20 per cent. According to Sengupta et al. (2008), rich households in India spend on education a higher proportion of their total consumption expenditure. The household expenditure on education seems to be a necessity for all, the coefficient of income elasticity being of the order of 0.2–0.3. In addition, they spend privately more than the state in order to prepare for the entrance examinations and while studying at the university. Among the families who actually spend money on their children's education, it is the low-income households that use a higher share of their household budget for education – overall as well as on individual items, this pattern is not universal. For example, Carsten et al. (2015) found that considering all families/households in Germany, higher-income families spend more on education, "*both in absolute and relative terms*" (emphasis added).

As this proportion is usually interpreted as the relative value or importance the families attach to education, one cannot exactly state that it is the poor or the rich income groups which attach higher value to education than others, though many have asserted that the poor families do attach higher value to education, as they do not possess much of any other capital. The household expenditure on education seems to be a necessity for all, the income elasticity being of the order of 0.2–0.3. In addition, they spend privately more than the state in order to prepare for the entrance examinations and while studying at the university. Family expenditures are income elasticity overall, but the coefficients of elasticity are very different in magnitude for lower-income compared to higher-income families. For example, Bayar (2016) observed low-income households having higher-income elasticity of education expenditures in African societies; Jenkins et al. (2019) have found in a study on Nigeria that the income elasticity of education expenditures are approximately four times higher for households in the bottom two-thirds of the income distribution than for those on the top one-third. Zhang and Zhou (2017), who analysed household expenditure on education in China, observed that the expenditure has a positive effect on the scores of students, particularly among those who are in top quintiles of academic achievement. Examining the determinants of household expenditure on school education in rural India, Tilak (2002a) has concluded that households tend to spend more on education with the increase of their income, the value of the coefficient of income elasticity being 0.2. Most of these studies found that household income is an important determinant of household expenditure on education.

There is, however, a threshold level of income for it to have an effect on household spending. For instance, Nahm and Hyung (2009) highlighted that households with relatively low education level do not increase investment on education than those with relatively high education level until their income level approaches some threshold level; once that is reached, investment on education begins to increase. Another finding by Nahm and Hyung (2009) on income elasticity tells us that private education is a 'normal' good, indicating that households invest more and more at any income levels as their income increases.

Several scholars have paid serious attention to examining gender differences in household expenditure on education (e.g. Tan, 1985; Panchamukhi, 1990; Hashimoto & Heath, 1995; Kanellopoulos & Psacharopoulos, 1997; Acevedo & Salinas, 2000; Psacharopoulos & Mattson, 2000; Tilak, 2000, 2002a, b; Li & Tsang, 2003; Gong et al., 2005; Kingdon, 2005; Tilak & Nalla Gounden, 2005; Chaudhuri & Roy, 2006; Tansel & Bircan, 2006; Yueh, 2006; Dang, 2007; Aslam & Kingdon, 2008; Lancaster et al., 2008;Himaz, 2010; Shafiq, 2011; Masterson, 2012; Zimmermann, 2012; Saha, 2013; Kumar, 2017; Iddrisu et al., 2018). Pro-male bias in spending on education was observed to be prominent in India and in several other countries (Subramanian & Deaton, 1991; Tilak, 2002a; Kingdon, 2005; Choudhury, 2012; Zimmermann, 2012; Azam & Kingdon, 2013). Datta and Kingdon (2019) further observe that gender bias in enrolment and expenditure on education are related; examination of one ignoring the other does not give a complete picture. Many studied these two separately as if they are independent of each other. Many of these studies are on school education. Such gender differences have been found to be high in higher education also (Chaudhuri & Roy, 2006; Lancaster et al., 2008; Kambhampati, 2008; Kaul, 2018). Quite a few studies (e.g. Aslam & Kingdon, 2008; Himaz, 2009) have confirmed that the variation in household investment in education by gender is due to the parents' preference for better quality education for boys over girls, as parents assume that higher spending means quality. Households' preference for boys as against girls in investing in education is widely prevalent; such a preference widens further at higher levels of education. But the preferences or biases are not the same in all countries or in all areas of a country or in all age groups of children in a country. For example, when geographical area and age group-specific regression models are run separately on the data of a district in Jammu & Kashmir (Beg & Bhatt, 2021), the results show that in the rural areas, in the age group of 15–18 years, there is a significant gender bias favouring boys in annual expenditure on education, and the results do not show any significant differences in household's education expenditure in urban areas. In urban China, there was a higher level of spending on younger boys (aged 13–15) and older girls (aged 16–18), based on which Yueh (2006) questions the general interpretation of pro-male (or pro-female) bias in household spending on education.

There are quite a few studies in which pro-female bias was observed (Acrenza & Gandelman, 2019). Some might feel that investment on girls' education might help in reducing dowry, as some boys might willingly marry higher educated girls with less or even without any dowry, anticipating that their total household earnings would be higher in the future because of the girl's higher education and corresponding employment. In Kerala, one finds a pattern of higher spending on girls than on boys (Layan, 2013). Expenditure per pupil is higher on girls' education than that on boys' in Maharashtra, Karnataka and Rajasthan (Panchamukhi, 1990), in Tamil Nadu (Tilak & Nalla Gounden, 2005) and in a few other states where a large-scale UNICEF survey was conducted on elementary education Mehrotra (2005). Similarly, households in urban Bangladesh were less likely to spend on education of the boys than of the girls, holding all else constant (Shafiq, 2011). Gender discrimination in the household expenditure on education does not necessarily exist in all cases (Acerenza & Gandelman, 2019; Tilak, 2000; Dang, 2007). Ganpule (2018), in a study on Mumbai, has found that household expenditure on education (from grade I to graduate level) of girls is related to household income, but not in the case of expenditure on boys. There is also some interactive effect of economic conditions and gender of the student on family spending. As Sarkar (2017b) has found, while household income has a significant effect on family spending on higher education of their children in India, the effect is higher in girls' education. According to Masterson (2012), asset ownership affects female bargaining power within households which result in gender bias in expenditure on education in Paraguay. Interplay of gender of the child with parental economic status has also been highlighted by some. An interesting hypothesis, known as Trivers-Willard (1973) hypothesis, has seen mothers in good economic conditions invest more in sons, whereas mothers in poorer conditions invest more in daughters (described by Hopcroft & Martin, 2016). On average, as Begum et al. (2014) have concluded, there is "no systematic inherent gender bias among parents, yet inherently biased parents allocate resources in a discriminatory manner" within the family. Moreover, bias against girls reflected in parental sexual selection which has been a wide spread phenomenon (Trivers, 1972), bias against girls' education and bias against spending on girls' education prevalent in many developing societies need to be distinguished. But it has been rarely attempted.

Apart from household income and gender, a variety of household factors are generally found to be very important determinants of household investments in education in many studies. Numerous studies have also highlighted the importance of caste in influencing family expenditure on education in India (Choudhury, 2012; Gangopadhyay & Sarkar, 2013; Sarkar, 2017b) and race in Sri Lanka (Asankha & Ajantha, 2020). Family expenditures on education differ across racial and ethnic groups in many countries, however, the differences are actually not found to be statistically significant in some studies. For example, Luo and Holden (2014a; also 2014b) have shown that when one compares families with similar household incomes and parental education levels, the household expenditures on higher education are essentially the same across all racial and ethnic groups; as parents' education and income level increase, so do the expenditure for higher education. They conclude from their study on the US that "from another perspective, socioeconomic differences, not differences in race or ethnicity, have a greater influence on how families value higher education investments".

Several empirical studies have shown that parental education has a significant positive influence on household investments on education (e.g. Brown, 2006; Quang, 2012; Acrenza & Gandelman, 2017; Kuvat & Ayvaz Kizilgöl, 2020). In a study on Cyprus (Andreou, 2012), it was found that in addition to household income, education of the head of the household, number of children in the household and region were the most important determinants of household expenditure on education. Among the many household factors, education of the head of the household figures prominently, apart from household income. That educated parents (and other educated adults) are likely to be more aware of the future benefits of education, and hence spend more on it, is established in a good number of studies in several countries (e.g. Tan, 1985; Kanellopoulos & Psacharopoulos, 1997; Tilak, 2002b; Chaudhuri & Roy, 2006; Dang, 2007; Omori, 2010; Masterson, 2012; Saha, 2013; Gangopadhyay & Sarkar, 2014; Minello & Blossfeld, 2017; Sarkar, 2017b). According to Psacharopoulos and Mattson (2000), an increase in the years of schooling of the head of household by one year leads to an increase in household expenditure on primary education by 8 per cent in Bolivia. The education level of the head of the household has an incremental effect on private spending in China (Yueh, 2006) and US (Omori, 2010). Differential effects of mother's and father's education on family spending on education are also widely noted. Some available research evidence also shows that the mother's education is having a higher effect on household expenditure on education than father's education (e.g. Tansel & Bircan, 2006; Kambhampati, 2008; Shafiq, 2011). Emerson and Souza (2007) also concluded that mother's education has a higher effect on daughters' school attendance than father's impact on sons' school attendance in Brazil. In general, as Saha (2013, p. 233) has reported, the higher the educational level of the parents/guardians, the greater is the level of expenditure on education of their offspring in India. There are very few exceptions to this on the importance of education of the parents/head of the household. According to Mahmood et al. (1992), education of the head of the household is not an important determinant of children's education; it only influences lifestyles of the people. Thus, it is not only gender of the child/student, but also the gender of the head of the household which also matters (Jenkins et al., 2019). In addition to household factors, macroeconomic factors like gross domestic product, public expenditure and availability of educational institutions and their quality are also found to be important by some scholars (Tilak, 2000; Layan, 2013).

Large households have to spend higher proportions of their income on essential items such as food, accommodation, clothing and other related items, leaving little amounts of resources for education, which also get diluted across number of siblings in the household, not necessarily uniformly (Downey, 1995). Hence, the per student expenditure made by the households on education and the size of the family or 'sibship' (Downey, 1995) can be expected to be inversely related, as has been found in a number of studies in many countries (e.g. McMahon, 1974; Psacharopoulos & Mattson, 2000; Tilak, 2000, 2002a; Tansel & Bircan, 2006). Demiroglari and Gürler (2020) have clearly found that there is a trade-off between the family investment made on the child and the number of children in the household. Single child households in China tend to spend more than the families with more than one child (Lin, 2019). We also find exceptions to this. In urban Bangladesh, the presence of older children in the family does not affect the decision of the households on the quantum of spending on education (Shafiq, 2011). It is not just the number of children in a household, more importantly, the characteristics of the children – gender, age, order, education status and so on – also matter in the distribution of family resources. For example, in Vietnam households with more primary school age or secondary school age children spend more on education, while households with pre-school age or college age children spend less on education (Quang, 2012). Parents may also be willing to spend more on the education of those children who perform better in their education than others (Asadi, 2020). According to Steelman and Powell (1991), in the US, parental investments in higher education of their children are shaped by their income, the number of children and also by many other characteristics, gender of parent and child, academic achievement of child, marital status, education and educational aspirations and so on. They may have mixed – stronger and weaker – effects. Thus, many studies confirm the influence of family structure on family investments in education.

Among the various items of household expenditure on education, expenditure on coaching or tutoring has been considered specifically by some and how this is influenced by various social, economic, educational and locational factors (Mitra & Sarkar, 2019). According to a CARE Ratings study (Sindhwani, 2019), Indian students are somewhat surprisingly found to be spending enormously on their higher education even when job prospects are not bright. As some (e.g. Chandrasekhar & Ghosh, 2020) have warned, this is "increasingly risky given the terrible state of the job market" and the high household expenditure and graduate unemployment "may well boomerang on society". Besides finding that professional/technical education costs to the households are much higher than general education, the study also highlights that between 2007 and 2018, household costs on professional education increased by more than 50 per cent. Among various professional disciplines in terms of household costs, the increasing order is law, management, information technology (IT), engineering and medicine, with law costing the least and medicine the highest. Choudhury (2019b) has examined the determinants separately of expenditure on fee and non-fee items in engineering education. While based on an analysis of National Sample Survey data in India, we noted in Chapter 3 that non-fee expenditure on engineering education forms only one-fourth of total (fee plus non-fee) expenditure. Choudhury and Kumar (2021) have found that non-fee expenditure on engineering education is almost the same as expenditure on fees in engineering education in Odisha. In a different study on engineering education in a backward state (Odisha) in India, Choudhury (2019b) has found that household expenditure constitutes about 30 per cent of the family income in the rural tribal population. Household expenditure in Turkey was sizeable on private schooling and tutoring, as a the study by Acar et al (2016). Further, analysing in the Engle curve framework, it has been found that for middle (and upper) income groups, education is a luxury good, as they spend higher amounts on quality, while low income groups consider it as a necessity. Further, as Choudhury has found, caste, religion and the type of institution in which the student is enrolled are the most significant determinants of household spending. In another study on engineering education in Delhi, the annual average household expenditure on undergraduate engineering education was observed to be higher for students interested in undertaking postgraduate study and beyond compared to the students who did not wish to pursue further education after their undergraduate degree studies (Choudhury, 2012).

Thus, one can note that though there are a good number of studies in many countries on family expenditure on education, in India such literature is not abundant; the small number also got confined to primary or school education. In the case of higher education, there are hardly a handful of studies, and it is further scanty in technical or engineering education. While family expenditure on education and its determinants have been examined in the literature, very few studies have focused on engineering education in India.

Since engineering education is relatively more expensive than general higher education and even other branches of professional/technical higher education, except medicine, engineering education may require special attention. But for the studies by Choudhury (2012, 2019b) Choudhury and Kumar (2021), there are very few studies on family expenditure on engineering education in India. Hence, the present examination may have to be seen as an important addition to the existing limited literature, though it does not claim any advances in theoretical or methodological aspects. It does, however, shed light on parental preferences expressed through expenditures on their children's engineering education.

Methodologically, while estimating simple income elasticity coefficients, double log regression equations are used extensively, and in most studies on determinants of household expenditure, ordinary least squares regression equation and in some cases logit or probit and also occasionally Tobit models have been used. Studies on India also used mostly the data of the National Sample Surveys; a few the India Human Development Surveys (National Council of Applied Economic Research) and National Family and Health Surveys; and very few are based on student-/graduate-based surveys conducted at micro level. Even with respect to studies on other countries, national-level consumption/expenditure and income surveys are extensively used. Very few studies are based on large student-based surveys.

Descriptive Aspects on Family Expenditure on Engineering Education

Family expenditure on education includes the expenditure incurred by students/their parents/families on education, on tuition fees, other fees (library fees, examination fees, fees on games and sports, etc.), accommodation, food, transport, textbooks, stationery, reference books and other study material, computers/laptops/ipads, internet connection, mobile phones and other necessay items. It also includes expendiure incurred on improving communications in English language, which has become an important essential component among many students in higher education in India in recent years. These expenses on various items are broadly classified into three categories: (a) expenditure on fees which includes tuition fees, library fees, examination fees, fees on games and sports and so on, which are compulsory payments to the institution; (b) non-fee expenditures like accommodation, food, transport, textbooks and reference books, stationery and other materials; and (c) 'additional' or extra expendture on items and activities such as improving communication skills in English language, computers, internet connection, mobile phones and so on. The total family expenditure on education is a sum total of all the three components; all three components of family expenditure are important as every item is strongly or otherwise related with the educational process. While household cost or investment includes opportunity costs of education, household expenditure does not include it.

Expenditure on both fees and non-fee items may vary by socio-economic background of the students, the institution one studies in and other characteristics, as some might get full or partial tuition waivers and some might get scholarships or some other financial assistance from the state or institution, which might reduce net family expenditure on education. But for tuition waivers – partial or full – expenditure on fee may not vary much by socio-economic background of the student in a given type of institution. On items of non-fee expenditure, some may spend higher or smaller amounts than others, but variations may not necessarily be very large. However, *additional* expenditure is more elastic to family income on the one hand and the needs of the students on the other, as in some cases students may avoid or spend higher or lower amounts on additional items. For example, some students may purchase reference books and laptops and others may use the facilities available in the institution or share the facilities available with other students. In some cases, institutions provide laptops to all the students 'free', the costs of which are often actually charged to the students under fee or different heads.

Table 6.2 presents a few descriptive aspects of family expenditure on engineering education in India, based on our survey. First, we note that family expenditure on engineering education in India is substantial, in absolute terms and as a share in the total family income. On average, families spend around ₹1.47 lakhs annually per student on undergraduate level of engineering education. Fee accounts for 35.2 per cent, non-fee items 33.6 per cent and additional items 31.2 per cent of the total. Annual average fee paid by the students on average was ₹51,700, which constituted 35 per cent of the total family expenditure on engineering education. Tuition fees account for as high as 80 per cent in total fees and the rest 20 per cent is accounted by library fees, examination fees, fees on games, sports and so forth. Tuition fee forming a large share in the total fees is common, though there exist some inter-institutional differences in the proportion of tuition fees and other fees to total fees. Tuition fee varies between government institutions and private institutions on the one hand and between several private institutions or between several public institutions even within a state, as explained later. Expenditure on non-fee-related items which is, on average, of the order of ₹49,400 per year, constitute nearly 34 per cent of the total expenditure. Almost 40 per cent of non-fee expenditure goes towards dormitory and food while the rest is incurred on textbooks, stationery and other items. As hostel facilities in public institutions are not adequate and may not exist in many institutions, students have to incur huge expenditure on accommodation and food.

As a result, students coming from outside have to take private accommodation on rent, which is normally costlier, and have to spend more. Further, as they stay away from the campus, they have to spend on transport also. Students are found to be spending 11 per cent of the non-fee (or 6 per cent of the total family) expenditure on daily transport. The expenditure on additional items was ₹45,800, which forms 31 per cent of the total. Coaching

Table 6.3 Family Expenditure on Engineering Education per Student, by Items of Expenditure (₹ per Annum)

Items of Expenditure	Per Student Family Expenditure	Percentage of Total	Percentage of Annual Family Income
Fees			
Tuition fees	42,089	28.65	13.49
Other fees	9,610	6.54	3.08
Total	51,699	35.19	16.57
Non-fee expenditure			
Dormitories/housing	18,952	12.90	6.08
Food	13,910	9.47	4.46
Textbooks and other study material	3,911	2.66	1.25
Transport	5,398	3.67	1.73
Others	7,221	4.92	2.31
Total	49,392	33.62	15.83
Additional expenditure			
Communication in English	9,378	6.38	3.01
Computer/laptop	11,883	8.09	3.81
Internet connection and mobiles	7,458	5.08	2.39
Entrainment/other related expenses	11,647	7.93	3.73
Others	5,457	3.71	1.75
Total	45,823	31.19	14.69
Grand Total	146,914	100.00	47.09

and tutoring for improving their communication skills in English language means an additional expenditure of ₹9,400 on average. All this takes away about half of the total family income. Expenditure per student on total fees accounts for 16.5 per cent of average family income – tuition fee 13.5 per cent and other fees 3 per cent.

Expenditure on non-fee items is also more or less equally sizeable: it amounts to 15.8 per cent of the family income; and *additional* expenditure, 14.6 per cent. It is quite possible that all the students do not necessarily spend on their education only from their family income; some might get educational loan, some might be lucky to get scholarships and others some financial assistance to support their studies.[4] Generally, scholarships are available in government institutions better than in private institutions.

Large differences exist in per student expenditure on higher education in India between public and private institutions (Salim, 1994). The family expenditure on engineering education is nearly 50 per cent higher if the wards are studying in private institutions than in the government institutions, as shown in Figure 6.2. It is ₹1.10 lakhs in government institutions and ₹1.65 lakhs in private institutions. Students studying in private institutions are

188 *Economics of Engineering Education in India*

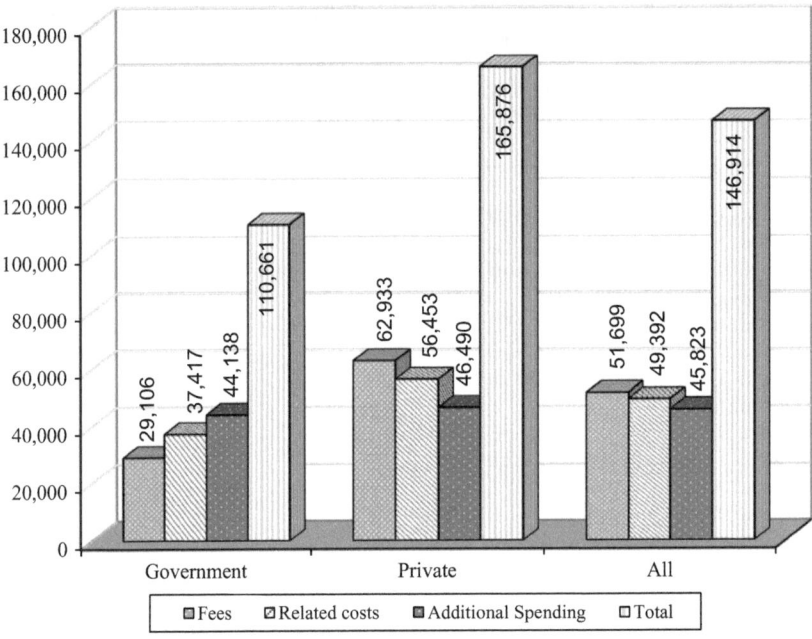

Figure 6.2 Family Expenditure (₹) on Engineering Education by Type of Educational Institutions

Table 6.4 Family Expenditure on Engineering Education per Student per Annum, by Gender, Caste and Type of Institution (₹ per Annum)

	Fees	Non-Fee Items	Additional Items	Total	Inter-Group Difference in Total
By Gender					
Male	52,479 (35.2)	50,516 (33.8)	46,263 (31.0)	149,258	1.07
Female	49,521 (35.4)	45,931 (32.9)	44,286 (31.7)	139,738	1.00
By social (caste) category					
Scheduled caste	32,760 (28.7)	40,619 (35.6)	40,625 (35.6)	114,004	1.17
Scheduled tribe	23,951 (24.8)	33,852 (35.0)	38,845 (40.2)	96,648	1.00
Other backward classes	40,584 (33.5)	41,708 (34.4)	38,888 (32.1)	121,180	1.25
General	57,226 (35.9)	53,445 (33.6)	48,540 (30.5)	159,211	1.65
By type of institution					
Government	29,106 (26.3)	37,417 (33.8)	44,138 (39.9)	110,661	1.00
Private	62,933 (37.9)	56,453 (34.0)	46,490 (28.0)	165,876	1.50
By stream of engineering					
Traditional	46,586 (35.9)	42,392 (32.6)	40,861 (31.5)	129,839	1.00
IT-related	53,930 (35.0)	52,367 (34.0)	47,839 (31.0)	154,136	1.19

Note: Figures in ( ) are percentages of total.

found to be spending 2.2 times higher than what the students in government institutions spend on fee alone. The difference in total fees is largely because of differences in tuition fees, which is ₹21,000 in public institutions and ₹52,700 in private institutions. Tuition fee, though partly regulated by the state,[5] is obviously much higher in private institutions compared to government institutions.

Expenditure on non-fee items such as accommodation/dormitory or housing, food, transport, textbooks and other study-related material is also higher for the students enrolled in private institutions (₹56,500) than those who are in government institutions (₹37,400). Much of the difference in the non-fee-related expenditure may be accounted by costs of accommodation, as already noted. There is no much difference in the expenditure on *additional* items, between the public and private institutions. On the whole, per student family expenditure on all the heads (fees, non-fee items and additional items) is higher in private than government institutions. Family expenditure also varies by the streams of engineering: IT-related subjects (e.g. electronics engineering, computer science engineering and IT) cost 19 per cent higher than standard traditional branches of engineering (e.g. mechanical, electrical and civil).

One of the striking features we note here relates to significant differences in family expenditures on education by social and economic classes. Family expenditure varies systematically with family income, as shown in Figure 6.3, and also by gender and caste groups. Students belonging to lower-income families incurred an expenditure on average of ₹70,300 per student, while the corresponding figure for the students belonging to higher-income families was ₹1.21 lakhs. The increasing pattern by rising family income holds in all the three categories of items of spending (fees, non-fee and additional).

After fees, students belonging to high-income families spend the second highest amount (₹40,166) on additional items like improving communication skills in English language, computers, internet connection, mobile phone and so on. As we have already noted, this pattern by household economic status – rich families spending more on the education of their children than the lower-income and poor families – is established in many studies in India and in other countries. Here too we note clearly that the higher the family income, higher is the expenditure per student. However, the family expenditure is less elastic to income, with the coefficient of elasticity being 0.138; it is higher in case of women, but still much below 1.

Gender differences also exist in the family expenditure on engineering education, though the differences are not very marked. Families spend ₹1.49 lakhs per student in the case of boys and ₹1.39 lakhs on the girls. On all the three heads – fee, non-fee and other expenditure – spending by the male students is higher than the female students. This pattern is also not uncommon among many countries, as we have already noted. It is widely noted that family investment on education of the girls is not at par with that on boys in many societies, including in India, partly attributable to intra-family

190 *Economics of Engineering Education in India*

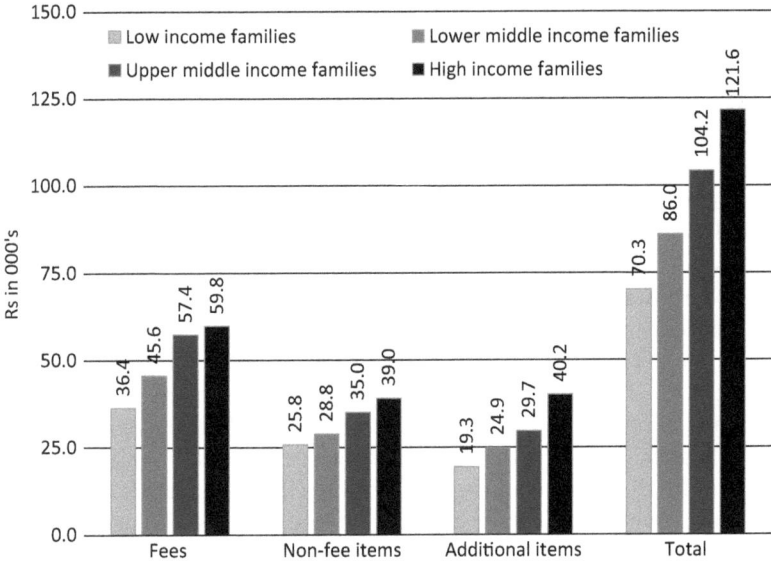

Figure 6.3 Family Expenditure (₹) on Engineering Education by Items and by Income Group

discrimination and gender bias against women. We find a similar picture here. Such a bias might originate from pre-existing beliefs or gender stereotyping due to socio-cultural or religious norms.

Table 6.3 also highlights the differences in family expenditure on education across social categories of population. Families belonging to scheduled tribes (STs) spend the least, that is, ₹96,648 per student per annum, while the expenditure of the families belonging to general category is the highest at ₹1.59 lakhs. Scheduled caste (SC) families spend a total of ₹1.14 lakhs and 'other backward classes' (OBCs) ₹1.21 lakhs. As the tuition and other fees for the students belonging to SCs and STs are subsidised, one finds a big difference, particularly in fees, paid by the various social groups. The expenditure incurred by ST students on fees on average is equal to about 37 per cent of the fees paid by the general category students. The corresponding figures are 58 per cent in the case of SCs and 72 per cent in the case of other backward castes.

Thus, we note wide variations in family expenditure on education by individual and family characteristics such as gender, caste, religion and family income. Variations in family expenditure represent inequalities with access to higher education. They also contribute to further widening of inequalities in the society.

Method

In the context of investigating the determinants of family expenditure on education, the main analytical tool used in the literature is the household expenditure function. A typical expenditure function is a regression equation that relates household expenditure to its determinants. Both from the point of view of empirical investigation and policy use, expenditure function facilitates analysis of the family expenditure in a framework appropriate for econometric estimation. The model that figures prominently in most of the literature on household decision-making behaviour, derived from the economic theory of consumer demand, which also forms the basis for the present investigation, is the model developed by Gary Becker (1975), which is mostly an 'individual' maximising model, and Behrman et al. (1982), which is described in the literature as the 'family' model.[6] It may not be possible to distinguish between the two, as some variables are common in both. Often, both models are considered by the researchers. McMahon (1984) has provided a more specific model on examining why families invest in education.

The conceptual model underlying a typical expenditure function can be expressed as a functional relationship that relates expenditures to its determinants:

$$HHEXPR = f(X_i)$$

Where HHEX refers to household expenditure on education and X_i a set of independent variables. Thus, it is a modified Engel function, expressing family expenditure on education as a function of household income and a set of household characteristics. A standard ordinary least squares regression equation, expressing dependent variable in terms of natural logarithm, of the following form is estimated:

$$ln HHEXPR = \alpha + \beta_i X_i + \varepsilon$$

where lnHHEXPR refers to logarithm of household annual expenditure on engineering education per student, β_i is a set of regression coefficients to be estimated that measures the extent to which various variables influence the household expenditure on education and ε the error term that is to be estimated by the equation. The coefficients β_i indicate the change in the levels of expenditures associated with a one-unit change in the given independent variable. The intercept term is α; it gives the mean effect on the dependent variable of all the variables excluded for the model or it is simply interpreted as the average value of the dependent variable when all the explanatory variables are set equal to zero.

A similar equation for student fees is also estimated separately, considering the fees as a function of a small set of variables:

$$ln FEES = f(X_i),$$

where X_i include type of institution, caste, gender, parental characteristics and rank in the competitive entrance examination and merit of the students.

Determinants of Family Expenditure

Given the pattern of family expenditure described earlier, one can expect economic and demographic characteristic features of the families to have considerable influence on the levels of family expenditures on education. Second, expected rates of return would considerably influence the family investments in education (Kambhampati, 2008), implying that the higher the rates of return to education, the higher would be the present levels of family investments and vice versa. But unfortunately, rates of return do not figure in our model here, mainly constrained by availability of data in a usable form. Gender and caste and size of the family – as an indicator of 'demographic burden' on the households apart from economic ability of the household – are also included in the function. In addition, as we have seen, the amount of expenditure incurred by the families on education to significantly vary with the type of institution, stream of engineering currently enrolled in and academic background of the students. Students who have studied in private schools at secondary level and/or in English medium (which is available mostly in private schools) might get habituated to higher levels of spending compared to their counterparts who have graduated from government schools and in local language as the medium. Similarly, students with higher educational aspirations – who have intentions or plans for further higher education (after completing bachelor's degree in engineering) – may spend higher amounts on acquiring additional knowledge and material. All these variables are considered here.

In all, constrained by the availability of data, only a few important socio-economic, demographic and educational variables are considered here, which are grouped into four categories: (a) individual characteristics such as gender, caste and religion; (b) household factors such as family's economic status, parental education, parental occupation and place of residence; (c) academic background of the students that includes type of school (public or private) attended, medium of instruction, board of examinations and academic performance in terms of percentage of marks secured at higher secondary level; and (d) current educational aspects of the students such as type of institution (public or private) currently attending, type of discipline (modern/IT-related or traditional), receipt of scholarship or educational loan or engagement in part-time work and further educational aspirations. Thus, while hypothesising which factors are related to family expenditures on education, we borrow, as suggested by Steelman and Powell (1991), mainly from the human capital theory (Becker, 1975), status-attainment model (Blau & Duncan, 1967) and also intra-family resource dilution hypothesis (Blake, 1989), each of which formed the basis for a large number of previous studies, apart from including a few other variables.

Results and Discussion: Determinants of Household Expenditure

Table 6.5 presents the OLS (ordinary least squares) results of regression equation of household expenditure on engineering education per student.[7]

First, our results support the general view about the prevalence of pro-male bias in family spending on engineering education in India, though it is not very high. Male students spend 11 per cent higher than the female students. Many families might still tend to feel that the return on the expenditure incurred by the families on girls' education would not accrue to their family; rather, it would flow to the in-laws' families after marriage. In addition, it is also common for the families to fear that investment in girls' education might work like 'negative dowry' in Indian society (Tilak, 1992a), as the higher educated girls look for further higher educated boys for their marriage, who, in turn, expect higher amounts of dowry. Though this countrywide phenomenon is changing rapidly, it is still perceived to be dominant in rural areas and among traditional and orthodox families.

Second important individual trait that determines family spending on engineering education is the social category. Confirming the general trend that students belonging to SC and ST categories spend significantly less than the students belonging to general category, here ST and SC students are found to be spending 44 per cent and 24 per cent, respectively, less than general category students (GENERAL). But the coefficient of OBC is found to be statistically not significant. It is also common knowledge that OBCs are not as backward as SCs/STs in education or in economic levels.

As in the case of many studies cited earlier, we find a positive relationship between the amount of family expenditure and annual income of the family. The annual income of the family influences positively it's spending on engineering education and the coefficient is statistically significant at 10 per cent level. The coefficient suggests that with an increase of ₹100 in income, the family spending on engineering education rises by 7 per cent. Economic status forms one of the most significant determinants of family expenditure on higher education. In addition to family income, we have also used ownership of a house by the family as an additional proxy for the economic status. But this variable turns out to be negatively related to family expenditure. Probably this is because the students whose family owns a house spend less as compared to the students whose family does not, as the former does not have to spend on boarding and lodging, particularly if the house is close to the institution where the student is studying.

As already noted, many earlier studies have shown that the parents' education or education of the head of the household has a significant positive effect on family expenditure on education. But in this, parents' – father's or mother's – education seems to have no significant effect on family expenditure on education; the coefficients are equivalent to almost zero in value and statistically not significant. This is indeed perplexing, needing further probe. The results do not validate the 'status maintenance model' (Blau & Duncan, 1967) in terms of education across generations.

Occupations of both the father and the mother (categorised as professional work, business and others) have been separately considered here to test their effect on family expenditure on engineering education. The results suggest that parents' occupation matters, if the father is engaged in business occupation (FATHEROCP_BUS), positively influencing the family expenditure. No other variable on occupation has any significant effect. The observed effects of the independent variables on the characteristics of the parents – occupation and education – are not consistent with many earlier studies. Like in a few studies (e.g. Shafiq, 2011), here too 'demographic burden' measured in terms of number of children in the family, turns out to be not a statistically significant factor in the expenditure on engineering education by the families in India. The intra-family resource-distribution hypothesis has perhaps no relevance in engineering education, while this has been found to be holding in the case of school education, as estimated by Tilak (2002a) and many others.

Another important household factor determining the family spending on engineering education is the residential status of the students (NATIVITY). As expected, the coefficient is negative in value and statistically significant. Students belonging to the same state where the institution is located spend less by 21 per cent than the students who in-migrate from other states. Those who come from other states have to obviously spend higher amounts.

Another set of variables considered here covers students' academic background (relating to senior secondary level of education). However, among the five variables considered in the equation under student's academic background, only SEC_SCH_LOCATION and SEC_BOARD are found to be statistically significantly related to family expenditure. Location of the secondary school from where the student graduated (SEC_SCH_LOCATION), considered here as a proxy for the rural/urban background of the students in the regression model, has been found to be statistically significant. However, quite interestingly, contrary to general understanding, the expenditure on engineering education is higher for students who have completed their senior secondary school located in rural areas than for those who studied in urban areas. While this needs to be probed further, it can be stated that probably this could be due to the background of the students who studied in rural/urban areas. A higher proportion of students from rural areas who come to engineering studies might be from relatively higher economic backgrounds, while in the case of urban areas they might include a good proportion of lower- and middle-income groups. Second, students from rural backgrounds may have to spend additionally on improving their communication skills in English language and skills with computers and other modern technology. The coefficients of other academic background variables like SEC_SCH_TYPE, SEC_MEDIUM and SEC_MARKS are statistically not significant.

Regression results in Table 6.4 show a positive relationship between the type of institution (public or private) the student is currently enrolled for undergraduate engineering education (ENGG_INST_TYPE) and family expenditure on education. More clearly, students in private institutions spend 61 per cent higher than students studying in public institutions and the regression coefficient is statistically significant at 1 per cent level of significance. This is one of the most important variables in terms of value of the

Table 6.5 OLS Estimate of the Determinants of Family Expenditure on Engineering Education

Variable	Coefficient	Robust Standard Error
Individual characteristics		
Gender	0.1134***	0.047
SC	−0.2439***	0.094
ST	−0.4407**	0.152
OBC	−0.0402	0.057
General	Reference	
Hindu	−0.1159**	0.056
Muslim	0.0826	0.102
Others	Reference	
Household factors		
lnHHY	0.0713*	0.026
Fathocp_prof	0.0088	0.050
Fathocp_bus	0.0933**	0.045
Fathocp_other	Reference	
Mothocp_prof	0.0087	0.050
Mothocp_bus	−0.0759	0.097
Mothocp_other	Reference	
Father_ED	0.0008	0.007
Mother_ED	0.0039	0.006
Siblings	0.0051	0.021
Nativity	−0.2146***	0.043
Own_house	−0.1876***	0.064
Student's academic background		
SEC_SCH_location	0.1517**	0.072
SEC_SCH_type	0.0328	0.043
SEC_medium	0.0623	0.062
SEC_board	−0.2459***	0.045
SEC_marks	0.0006	0.002
Student's current education status		
Engg_inst_type	0.6141***	0.0048
Stream_study	−0.0166	0.042
Part_time	0.0990*	0.056
Scholarship	0.0306	0.052
Loan	0.0870*	0.060
ED_ASP	−0.0478	0.037
Intercept	3.3195***	0.355
R Square	0.219	
F-Value (27,1603)	17.39***	
Number of observations	6,131	

Note: *** = statistically significant at 0.01 level of significance; ** = 0.05 significance level; * = 0.10 significance level

coefficient and also the standard error. This may suggest the need to effectively regulate fees in private institutions and at the same time to increase the number of public institutions and their intake. However, the other important variable, the stream of discipline of study (STREAM_STUDY), has no statistically significant influence on family expenditure in engineering education.

But the other two variables, viz. part-time engagement in work and availing of student loans, matter, both having positive effect on family expenditure. Educational loan increases the total family expenditure on education. Students who take loans spend 9 per cent higher than the students who do not avail educational loan. But SCHOLARSHIP has no significant effect on family expenditure, though it seems to be marginally but positively influencing the expenditure. Scholarship may be partly substituting family expenditure. Only a small fraction of students gets scholarships, as we note in Chapter 7, and the amount of scholarship may not be very high compared to the fee and other costs of education. Last, the results show that students' engagement in part-time work increases the family spending by 10 per cent. The additional earnings made with part-time work are probably incurred as additional expenditure on engineering education.

We have already noted that fee is an important item of total family expenditure on education and that it varies by different characteristics of the students and the institutions. Interestingly, fee also varies not only between different institutions, but also between different institutions within a state – particularly among different private institutions. Fees used to be uniformly same for long in all private institutions in a state, as determined by a state-level fee regulating committee at regular intervals, often every year, and another

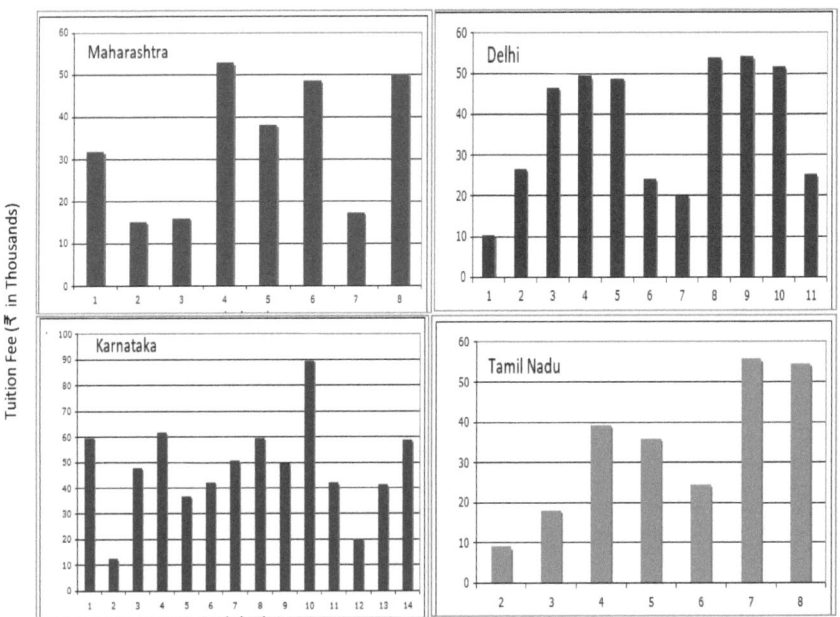

Serial Number of Institution

Figure 6.4 Average Tuition Fees by Students in Selected Engineering Education Institutions (₹ per annum)

level of fee is charged uniformly in all public institutions. But subsequently, the committee began setting fee levels for each private institution separately. All government colleges in a state levy a uniform level of fees, while each university sets its own fee level; and IITs (Indian Institutes of Technology) and NITs (National Institutes of Technology) decide independently of other institutions. As a result of all this, one notices wide variations in fee levels between several institutions, as shown in Figure 6.4 in the case of the institutions in our sample in the four states.

The regression estimates of the fee equation given in Table 6.5 also lead us to make a few interesting observations. As one expects, higher the rank of the student in the entrance examination, lower could be the fees, as students get admitted in public institutions or at subsidised fee rates in private institutions. If one belongs to the disadvantaged sections of students – SCs, STs, OBCs, the fee she/he has to pay would be lower (Table 6.6). These students get either fee waivers or are charged reduced rates. Fee is lower also if one is a female. Interestingly, mother's education (proxy for economic and social status) has a positive effect on the tuition fees paid by the students: higher the level of education – general or professional – higher would be the fees. Probably higher educated parents prefer private institutions that charge high levels of fees, as described in Chapter 4. But as we have noted in the household expenditure function, education of parents turns out to be statistically not significant.

Table 6.6 Tuition Fees Paid by Students as a Function of Student Characteristics and Type of Institution

Variable	Eqn. 1	Eqn. 2	Eqn. 3	Eqn. 4
ENT_score	−0.61***	−0.66***	−0.69***	−0.37***
SC	−26.50***	−23.28***	−31.52**	−43.48***
ST	−33.19***	−29.34***	−81.17***	−49.29***
OBC	−17.02***	−13.39***	−0.40	−15.00
Gender	−1.62	−2.30	−2.30*	−3.64***
Mother_HR_gen		9.06***	8.98***	7.17***
Mother_HR_profl		8.46***	8.41***	7.43***
Father_HR_gen		3.28	3.43*	4.26**
Father_HR_profl		3.64	3.90*	5.15**
ENT_score_SC			0.11	0.38*
ENT_score_ST			0.72**	0.47
ENT_score_SC OBCs			−0.16	0.06
engg_inst_type				28.79***
Intercept	96.71***	92.26***	94.03***	75.65***
Number of observations	4117	4097	4097	4097
R-square	0.08	0.09	0.10	0.17

*** Statistically significant at 0.01 level, ** at 0.05 level and * at 0.10 significance level.

As it is understood, if one goes to a public institution, she/he has to pay lower levels of fees than those who go to private institutions. Though these results are in expected directions, it is important to note that there are variations in tuition fee levels even among public institutions. This is, of course, common in private institutions. The explanation of varying effect of various factors helps in making more effective and equitable policies in engineering education.

Concluding Observations

Analysis of patterns and determinants of family expenditure on higher education provides valuable insights into families' preferences that would be useful for decision-making at household level as well as for public policy making regarding funding of higher education. As more than four-fifths of the students in engineering education in India are enrolled in the private self-financing universities and colleges, one can infer that more than 80 per cent of the engineering education is substantially funded by families rather than through the public exchequer. The families are no more 'hidden' funders of education. This makes it more important to analyse the pattern of family expenditure on engineering education, as families meeting a disproportionately high proportion of the costs of education have a lot of implications for access, quality and equity, which, in turn, have their own effects on the entire social fabric. However, here, only a few aspects of family expenditure are analysed, and in analysing its determinants only a few important factors could be considered. There are many other important factors that determine the family expenditure on education, but we could not consider them in the estimation of the multiple regression equation. Important omissions include level of government expenditure, employment rates and rates of return associated with engineering education. We could not consider specifically any supply side factors, constrained by the availability of data. Second, we have considered total (gross) family expenditure on education. It would have been more appropriate to consider net expenditure, after adjusting for scholarships on which unfortunately we do not have the required data.

Some of the findings that we have arrived here conform and a few contrast to theoretical postulates and some of the earlier research evidence; and some results require further probing. Families spend considerably high amounts on engineering education of their children. On average, a family spends nearly half of the average income of the family on its ward's engineering education. Of the total, fee alone accounts for nearly one-third of the income. Expenditure of students enrolled in private institutions is much higher than in the case of those enrolled in government institutions. Given that a large part of engineering education is in private sector, a majority of students spend a lot on engineering education. There exists a small degree of pro-male bias in household investment on engineering education. There are also wide variations in family spending by social (caste and religion) and economic characteristics. Family's economic, educational and social factors exercise significant influence on the levels of family expenditures on engineering education in India. These factors reflect the ability and willingness of families to spend on education.

A high level of family expenditure on higher education will have negative effect on access to higher education; and second, wide variations in it reflect high levels of inequalities in access to higher education. In fact, as Lunn and Kornrich (2018, p. 147) have observed, household spending on education is 'a mechanism of social stratification"; hence, egalitarian societies should not allow high levels of family expenditures on education. Societies that would like to expand higher education and aim at providing equitable access to higher education have to think of effective public subsidisation policies that reduce the need for high level of family expenditures on education.

Notes

1 OECD and a few others refer to family (or household) expenditure on education as private expenditure, some others use terms such as 'consumption expenditure', 'out-of-pocket expenditure', 'parental expenditure' and 'student expenditure'. They are broadly the same, but for minor differences in some cases.
2 Based on the same source, a few aspects at macro level are briefly described in Chapter 3.
3 While 'household' is the term used extensively in the literature and some used 'family' and 'household' interchangeably, 'family' defined as consisting of two or more members who live in the same home and are related by birth, marriage or adoption is a more appropriate term in Indian society than household, which is normally defined as consisting of one or more persons living in the same house, condominium or apartment, *who may or may not be related* (United Nations: *Multilingual Demographic Dictionary*, New York, 1958), though the term 'household' is extensively used in Indian literature too, including in the *National Sample Surveys*. However, the distinction between the two is not strictly maintained here; they are interchangeably used.
4 In our sample, 4.4 per cent of the students received tuition waivers and 12 per cent scholarships. We do not have data on the corresponding amounts. See Chapter 7 for details on some of these aspects.
5 Fees in universities are fixed by the universities; in the government colleges, they are decided by the state, and in private institutions, fees are determined by state-appointed fee regulating committees in respective states.
6 For discussion on the two methods, see Ermisch and Francesconi (2001).
7 The problem of multi-collinearity is not expected to be serious because of large sample size; double log regression equation is used, considering logarithmic form of variables that are measured in continuous cardinal numbers and others in binary form, in the estimation here to avoid the problem of heteroscedasticity. See Gujarati (1985). Further, if the interrelationship among the collinear variables is stable, it does not post any problem for prediction purposes (Maddala, 1977).

7 Funding of Engineering Education

Scholarships, Other Financial Assistance and Education Loans

Introduction

Funding policies in higher education have undergone drastic changes over the years in many developing as well as advanced countries, including India. Higher education, which used to be nearly fully or heavily subsidised by the state, is increasingly becoming dependent on cost recovery measures such as student fee and student loans, both of which have become very popular methods in the neoliberal era in most societies, specifically in India since the beginning of the 1990s. Both have contributed to making higher education increasingly costlier for the students, raising questions of affordability, access and inequality. This is more so in the case of engineering (other technical and professional) education in India, which is generally more expensive than general higher education, both from the point of view of the state and the student. But the problems of financing engineering education are also assuming different dimensions in quantum and nature (Tilak, 1999). To add further to this, a very high proportion of engineering education is also in private sector, making it further costlier. Though state subsidises higher education through general (universal subsidies) and specific subsidies, students incur, for example, on engineering education in India ₹1.5 lakhs per student on average per year, as noted in Chapter 6. How do the students finance their education? While families take responsibility for funding education of their children, those from the disadvantaged strata of society find it difficult to finance on their own. They critically depend on state subsidies – financial assistance in terms of scholarships – and on student loans and/or on work opportunities while studying (on-campus engagement in part-time work).

In the literature, theoretical rationale for and practical problems in public and private financing of higher education, including financing through direct and indirect subsidies (grants, scholarships, student fees and loans), are well discussed (Psacharopoulos & Woodhall, 1985; World Bank, 1986; Tilak, 1997, 2004; Ziderman, 2020). While theoretical and philosophical underpinnings such as externalities, public good nature, social responsibility of higher education, market failures in providing public goods, imperfections in capital market and so on formed the basis for public financing of education, fiscal constraints, competing demands, political commitments inadequacy of public resources, market efficiency and other practical constraints and ideological underpinnings favour private financing of education, specifically fees and student loans (Tilak, 2004). Apart from general subsidies in terms of grants to institutions, scholarships and other financial assistance to students play an important role in improving access to higher education, particularly for the students belonging to disadvantaged groups. According to a large number of studies (e.g. Schwartz, 1985; Moore et al., 1991; Glocker, 2011), enrolment and persistence in higher education and also student success are significantly and positively influenced by student aid or financial assistance received from the stat. With respect to student loans, the most common argument made in its favour is that students from poor households are not able to enrol themselves in higher education due to their financial problems, and so educational loan enables them to pursue higher education by deferring the current costs and to repay the same in future when they have secure jobs. But available evidence (e.g. Boatman et al., 2017; Callender & Mason, 2017) also shows that prospective undergraduates, especially from low social and economic classes, feel deterred from applying to university education because of fear of debt.

Scholarships and other measures of financial assistance to students have been used as an important measure of promoting equitable access to higher education for a long period, but the allocation of public resources to scholarships has suffered a severe decline in India over the years (Tilak, 2005; Narayana, 2019). The share of scholarships in total expenditure on higher and technical education has been less than 1 per cent in the most recent period, as described in Chapter 3. Public policy seems to favour a shift from scholarships to loans, as if the latter is a substitute to the former. India restructured its loan programme (Tilak, 1992a) in the 1990s, and the new scheme (Tilak, 2009b) has become gradually popular over the years, as an increasing number of students tend to opt for educational loans. Yet, access to educational loans seems to be severely constrained by a variety of factors, and students from lower socio-economic strata find it difficult to secure loans. All students do not go for and/or get loans. Hence, understanding the determinants of who get/take loans becomes important.

This chapter examines the pattern of financial support received by the students in the form of scholarships, fee waivers, boarding/lodging allowances and also through part-time work and student loans in engineering education in India. First, we briefly examine the pattern of financial assistance being received by students in engineering education in India. Next, a description of a profile of students who took educational loan by socio-economic and institutional characteristics (gender, family income, type of educational institution and department of study) is presented. Then, using a logit model, we also examine the factors determining the receipt of loan by students. Determinants of the amount of loan received by students is also analysed with the help of ordinary least squares (OLS) equation.

Financial Support to Students in Engineering Education

The financial support received by the students consists of merit or merit-cum-means scholarships, simply referred here as scholarships, tuition and other fee waivers and room or board allowances. We also considered part-time work opportunities in their own departments or institutions as yet another measure of financial assistance or as a means of self-financing. As per our survey, a bare 9 per cent of the students have received scholarships, 6.3 per cent received tuition waivers, 2.7 per cent received room/board allowances and only 2.3 per cent students were engaged in on-campus work. In all the four cases of financial assistance, students enrolled in government institutions benefited marginally higher than those in private institutions. As shown in Table 7.1, 11.4 per cent of the students in government colleges have received scholarships, while the corresponding figure is 7.9 per cent in private colleges. Girl students fare better than boys in securing scholarships, while in the case of the other three, viz. fee waivers, room/board allowances and on-campus work opportunities, boys are marginally at an advantage. Around 10 per cent of students enrolled in conventional/traditional departments received scholarships in comparison to 8.8 per cent of those enrolled in information technology (IT)-related departments. It may be noted that traditional streams of engineering are offered more in government institutions, while many private institutions focus on offering IT-related streams. Private institutions have fewer programmes of financial assistance.

The distribution of scholarships varies by family income. Fourteen per cent of students belonging to low-income group[1] received scholarships; the corresponding figures for other groups varied between 7.5 per cent and 12.3 per cent. Excluding the lowest income group, the distribution does not seem

Table 7.1 Percentage of Students Who Received Financial Assistance by Type of Institution and Department of Study

	Scholarship	Tuition/Fee Waiver	Room/Board Allowances	On-Campus Work
Type of Institution				
Government	11.40	9.09	2.80	3.64
Private	7.85	4.81	1.95	2.18
Department of Study				
Traditional	9.93	9.11	3.34	3.74
Modern/IT-related	8.75	5.14	1.81	2.26
Income Groups				
Low	13.95	8.96	4.45	3.18
Lower middle	7.53	6.58	1.66	2.25
Upper middle	8.06	2.45	1.79	3.46
High income	12.30	3.57	1.22	3.85
Total	9.09	6.29	2.25	2.69
	(472)	(322)	(113)	(132)

Note: Figures in parentheses refer to total number of students.

to be progressive. On the other hand, tuition waivers and room/board allowances are relatively more progressively distributed – distribution favouring relatively more the low- and lower-income groups. Very few students take up on-campus jobs, and those very few are distributed somewhat evenly among all income groups – nearly 4 per cent among the top income group and 3 per cent among the low-income group. Students from high-income groups also take up on-campus part-time jobs to support their studies or to meet additional expenses.

It is not only the number (percentage) of students but also the distribution of amount of financial assistance that depicts a similar pattern. The annual average amount of financial assistance received by students from scholarships was ₹15,800, tuition waiver was ₹23,600, room/board allowances ₹14,000 and through on-campus work, a student on average earned ₹23,500 per year. The amounts of scholarship, and other assistance in the form of fee waivers, allowances and earnings from campus work – received by the students in private institutions were higher than those in government institutions.

Students enrolled in IT-related departments received an annual average amount of ₹15,700 as scholarship, whereas students in traditional departments could get an annual average scholarship amount of ₹16,200 (Table 7.2). But in the case of tuition/fee waiver, students in IT-related departments received higher financial assistance than students in traditional departments. Similar is the pattern in the case of room/board allowances and earnings from on-campus work.

The scholarships seem to be more progressively distributed in terms of the amount of scholarship. Students belonging to high-income households have received the lowest amount of scholarship (₹12,300 per student), followed by upper middle-income households (₹12,400), low-income households (₹15,500) and lower middle-income households (₹17,300). But the pattern of distribution of tuition and fee waivers and other allowances was different: students from high-income groups received the highest amounts of tuition/fee waiver and room/board allowances. With respect to on-campus work,

Table 7.2 Average Amount of Financial Assistance Received by Students by Type of Institution and Department of Study (₹ per Annum)

	Scholarship	Tuition/Fee Waiver	Room/Board Allowances	Earnings from On-Campus Work
Type of Institution				
Government	12,489	14,525	6,500	9,353
Private	18,488	33,095	12,670	17,542
Department of Study				
Traditional	16,160	18,404	9,575	12,585
Modern/IT-related	15,672	27,156	17,374	31,769
All: Per student financial assistance	15,828	23,619	14,010	23,515

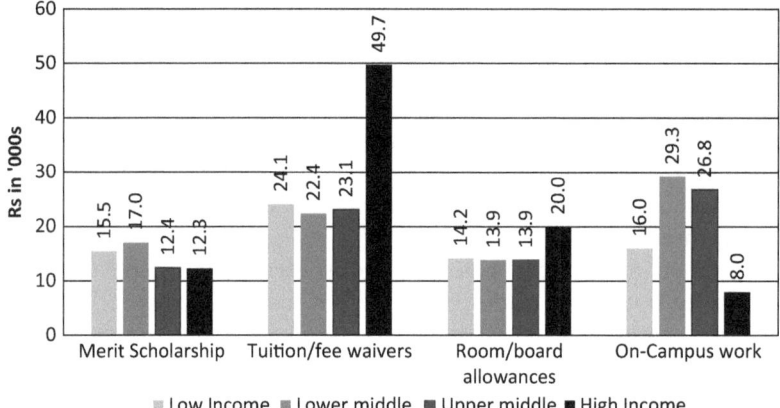

Figure 7.1 Annual Average Amount of Financial Assistance Received by the Students by Annual Income of the Family (₹ in Thousands)

students belonging to high-income households earned the least amounts of all the income groups (Figure 7.1).

Student Loans

As noted earlier, scholarships, fee waivers and more benefit only a small fraction of student community. A large number of students even among the low- and middle-income groups entering into the higher and professional education are either left out of these benefits, and/or even after receiving such a kind of assistance are not in a position to cover their remaining costs (tuition fees, costs of living and other additional expenses) on their own, and hence they search for alternative sources. One major alternative is borrowing – educational loan.

The Government of India introduced a restructured student loans scheme as a method of financing higher education in the mid-1990s. As per the restructured scheme, it is not the government but commercial banks that provide loans to the students. The loan covers the expenses on tuition fees and other fees payable to the institution, travel expenses, purchase of books and other equipment and other necessary expenditure, total with a fixed upper limit of ₹10 lakhs for the students studying within India and ₹20 lakhs for the students studying abroad. This scheme is getting popular nowadays. As per the latest statistics available, in 2018–19, there were about 2.5 lakh student loan accounts with the banking system in India, which, however, used to be 3.3 lakhs in 2015. The total amount of loans distributed to students in 2019 was of the order of ₹22,500 crore (TOI, 2019). Many commercial banks are operating this scheme with a common set of conditions, within the broad framework of rules, regulations and procedures agreed by the Indian Bankers' Association with the Reserve Bank of India.[2] For example, the State

Bank of India provides student loans to Indian nationals for pursuing higher education in India or abroad where admission has been secured. The repayment commences one year after completion of course of study or six months after securing a job, whichever is earlier, and the entire loan amount with interest is to be repaid in five to seven years of commencement of repayment. The Government of India has also introduced in recent years several measures to make educational loan programme popular among the students, with interest subsidies (for the duration of the studies plus one year) as an incentive to the disadvantaged sections of the society.

While the number of students opting for student loans is rapidly increasing, the total number is still very small compared to the student numbers in higher education. Hardly three lakh students out of nearly 36 million total enrolments in higher education get educational loans from institutional sources[3] (2017–18) (see also Narayana 2005; Tilak 2009b). Despite a few measures taken by the government to make it attractive, loans are still found to be not easily accessible to the weaker sections of the society, who may actually need them more. It is often observed that commercial banks discriminate against those whose loan repaying capacity is low, and against those types of higher education that do not necessarily promise high wage employment to the graduates and against those higher education institutions that do not have a good brand name or reputation. Banks might, however, prefer engineering or professional education to other areas of higher education, as it is more closely related to employment. From the demand side, it is also generally observed that students belonging to lower-socio-economic strata do not prefer taking educational loans for some of the familiar reasons – they are risk-aversive; employment and economic returns from higher education are not certain; and loan is still culturally not popular among all (Chandrasekhar et al., 2019). Lack of credit constraint due to capital market imperfections on the one hand and the individual characteristics, family circumstances, preferences and attitudes and other factors on the other make access to educational loans difficult. While in principle, many students in general higher education and professional/technical higher education opt for student loans to finance their education, usually the probability of opting/getting educational loans is higher for a student pursuing an engineering degree in India as engineering education (and also professional education like medical education) is expensive. Hence, it will be useful to examine factors that determine who take/receive educational loans in higher education in India.

There are a few important studies on the issue of determinants of loans in a few countries, but not many on India. In a study on the UK, Johnes (1994) established that women are significantly less likely to take out a loan than are men, and that quite interestingly, low parental occupational status does not deter students from taking out a loan. In studies on loans in Italy and England, Perali and Barzi (2011) and de Gayardon et al. (2019) found that family circumstances, such as family income, indicators of family wealth (home ownership), private education, living area, parental education, gender, ethnicity, debt aversion, individual characteristics, preferences and attitudes, outcomes and efforts are found to be very significant determinants of student loan take-up. In the study on England (de Gayardon et al., 2019), only social class was found to have no independent effect. Among the determinants of the amount of loan, tuition and fees were found to be the most important ones in the USA (Macy & Terry, 2007). The amount of loan taken also varies by several individual characteristics (Avery & Turner, 2012). Such studies are rare in India, as data available from the banks do not include student and other background factors, and very few surveys are conducted of students who applied/got/did not get loans. Mostly, available data at macro level (from Reserve Bank of India or from other banks) on educational loans in India include the number of students getting loans, amount of loans disbursed, number of existing loan accounts, amount of loss due to non-repayment and so on, and hence only these aspects were analysed by scholars (e.g. Narayana, 2005; Rani, 2014); and on the socio-economic profile of the loanees, no studies are made.[4]

A Short Profile of Educational Loanees

Our survey gives information on some important aspects on who gets loans. It is generally expected that a large number of students in engineering education would have got loans from banks, as engineering education is considered expensive; most students apply for loans and the banks prefer giving loans to engineering students compared to the students enrolled in other disciplines of higher education. However, in this study, we find that only 10.3 per cent of students have taken loans from banks to pursue their engineering degree studies (Table 7.3).

The smaller number of students availing loans may be due to the non-availability or the rigid structure of the loan scheme or due to lack of demand for loans by the students and/or their families or both. It is quite possible that many students might not have applied for educational loans. Generally, it is also expected that students do seek loans as engineering education is one of the costliest branches of higher education, and it is further costlier in private

Table 7.3 Number of Students Who Received Educational Loan by Type of Institution and Department of Study

	Total Number of Students Responded	Percentage of Students Who Received Loans
Type of Institution		
Government	1,852	8.37
Private	4,181	11.22
Department of Study		
Traditional	1,963	11.21
Modern/IT-related	4,070	9.93
Total	6,033	10.34

institutions than in public institutions. But we note that only 11 per cent of students studying in public (government) institutions received loans from banks, whereas the corresponding figure is 8.4 per cent of students studying in private institutions. Coming from relatively higher socio-economic background, students in private institutions might not need loans. That the quality of public institutions is higher and that accordingly graduates from public institutions would have higher probability of securing employment compared to the others might influence the banks in according preferential treatment in the sanctioning of loans.

Generally, it is also presumed that banks prefer giving loans to the students in IT-related departments like computer science engineering, electronics and communication engineering or IT to students enrolled in traditional areas of engineering, assuming higher probability of employment of graduates of the IT-related disciplines of engineering. But contrary to this, a marginally higher proportion of students enrolled in traditional streams of engineering (11.2 per cent) have got educational loans than the students enrolled in IT-related courses of study (9.9 per cent). We also find that a higher number of male students received educational loans than women (11.2 per cent against 8.1 per cent). It is generally felt that parents in India are more willing to go for loans for their sons' than for their daughters' education. For a long time, it is widely felt that loan works as a 'negative dowry' and hence there is a serious disincentive in taking loans for girls' education, though the situation is changing slowly over the years.

Last, loan facilities are availed by a higher proportion of students belonging to low-income group than middle- and upper-income groups. As per our survey, 16 per cent of the students from low-income group could secure educational loans from banks and only 3 per cent of students from top income group have taken loans. The corresponding figures are 10 per cent for lower middle-income households and 5.5 per cent for upper middle-income

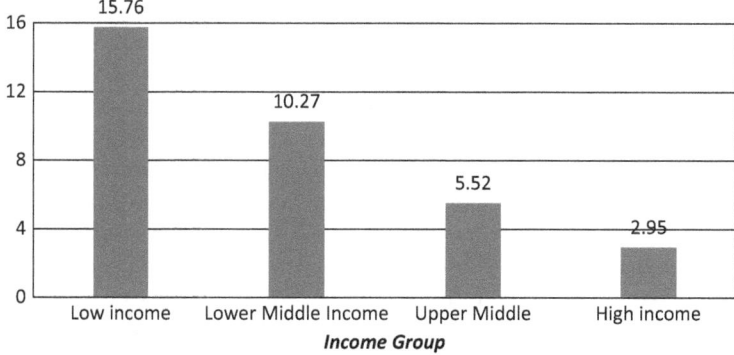

Figure 7.2 Percentage of Students Availing Educational Loans by Annual Income of the Family

208   *Economics of Engineering Education in India*

households (Figure 7.2), based on which one might say that distribution of educational loans is somewhat progressive.

Who Gets Education Loans? Determinants of Education Loans

Now we analyse the probability of getting educational loan by engineering students using a logit model. The model considers "whether the students has taken/received an educational loan or not" as the dependent variable and individual characteristics, household factors, academic background of the students and factors related to current education of the students as explanatory variables.[5] Though there are many other relevant variables, the selection of the variables is constrained by the availability of information collected in the survey. In the survey, information was collected from the students, not from the banks or the higher education institutions. Further, there is one major limitation. The survey provides only information on whether the student has received loan or not and how much, besides on background and other characteristics of the students and their families. Information was not collected on whether a student has applied for loan or not. So it is assumed that all the students have opted for but only some got loans and others did not. This may be noted as an important limitation of our analysis.

The results of the logistic regression are given in Table 7.4. Two individual factors – social category (CASTE) and gender – are found to be statistically significant in determining students' decision to take/get a loan. As expected, female students are less likely to prefer taking educational loan than male students. Similarly, students belonging to backward social category find difficulty in accessing the credit market for education. This is found to be true here in the scheduled tribe (ST) students. Students belonging to STs are less likely to get educational loan than the students belonging to general category. The other two caste dummies (SCs [scheduled castes] and OBCs [other backward classes]) are found to be statistically not significant. The probability of getting an educational loan is inversely related to the economic conditions of the household: a one unit increase in income reduces the probability of getting educational loan by 3 percentage points. It implies that higher the income, lower will be the requirements or demand for educational loan and vice versa. Similarly, families having no house of their own – another measure of economic conditions – are more likely to get loans from banks than the families owning a house. But it is also possible that those who own houses may offer them as collateral and may accordingly have better chances of securing a loan. The results seem to confirm the latter view, though collateral is not strictly required for most educational loans in general. Parental occupation also seems to be influencing the probability of securing a loan.

The student whose father is a professional worker or involved in business activities is less likely to go for educational loan than the student whose father is engaged in 'other' occupations such as clerical work, service work, skilled and unskilled work or is a retired person. But the variable mother's occupation is found to be statistically not significant.

Table 7.4 Who Gets Educational Loans? Logit Estimates of Determinants

Variables	Coefficient	Odds Ratio	Standard Error	Marginal Effect (dy/dx)
Individual Characteristics				
Gender	−0.336**	0.715	0.152	−0.030
SCs	0.092	1.096	0.238	0.009
STs	−1.954*	0.142	1.037	−0.093
OBCs	−0.044	0.957	0.172	−0.004
General	Reference			
Hindu	0.162	1.176	0.234	0.015
Muslim	−0.386	0.680	0.453	−0.032
Others	Reference			
Household Factors				
LnHHY	−0.319***	0.727	0.074	−0.030
Fathocp_prof	−0.524***	0.592	0.176	−0.045
Fathocp_bus	−0.478***	0.621	0.163	−0.041
Fathocp_other	Reference			
Mothocp_prof	−0.250	0.770	0.200	−0.022
Mothocp_bus	0.080	0.770	0.290	0.007
Mothocp_other	Reference			
Father_ED	−0.0002	1.070	0.022	−0.00002
Mother_ED	−0.006	0.994	0.019	−0.0005
Own_house	0.246**	1.278	0.120	0.023
Own_land	−0.118	0.888	0.082	−0.011
Siblings	0.158**	1.171	0.070	0.015
Student's Academic Background				
SEC_Marks	−0.008	0.992	0.006	−0.0007
SEC_SCH_location	0.253	1.288	0.193	0.026
SEC_SCH_tYPE	0.007	1.008	0.136	0.0007
SEC_medium	0.058	1.059	0.182	0.006
SEC_board	0.252*	1.286	0.146	0.023
Student's Current Education Status				
LnHHEXPR	0.164*	1.178	0.086	0.016
Engg_inst_type	0.149	1.160	0.161	−0.014
Stream_study	0.024	1.024	0.141	0.002
Employment	−0.038	0.963	0.142	−0.004
Constant	1.903		1.422	
Log likelihood	−929.85			
Pseudo R²	0.058			
Number of observations	2657			

Notes: Level of Significance: *** $p < 0.01$; ** $p < 0.05$; and * $p < 0.1$.

Other household factors included in the model such as educational level of the parents and family wealth in terms of ownership of land turned out to be statistically not significant. The probability of securing an educational loan increases with the increase in the number of siblings in the family. After all, as family size increases, family burden increases, necessitating households to resort to loans – educational loans in this case.

Expecting previous academic background of the students to have an effect on getting educational loan from banks, variables such as percentage of marks secured in senior secondary examination, location of the school (rural or urban), type of school (government or private), the medium of instruction followed in the school (English or others) and the examination board (central board or state board) are included in the equation. All these reflect some key aspects relating to students' academic background. Results presented in Table 7.5 show that students who completed their senior secondary schooling in schools affiliated to central boards (SEC_BOARD) are more likely to get a loan than students graduating from state boards. Students of central board schools are likely to be more informed about the scope and availability of loans than others. Academic background of the students does not seem to matter much in securing loans, as other four academic variables on academic background are found to be statistically not significant. In the pre-restructured scheme of educational loans in India, academic merit of the student was an important consideration in granting loans by the government. But, as per the new scheme operated by the commercial banks, merit is not a condition, nor does it seem to influence the banks in their decision-making regarding awarding of student loans.

Among the factors included on students' current education status, household expenditure on education, a proxy for the household cost of education, which includes fees, living expenses and other expenditures, is found to be statistically significant. The higher the cost of engineering education, which the families have to bear, higher is the probability of going for and/or getting an educational loan. Surprisingly, other factors such as the type of institution the student is currently studying in (public or private), or type of engineering stream the student has chosen or even the employment prospects do not seem to have any statistically significant effect on securing a loan.

Amount of Educational Loan Received by the Students

In addition to examining the question of who gets educational loans, it is analysed here to assess which types of students are likely to be borrowing/receiving too much or too little as loans. commercial banks consider, in addition to the amount of loan sought by the student, the costs of education (fees, living and other costs that students have to incur) while deciding on the amount of loan to be sanctioned. On average, according to our study, students in engineering education in India have received ₹80,300 as loan per annum per student during their programme of study. Women students received higher amounts than men – ₹97,700 as against ₹73,200 in case of men. As the fees in government institutions is much less than that in private institutions, obviously students studying in public institutions receive less amount as loan from the banks. Students enrolled in government institutions received on average ₹69,700, while it is ₹90,800 in the case of students enrolled in private institutions (Table 7.5). The amount of student loan is expected to vary by the stream of engineering education that a student is enrolled in, as fees (and even other expenditure) also differ by the stream of engineering. Students enrolled in traditional or conventional departments are found to have received higher amount of loan per annum than students enrolled in IT-related departments. Students in traditional departments received ₹85,000 as loan compared to ₹78,000 for students of IT-related departments.

The amount of loan received by the student may be expected to be inversely related to the economic condition of the household. In a sense, students from low-income families require more amounts of loan to bear the costs associated with engineering education, as they may not be able to afford to spend much out of their own pockets. But do they get higher amounts? The results here reveal that the amount of loan received by the students increases with the increase in the annual income of the family, excepting in the upper middle-income group. While a student on average belonging to low-income families received ₹61,500 as loan, those from lower middle-income families received ₹95,200 and those from high-income families ₹108,300. Banks might tend to be guided more by creditworthiness and repayment capacities, apart from mortgage (surety) provided by loanees, than genuine requirements of the loan seekers and may discriminate against low-income families in granting higher loan amounts. Though comparatively higher number of students from low-income households received loans as noted earlier, the amount of loan received by them seems to be significantly less than what the high-income households received.

What are the factors that determine the amount of educational loan taken by the students? As already stated, while tuition fees and other costs of education are necessarily considered by the banks while deciding on the amount of loan to be sanctioned, many other factors – individual characteristics, socio-economic background and previous and current education-related aspects – might also influence the amount of loan. Otherwise, the amount

Table 7.5 Amount of Educational Loan Received by Students and by Type of Institution and Department of Study

	Amount of Loan (₹ in '000s)
Type of Institution	
Government	69.68
Private	90.77
Department of Study	
Traditional	85.39
Modern/IT-related	78.23
Family Income	
Lower	61.51
Lower middle	95.15
Upper middle	56.86
Higher	108.33
Total	80.29

of loan would be the same for all students in an institution or same for all, at least in a given department in a given institution. But that is not the case.

Using OLS technique, the factors that determine the amount of loan are examined here estimating the following equation:

$$ln\text{LOAN AMOUNT} = \alpha + \beta_i + \varepsilon$$

where LOAN AMOUNT is the amount (₹) of loan received by the student and β_i are a set of independent variables.

The independent variables are already described and defined in Table B1 in the Appendix to Part II. The Appendix also gives more details on the variables. The estimated results of the OLS equation are presented in Table 7.6.

Among the individual characteristics, social category of the student turns out to be statistically significant. As expected, caste matters: one's belonging to SCs reduces the amount of educational loan the banks sanction. Banks might doubt their repaying capacity. Female students get higher amount as educational loan than male students, but the variable GENDER turns out to be statistically not significant. There does not seem to be much gender discrimination in sanctioning the amount of loan. Student whose father is involved in business activities gets less amount of loan than the student whose father is engaged in other occupations such as farmer, teacher and self-employed. The other significant factor determining the amount of loan received by the engineering students is the ownership of land by their families: families that own land get/take less amount as loan from the banks than the families without land. However, contradicting this, students having their own house received higher amount as loan than their counterparts. It appears ownership of land and ownership of house do not represent economic status in a similar way. Ownership of land may mean much more than owning a house.[6]

It is expected that the households with a larger number of siblings go for higher amount of loan than the households with less number of siblings to finance the expensive engineering education of their children. The results show the same, but the coefficient is statistically not significant.

Interestingly, the type of school students graduated from (public or private) has a significant effect on the amount of loan. Though the probability of getting loans is not influenced by students' academic background, the amount of loan the students get seems to be influenced by some factors relating to students' background. Students graduated from private schools in their senior secondary schooling get/take higher amounts of loan than students coming from government schools. This may be due to the fact that students who studied in private schools might belong to rich households and are accustomed to spending higher amounts. Similarly, students graduating from secondary schools located in rural areas get smaller amounts of loans than their counterparts.

The needs as well as the level of spending of the students from rural background may be less. Students from private schools and from urban

Table 7.6 OLS Estimates of the Determinants of Amount of Educational Loan Received by Students

Variables	Coefficient	Standard Error
Individual Characteristics		
Gender	0.163	0.373
SCs	-1.711***	0.581
STs	0.835	2.611
OBCs	-0.227	0.402
General	Reference	
Hindu	-0.192	0.580
Muslim	0.779	1.081
Others	Reference	
Household Factors		
*ln*HHY	-0.043	0.188
Fathocp_prof	0.00009	0.420
Fathocp_bus	-0.681*	0.420
Fathocp_other	Reference	
Mothocp_prof	-0.200	0.478
Mothocp_bus	0.388	0.687
Mothocp_other	Reference	
Father_ED	-0.075	0.054
Mother_ED	-0.041	0.045
Own_house	0.470*	0.279
Own_land	-0.687**	0.202
Siblings	0.074	0.159
Student's Academic Background		
SEC_Marks	0.018	0.015
SEC_SCH_location	-0.489*	0.476
SEC_SCH_type	-0.671	0.326
SEC_medium	0.585	0.472
SEC_board	-0.072	0.365
Student's Current Education Status		
*ln*HHEXPR	-0.058	0.193
Engg_inst_type	0.379	0.406
Stream_study	0.488	0.338
Employment	0.734**	0.335
Constant	2.099**	2.588
R^2	0.17	
Adjusted R^2	0.10	
F-Value	2.23***	
Number of observations	286	

Note: Level of Significance: *** $p < 0.01$; ** $p < 0.05$; and * $p < 0.1$.

areas are perhaps relatively smarter in getting higher amount of loans. Their levels of spending may also be generally high. Though the results on a few other factors relating to current educational background of students show expected results, they are found to be statistically not significant. Employment potential of engineering discipline is also expected to have a positive effect on the amount of loan the banks give. This is found to be true here, as the coefficient is positive in value and statistically significant. Banks seem to give much weightage to the employment prospects of the graduates.

Thus, some of the results we find here are on expected directions and some contradict general understanding of the issues, requiring further investigation.

Summary and Conclusions

Financing of higher education has undergone dramatic changes in India, like in many countries since the 1990s. Public funding for higher education has not kept pace with growth in enrolments; and cost recovery measures, particularly fees, have been used to generate more and more private resources. But since a majority of students in general and those belonging to lower-socio-economic strata in particular cannot afford high fee levels, scholarships and more importantly student loans have been thought of as measures that can mitigate the potential regressive effects of student fees and as those that can improve access to higher education. Based on the student survey, we have examined in this chapter, with the help of logit and OLS equations, the question of who gets educational loans and how much, besides briefly analysing the kind of financial assistance in the form of scholarships and allowances that students get. Following are some of the key findings of the analysis:

- According to our survey, only a very small proportion of students in engineering education in India receives scholarships, fee waivers and other kinds of financial assistance. Students, particularly those who are not able to get any kind of financial assistance, take part-time work on the campus to partly finance their education. Their number is also very small: 2.7 per cent of the total. All the corresponding numbers are smaller in private institutions than public institutions.
- Given the high private (household) costs of engineering education, many students opt for educational loans. While loans are taken from institutional sources (commercial banks) or from non-institutional sources (family and friends) to finance their education, we concentrated here on institutional sources. All students do not necessarily get loans, even if they are eligible to get loans as per the criteria set by the banks or the government and even if they apply for loans. While educational loans are considered as an important means of financing engineering education in India, we found that only about 10 per cent of students have got educational loans from banks. Descriptive statistics show that of the total, higher number of male students got loans compared to women. Further, comparatively a higher number of students enrolled in private institutions get loans than the students in government institutions. Similarly, a higher proportion of students enrolled in conventional/traditional disciplines of engineering study get loans compared to those enrolled in IT-related modern streams of engineering education.

- Among the factors that explain the probability of getting loans, social category, family income, ownership of assets (house), parents' occupation and costs of education (that students have to incur) are significant.
- Family income of the students is found to be a significant factor in determining the student's probability to get a loan. More clearly, the value of the coefficient suggests that a student belonging to a rich family is less likely to get loan than a student from a poor family. Furthermore, as revealed by the corresponding marginal effect, a student belonging to a rich household is less probable by 3 percentage points of getting a loan than a student from a poor household. But students from high-income groups are found to receive higher amounts of loans compared to others. So the distribution of loans seems to be somewhat progressive, but not the distribution of amount of loans.
- Other things being constant, socially backward (schedule caste) students, who may actually require more, are less likely to get educational loans than other students. The amount of loan provided to these students is also less. Perhaps banks are more willing to give loans to the students belonging to the higher social category.

Reasons for many of the findings arrived at here need to be probed with further research. In this analysis, some of the important factors turned out to be statistically not significant as a determinant of receipt of educational loan and also the amount of loan. These include: educational level of the parents, department of the study, type of institution and so on. Probable reasons need further probing. An important limitation that one has to note about this analysis is: the statistical analysis here considered some of the important quantifiable variables only on which data are available; there are many other important factors on which the survey has not provided needed data and hence could not be incorporated in our analysis. So is the case with respect to many other non-quantifiable qualitative factors. Besides stressing the need for more in-depth studies in this direction, this analysis is still very useful in shedding light on quite a few important dimensions on higher education policy, particularly the scholarships and loan financing.

The conclusions arrived here have valuable policy implications for modifying or redesigning the educational loan programme in India and in other countries, besides stressing the need to expand other kinds of financial assistance to improve access to higher education. Policy makers may need to note that educational loans are not so popular as generally believed. There may be constraints on both supply and demand side. They need to be addressed. It also appears that loans cannot substitute scholarships and other financial assistance, not only theoretically but also in practice. Given the resource constraints, we may need both, even though liberal scholarship programmes (and general subsidies) are a more effective method of financing higher education. Third, all specific subsidies like scholarships, loans, fee waivers and so on need to be designed in such a way that they will be progressive in effect, benefiting the relatively deprived sections more than the others. Generally, administration of specific or targeted subsidies suffers from errors of omission and commission. Efforts need to be made to reduce scope for such errors while designing them.

Notes

1 Details on classification of income groups and on other variables, including their definitions and measurements, are given in Chapter 4. Also see Appendix B.
2 For detailed information on eligibility, rate of interest, security deposit and repayment and related conditions and features of the scheme, see *http://www.iba.org.in/educational_loans.asp*.
3 There is hardly any information in India on non-institutional loan financing of higher education like family and friends.
4 Choudhury (2012), however, analysed, drawing from a sub-sample of the survey data used here in this study, some of these aspects relating to student characteristics and other factors in Delhi.
5 In Appendix B, the definitions and the way they are measured are given.
6 Land may yield money income regularly, while ownership of house does not necessarily yield such tangible incomes, particularly if it is not rented out.

8 Students' Perceptions on Quality of Engineering Education

The Problem

It is widely felt that this massive expansion in engineering education that has taken place during the post-independence period in India has been at the cost of quality of education. As noted earlier, except for a small number of graduates produced by a few institutions like the IITs and NITs, a vast majority of graduates are regarded 'unemployable' in any appropriate occupation (Aspiring Minds, 2019); in the global university ranking systems, very few institutions figure with high ranks, except a few IITs which also figure after top 100 or 200; in the national system of ranking (National Institute of Ranking Framework), a little less than 2 per cent of the institutions have been found to have scored above 50 per cent marks; less than 5 per cent of the engineering graduates are found to have been qualified in the graduate attitude test in engineering (GATE); and hardly 5 per cent of the colleges received 'full accreditation' by the national accreditation body, the National Board of Accreditation (NBA) (VIF, 2019); even the pass rates in undergraduate studies are very low (Mani & Arun, 2012). Thus, there are strong and well-articulated views on the poor quality of engineering education in the country. Further, international comparative studies (Loyalka et al., 2019, 2021) have shown that Indian engineering institutions compare poorly with those in the US in equipping students with higher-order thinking abilities and academic skills; though elite institutions in India do better, they still perform very poorly compared to elite institutions in the US. The widely prevalent views on the quality of education are also based on robust empirical evidence, but mostly based on the information collected from the educational institutions, employers and other stakeholders, but for studies by Loyalka et al. (2019, 2021), which are based on large surveys of skill acquired by students. Experts and several committees (e.g. AICTE, 2003, 2018; Banerjee & Muley, 2009; Biswas et al., 2010; MHRD, 2011; World Bank, 2013; Anandkrishnan, 2014; Loyalka et al., 2016; Government of India, 2019, 2020) that examined the status of engineering education in India have also commented in this context on institutional expansion, poor infrastructure, less provision of postgraduate and research programmes, commercialisation, ineffective regulation, lack of

DOI: 10.4324/9781003430223-10

governance, state control and absence of autonomy, lack of qualified teachers, inadequate public funding, policy vacuum, outdated curriculum, old-fashioned teaching methods, irrelevant skills and knowledge provided by the engineering colleges and universities, weak linkages between universities and industry and so on. They also made valuable recommendations on these aspects. Many recommended improvement in infrastructure, faculty recruitment, autonomy, increased public funding, raise in fees, faculty training, restructuring of regulatory institutions, planned and regulated growth, focus on research and postgraduate programmes, restructuring of curriculum, including increase in market relevance of curriculum and introduction of ethics, and so on. A majority of such studies are based on surveys of institutions, so are many of the reports of the expert committees, but not necessarily of students. There are a few studies in India that are based on student surveys; but these surveys covered several aspects relating to their socio-economic background, expenditures on education and employment/unemployment (Rao, 1961; Bose et al., 1983; Senthilkumar & Arulraj, 2011), but they rarely focused on quality-related aspects and how students perceived the quality of their education. Using students' surveys, Uplaonkar (1983) analysed occupational preferences by gender and Singh (1993) examined costs of higher education in University of Delhi. Vijay (2013) analysed student ratings of quality of higher education using sigma model approach in India.

In this chapter, the attempt is to contrast these macro-level perspectives of the stakeholders – the employers, the economic and educational planners and policy makers, higher education bodies and other wings of the government, and the society at large with micro-level evidence, essentially the students' perspectives collected in the student's survey that we conducted. Rarely students' experiences and views on the quality of education were analysed, though they are the main stakeholders. In this sense, this analysis contributes a new dimension of examining quality dimensions, as it largely depends upon students' perspectives on about a dozen aspects of quality, and supplements the existing knowledge on the quality of engineering education in India. This chapter also highlights the differences between public (government and government-aided private) and private institutions and also between 'traditional' and 'modern' branches of engineering. The latter is a new facet that is added here, which has been rarely studied. Merely the results of the survey are presented here, and no claim is made of any advances in theoretical knowledge or any contribution to methodology, but the empirical evidence is indeed rich and unique. The mere descriptive empirical evidence provided should be of interest to many scholars, administrators and policy makers for their better reflection on the quality and related aspects of engineering education in India.

Analysis of Survey Results

The survey data provided valuable information on students' views on four important aspects, viz. teaching methods used in the classroom, evaluation pattern, skills acquired by students during the course and the involvement of students in different activities. In fact, the questionnaire used for the students' survey includes a variety of questions on students' perceptions and experiences in the colleges and universities. They relate to their views on the quality of the institution the student was enrolled in, the quality of education she/he was receiving, the level of skills and knowledge acquired during the studies, the level of confidence or preparedness for the future, the students' participation in various academic and related activities, number and type of major and non-major subjects taken as a part of their study and so on. We also obtained information through them on the pedagogic methods and the methods of evaluation adopted in the respective institutions. Finally, information is also collected on how the students use their time. The descriptive analysis attempted here is based on such information collected from the students' survey and interviews with them, supplemented with the information collected through a questionnaire and interviews with heads/deans of departments/institutions on general, academic, faculty, financial and governance aspects of the institutions and from information collected from a small number of major employers of graduates. So there are some direct and indirect measures that are used here to understand quality and related aspects of engineering education in India. Attempt has been to cover comprehensively the quality aspects of education.

How do Students Feel about the Quality of Their Engineering Education?

First, we analyse students' perceptions on the quality of education. Reports of many expert committees and media reports often complained about the poor quality of education imparted to the students in engineering institutions, particularly in private institutions, which actually dominate the whole engineering education scene in the country. They commented on the poor quality attributes of the engineering graduates and their lack of knowledge, skills and proper attitudes. How do the students feel about it? Do they know that they are receiving substandard education that does not provide any knowledge and skills relevant for employment or for the society at large? One of the most interesting results of our student survey is that students are largely 'satisfied' with the quality of their engineering. Evidence can be cited on quite a few aspects relating to this issue.

Improvement in Knowledge, Skills and Abilities

First, students were asked how they felt about their technical knowhow at the time of survey/interviews compared to the time of admission, that is, after three to three and half years of studies. Most students responded that they felt 'stronger' or 'much stronger' (Figure 8.1). The knowledge-related aspects include essentially knowledge of technology, knowledge of new technology, and knowledge of engineering practices. Details are discussed in the following pages.

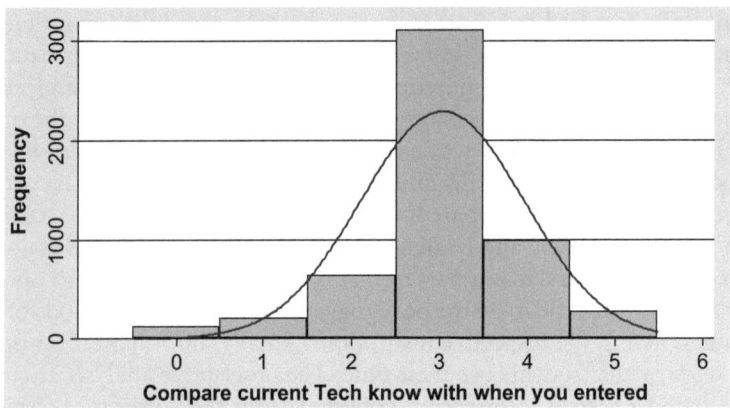

Figure 8.1 Students' Opinion of Current Subject Knowledge Compared to When They Entered the Institution (Distribution of Frequency)

Note: 0 = much weaker; 1 = weaker; 2 = same; 3 = stronger; 4 = much stronger; 5 = don't know.

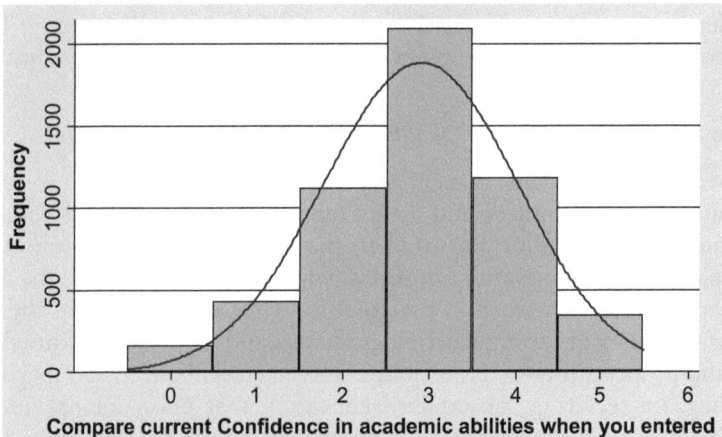

Figure 8.2 Students' Opinion on Confidence in Academic Abilities Compared to When They Entered the Institution (Distribution of Frequency)

Note: 0 = much weaker; 1 = weaker; 2 = same; 3 = stronger; 4 = much stronger; 5 = don't know.

Similarly, when asked about their current level of abilities and skills compared to when they entered the institution, they also felt stronger or much stronger, on average (Figure 8.2). The abilities and skills on which enquiry was made include ability for collaborative work, problem-solving skills, writing skills, communication skills, academic skills, leadership abilities, intercultural understanding and knowledge of global affairs.

It will be interesting to look into the details on some of these aspects. Fourteen attributes relating to knowledge, skills and abilities have been identified for assessment. They are: knowledge of technology, knowledge of new technology, knowledge of engineering practices, knowledge about global markets/economies, ability to communicate in a foreign language, leadership ability, problem-solving ability, academic ability, ability and skills for collaboration for work, writing skills, oral communication skills, intercultural skills, entrepreneurial skills and ability to appreciate the importance of lifelong learning.

As expected, the response of the students varies across these several attributes, as one can note from Figure 8.3. The students responded differently to different questions. They claimed that they acquired more knowledge and advanced considerably their knowledge, skills and abilities with respect to many aspects. Seventy-five per cent of the students felt that they advanced their knowledge of technology and knowledge of engineering practices. More than 50 per cent of the graduates stated that their knowledge and abilities are 'stronger' and even 'much stronger' than when they entered the engineering colleges/universities. Among the abilities and skills in other areas, only in the case of foreign languages, the improvement has been poor: about 75 per cent of the students did not feel to have improved considerably in case of ability and skills in foreign language, after starting their studies in engineering education. The areas in which they felt about the same as when they entered were in foreign language skills and entrepreneurial skills. For others, the change is marginal or towards worsening of the levels of abilities, as given in Table 8.1. In the cases of the others, it is only a small proportion of students

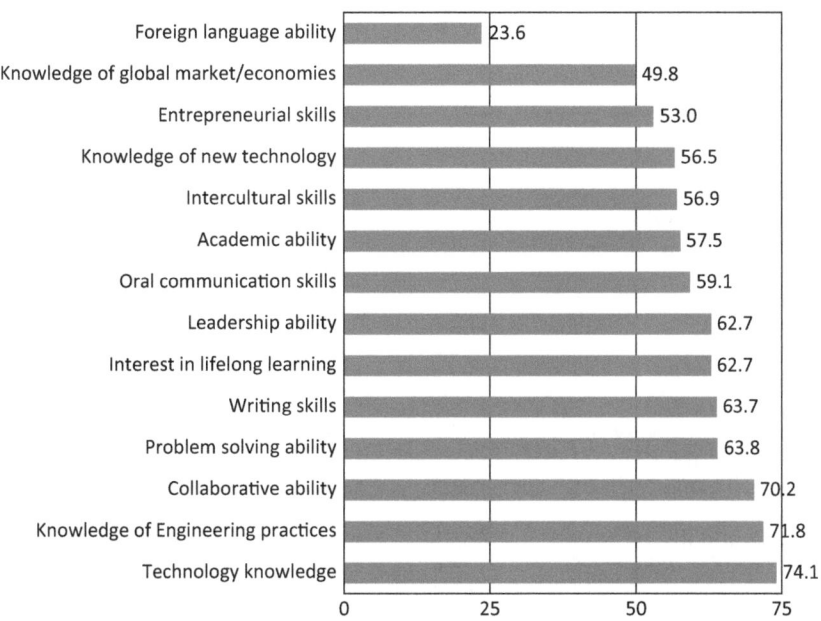

Figure 8.3 Percentage of Students Reporting That Their Current Knowledge and Abilities are 'Stronger' or 'Much Stronger' than at the Time of Admission in the Institution

who reported 'weaker' or 'much weaker' or 'the same' than what they were at the time of admission in the institutions.

Table 8.1 gives these details of responses of students separately by public and private institutions and by streams of engineering – modern and traditional. With respect to almost every aspect, students of public institutions score higher than students in private institutions. Similarly students in 'modern' streams of engineering feel stronger (+ very stronger) than students of traditional streams. This is true with respect to knowledge, skills and abilities in different aspects. Table 8A.1 gives further details in responses, such as how many felt 'average' or 'worsened'.

Thus, a majority of students feel that they learnt a lot during their studies and improved their knowledge levels, skills and abilities considerably. With respect to a variety of aspects of knowledge and skills, they felt 'stronger' or 'much stronger' when they were in the fourth year of their studies compared to the levels with which they entered engineering institutions four years earlier. This is true not only in the case of knowledge of technology and knowledge of engineering practices, but also with respect to abilities and skills for collaboration, problem solving, writing, communication and leadership. As most projects nowadays require efforts of teams of engineers, collaboration and skills

Table 8.1 Current Knowledge and Abilities Compared to the Time of Admission in Engineering Studies (Percentage of Students Who Reported 'Stronger' or 'Much Stronger')

	Institutions		Branches		All
	Public	Private	Traditional	Modern	
Knowledge of technology	76.7	72.8	70.9	75.6	74.1
Knowledge of engineering practices	74.7	70.3	68.2	73.4	71.8
Knowledge of new technology	60.1	54.7	52.4	58.4	56.5
Leadership ability	65.4	61.3	58.3	64.7	62.7
Writing skills	65.0	63.0	62.3	64.3	63.7
Academic ability	59.1	56.6	56.2	58.0	57.5
Oral communication skills	64.3	56.5	55.0	60.9	59.1
Problem-solving ability	66.4	62.5	60.0	65.5	63.8
Collaborative ability	72.0	69.3	66.2	72.0	70.2
Interest in lifelong learning	65.2	61.5	60.0	63.9	62.7
Intercultural skills	59.0	55.8	54.2	58.1	56.9
Entrepreneurial skills	55.7	51.6	49.3	54.6	53.0
Knowledge about global markets/ economies	53.3	48.1	47.3	51.0	49.8
Foreign language ability	25.9	22.4	24.5	23.2	23.6

for collaboration are important in engineering education. About one-fourth of the students felt that there was no improvement or deterioration, while about 10 per cent felt that there was deterioration in their skills, knowledge and abilities in most of the identified areas. A majority of the students felt that their abilities to learn/communicate in any foreign language worsened. Many institutions in India might not offer any scope for learning foreign languages, unlike in the western universities. On the whole, the variations in responses to being 'stronger' or 'much stronger' or otherwise, compared to what they were at the time of admission in the colleges, also depends upon the varying levels of knowledge/confidence base with which they entered the campuses.

Assessments by Institutions

We asked similar questions to the heads of departments/deans to make an assessment of their graduates on various parameters of competence. Such an assessment may raise questions of bias. However, we also asked recruiters to provide their assessment of the average recruit, who is primarily a fresh graduate of a private college. The assessments are ranked low, medium and high. The results are shown in Table 8.2. It appears that there is a remarkable similarity between the attributes of students assessed by recruiters and colleges. However, we need to keep in mind that these three firms were large employers and therefore had the "pick of the crop" — the best from the public, government-aided private and private colleges. The opinion of smaller firms, which may actually be predominant in the market that offer lower salaries and hire more average students, might be quite different. Yet, at least as far as the larger firms are concerned, it appears that the objective of engineering colleges to produce an employment-worthy graduate is being met.

Overall Quality of Education

Second, how do the students perceive the overall quality of education they were receiving? The response has been mixed. The non-response rate is high: one-third of the students did not answer this question or stated, "do not know" – more students in public institutions and traditional branches saying so than their respective counterparts. If the non-responses are excluded, then out of the total, 66 per cent of the students felt that the quality was above average (including good, very good and excellent). Thirty per cent of the students felt the quality was just average, and according to a very small proportion of students, the quality of the education they were receiving was poor/very poor (Figure 8.4). Surprisingly, we also did not find much noticeable difference between the perceptions of students enrolled in public and private institutions or between traditional and modern departments (Table 8.3). Note that in Table 8.3, non-response category is also included.

There are differences between traditional and modern departments, though the differences are not very high. Those who felt that the quality of their education was 'good' are also high in modern departments, which is about 5

Table 8.2 Assessment of Quality of Their Graduates by Engineering Institutions and by Employers

Competence of Students	Engineering Institutions			Employers		
	Public	Government-Aided Private	Private (Unaided)	Firm 1	Firm 2	Firm 3
Core science and engineering	High	High	Medium	High	High	High
Science and engineering knowledge in Major	High	High	Medium	High	High	High
English	High	High	Medium	High	High	High
Basic use of computers	High	High	High	High	High	High
Programming	High	High	Medium	High	High	Medium
Communication	High	High	Medium	High	High	High
Management	High	High	Medium	High	High	High
Sales	Medium	Medium	Medium	High	Medium	High
Organisation	High	Medium	Medium	High	High	Low
Teamwork	High	Medium	Low	High	High	High
Local networks	Medium	Medium	Medium	High	High	High
Global networks	Medium	Medium	Medium	High	High	High
Problem-solving	High	High	Medium	Medium	High	Low
Innovativeness	High	High	High	Medium	High	High
Multicultural awareness	Medium	Medium	Medium	Medium	High	Medium

Note: The last three columns refer to opinions of three IT firms in India, which together employ 235,000 persons as of April 2010. Firm 1 is a product company in ICT design, while firms 2 and 3 are IT services firms.

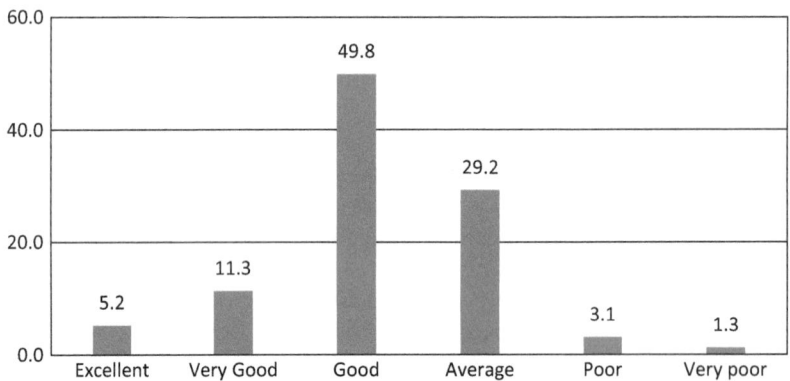

Figure 8.4 Students' Perceptions about the Quality of Their Education

Note: Non-responses/'Do Not Know' are excluded here. (They are included in Table 8.3).

Table 8.3 Students' Perceptions about Quality of Their Education

	Excellent	Very Good	Good	Average	Poor	No Response/ Do not Know	Total
Institutions							
Public	3.2	8.4	31.5	15.9	3,1	37.9	100
Private	3.5	7.0	33.3	20.7	2.7	32.7	100
Branches							
Traditional	3.0	7.7	29.2	17.9	2.7	40.7	100
Modern	3.6	7.4	34.5	19.9	3.5	31.2	100
Total	3.4	7.5	32.7	19.2	2.8	34.3	100

percentage points higher than traditional departments. About 45.5 per cent of students in modern departments felt that their education was 'good' (and above) compared to 40 per cent in traditional branches of engineering.

Preparedness for Future and the Level of Confidence

Third, what about the confidence levels of the students regarding their preparedness to enter the world of work or further education? We asked in the survey whether the student agrees with the statement "I am well prepared for ..." Given the responses in the earlier sections, one may not be surprised to note that a majority answered that they 'agreed', with some answering that they 'strongly agree' than those who had no opinion one way or the other. As high as three-fourths of the students claimed to have acquired technical abilities to enter the next phase of life. Two-thirds of the students were confident that they were well prepared for a good career in engineering; a similar proportion also stated that they were well prepared for managerial jobs; 60 per cent of the students are confident that they were well prepared for jobs in foreign lands; and only 54 per cent of the students 'strongly agreed' or 'agreed' with a view that that they were prepared for further education (Table 8.4). It is possible that the students are inherently not interested in further higher education or research for many reasons, the main reason, in addition to lack of research aptitude, is the academic environment in most places, which is not necessarily promotive of postgraduate education and research (Figure 8.5).

The branches of study do not matter much with respect to the confidence levels of students, as we find no big differences between students in modern areas and traditional departments. The only exception is in the case of preparedness to go abroad, a higher proportion of students (64 per cent) in modern branches claimed to have been well prepared than others (55 per cent) (Table 8.4). Students might get influenced while expressing this opinion by the general trends: larger number of graduates in electronics, computer sciences and IT (information technology)-related engineering going abroad compared to graduates in traditional branches of engineering.

While we do not find much difference between the students of public and private institutions, a marginally higher proportion of students in public

226 Economics of Engineering Education in India

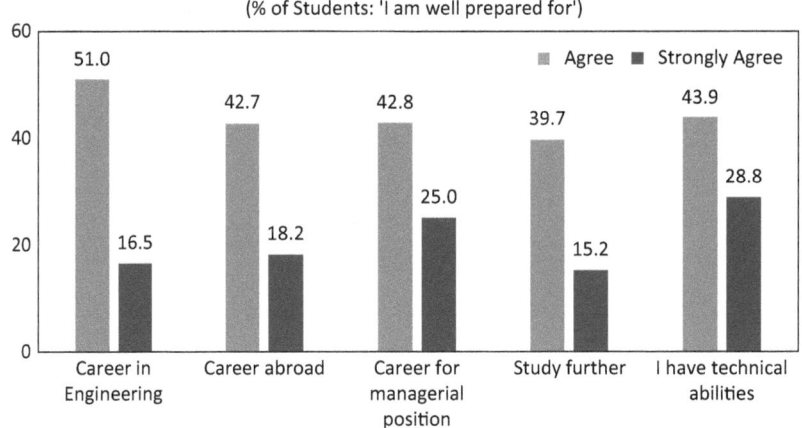

Figure 8.5 Overall Confidence of Engineering Students (in All Branches in All Institutions)

Table 8.4 Confidence of the Students on Their Preparedness for Future

	Public		Private		Traditional Branches		Modern Branches	
	Agree	Strongly agree	Agree	Strongly agree	Agree	Strongly Agree	Agree	Strongly Agree
'I am well prepared for'								
Career in engineering	54.3	15.2	49.4	17.1	48.3	16.7	52.3	16.4
Career abroad	46.4	14.7	40.8	20.0	39.2	15.6	44.3	19.4
Career goal for managerial position	46.7	20.4	40.8	27.4	42.4	21.6	43.0	26.5
Study engineering further	45.4	13.7	36.8	16.0	36.4	14.5	41.2	15.5
'I have technical abilities'	45.6	24.9	43.1	30.8	44	21.6	43.9	29.3

institutions feel more confident; but with respect to technical abilities, students in private institutions feel better than others. Nearly two-thirds of students were also optimistic about the availability of jobs for graduate engineers in India in the near future.

Curriculum and Course Structure

Now we look at some selected aspects of curricula the students undergo during their studies. As per our survey and interviews, students in engineering studies take four to six courses and two to three courses of practical training which are laboratory-based every semester for four years – a total of 36–40 courses and 16–18 laboratory-based courses in their undergraduate training. Students are in classroom and/or laboratories for about 25 hours per week and 13 hours on computers. According to our interviews with students, they spend relatively little time working on their studies at home. As shown later, students spend about 9 hours a week on homework. Tables 8.5 and 8.6 provide some important details on course structure in the IIT Madras.

There is one lab for every two to three courses, depending on the institution, compared to each technical subject course having laboratory work associated with it in countries like the USA.[1] Students in India are required to take more courses in sciences and engineering. For example, at IIT Madras, in the computer science engineering department, the core requirement (in sciences) consists of two classes in physics, two in chemistry and four in mathematics. The core subject classes are spread over three years. Further, with respect to course content, it has been found in our interviews that IIT Madras begins its programming sequence with training in Pascal, a language no longer taught in most American universities like Stanford, where the introductory course on computer science engineering emphasise modelling. In India, it appears the focus is on numerical analysis, such as Gaussian eliminations or Euler's method. In IIT Madras, all the classes in the first year are in core sciences or the major. In the second year, the student takes one humanities class (out of six) each semester and one more in the final year. The range of courses described under the term 'humanities' is wide, which includes the social sciences. While the class time for the humanities accounts for about 6 per cent, its share in total time spent is much less. There is need to integrate courses from humanities and social sciences with engineering curricula, as there is interdependence between technology and the social and economic foundations of the society, and it will help the engineers' understanding of the societal norms of the workplace better (Sharan, 2004; Sheppard et al., 2009; Government of India, 2019).

Table 8.5 Subjects Studied in Computer Science Engineering Course

Courses	Indian Institute of Technology Madras
Engineering Fundamentals	5
Computer Science Classes	16
Senior Project	1
Minor (Engineering)	3
Mathematics	4
Physics	2
Chemistry	2
Humanities and Social Sciences	3
Total	36 (8 semesters)

Table 8.6 Structure of Coursework and Student Study Patterns

Category	Structure
Lecture: Laboratory	3 : 1
Supervised: Unsupervised	3 : 1
Total hours/week on major	40
Total hours/week on other subjects	3
Lecture: Small group work/group discussion	2 : 3 : 1
Total units in major, including prerequisites	88%

Table 8.6 gives further details on course structure. It shows the distribution of work between lecture courses and laboratory courses, lectures and group work and time spent by students in classrooms/laboratories versus work outside the classroom. The ratio of classes to supervised labs is 3:1 and the ratio of unsupervised work (outside class hours) to supervised hours (in classroom lectures and laboratories) is 1:3. Students learn less on their own and depend extensively on classroom lectures. Within supervised teaching, the lecture method dominates.

Let us look at some more details on the same based on our four-state survey.

First, what kinds of courses are chosen by the students while studying engineering education for their undergraduate degree? Students seemed to be focusing on major subjects only, and very few students were found to have opted for any courses outside their major/primary course. More students in public institutions took courses outside their majors than students in private institutions (Table 8.7). When it comes to students in modern branches of engineering, still fewer students took courses outside their major. Perhaps many institutions do not offer courses outside their majors and students might not have many choices or might not necessarily be aware of such probable choices. Note the high non-response rate – nearly 50 per cent. The courses that engineering students can take in addition to major courses and laboratory courses are design courses, oral or written communication courses and professional courses such as business ethics, collaboration, entrepreneurship, leadership, management, preparation of projects for grants, international courses and so on (Figure 8.6).

They can choose the type of course and number of courses in each category. Very few students seemed to have taken design courses, or courses in communication skills, or courses in business ethics and so on. Fewer students, 17 per cent, opted for international courses and those few might take just one such course (Table 8.7).

Second, even among the core courses, students have options to choose a number of majors, laboratory courses, design course, communication courses and professional courses such as courses in ethics, leadership, communication skills and also international courses. We examined what is the

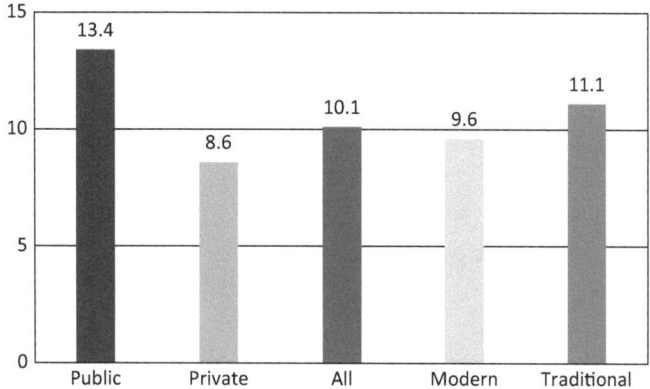

Figure 8.6 How Many Students Have Taken Courses Outside Primary/Major? *(%)*

course combination the students choose. We found that 34 per cent of the students took 27 majors, 33 per cent 14 laboratory courses, and three design courses by one-fourth of the students. Both a higher proportion of students and in terms of number of courses – majors, laboratory and design courses – students in public institutions excel the students in private institutions. While students in private institutions chose 23 major courses and 12 laboratory courses, their counterparts in public institutions chose 30 major courses and 15 laboratory courses. In public institutions, more than 45 per cent of the students took courses likewise, while the corresponding number was just above 25 per cent in private institutions.

'Quality' as Reflected in Student Practices

What are the major academic activities the students are engaged in? As the responses summarised in Table 8.8 show, hardly one-fourth of the students were found to have ever participated in internship programmes. Except for active participation in activities of student organisations, a vast majority of students were not involved in any activity and did not take up or get a chance to work on teachers' research projects, did not participate in any programme abroad, took any interdisciplinary courses of study in sciences or studied any foreign language. Very few teachers may have their own research projects. In an interesting study on science and technology students in India, China and Russia, Loyalka et al. (2022) found that faculty research may have a negative effect on student learning. Further, foreign languages are not offered in many institutions of engineering education in India. The students also did not seem to be interested in leadership programmes/classes. We also note that this was, more or less, the same situation in the case of students enrolled in traditional and modern streams, differences between the two being very marginal. Students in public institutions were marginally at an advantage almost in every aspect than those who were in private institutions. On the

Table 8.7 How Many Students have Taken the following Types of Courses and How Many Courses?

		Major Courses	Laboratory Courses	Design Courses	Oral Communication Courses	Professional Courses	International Courses
By Type of Institution							
Public	No. of courses	30	15	4	3	2	1
	Percentage of students	46.2	45.4	31.4	39.0	36.8	17.1
Private	No. of courses	23	12	3	2	2	1
	Percentage of students	27.6	26.3	21.9	22.8	21.0	16.1
By Branches of Study							
Traditional	No. of courses	25	14	3	3	2	1
	Percentage of students	26.6	25.4	21.8	21.4	20.0	12.5
Modern	No. of courses	27	14	4	2	2	1
	Percentage of students	37.6	36.4	26.9	31.7	29.5	18.4
All	No. of courses	27	14	3	2	2	1
	Percentage of students	34.1	33.0	25.3	28.5	26.5	16.6

whole, that more than 75 percent of the students have not worked in any internship programme, and that more than 85 percent of the students have not worked on any research project of their teachers must be a matter of serious concern, as they have direct impact on the quality of education they receive. The exception is only in the case of IITs and to some extent NITs. It is important to recognise that internships provide some valuable exposure to the industry and it is essential in transforming fresh engineering graduates to ready-to-use professionals (Prabhu & Kudva, 2016). After all, exposure to industry through a variety of ways helps in developing abilities to solve practical problems (Figure 8.7).

Then, one may be curious to understand the academic activities of the students. Writing laboratory/technical reports seemed to be the major academic activity that the students were involved in. Laboratories are the best places that help in integration and synthesis of knowledge development, skills of solving problems and skills of collaboration. Learning from preparing lab reports is very valuable. The next important activity the students were engaged in was participation in group projects. Project-based and problem-based learning is generally regarded as very effective in engineering education. But they were least used practices, as per our survey. Students also make oral presentation of the technical reports. Half the students never had any opportunity to work with any firm. Occasionally, students prepared some technical reports or participated in group projects. Thirty-seven to forty-three per cent of the students never discussed issues relating to the global economy, markets and

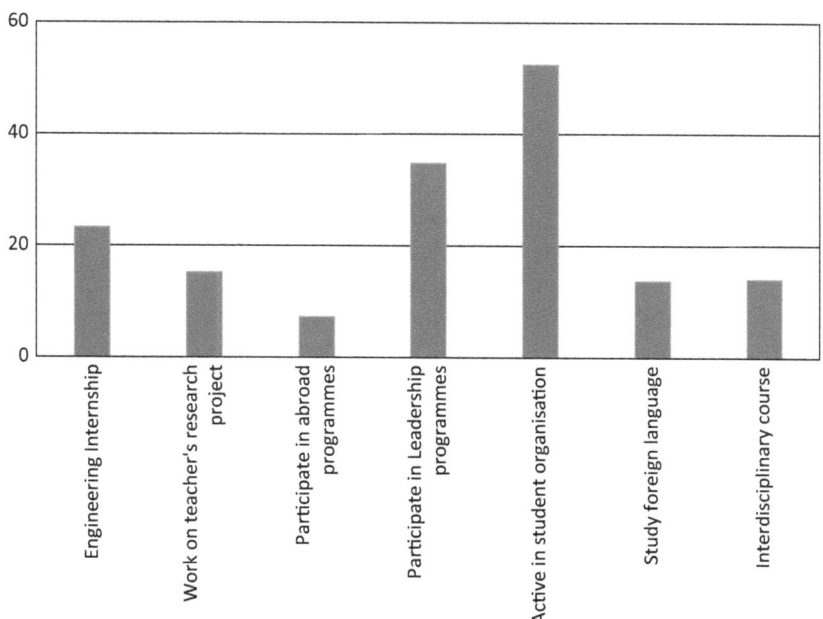

Figure 8.7 Students' Participation in Various Study-Related Activities

Table 8.8 Students' Participation in Internships and Other Programmes (% of All Students)

	Public	Private	Traditional	Modern	All
Internship in engineering projects	25.4	22.1	21.2	24.2	23.2
Work on teacher's research project	17.0	11.8	15.4	15.1	15.2
Participated in abroad program	6.4	7.6	7.8	6.9	7.2
Participate in leadership programmes/classes	36.9	33.7	32.1	36.0	34.8
Active in student organisation	55.1	51.1	50.4	53.4	52.4
Study a foreign language	14.1	13.5	13.4	13.9	13.7
Interdisciplinary course	16.6	12.7	14.4	13.9	14.0

so on among themselves or with others. They might be least concerned with global (and even national) issues, being caught up with tight academic work relating to their studies. They do, however, discuss about their profession (Figure 8.8). It seems that a majority of the students seemed to be focused on their basic studies and participated in the essential activities related to their academic studies. Laboratory and design experiences are valuable. Design projects offer opportunities to approximate professional practice. But involvement in designing of projects is limited. The students also do not seem to be much interested in co-curricular and additional activities that may also impact the overall quality of the students and their personality development.

Table 8A.2 gives details by type of institutions and by branches of engineering. Students in public institutions were found to be performing better than their counterparts in private institutions with respect to writing laboratory reports, developing technical designs and working in group projects. With respect to other activities, there was no big different between the two. Likewise, the students in modern departments were engaged more frequently than those in traditional departments in writing laboratory reports, working in group projects, developing technical designs and presenting reports orally. But in the case of working with firms or discussing global issues or their profession, they were involved less frequently.

It is often stated that students in engineering education do not take interest in social and political issues at national and global levels. We have not collected any information on this, except discussions on global markets/economy and related issues. However, we collected information on students' voting behaviour in general elections at the local/state/national levels as a civic attribute. Only 55 per cent of the students have mentioned that they voted in the elections. The differences between public and private institutions or departments were marginal. There were differences between the four states:

Students' Perceptions on Quality of Education 233

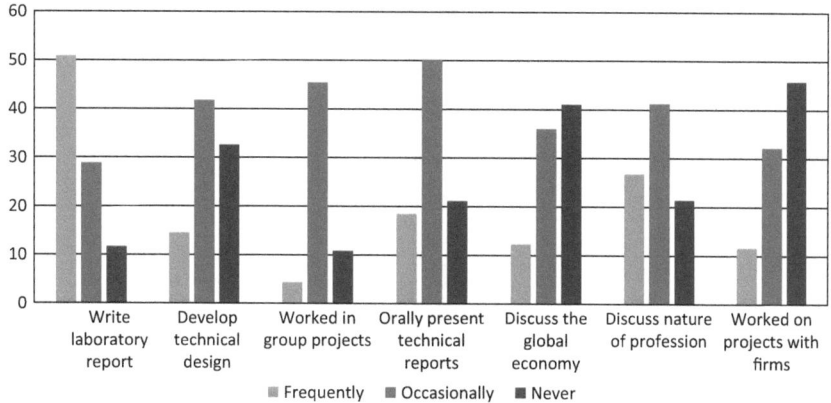

Figure 8.8 Participation of Students in Academic Activities (% of All Students)

while 70 per cent of the students voted in Delhi, only 51 per cent did so in Maharashtra. This is not much different from the voting behaviour among the overall population in India.

Time Use by the Students

How do the students in undergraduate engineering studies spend their time? Figure 8.9 shows the activities that engineering students spent their time on. These data support the data in Table 8.9 showing that a much higher fraction of student time on academic work is devoted to attending classroom lectures and supervised work rather than studying on their own or at home. The remaining time is distributed across socialising with friends, entertainment, sports, clubs and 'other' activities such as voluntary/paid work and transport.

While we cannot comment whether this was an efficient pattern of time use or not, we note that the time spent on homework on self-learning is relatively very small compared to time spent in classrooms. This also means that classroom is the main place for learning by the engineering graduates like in the rest of higher education. Long ago, the Radhakrishnan Commission (1949) expressed concerns that mass lecture is the most common in higher education and it was not supplemented by any regular work by students post lecture (Mathew 2016). This continues to be the case.
Note: Other activities include volunteer work, paid work, transport, clubs and 'others'.

We have not found major differences in student's time use between traditional and modern departments or between types of institutions. Even by gender, there are not much differences. But we find differences between the four different states in the total number of hours and their distribution as well. Students in Tamil Nadu used to spend 27 hours on attending classes/labs and 13 hours on entertainment, while students in Delhi spent 17 hours on classes/

234 *Economics of Engineering Education in India*

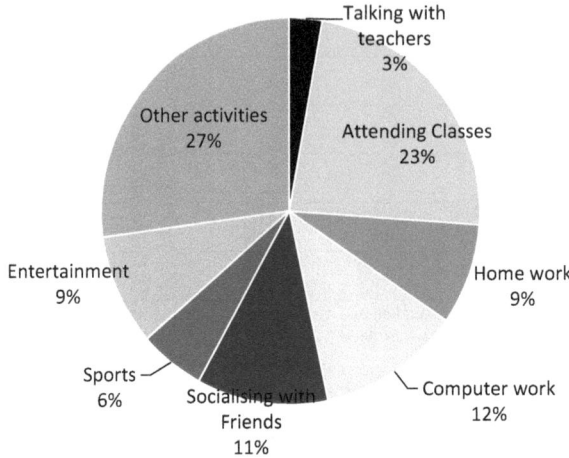

Figure 8.9 Time Use by the Engineering Students in India

Table 8.9 How Do Engineering Students Spend Their Time (Hours per Week)

Category of Activity	Delhi	Karnataka	Maharashtra	Tamil Nadu	All
Attending classes/labs	17.9	29.8	27.4	33.4	27.0
Studying/homework	9.2	10.1	9.3	9.3	9.6
Socialising with friends	12.3	13.1	11.8	10.5	12.4
Meeting teachers outside classroom	2.5	2.4	1.8	3.0	2.3
Computer work	13.6	13.7	12.3	12.0	13.2
Volunteer work	2.9	3.4	2.7	4.4	3.3
Student clubs/groups	3.9	3.6	4.1	4.6	3.9
Sports/Exercise	6.2	6.7	6.0	6.2	6.4
Entertainment (movies, games, going out etc.)	9.2	12.4	10.0	13.0	11.3
Paid work	2.3	1.4	1.4	1.5	1.6
Transport	8.3	6.9	8.0	7.0	7.6
Total	95	113	106	112	108

labs and 9 hours on entertainment. Students of Tamil Nadu also spent less time than their counterparts in other states on computers and with friends.

Teaching Practices and Methods of Evaluation

Teaching, learning and evaluation are inseparably linked together and the results depend upon the methods adopted for each of them. Evaluation tools are the measures of the pedagogy's ability to contribute to learning on the one hand, and on the other students' level of assimilation of knowledge. An important aspect on which we obtained valuable information from the survey of students and interviews with them refers to the pedagogic methods of teaching and methods of evaluation followed in their institutions, which have their own implications for quality of education.

Teaching and Instructional Practices

As the UGC (University Grants Commission) (1973) listed, the objectives of teaching in higher education are many folds, not just confined to transmission of knowledge.[2] To fulfil the objectives, one needs an appropriate blend of various methods and practices in the delivery of education. Lecture in classrooms is the most commonly used method of teaching in all levels of education, including higher education in India. One may expect that engineering institutions may focus relatively more on technical demonstrations, laboratory work, field visits to industries and so forth, as the more effective pedagogic tools. But as per our survey, the traditional lecture method in the classroom, often known as chalk-and-talk method, seemed to be the most frequently used method in engineering colleges as well, whether it is teaching in traditional areas of engineering or modern (IT-related) areas or in public or private institutions. We noted during our survey that many institutions have smart classrooms, smart boards, computers and computer labs. The classroom lecture method is followed by use of laboratory for teaching as the second most common method of teaching. Other methods like students' oral presentations and discussions or work in small groups are only occasionally used. Technical demonstration is also only occasionally used by teachers. Field visit to industries and/or work is also a tool not used much in the teaching/learning pedagogy in the traditional departments. On the whole, no major innovative pedagogic methods seemed to have been adopted in engineering institutions in India that will stimulate creative and imaginative thinking among students or teachers. Presently, teachers seem to be primarily engaged with imparting technical knowledge and the teaching strategies are confined to structured problems and demonstrations.

Compared to public institutions, private institutions appeared to be using technical demonstrations, discussions in small groups and laboratories more frequently than public institutions. But presentations by students and work in small groups were more frequently used in public institutions than in private institutions. Surprisingly, modern departments relied more on classroom lectures than traditional departments. With respect to every other method, traditional departments seemed to be performing better than modern departments (Figure 8.10).

Methods of Evaluation

The method of evaluation of students' performance is generally regarded as one of the most important dimensions, reflecting on the quality of education. Evaluation or assessment is a very important part of the constructive alignment process in education. A well-designed evaluation system helps in understanding the level of mastery attained by students in a subject. The assessments help teachers in further improvement in their teaching practices. If the methods are defective, they may not be able to give any proper picture

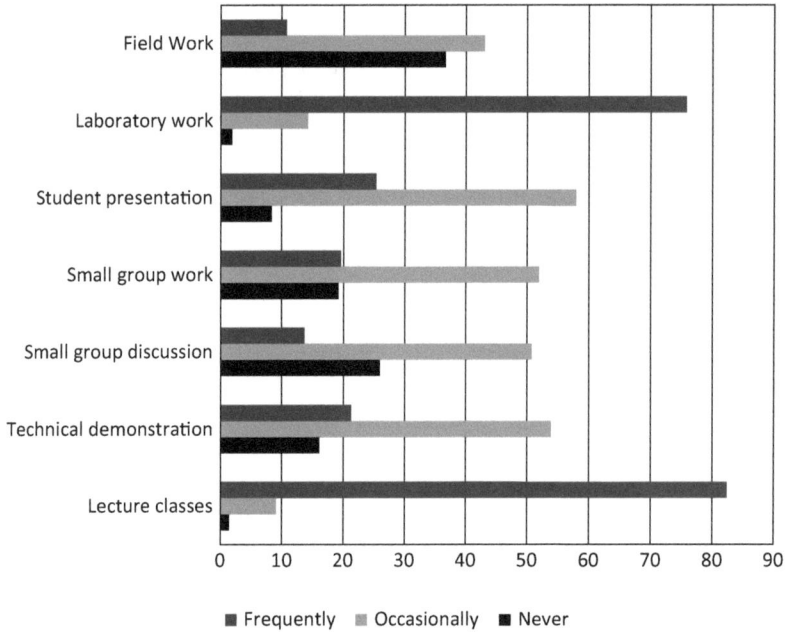

Figure 8.10 'Used' and 'Never Used' Teaching Methods

about the quality of teaching, quality of education or of the graduates. Year/semester-end examinations are the most traditionally used methods of evaluation in education in India. Continuous evaluation through assignments, group discussions, work in small groups, seminar presentations, project work and so on is extensively used in universities, mostly supplementing semester/year end examinations. Some reforms in examinations are attempted in higher education in India. It is widely agreed that a harmonious set of tests, quizzes, tutorials, home assignments, seminar presentations, group discussions, orals, project work and so forth have to be designed if an all-round assessment of the fulfilment of the objectives of a course has to be made. What are the practices in engineering institutions in India? (Figure 8.11) According to our survey, the semester-end examination was the most frequently used method in all institutions and branches. It is used more frequently in public institutions and also in modern departments than in private institutions and traditional departments, respectively. Problem-solving test was the second most frequently used method, again more frequently in public institutions and modern branches than in others. In other methods, no big differences can be found between the several categories. Multiple choice tests are not common; they are least used. Oral presentations for evaluation were also only occasionally used.

It appears that the engineering education system, like the rest of higher education, needs drastic reforms in teaching and evaluation. The parameters

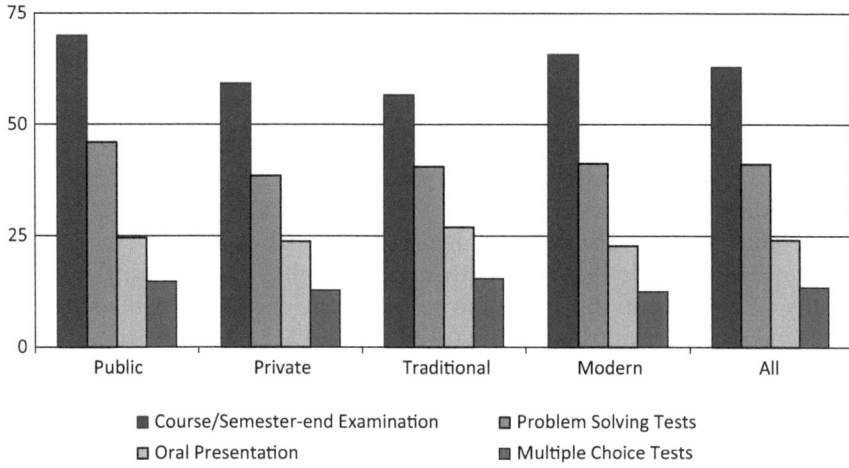

Figure 8.11 'Frequently' Used Methods of Evaluation in Engineering Education, Response by Students (%)

Note: 'Occasionally used' is not included here.

of testing and evaluation that are in practice need a relook and reorientation, so that the system creates a new generation of technically competent, professionally knowledgeable and socially progressive knowledge citizens for the emerging national and global knowledge society.

Now based on survey of the institutions and interviews with deans/heads of departments, let us look at a couple of related dimensions of quality of education.

Faculty with PhD Degree and Research Orientation

A PhD degree is an essential condition for teaching in higher education institutions in India. A simple measure of faculty quality is the proportion of faculty with PhDs. But a large number of teachers in higher education in India do not have a research degree. Assuming that a research degree increases the quality of teaching and research in an institution, we examine how many teachers in engineering institutions possess PhD degrees. Except in the three IITs we surveyed, in the engineering colleges and universities, the proportion of PhDs among the teaching faculty varied between 4 per cent and 26 per cent (Table 8.10).

However, these figures represent the percentages in the entire institution. Some departments may have higher proportions. It is likely that the departments like electrical engineering and computer science have much lower proportions of teachers with PhD degree compared to more traditional fields such as civil and mechanical engineering. For example, in one private college, of the 70 professors with PhDs, only 5 (7 per cent) were in electrical engineering, even though 17 per cent of total students were in that field of study. In a government college, of the 68 faculty members, 15 (22 per cent) were in electrical engineering and computer science, whereas 40 per cent of total students were in those two fields.

The share of faculty with PhD degrees was lower in private institutions, averaging 13 per cent in our sample, versus 49 per cent for state and state-aided institutions. We note clear differences in the quality of faculty between public and private institutions. Public institutions are also able to attract better qualified faculty because of higher job stability and salary parity. The quality of an institution can be further assessed by observing the share of part-timers in the faculty. As summarised in Table 8.11, the part-timers were fewer in public and government-aided private institutions than in private self-financing institutions.

The quality of instruction is also likely to be influenced by the student-faculty ratio. According to the AICTE guidelines, it is expected to be 15. In our interviews, this ratio was seen to have been largely met by all institutions, and the median was 14.62. However, the ratio was higher in private institutions than in state-aided colleges, which, in turn, was higher than in public institutions.

The major reason that there are relatively only a few teachers with PhDs in engineering institutions is the more general shortage of PhDs in general and in engineering education in particular. PhD programmes are available

Table 8.10 Faculty with PhD Degree in Selected Engineering Institutions in Three States

State/Engineering Institutions	Total Faculty	Total Students	Number of PhDs	Student/ Faculty	Percentage PhDs
Karnataka (private)	348	4,473	48	12.9	13.8
Karnataka (private)	381	5,465	94	14.3	24.7
Karnataka (private)	107	1,584	...	14.8	0.0
Karnataka (private)	91	1,440	7	15.8	7.7
Karnataka (private)	106	1,600	10	15.1	9.4
Maharashtra (public)	520	6,000	470	11.5	90.4
Maharashtra (public)	165	3,700	38	22.4	23.0
Maharashtra (public)	55	860	...	15.6	0.0
Maharashtra (private)	113	1,671	9	14.8	8.0
Maharashtra (public)	141	1,902	14	13.5	9.9
Maharashtra (public)	46	458	33	10.0	71.7
Maharashtra (public)	222	3,082	38	13.9	17.1
Maharashtra (private)	222	3,112	...	14.0	0.0
Delhi (public)	28	1,384	14	49.4	50.0
Delhi (private)	64	960	5	15.0	7.8
Delhi (private)	97	1,440	5	14.8	5.2
Delhi (private)	137	1,880	...	13.7	0.0
Delhi (public)	251	3,500	129	13.9	51.4
Delhi (public)	136	2,050	18	15.1	13.2
Delhi (private)	86	1,386	11	16.1	12.8
Delhi (public)	357	4,382	351	12.3	98.3

Table 8.11 Faculty in Public versus Private Institutions (Proportion of Faculty)

	Public	Government-Aided Private	Private
PhDs in faculty	High	High	Low
Part-time faculty	Low	Low	High
Undergraduates	Low	Medium	High
Ratio of students/faculty	Low	Medium	High

in public universities, and in the case of engineering, almost exclusively in IITs and NITs and some universities, but annual production of these institutions is extremely small in number. They hardly cater to the needs of even the government engineering colleges in the entire country. Private institutions, both aided and self-financing, tend to focus more on undergraduate education, while public institutions which are also relatively older have a mandate to develop postgraduate education and research programmes. The average proportion of undergraduate students in the total enrolment was 76 per cent in state institutions and 94 per cent in private institutions in the country as a whole.

Although having a PhD does not necessarily imply that a teacher will be a more competent teacher, some positive relation between completion of a research degree and being able to teach a subject more competently can be expected, even at the undergraduate level. If this is the case, it seems to be difficult in the future to increase the quality of undergraduate engineering education significantly, unless some major initiatives are taken to promote research programmes and teacher recruitment.

Summary and Concluding Interpretations

This chapter presented students' perspectives on the quality of undergraduate engineering education in India. The analysis presented here covered nearly a dozen aspects of quality of education, and the findings are described in detail.

Of all, most strikingly, in contrast to predominant experts' views, engineering students who were interviewed in a wide range of institutions, including many private ones, appeared quite satisfied with their education and with their choice of engineering and the institution. This is largely the case whether they are in the prestigious IITs or in less notable private institutions. As far as these students are concerned, in their opinion, the higher engineering education system has done 'right' for them. How do we reconcile these somewhat highly positive views of the students with the general perceptions and perceptive views based on rigorous analytical studies of the experts and committees on engineering education in India, all of which condemn engineering education in India as deplorable in quality?

The 'overall' assessment of quality of education/institution by the students presented here is not really 'summative' assessment, as on several individual parameters, students admitted otherwise. For example, the majority of students reported not to have participated in internships programmes, or got any exposure to industry, or got any opportunities to participate in research projects, or in leadership programmes and so on. Students have also stated that they did not develop technical designs, or participate in projects with firms and so on. They have also mentioned that classroom lecture is the most relied method of teaching and semester/course end examination the main tool of evaluation. The question remains whether at all the students know that these are indeed not positive aspects of their education. It is likely that students are aware of some of these problems, but have reconciled to the situation to the extent of viewing the systems as satisfactory or good or even very good. After all, there was no choice for the students. Clearly, no strong evidence could be found from the survey to say that a majority of students acquire essential attributes of engineers for the twenty-first century that include strong analytical skills, practical ingenuity, creativity, mastery of business and management – awareness of interdependence between technology and the social and economic foundations of the society (Sheppard et al., 2009). At least, some students are aware of these aspects, and their expectations and aspirations accordingly are conditioned.[3] Further, students might also feel hesitant to admit that they did not learn much during their studies. So many claimed that their current levels of knowledge and skills are 'stronger'/'much stronger' than what they were earlier.

While there is no basis to doubt the integrity and honesty of the students, though some feel that many private institutions do not encourage, in fact, prohibit, their students or faculty to speak honestly about their institutions,[4] one has to note that given the asymmetry of information, students' knowledge of 'good-quality' engineering education, what a high-quality institution, like say an IIT, in India looks like, let alone world class universities abroad and even the labour market conditions in the country and at global level, including the professional knowledge, skills, abilities, competencies, attitudes and other values that the modern employers value, may not necessarily be of reasonable level.[5] Immediately after their senior secondary-level examination, students join a particular engineering college/university, having no opportunity to interact with students and faculty of other (good and bad) institutions. Second, they have not yet entered the labour market, and with little participation in engineering internship and similar programmes that might provide some exposure to the world of work, they are yet to understand what the profession requires. They may have very limited or narrow view of employability (Tymon, 2011). Hence their expectations and aspirations are not high. For the same reason, the students' perceptions on some of the issues may have to be discounted. So one extreme interpretation is: many students are like frogs in the well and are very happy with what they have without necessarily knowing what is good and what is going on outside.

An alternative explanation can be as follows: the expert's conclusions are based on an examination of input indicators like the quality of teachers and infrastructure, process indicators such as methods of teaching, learning and evaluation and outcomes such as employability and graduate attributes. In contrast, it is likely that the students' reflections are essentially based on certain other outcomes: they are assured of a degree, which has an immediate value in the market – labour market as well as marriage market, besides enhancing the social status. The experts may be concerned, for example, with the PhD degree holders among faculty and their research output. Students may be least bothered about these aspects; they would be content if a teacher takes the class and finally helps them in going through semester/year end examinations successfully, which an under-qualified instructor in a coaching institution might as well do.[6] The experts may be interested in the adoption of sustainable knowledge development practices, but the students may be worried about their immediate success in examinations and in securing employment. The experts' long-term considerations may not figure in students' short-term perspectives. Thus the expectations and considerations of the experts and the students while making their respective assessment of quality of education can be different.

While it cannot be concluded that one is right and the other group is wrong, we feel that both perspectives are important for a proper understanding of the quality of engineering education in India. The students' perspectives analysed here may compel researchers to widen their approach to study quality-related problems and administrators and policy makers to rethink on their perspectives and policy initiatives. Obviously, quality improvement requires multiple interventions and multiple perspectives need to be taken into account. We need a fresh broader perspective.

Notes

1 The inputs provided by Martin Carnoy on US universities, described here, and the notes taken at the time of discussions with students and faculty in Indian institutions, which are used here, are gratefully acknowledged.
2 They are: to transmit a body of facts, figures, theories and so on; to create a grasp and an understanding of the theories and principles so that one may apply them to new situations; to produce a capacity of critically evaluating hypotheses when they are presented; to cultivate an open and flexible mind, so that one may retain the capacity to learn new things in the future; to cultivate an urge for perfection, an appreciation of beauty and inclination to search for newer and better solutions to problems, to discover and invent; to train the mind for imagination, intuition and speculation into the realm of the unknown; to produce motivation and drive in the individual to result in capacity for sustained intellectual effort, to possibly cultivate qualities of leadership as well as team work; to cultivate specific manual, technical, intellectual and other soft skills; to train in the ability to communicate at a high intellectual level through specific media; and so on (UGC, 1973).
3 For the same reasons, students from 'tier 2' and 'tier 3' colleges have lower expectations on future employment conditions and salaries (Aspiring Minds, 2019). See Chapter 2.
4 Quite a few private institutions – universities and colleges – in the National Capital Region of Delhi and other states have flatly refused permission to conduct our survey in their institutions, despite our having an official letter seeking their co-operation in the conduct of the survey.
5 In a study on Karnataka, based on student survey of students, it was concluded that students could not connect to the industry expectations only through the classroom teaching model predominantly used on campus (Kulkarni, 2017).
6 Many of the students undergo coaching from such institutions while preparing for common entrance examinations for admission in engineering institutions.

Appendix (to Chapter 8)

Table 8A.1 Current Knowledge, Abilities and Skills of Students Compared to the Time of Entry into This Institution

	Much Weaker	Weaker	Same	Stronger	Much Stronger	No Response/ Do Not Know	Total
Public Institutions							
Knowledge of technology	2.5	4.3	11.2	55.0	21.7	5.4	100
Knowledge of engineering practices	1.5	4.0	13.6	59.1	15.7	6.2	100
Foreign language ability	7.0	11.2	48.9	19.8	6.1	7.0	100
Leadership ability	1.9	3.6	22.6	43.0	22.5	6.4	100
Writing skills	1.8	4.5	22.6	47.8	17.1	6.1	100
Academic ability	3.1	6.4	21.7	38.3	20.9	9.7	100
Knowledge of new technology	2.3	5.1	18.4	45.9	14.2	14.1	100
Knowledge about global markets/ economies	2.9	6.6	29.2	40.8	12.5	8.0	100
Oral communication skills	1.8	4.9	21.6	45.9	18.3	7.6	100
Problem-solving ability	1.5	4.4	16.3	41.7	24.6	11.4	100
Collaborative ability	1.9	3.0	14.5	41.2	30.9	8.5	100
Interest in lifelong learning	3.2	5.5	18.6	42.3	22.9	7.5	100
Intercultural skills	2.3	5.0	26.0	41.8	17.2	7.8	100
Entrepreneurial skills	3.0	4.9	26.4	39.9	15.8	10.0	100
Private Institutions							
Knowledge of technology	2.3	3.9	12.8	57.6	15.2	8.2	100

(*Continued*)

Table 8A.1 (Continued)

	Much Weaker	Weaker	Same	Stronger	Much Stronger	No Response/ Do Not Know	Total
Knowledge of engineering practices	1.7	4.2	14.7	56.4	13.9	9.1	100
Foreign language ability	8.7	12.7	46.0	16.6	5.9	10.2	100
Leadership ability	1.8	4.8	22.9	42.5	18.8	9.2	100
Writing skills	1.7	4.5	21.9	44.2	18.9	9.0	100
Academic ability	3.2	9.0	21.5	35.1	21.6	9.6	100
Knowledge of new technology	2.2	6.2	24.3	36.2	18.5	12.6	100
Knowledge about global markets/economies	3.5	7.7	29.8	34.4	13.7	11.0	100
Oral communication skills	2.1	5.3	22.9	35.6	20.9	13.2	100
Problem-solving ability	1.6	3.5	16.0	42.3	20.2	16.5	100
Collaborative ability	1.5	3.2	14.4	42.9	26.4	11.6	100
Interest in lifelong learning	3.1	5.4	19.5	38.3	23.2	10.6	100
Intercultural skills	2.2	5.1	25.2	36.1	19.7	11.7	100
Entrepreneurial skills	2.8	5.4	26.0	35.2	16.3	14.3	100
Traditional Departments							
Technology knowledge	2.9	3.8	12.7	57.5	13.4	9.6	100
Engineering practice knowledge	1.7	3.7	15.4	54.3	13.9	11.1	100
Foreign language ability	9.0	13.6	40.7	18.8	5.7	12.2	100
Leadership ability	2.0	4.5	24.0	39.6	18.8	11.3	100
Writing skill	1.6	4.2	21.4	44.2	18.1	10.6	100
Academic ability	3.1	8.0	19.1	35.5	20.8	13.6	100
Knowledge about new technology	2.6	5.8	22.1	36.3	16.1	17.1	100
Knowledge about global market/economies	3.8	7.4	27.3	35.2	12.1	14.3	100
Oral communication skill	1.9	5.5	22.2	37.5	17.5	15.4	100
Problem-solving ability	2.1	3.8	15.8	42.1	17.9	18.3	100
Collaborative ability	1.6	3.4	14.2	42.3	23.9	14.6	100

(*Continued*)

Table 8A.1 (Continued)

	Much Weaker	Weaker	Same	Stronger	Much Stronger	No Response/ Do Not Know	Total
Interest in lifelong learning	2.6	5.1	18.6	38.8	21.2	13.7	100
Intercultural skill	2.2	4.8	24.1	36.5	17.7	14.8	100
Entrepreneurial skill	3.1	5.0	24.9	33.3	16.0	17.8	100
Modern Departments							
Technology knowledge	2.1	4.1	12.1	56.3	19.2	6.2	100
Engineering practice knowledge	1.6	4.3	13.9	58.6	14.8	6.8	100
Foreign language ability	7.7	11.6	49.8	17.2	6.0	7.7	100
Leadership ability	1.8	4.4	22.3	44.1	20.6	6.9	100
Writing skill	1.8	4.6	22.5	45.9	18.4	6.8	100
Academic ability	3.2	8.3	22.7	36.5	21.6	7.9	100
Knowledge about new technology	2.1	5.8	22.4	40.9	17.5	11.3	100
Knowledge about global market/ economies	3.1	7.3	30.7	37.1	13.8	8.0	100
Oral communication skill	2.0	5.0	22.6	39.8	21.2	9.5	100
Problem-solving ability	1.3	3.8	16.2	42.1	23.4	13.2	100
Collaborative ability	1.7	3.0	14.5	42.4	29.7	8.7	100
Interest in lifelong learning	3.3	5.6	19.5	40.0	23.9	7.7	100
Intercultural skill	2.3	5.2	26.1	38.7	19.4	8.4	100
Entrepreneurial skill	2.8	5.3	26.6	38.4	16.2	10.7	100
All							
Technology knowledge	2.3	4.0	12.3	56.7	17.4	7.3	100
Engineering practice knowledge	1.6	4.1	14.3	57.3	14.5	8.1	100
Foreign language ability	8.1	12.2	47.0	17.7	6.0	9.1	100
Leadership ability	1.8	4.4	22.8	42.7	20.1	8.2	100
Writing skill	1.7	4.5	22.1	45.4	18.3	8.0	100
Academic ability	3.1	8.2	21.6	36.1	21.3	9.7	100
Knowledge about new technology	2.3	5.8	22.3	39.4	17.1	13.1	100

(*Continued*)

Table 8A.1 (Continued)

	Much Weaker	Weaker	Same	Stronger	Much Stronger	No Response/ Do Not Know	Total
Knowledge about global market/economies	3.3	7.3	29.6	36.5	13.3	10.0	100
Oral communication skill	2.0	5.2	22.5	39.1	20.0	11.3	100
Problem-solving ability	1.6	3.8	16.1	42.1	21.7	14.8	100
Collaborative ability	1.7	3.2	14.4	42.3	27.9	10.5	100
Interest in lifelong learning	3.1	5.4	19.2	39.6	23.1	9.5	100
Intercultural skill	2.2	5.1	25.4	38.0	18.9	10.4	100
Entrepreneurial skill	2.9	5.2	26.1	36.8	16.1	12.9	100

Table 8A.2 Participation of Students in Academic Activities

	Frequently	Occasionally	Never	No Response/Do Not Know	Total
Public Institutions					
Write laboratory report	56.7	28.2	8.3	6.8	100
Develop technical design	16.3	49.1	26.3	8.4	100
Worked in group projects	41.1	40.4	11.2	7.4	100
Orally present technical reports	17.0	54.3	20.3	8.4	100
Discuss the global economy	12.3	35.7	43.4	8.6	100
Discuss nature of profession	26.5	41.9	23.4	8.2	100
Worked on projects with firms	11.0	34.1	46.7	8.2	100
Private Institutions					
Write laboratory report	47.9	29.1	13.2	9.8	100
Develop technical design	13.6	38.0	35.9	12.6	100
Worked in group projects	30.9	48.0	10.6	10.5	100
Orally present technical reports	19.1	48.1	21.4	11.4	100
Discuss the global economy	12.2	36.2	39.8	11.9	100

(*Continued*)

Table 8A.2 (Continued)

	Frequently	Occasionally	Never	No Response/Do Not Know	Total
Discuss nature of profession	26.9	40.8	20.3	12.0	100
Worked on projects with firms	11.9	31.2	45.3	11.7	100
Traditional Departments					
Write laboratory report	45.6	30.7	11.9	11.8	100
Develop technical design	13.9	37.5	32.8	15.8	100
Worked in group projects	28.6	46.4	12.7	12.3	100
Orally present technical reports	16.8	47.2	20.8	15.2	100
Discuss the global economy	13.4	35.5	36.6	14.6	100
Discuss nature of profession	27.1	38.9	19.1	14.9	100
Worked on projects with firms	12.1	33.9	40.5	14.0	100
Modern Departments					
Write laboratory report	53.2	28.0	11.4	7.4	100
Develop technical design	14.8	43.7	32.5	9.1	100
Worked in group projects	36.9	45.0	9.9	8.2	100
Orally present technical reports	19.2	51.5	21.2	8.2	100
Discuss the global economy	11.7	36.2	43.0	9.1	100
Discuss nature of profession	26.6	42.3	22.3	8.8	100
Worked on projects with firms	11.4	31.6	48.0	9.0	100
All					
Write laboratory report	50.9	28.8	11.6	8.8	100
Develop technical design	14.5	41.8	32.6	11.1	100
Worked in group projects	34.3	45.4	10.8	9.5	100
Orally present technical reports	18.4	50.2	21.1	10.4	100
Discuss the global economy	12.2	36.0	41.0	10.8	100
Discuss nature of profession	26.8	41.2	21.3	10.7	100
Worked on projects with firms	11.6	32.2	45.7	10.5	100

Table 8A.3 Teaching Methods Used in Public versus Private Engineering Institutions

	Frequently	Occasionally	Never	No Response	Total
Public Institutions					
Lecture classes	83.3	9.1	2.0	5.7	100
Technical demonstration	18.9	56.8	16.6	7.7	100
Small group discussion	12.9	51.0	28.2	8.0	100
Small group work	24.7	51.7	15.7	7.8	100
Student presentation	30.0	53.7	9.3	7.1	100
Laboratory work	74.2	16.7	2.2	6.9	100
Field work	11.4	44.3	33.9	10.4	100
Private Institutions					
Lecture classes	82.0	9.1	1.2	7.7	100
Technical demonstration	22.6	52.5	15.8	9.2	100
Small group discussion	14.1	50.7	24.9	10.4	100
Small group work	17.0	52.0	21.0	10.0	100
Student presentation	23.0	60.2	7.9	8.8	100
Laboratory work	76.7	13.0	1.7	8.7	100
Field work	10.6	42.6	37.7	9.2	100
Traditional Streams					
Lecture classes	79.1	10.4	1.8	8.8	100
Technical demonstration	23.2	49.4	15.4	12.0	100
Discussion in small groups	16.0	47.8	23.8	12.4	100
Work in small groups	20.4	48.8	17.8	13.0	100
Student presentations	25.4	55.7	8.3	10.6	100
Laboratory work	73.4	14.6	1.9	10.0	100
Field Visit/work (in industries)	14.7	50.5	23.5	11.4	100
Modern Streams					
Lecture classes	83.9	8.5	1.3	6.3	100
Technical demonstration	20.5	55.9	16.4	7.2	100
Discussion in small groups	12.7	52.1	27.0	8.3	100
Work in small groups	19.3	53.3	19.8	7.6	100
Student presentations	25.4	59.1	8.4	7.2	100
Laboratory work	76.9	14.1	1.8	7.2	100
Field visit/work (in industries)	9.0	39.7	42.7	8.6	100
All					
Lecture classes	82.4	9.1	1.4	7.0	100
Technical demonstration	21.3	53.9	16.1	8.7	100
Discussion in small groups	13.7	50.8	26.0	9.6	100
Work in small groups	19.6	51.9	19.2	9.2	100
Student presentations	25.4	58.0	8.4	8.2	100
Laboratory work	75.8	14.2	1.9	8.1	100
Field visit/work (in industries)	10.8	43.1	36.6	9.5	100

Table 8A.4 Frequency in the Use of Methods of Evaluation

	Frequently	Occasionally	Never	No response	Total
Public Institutions					
Multiple choice tests	14.8	43.9	34.4	6.9	100
Test with problem-solving	46.1	36.9	10.4	6.6	100
Course/semester end examination	70.0	17.5	5.4	7.1	100
Oral presentation	24.6	52.5	15.8	7.1	100
Private Institutions					
Multiple choice tests	12.8	34.7	43.2	9.3	100
Test with problem-solving	38.6	39.8	12.9	8.8	100
Course/semester end examination	59.2	22.9	7.1	10.8	100
Oral presentation	23.8	48.7	17.9	9.6	100
Traditional Branches					
Multiple choice tests	15.5	38.8	34.2	11.5	100
Test with problem-solving	40.6	36.8	10.8	11.8	100
Course/semester end examination	56.6	22.0	7.4	14.0	100
Oral presentation	26.9	44.9	15.5	12.7	100
Modern Branches					
Multiple choice tests	12.6	37.4	42.9	7.1	100
Test with problem-solving	41.3	39.7	12.6	6.4	100
Course/semester end examination	65.7	20.7	6.2	7.5	100
Oral presentation	22.8	52.3	18.0	7.0	100
All					
Multiple choice tests	13.5	37.8	40.2	8.5	100
Test with problem-solving	41.1	38.8	12.1	8.1	100
Course/semester end examination	62.9	21.1	6.5	9.5	100
Oral presentation	24.1	50.0	17.2	8.8	100

9 Employability, Employment and Earnings of Engineering Graduates

Eighty percent of engineers are not employable for any job in the knowledge economy.

(*National Employability Report*, 2019, p. 5)

Only forty nine percent of engineering graduates have 'employable talent'.

(*India Skill Report*, 2020, p. 13)

Introduction

The growing trend towards massification of higher education signifies a change in the aspirations of students. The pursuit of higher education is no more based on the traditional principle of 'knowledge for knowledge sake', but on 'higher education for employment/economic returns'. Nowadays employability dominates the agenda of higher education institutions. This is more so understandably in the case of professional/technical streams of higher education like engineering and technology. The current labour market situation is characterised by excess supply of graduates, shortages of skilled manpower, mismatches, disguised unemployment and mis-/mal-employment (Tilak, 2023). How is the labour market situation for engineering graduates? What is the employment potential of engineering graduates? As reported in Chapter 2, among major disciplines, the employability of graduates in engineering seems to be the highest. The private rate of return to first degree in engineering education in India was above 20 per cent in 2006; even the social rate of return was above 16 per cent (Carnoy et al., 2012, p. 23). The estimates of rates of return given in Tables 9.1 and 9.2 are somewhat dated; more recent estimates are not available.

Even if the returns have fallen in recent years, one can expect reasonably attractive rates of return to engineering education even now, and more importantly, such returns to be relatively higher than returns to general higher education. Hence, this may still be the reason why there exists a huge demand for engineering education in India,[1] even though quite a few

Table 9.1 Private and Social Rates of Return to Higher Education by Gender in India, 2006 (%)

Level of Education	Earnings Forgone	Earnings Foregone + Tuition	Private + Public Costs (Social Rate of Return)
	(Private Rates of Return)		
Men			
Diploma (All)	19.0	13.7	12.0
Graduate (All)	19.5	14.1	12.3
Diploma (Technical)	21.0	11.0–13.2	8.7–10.0
Graduate Engineer	36.8	20.4–24.1	16.0–18.6
Women			
Diploma (All)	18.6	12.6	10.7
Graduate (All)	18.0	12.4	10.6
Diploma (Technical)	30.0	12.1–16.0	7.8 –10.2
Graduate Engineer	…	…	…

Source: Carnoy et al. (2010), based on the National Sample Survey, 2006.

Table 9.2 Estimates of Mincerian Rates of Return by Gender in India, 2006

Variable	Model I		Model II	
	Male	Female	Male	Female
Age	0.07***	0.05***	0.07***	0.05***
	(0.00)	(0.00)	(0.00)	(0.00)
Age-squared	–0.00***	–0.00***	–0.00***	–0.00***
	(0.00)	(0.00)	(0.00)	(0.00)
General education (left out = higher secondary)				
\Not literate	–0.96***	–1.24***	–0.95***	–1.24***
	(0.01)	(0.03)	(0.01)	(0.03)
\Literate without formal schooling (EGS/NFEC/AEC)	–0.81***	–1.16***	–0.80***	–1.16***
	(0.05)	(0.13)	(0.05)	(0.13)
Literate without formal schooling (TLC)	–0.85***	–0.99***	–0.84***	–0.99***
	(0.06)	(0.12)	(0.06)	(0.12)
Literate without formal schooling (Others)	–0.71***	–0.61***	–0.70***	–0.61***
	(0.05)	(0.11)	(0.05)	(0.11)
Below primary	–0.75***	–1.00***	–0.74***	–1.00***
	(0.02)	(0.04)	(0.02)	(0.04)
Primary	–0.61***	–0.99***	–0.60***	–0.98***
	(0.01)	(0.04)	(0.01)	(0.04)
Middle	–0.43***	–0.74***	–0.42***	–0.74***
	(0.01)	(0.04)	(0.01)	(0.04)
Secondary	–0.21***	–0.30***	–0.21***	–0.30***
	(0.01)	(0.04)	(0.01)	(0.04)

(*Continued*)

Table 9.2 (Continued)

Variable	Model I		Model II	
	Male	Female	Male	Female
Diploma/certificate course	0.36*** (0.02)	0.48*** (0.06)	0.14*** (0.03)	0.36*** (0.07)
Graduate	0.48*** (0.02)	0.52*** (0.04)	0.41*** (0.02)	0.46*** (0.04)
Postgraduate and above	0.75*** (0.01)	0.66*** (0.01)	0.69*** (0.02)	0.61*** (0.01)
Technical education (left out = no technical education)				
Technical degrees (all fields) and diploma or certificate (below graduate level) in other technical fields			0.34*** (0.03)	0.15*** (0.05)
Diploma or certificate (below graduate level) in engineering/technology			0.23*** (0.03)	0.11 (0.09)
Diploma or certificate (below graduate level) in medicine			0.27*** (0.08)	0.19** (0.09)
Diploma or certificate (graduate level) in other tech fields			0.18*** (0.05)	0.22*** (0.07)
Diploma or certificate (graduate level) in engineering/technology			0.55*** (0.04)	0.12 (0.11)
Diploma or certificate (graduate level) in medicine			0.69*** (0.09)	0.76*** (0.12)
Constant	5.08*** (0.03)	5.32*** (0.06)	5.07*** (0.03)	5.32*** (0.06)
R-squared	0.39	0.43	0.40	0.44
No. of observations	49351	13266	49198	13244

Notes: Standard errors in parentheses; *** $p < 0.01$, ** $p < 0.05$ and * $p < 0.1$.
Source: Carnoy et al. (2010). Based on the National Sample Survey, 2006.

cracks are being noted both with respect to employment and also associated earnings in the markets: employment opportunities begin to be not so good or salaries as attractive as they were about one to two decades ago. In this chapter, we wish to explore the factors that predict employment of engineering graduates and determinants of their earnings.

It is widely perceived that the massive expansion of higher education, engineering education in particular, has been at the cost of quality of the education and employability of graduates. Based upon the data collected through the primary survey, the attempt in this chapter is to analyse the employment and related aspects of engineering graduates in India. After describing the methodology in the next section, labour market profile of engineering graduates based on the primary survey, the determinants of employment probabilities of engineering graduates are analysed. This is done with the help of logistic regression, considering 'whether the engineering graduates have been employed or not' as the dependent variable. Then, the determinants of earnings of engineering graduates are estimated, using the ordinary least squares (OLS) technique. This chapter ends with presenting a short summary of findings and their implications for public policy on engineering education.

Methodology

We do not have the data on actual employment of the graduates or on their earnings. Students in the final year of their studies were the respondents in our survey. They were yet to formally enter the job market. Campus recruitment is a very common practice in many higher education institutions in India.[2] Recruitment of undergraduate engineering students through campus recruitment drive by engineering companies has become very popular, in which a variety of companies – foreign, domestic and joint ventures – participate. Students are recruited by prospective employers before they complete their studies. Generally, the recruitment takes place through placement cells of the institution, when the students are in the final year/semester of studies. A variety of firms, companies or organisations interested in recruiting engineering graduates belonging to different streams visit institutions for on-campus recruitment of graduates as per their needs. They use face-to-face interviews, group discussions or some other selection method. They consider it as the best method of catching the talent early. Selected students are given a job offer that describes conditions relating to the job, including starting annual salary. So, in our survey, students were asked a question, 'whether she/he has got job offer' in the on-campus recruitment. Students who have received job offers are considered here as 'employed' and who have not as 'unemployed'. Similarly, the first annual salary offered to the students (by the employers) is taken as the actual earnings from their jobs in the first year or as starting salaries. It would have been ideal to use information on graduates who are actually employed, but the survey has not considered employed graduates. Consideration of the variables for the statistical analysis is seriously constrained by the availability of data. We could consider only those variables that could be generated from the survey data. The survey did not include many relevant variables. There are several other probable determinants of employment and earnings of engineering graduates that could not be considered.

After a brief discussion on the employment and earnings profiles of the graduates surveyed in the next section, the predictors of employment and determinants of earnings of engineering graduates are estimated using logistic regression and OLS equations, respectively, which are also used in the earlier chapters.

Employment and Earnings Profile of Engineering Graduates

Employment Profile

Unemployment of engineering graduates accounts for a huge loss in terms of manpower and economy. As per our survey, only 26 per cent of the graduates succeed in getting employment offers through on-campus recruitment, as shown in Table 9.3; others could not make it.[3] There may be many reasons for such a low rate of employment. A good number of firms/organisations/companies/industries visit universities, colleges and other institutions of engineering education in search of talent and select students as per their requirements.[4] Job offers are conditioned by the requirements of the organisations – number and nature. It is also possible that some students might not like the jobs and associated conditions offered by the companies, including pay, location and job profile or the goodwill of the company, or they may have some preference to go for further studies, and they may not finally take up those jobs. But quite probably, in such cases also, the students take the offers but may not finally join the given job. On the whole, since a large number of engineering institutions are visited by prospective employers and a majority of students participate in the recruitment process, it may not be far from correct to assume that the results of campus recruitment reflect employment and unemployment (including voluntary unemployment) conditions of engineering graduates in the country. As noted, the employment rate at national level is also close to our estimate. It is widely stated that 75 per cent to 80 per cent of the graduates are not employable.

Gender discrimination in job market is a matter of concern in many countries, including India. Further, it is predominately visible in the engineering sector, where men are traditionally preferred to female graduates (Duraisamy & Duraisamy, 1999). However, according to our survey, gender differences in the labour market are very marginal, favouring women: around 25 per cent of male students have got job offers compared to 27 per cent among females. However, we find noticeable gender differences when it comes to employment by different types of organisations – foreign, joint ventures and domestic.

A student's choice of enrolment in an engineering institution depends, inter alia, on the job placement record of the institution. Engineering institutions which have higher placement records in recent years obviously attract more students than the institutions which have performed poorly in the campus placement/recruitment. This is truer in the case of private engineering institutions than public universities/engineering institutions. While students mostly prefer government institutions to private ones for various reasons, as described in Chapter 4, between the several private universities and colleges, students prefer enrolling in those institutions which have better campus placement records to others. As the numbers of private universities and colleges of engineering in India are very high, students have more options among these institutions. Private institutions use various methods to attract companies to recruit their students and to have a record of high campus placement. On the other hand, as the public engineering institutions are small in number, their quality is high and tuition low, students face fierce competition for admission in these institutions. Hence the record of campus placements does not matter much in the enrolment in the public institutions, though generally these institutions are considered to be faring better than private ones in placement as well.

We note that in our survey, the number of students who have got job offers is nearly two times higher in government institutions than in private institutions (Table 9.1). The employers may obviously be concerned with quality of the institutions and the graduates. Public institutions, with better trained and qualified faculty and good academic infrastructure, could produce better trained graduates than private universities and colleges. The latter are known to be having poorer quality teachers and in smaller numbers than required, and not necessarily good infrastructure in terms of libraries and laboratories. The facilities and structures provided for campus recruitment in government institutions may also be more transparent and on the whole better than in private institutions. As a result, government institutions have a better placement record than private institutions. That a higher proportion of students studying in public institutions secure job offers than students enrolled in private institutions confirms the quality advantage that public institutions have over private institutions and the employer's recognition of the same.

The stream/department of engineering that one is enrolled in carries a high value in the labour market. Jobs in the engineering and technical areas are highly specialised and the scope for substitution between different specialisations or streams of study in the recruitment market is to some extent restricted, as the job requirements and the area of specialisation in engineering education are somewhat closely related. For example, the requirement of a company for a graduate in electronics engineering cannot be substituted with a graduate in civil or mechanical engineering or vice versa. Hence, it can be stated that employment of engineering graduates also depends upon the stream of study one is graduated in and the level of employment might depend upon the jobs available under each category. As the electronics and IT (information technology)-related firms seemed to be growing fast, higher number of graduates in these areas might get employment than those specialised in other engineering subjects. That the rates of employment vary widely by the stream of engineering and that they also change overtime is well documented. For example, according to *India Skill Report 2022*, the employability of graduates in electronics and communications engineering is the highest – 69 per cent – compared to 35 per cent among graduates of civil engineering in 2022 (Figure 9.1). Further, employability has declined

Table 9.3 Employment Profile of Engineering Graduates (Engineering Students Who Have Got Job Offers in Campus Recruitment)

Category	Percentage	Field of Employment		Region of Placement		Type of Enterprise		
		Engineering	Non-Engineering	Within State	Outside State	Foreign	Joint Venture	Domestic
GENDER								
Male	25.35	88.92	11.08	59.60	40.40	34.65	37.36	27.99
Female	26.69	90.17	9.83	50.58	49.42	30.56	44.84	24.60
NATIVITY*								
Native of the state	23.88	85.08	14.92	51.41	48.59	37.33	35.08	27.59
Outside state	21.53	88.56	11.44	59.45	40.55	31.16	42.15	26.69
TYPE OF Educational Institution								
Government	37.12	88.99	11.01	56.35	43.65	33.77	33.08	33.15
Private	20.03	89.62	10.38	57.37	42.63	33.38	42.31	24.31
STREAM of Engineering Study								
Traditional	16.68	81.00	19.00	56.27	43.73	27.46	41.98	30.56
IT-related	29.77	91.35	8.65	57.37	42.63	36.07	38.40	25.53
Total	(1657)	89.31	10.69	57.03	42.97	33.50	39.47	27.03
Percentage of all who secured placement offers	25.74							

* Whether the student belongs to the same state where the education institution is located or she/he is a native of some other state in India.
Total: Figures in ( ) refer to number of students who secured placement offers.

in civil and mechanical engineering graduates, while it increased in all other graduates.

There are similar significant differences in rates of employment, as per our survey, between the graduates of various sub-streams of engineering: 17 per cent of the graduates in traditional streams have received job offers, while the corresponding figure was almost double – 30 per cent – of those pursuing studies in IT and related branches. Coinciding with popular perceptions, employment conditions seem to favour graduates in modern streams of engineering as against those graduating in traditional areas, though domestic and joint ventures recruit higher proportions of graduates in traditional streams of engineering. Joint ventures seem to have a higher demand for graduates in both IT-related and traditional streams.

Nearly one-fourth, that is, 24 per cent, of the 'native' students[5] have got job offers in their native states and 22 per cent of the non-natives have got job offers in 'other states'. Surprisingly, more male students have got jobs within their state of domicile as compared to females, the shares being 60 per cent for males and 51 per cent for females. There is no much difference in this between the graduates of private and public institutions or between those who graduated in traditional and modern streams of engineering. Surprisingly, only half of the engineering students (51 per cent) belonging to 'within state' could get job offers in the same state. The other half had to migrate to other states for employment. This also depends on the employment conditions in various states, which widely vary in India.

Different kinds of engineering firms go to the educational institutions for campus recruitment for some jobs in engineering and some jobs in non-engineering activities like administration and management in engineering and non-engineering firms. The jobs in the engineering category includes civil, mechanical, electrical, electronics, computers, IT and so on, while jobs of non-engineering category include executive posts in human resources, marketing, management, finances, administration, planning, development and so on. Graduates who are not successful (or uninterested) in getting a suitable job in their parent discipline of engineering may choose different jobs in non-engineering categories. Firms that come for campus recruitment to engineering institutions might offer the students jobs in either engineering or non-engineering trades, depending upon their requirements. If engineers are employed in non-engineering jobs, including in civil services and public administration, this, generally known as 'mal-employment' is considered by some as a waste of resources – financial and human. This is also considered as a mismatch between education and qualifications. We find that nine out of every ten of the students who got jobs on-campus recruitment have taken jobs in areas of engineering and closely related areas and only 10 per cent have gone for non-engineering jobs. Those who leave engineering in favour of jobs in non-engineering activities are very few in number. In contrast to general perceptions, relatively a higher number of female students have taken engineering-related jobs than male students. There is no much variation in

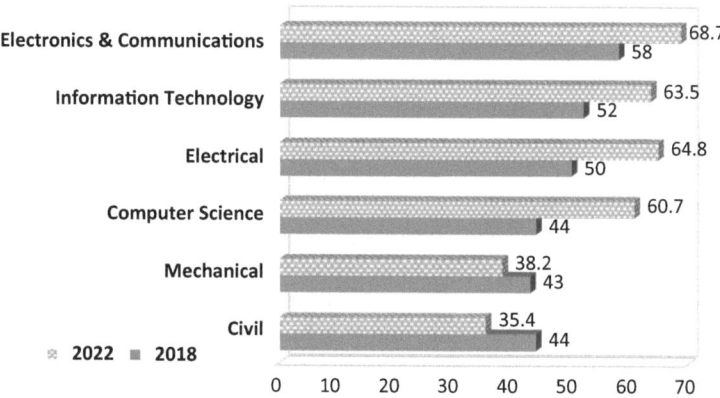

Figure 9.1 Employability of Engineering (%) Graduates by Stream of Study, 2018 and 2022
Source: Based on *India Skills Report* 2020 and 2022.

this between students from government and private engineering institutions. But we find some difference in the pattern between students in conventional streams of engineering and IT-related modern streams. As high as 91 per cent of the students in modern branches of engineering who have got their job offer have taken up (or selected for) the engineering-related jobs, whereas only 81 per cent students enrolled in traditional departments of engineering (mechanical engineering and electrical engineering) have done the same. That is, nearly 20 per cent of students in traditional disciplines chose non-engineering jobs for their employment.

Among the several companies that go for campus recruitment drive, domestic companies do not seem to perform so well. Foreign companies attracted as many as 43 per cent of the students and joint venture companies another 40 per cent. This is the same pattern in the case of male students who received job offers. But in the case of female graduates, joint ventures recruited them more than others. Joint ventures also attracted students from private educational institutions more than foreign and domestic companies. Hence, a higher number of students from private universities/colleges have got job offers in joint venture companies, whereas the students from government institutions received offers mostly from domestic companies. Joint ventures and foreign firms together account for 70 per cent of the employment of graduates in traditional areas of engineering and 75 per cent in IT-related modern areas, the rest being accounted by domestic enterprises.

Earnings Profile of the Graduates

Graduates in engineering earn substantially higher than other graduates, and even than those with master's degree in India. Based on the National Sample

Survey, 2006, Carnoy et al. (2012) estimated that the annual earnings of male graduates in engineering earn consistently higher than those with master's degree for the entire life time, as shown in Figure 9.2. But they are not the same for all. They differ by gender, by the type of institution they studied, by the nature of organisation they are employed and so on. Based on our survey, some such details on how do they differ by different characteristics of the graduates are presented.

As stated earlier, the wages/salaries offered for the first year of employment at the time of on-campus recruitment are considered here as the earnings of the graduates. Though they are not actual earnings, nor, of course, are they lifetime earnings, they are used by many scholars in such contexts. They can certainly be considered as starting salaries of the graduates, but not as lifetime earnings. On average, such earnings amounted to ₹3.9 lakhs per annum per person. There is no much gender difference in the earnings: both men and women receive more or less the same.[6] Graduates from public institutions of higher education seem to receive better treatment with an offer of higher earnings than graduates from private institutions, which is partly reflective of the differences in quality of education the graduates receive. Annual earnings offered to graduates of public institutions were of the order of ₹4.1 lakhs compared to ₹3.6 lakhs offered to graduates of private institutions. As stated earlier, this reflects partly the employers' acknowledgement of the quality of public institutions. Generally, it is observed that students are better trained in government institutions and hence, come out better skilled and more competent than the students of private institutions and hence, they may even be able to bargain for higher wages. Availability of trained faculty, better physical infrastructure such as laboratories, classrooms and hostels and overall academic atmosphere are often cited as major reasons for superior quality of education provided in government institutions in India.[7]

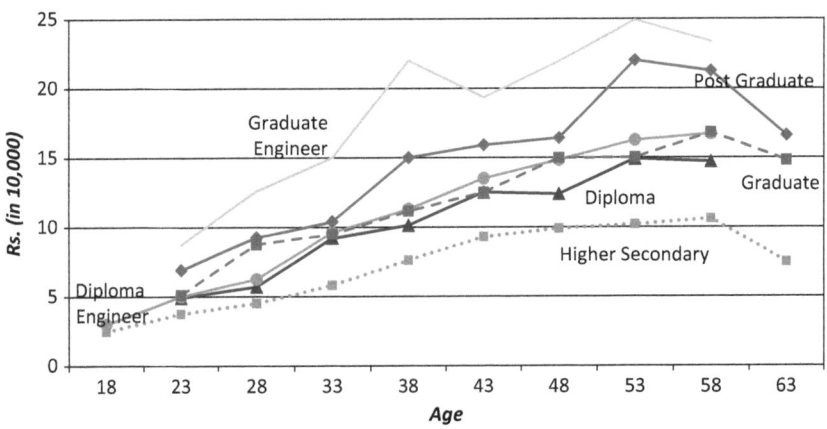

Figure 9.2 Annual Earnings of Males in India by Educational Level, 2006 (₹)
Source: Carnoy et al. (2012, p. 22).

Employability, Employment and Earnings 259

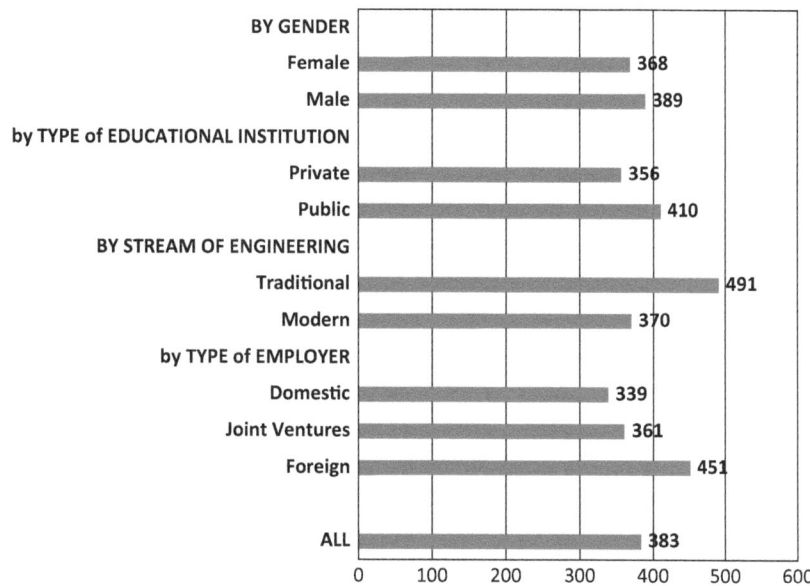

Figure 9.3 Starting Average Annual Salaries of Engineering Graduates in India (₹ in Thousands)

Further, somewhat contrary to general opinion, graduates in traditional streams of engineering like mechanical, civil and electrical are offered higher wages – about 33 per cent higher – than those who graduated in modern IT related streams, as shown in Figure 9.3. While graduates of modern disciplines get better treatment in terms of employment, in the case of paychecks, graduates in traditional branches get a better deal. Students seem to have strong preferences in favour of modern areas, expecting quick employment and high wages.

Foreign companies obviously pay higher levels of salaries than joint ventures and domestic companies. The pay in foreign companies is 33 per cent higher than the pay offered by domestic organisations, which, in turn, is 7 per cent less than what joint ventures offer.

Who Gets the Jobs? Determinants of Graduate Employment

Which individual traits and social, economic and institutional factors predict graduate employment? The literature on determinants of unemployment/employment is dominated by studies at macro level, wherein rates of unemployment/employment are considered as a function of economic growth, level of technology, structural and other factors. Drawing from 21 case studies of developing and developed countries, sponsored by UNESCO-IIEP, Sanyal (1987a, b) concluded that the stagnant economic growth is the most dominant factor that explains graduate unemployment. There are also, of course, a good number of studies based on graduate surveys which analysed individual employment as a function of household factors – social, economic and more, individual factors, academic background of the students and more. As Atkinson and Pennington (2012) found, analysing unemployment of engineering graduates in UK, there is no single reason for unemployment. A multitude of factors explain why graduates are employed or unemployed. Macmillan et al. (2015) highlighted the importance of several factors in access to good employment in UK that include family background, networks and the pubic/private school the graduates attended. They have also shown that graduates from private schools are more likely to enter 'high status' occupations.

Several studies concluded that the subject or the major the students chose in their studies matter a lot in employment market. For example, Kong (2011) analysed employment of graduates in Beijing, China, and finds that employment of graduates is considerably influenced by the 'major' chosen by the student during their studies, apart from the reputation of the college and gender of the graduate; and that women find jobs more easily. On the other hand, in a study on Korea, Park (2015) concluded that, based on a hierarchical liner regression model, the curriculum – the major subject chosen – was not statistically significant, nor were the household income, club activities and employment preparation activities. In a study of a small township in South Africa, education level, age, marital status, household labour force and total government grants were significant determinants of employment status, according to Dunga (2014). As one would expect, university scores are used by the employers as a selection criterion to filter through the competition among job applicants in many cases (Boissiere et al., 1985). After all, an important function of higher education is filtering or screening or signalling and arranging graduates in a queue in the labour market (Arrow, 1973; Spence, 1973; Thurow, 1975). Students with good academic records are viewed more productive, as being better prepared for their first jobs (Jones & Jackson, 1990). Preference for employment in public sector also keeps many graduates unemployed, as employment in public sector is relatively limited, as Panchamukhi (1987) has shown in the case of India about two decades ago. Analysing educated unemployment in India, researchers (e.g. Bairagya, 2015) identified socio-economic, regional and other factors and used probit or logit regression technique. Choudhury (2012), in a study of engineering graduates in Delhi that used a sub-sample of the database of the present research study, concluded that while the type of the institution (public or private), caste, academic merit of the student and the loan status of the student were significant determinants of employment, the major stream of engineering, parental occupation or education were not having any influence on the employment probabilities of the graduates.

While there is a good number of studies on employment of the graduates in India, many were conducted in the 1970s and 1980s (e.g. Blaug et al., 1969; Panchamukhi, 1987; Azad, 1991) when the economic and educational conditions were altogether different. While many studies tend to explain employment/unemployment with the help of national economic factors, including industrial production and growth in gross domestic product, few concentrated on graduates' traits and the quality of education they received and related aspects. Some research has focused on specific disciplines like economics. There is need to examine the determinants separately for each major discipline. There are practically no studies focusing on engineering education in India. Hence this study may be seen as a modest contribution in this direction.

Based on a quick review of the literature and considering the availability of data in our survey, a set of predictors of employment of engineering graduates is identified. The set includes 15 variables grouped into three categories: (i) personal attributes (individual factors) – gender and caste; (ii) household factors that include household income, parental occupation and parental schooling; and (iii) academic aspects – academic performance at the senior secondary level (before entering undergraduate engineering studies), the medium of instruction at secondary level, the type of education institution currently attending (public or private) and the 'major', the mainstream of engineering: modern or traditional. We have also included in category (iii) a variable that reflects the student's educational loan status – whether she/he has taken any educational loan for the engineering studies. These are described in Chapter 4 and are used in other chapters of this study as well.

The hypothesis examined is: factors relating to educational background of the students are the most important determinants of employment of engineering graduates in India; and socio-economic background of the students, including individual factors such as gender and caste, and household conditions do not influence much the employment probabilities of graduates.

The statistical results are given in Table 9.4.

What do the Results Suggest?

Given the general gender preferences and discrimination in labour market, it is generally presumed that employers coming for on-campus recruitment will have a bias against female candidates and accordingly prefer recruiting male graduates. They might presume rightly or wrongly that male employees would not mind staying in office and work longer hours, while females having family obligations would not do so. The problem of gender discrimination in the job market is said to be predominantly in the engineering sector, where male applicants get better treatment than female graduates. The popular perception is that engineering and technical education is a masculine domain (Goel, 2007). But it was also found that women perform better in campus recruitment drive in engineering colleges in India (Gokuladas, 2011). Given some of these popular views, some of which were supported by research, one can hypothesise that *ceteris pari bus*, companies coming for on-campus recruitment prefer hiring male graduates to women. We find here that the probability of getting employment for a woman is less than that for a male student, but the difference is statistically not significant. We have already noted that the absolute difference in employment rates is also very small.

Caste is included as an explanatory variable to see whether employers have any preference towards or bias against students belonging to lower social background (e.g. scheduled castes [SCs], scheduled tribes [STs] and other backward castes [OBCs]) in providing jobs. When caste is included in the equation in the form of binary variables for SCs, STs and OBCs, with general population as a reference category, the results show that caste does not matter, as it turns out to be statistically not significant. Generally, it seems that the majority of firms going for on-campus recruitment belongs to private sector, which does not necessarily provide the constitutionally guaranteed reservations (quotas) to the students belonging to disadvantaged sections of population such as SCs, STs and OBCs. The employers may not give any preference or discriminate against graduates of these caste groups.

Then, we consider three important dimensions relating to socio-economic conditions of households – household income, father's occupation and father's education. Household income is measured in logarithmic form to even out extreme differences. Father's occupation is defined in three categories: (a) professional or technical worker; (b) businessmen; and (c) others; and years of schooling of the father is taken for father's education. It is hoped that these three dimensions reflect economic and some kind of 'social capital' that the students possess. Household income represents its economic status. The higher the economic status of a household, the greater could be the chances of getting employment by a graduate, as rich households might be able to invest additional resources on improving English language, skills on computers and so on, which seem to have been highly valued by the employers in the job selection processes, besides the formal education and training one receives.

Similarly, parental occupation and education can be expected to be of help for the student to access better information on labour market and to make a wise decision in selecting the jobs. So, one may expect all the three household factors to have a positive effect on employment of graduates. Surprisingly, the results show the other way. The coefficients of all the variables are negative in value: higher family income, parents' higher occupational status or parent's higher education reduce the probability of employment. While the coefficient of occupation is not statistically significant, the other two – lnHHY and FATHER_ED – are statistically significant.

The third group of variables that can be expected to have considerable influence on graduate employment relates to the educational background of the students. We do not have information on the quality of engineering education that the students receive or the quality of the institution, though they are generally found to be very important. Instead, we use two indicators of academic performance of the students at senior secondary level, which are highly related to admission and may also be related to the performance in undergraduate engineering studies. They are: the marks secured in the senior

Table 9.4 Logit Estimates of the Employment Probabilities of Engineering Graduates

Variables	Coefficient	Odds Ratio	Standard Error	Marginal Effect (dy/dx)
Individual Characteristics				
Gender	-0.0985	0.9062	0.080	-0.020
SC	0.1675	1.1824	0.168	0.030
ST	0.3409	1.4062	0.320	0.050
OBC	-0.0037	0.9964	0.108	0.000
Others	Reference category			
Household Factors				
L*n*HHY	-0.0847*	0.9189	0.045	-0.010
Fathocp_prof	-0.1143	0.8920	0.092	-0.020
Fathocp_bus	-0.1025	0.9026	0.094	-0.020
Fathocp_others	Reference category			
Father_ED	-0.0373***	0.9634	0.013	-0.010
Educational Background				
Engg_inst_type	0.3511***	1.4207	0.082	0.060
Stream_study	-0.2662***	0.7662	0.087	-0.440
SEC_marks	-0.0642***	0.9378	0.004	-0.010
SEC_medium	-0.1873*	0.8292	0.111	-0.030
Loan	-0.3052**	0.7370	0.118	-0.060
Intercept	7.9395**		0.634	
Log likelihood	-2283.79			
Pseudo R²	0.0808			
Number of observations	4,432			

Note: Significance level: *** $p < 0.01$; ** $p < 0.05$; and * $p < 0.1$.

secondary examination (SEC_MARKS) and the medium of instruction (English/non-English) at senior secondary level (SEC_MEDIUM). It can be argued that graduates having higher scores in senior secondary examination may have better chance in job market than the students scoring comparatively lower percentage of marks.[8]

Prospective employers obviously consider the previous academic background of the graduates in their selection process. In the absence of information on performance of graduates in degree-level examination, they might consider records at school level. Similarly, it is widely felt that communication skills in English carry a premium in employment market (see also Gokuldas, 2011). It is assumed that school graduates with English as a medium of instruction will have a good command over English language and will be able to perform better compared to those with Hindi or regional language as their medium of study. Hence, employers may favour those who had English as the medium of instruction than others. Graduates may also feel that proficiency in English language is acquired better when English is used as a medium of instruction rather than if it is merely a subject. Proficiency in speaking English is considered as a good qualification for good employment.

This has been the view for a long period (Allen, 1854) and still continues to be so, supported by robust research as well (Azam et al., 2013; Pandey & Pandey, 2014).

Both the explanatory variables included in the equation to represent academic background of the student, viz. percentage of marks scored in the senior secondary examination (SEC_MARKS) and medium of instruction at senior secondary school, are found to be statistically significant in determining the probability of getting employment, confirming our view that firms going for on-campus recruitment consider the performance of the prospective employees at higher secondary school level and they assign a positive value to the same; but they seem to be not necessarily bothered much about the medium of instruction in which the student studied at school level. Perhaps they would be content with the knowledge and skills in English language, as displayed in the interview/group discussions. The variable SEC_MEDIUM has a negative value and is statistically significant at 10 per cent level. It is also possible that command over English can be acquired not necessarily when it is used as a medium of instruction, but when it is taught and learnt properly. In fact, apart from this, firms may be interested in non-technical knowledge of the graduates, including their attitudes and values (Gokuladas, 2010).

Two aspects relating to current education, the type of engineering institution the student is studying in (public or private) and the stream of engineering (traditional or modern) the student is enrolled in, are considered here. While many earlier studies have considered the prestige or reputation of the college in this context, we do not have data on the same. Hence, simply the type of institution (public or private) is considered. Note that in general, public institutions in engineering education are generally regarded to be better and high in reputation than private ones. Second, as already described, as employment varies widely by the stream of engineering, the stream is also included in the model as an explanatory variable. Another important variable that is considered here is the loan status of the student – whether the student has taken any educational loan or not. Employers may either favour or discriminate against those carrying a debt owing to the educational loan taken for the studies. Employers may feel that employees with student loan debts would have financial stress, which might interfere with their job performance and finally their productivity at work might get affected, as they might spend considerable time worrying about repayment of their loans, and that in the process, they might also continuously look for a better job. Or alternatively, employers may feel that employees with such debts cannot risk even frictional unemployment or pay cuts for inefficiency, and hence, will be loyal to the organisation and work sincerely so as to earn and repay the loan fast (Mercer Survey, 2017).

According to the logit estimates in Table 9.4, the stream/branch of engineering the graduates have enrolled in (STREAM_STUDY) has the strongest influence on their employment probabilities. Contrary to general perceptions, as revealed from the estimates of marginal effects (given in the last column in Table 9.4), graduates of IT-related streams – computer science engineering, electronics and communication engineering and IT engineering – have 44 percentage points less chance of getting employment than the graduates of traditional branches. Similarly, the results show that students of private engineering institutions have higher likelihood of getting jobs compared to the students enrolled in government engineering institutions, though the private advantage is not very high: the advantage the graduates in private institutions have is only by 6 percentage points. Both these aspects need further examination, as they also contradict common perceptions as well as the inferences from the descriptive statistics given earlier in Table 9.3.

The other important variable that turns out to be statistically significant is the loan status of the students. The results show that students who availed educational loan are at a disadvantage in the labour market: they are less likely to get employment than the students who have no debt obligations. As per the estimate of marginal effect, students taking educational loan have 6 percentage points less chance to get employment than the students who have not taken educational loan. There may be many more factors than what we noted in the literature described earlier, which explain the individual differences in employment of graduates. But lack of data has prevented us in including them here in the statistical analysis.

Determinants of Earnings

The literature on economics of education is abundantly rich with studies on earnings function. Typical or standard earnings function also known as Mincerian Equation (Mincer, 1974) included schooling and job experience as the only explanatory variables and both were found to be important in a large number of studies (see, e.g., Psacharopoulos & Tilak, 1992). Extended or augmented Mincerian earning functions include a variety of factors – personal, market and environmental. They cover individual, social, household characteristics, education variables and factors relating to job, the organisation and many more. Researchers used essentially the OLS technique in such contexts, including stepwise repression analysis (e.g. Tilak, 1980). The applications of human capital earnings function have grown manyfold over the years (Willis, 2016).

Some recent research has guided us to identify a few important possible determinants of earnings. The relationship between academic performance and starting salary has been examined by a number of researchers in various experimental settings. A few of the earlier studies in context include James et al. (1989), Weisbrod and Karpoff (1968) and Murnane et al. (1995). Apart from Choudhury (2012), quite a few researchers identified in such contexts variables like knowledge of English, academic performance, quality of college, subjects of study, etc., apart from individual, social, economic and household factors. Chevalier (2011) found significant differences in earnings by the subject studied by the UK graduates. Earnings of graduates in Canada are reported to vary widely by field of study (Frenette & Rank, 2016); the differences are also marked between several streams of engineering, general engineering, civil and mechanical engineering graduates earning higher than electronics engineering, computer engineering, etc. The majors chosen seem to explain a large part of the gender gap in earnings in US (Daymont & Andrisani, 1984). That female graduates earn less than male graduates is well documented in the literature. Ramsey (2008) highlighted this in the case of UK. Ramsey also found that earnings vary by type of university. In India, Duraisamy and Duraisamy (1999) found that women graduates of professional and technical higher education were discriminated in the labour market with respect to wages, and the magnitude of discrimination ranged between 55 per cent and 70 per cent, depending on the level of education and sector of employment (public/private sector). Madheswaran and Shroff (2000) also found that women graduates with scientific and technical education face discrimination in the labour market. Parikh and Sukhatme (2004) reported that women engineers in India encounter hindrances in rise in wages and career promotions. Focusing on starting salaries of the fresh engineering graduates in IT-related majors in India, Singh (2016) found that the academic performance in school and college, college reputation, school affiliation and engineering major are key predictors of starting salaries. Using the *India Human Development Survey* (of the National Council of Applied Economic Research), Azam et al. (2013) attempted to quantify the effects of English language skills on wages in terms of rates of return, and concluded that returns to English language skills in the Indian labour market were very high. After controlling for age, social group, schooling, geography and proxies for ability, they found that hourly wages are on average 34 per cent higher for men who speak fluent English and 13 per cent higher for men who speak a little English relative to men who do not speak English at all. Earnings are not only different for graduates of different subjects, they are also determined differently for graduates of different subjects (Dolton & Makepece, 1990). Jack Britton et al. (2016) found, based on data on 260,000 graduates in the UK, the subjects one studied and the university one attended have strong influence on earnings of graduates. Then comes the finding that the individual variables such as socio-economic class, region and ethnicity matter, even after controlling for academic-related variables. Chakravarty and Somanathan (2008), using data of 242 final year students of IIM Ahmedabad, have also found that academic performance of the students is an important determinant of salary offered to them. An increase of one grade point in the performance during the first year (measured in terms of Grade Point Average [GPA]) is estimated to raise the wages by more than 40 per cent. Academic performance was found to be the most important determinant of starting salaries in Australia too (Chia & Miller, 2008). In the same study, it was also found that science graduates earn less than general graduates. According to Panchamukhi (1987), about one-third of variation in graduate earnings in India could be explained by family characteristics.

Taking the clue from available research, incorporating some of these variables, an attempt has been made here to find out the determinants of annual earnings of graduates using the OLS technique. In such a context, a typical Mincerian (Mincer, 1974) log earnings function is extensively used by a majority of the researchers, including those cited above. We also use the same, the augmented Mincerian Equation. The selection of the variables is subject to the same constraints as in the case of the employment equation estimated in the previous section.[9] Variables on gender and parental occupation and education as household background factors, education-related factors that include current and past education and factors relating to the job – the field of employment (engineering or non-engineering) and type of employment organisation (foreign, joint venture or domestic) – are regressed on earnings. Other variables like caste and household income have been tested and are found to be not relevant, being statistically not significant and having no effect on the explanatory power of the equation.

Discussion of the Results on Earnings Function

Some of the results of the earnings functions given in Table 9.5 are similar to the results obtained in the logit regressions on employment, while some contradict them. Gender is not an important predictor of employment, as we have already seen, but it turns out to be a significant factor in the OLS estimation of earnings equation and it works adversely for women. Parent's occupation or education does not have any significant effect on the earnings of the graduates, though father's education has a small positive effect. Interestingly, the higher the level of parent's occupation (professional or business), lower would be the earnings of the graduates.

Among the variables chosen to refer to current and past education background of the students, the OLS results show that the type of institution (public or private) is the most significant factor in the determination of earnings of graduates. The coefficient of the variable (ENGG_INST_TYPE) is negative and significant at 99 per cent level of confidence. Being a graduate from a private institution pushes down the wages by about 15 per cent, below the earnings of the graduates of government institutions.

It may be pertinent to note here that the students of private universities/colleges make higher Investments (in terms of household expenditure) than the students of government institutions in their engineering education, as noted in Chapter 6, and their probability of getting employment through on-campus recruitment is comparatively high. But more important to note is the fact that the graduates of private institutions earn less than the graduates of public institutions, though it can be the other way in other countries (e.g. Crawford & Vignoles, 2014). In contrast, Macmillan et al. (2015)

have found that graduates form private schools earn higher than those from public institutions. It may depend upon the quality of education a graduate receives.

Almost similar to the estimates of logit Equation on employment, English medium has a small value negatively influencing the earnings; the coefficient is significant at 10 per cent level. While most literature suggests that communication skills in English language matters a lot in employment and earnings, we found here in both the equations that the coefficient of the variable SEC_MEDIUM being negative in value. Perhaps the medium of instruction at secondary level does not matter as long as the students have good domain knowledge in the subject (reflected in SEC_MARKS), good analytical and quantitative skills and good communication abilities in English. Perhaps none of them is related to the medium of instruction. Possibly it is not the medium of instruction that improves the student's knowledge and skills in a language, but it is how a language is taught and learnt as a subject. After all, English is highly valued by the employers and it is English that is found to explain a substantial part of the gap in employability of engineering graduates (AspringMinds, 2020, p. 36). It is generally observed by pedagogues that English when taught as a subject, the grammar, the syntax, the linguistics and more, besides the literature, are much better valued than when it is merely a medium of instruction.

The stream of study in engineering – modern or conventional – also does not matter in earnings, though it matters in the case of employment. The regression coefficient is positive in value but not statistically significant. The percentage of marks scored by the student in higher secondary examination (taken as a proxy of quality of the graduates) is positively related with the probability of employment as well as the annual earnings of graduates. More clearly, with the increase in higher secondary examination marks by 1 per cent, the annual earnings of graduates increase proportionately by 1 per cent.

Though the common tendency is one to accept a job that offers higher earnings (in fact, higher lifetime earnings), graduates in some cases may have overriding preferences relating to the nature and field of job, place of occupation, type and reputation of the firm and so on. For example, one might take up a job, even if earnings are relatively less, but if it is a foreign company with a high brand value, or if the location of work is their native city or state instead of a job with higher earnings in a faraway place. Hence, it is expected that the earnings of the graduates vary significantly with the nature and field of employment. Considering this, in the OLS estimation, we included two factors related to job market, namely field of employment – engineering or non-engineering – and type of enterprise that offers a job. One can expect the students employed in engineering-related fields to make higher earnings than those in non-engineering-related jobs. The underlying hypothesis in including the 'type of enterprise' as an explanatory variable in the earnings function is that the graduates employed in foreign firms will earn high wages, followed

Table 9.5 OLS Estimate of the Annual Earnings of Engineering Graduates

Variables	Coefficient	Standard Error
Individual and Household Factors		
Gender	−0.0861**	0.0319
Fathocp_prof	−0.0467	0.0347
Fathocp_bus	−0.0387	0.0367
Fathocp_others	Reference	
Father_ED	0.0005	0.0053
Past and Current Educational Background of Students		
Engg_inst_type	−0.1484***	0.0310
Stream_study	0.0268	0.0350
SEC_marks	0.0069***	0.0018
SEC_medium	−0.0811*	0.0428
Job Characteristics		
field_employment	0.1427**	0.0438
Type_joint	−0.1232***	0.0383
Type_dome	−0.1242***	0.0326
Type_foreign	Reference	
Intercept	0.8466*	0.1713
R-squared	0.0912	
Adjusted R-squared	0.0804	
F-Value	8.4600***	
Number of observations	940	

Note: Significance level: *** $p < 0.01$; ** $p < 0.05$; and * $p < 0.1$.

by the employees of joint venture companies and then those in domestic companies.

Our results show that these two factors matter most in explaining earnings of the graduates. After controlling for other factors, jobs in engineering activities give 15 per cent higher earnings than if employed in non-engineering activities. Or in other words, engineering graduates employed in non-engineering firms earn 15 per cent less than the graduates employed in engineering fields. It supports the general presumption that the earnings in engineering-related jobs are higher than non-engineering-related jobs. Second, if one chooses a domestic unit or a joint venture for employment, she/he would receive about 12 per cent less earnings than those employed in foreign establishments, as far as starting salaries are concerned.

Summary Conclusions and Implications

Based on the student survey, in this chapter, an investigation into the determinants of employment and determination of earnings of engineering graduates is attempted. Students in the final year of the undergraduate studies have gone through campus recruitment. The job offers and the starting salaries offered in the on-campus recruitment are used as employment and earnings of the graduates in this study, though they are not the perfect measures. Logistic and OLS regression equations are estimated to examine the probabilities of employment and the determinants of earnings, respectively. We have hypothesised that academic performance and related educational variables are the most important predictors of graduate employment, and similar variables and employer-/job-related characteristics together account for most of the variance in earnings of engineering graduates.

To briefly sum up, our results confirm our hypotheses: educational characteristics of graduates and their fathers' education are the most important predictors of employment. Second, education characteristics explain a substantial part of the variance in earnings. Interestingly, factors such as caste and gender or even family characteristics like father's occupation have no significant role in employment, and caste and parental occupation have no significant influence on earnings.

As a limitation, it must be noted that quite a few important factors could not be considered in this exercise due to constraints on data availability. Further research with a larger set of variables with data on actual employment earnings of those who are already employed with varying duration of experience may give more robust results. Yet the results arrived here have important implications for further research and policy making relating to engineering education, private education and employment of engineering graduates. With respect to further research, this study highlights the need to recognise the difference between public and private institutions and if possible, elite and mass institutions. Second, a survey of employers going for campus recruitment may yield interesting insights into the criteria that they actually focus in recruitment. Such a survey, if followed upon, may also indicate the durability of employment offered in campus recruitment, as practices of other kind are often reported in media.

How to enable the employability of graduate engineers? The analysis made here will inform public policy. One can draw quite a few important implications. First, the mushrooming of a large number of low-quality private institutions of engineering education will not help employment or economic growth. There needs to be strong checks on the growth of low quality of institutions. AICTE has closed as many as 778 private institutions during 2012–13 to 2019–20. This measure and the number do not seem to be enough. Effective mechanisms of quality control are necessary. Curricular and pedagogical arrangements need to be strengthened and restructured to prepare better quality graduates. The quality of engineering education has to be substantially raised with inculcation of a variety of skills so that the graduates become immediately employable and succeed in the dynamically changing labour market (Gaurav, 2020). Graduates require three types of skills: skills to acquire a job, skills to perform a job efficiently, and skills to face upheavals and uncertainty and progress in career. Presently there seems to be a wide gap between the requirements of the graduates/employers and what the institutions provide, Basically, graduates should be equipped with a variety of twenty-first century skills (beyond core academic subjects), such as artificial intelligence, cloud computing, 3D (three-dimensional) machining, data analytics, data engineering, data sciences, machine learning, deep learning, robotic process automation and so on, along with professional engineering knowledge. Modern engineering problems require students to master engineering knowledge, while the ability to work with others across contexts requires professional skills. Both are interdependent and important for success in the labour market (Winberg et al., 2020). Soft social and emotional skills such as communication, collaboration, leadership, resilience, cultural competency and more are increasingly valued. Unless sufficient focus is given to develop such skills along with abilities, there will be a huge wastage of human resources and the investment made in engineering education from public as well as private, including household sources (Swaminathan, 2014). Interestingly, though most private institutions in India are found to be offering very poor quality education, probability of getting employment is higher for graduates of private institutions, but they get very low starting salaries compared to those who graduate from public institutions. It is possible that many engineering graduates from low quality institutions, though prefer engineering jobs, end up in non-engineering jobs and/or low-paying jobs, which reflects yet another form of wastage of resources. Private colleges also focus on their records of campus recruitment, but not much on salaries the graduates would receive, that is, the quality of employment might be less cared for. Similarly, graduates in modern streams of engineering like electronics and computer science, if employed, are likely to earn more than those who graduated in traditional streams of engineering; but they are at a disadvantage in employment market compared to the graduates in traditional streams. This may partly reflect the glut in the labour market. There is overproduction of graduates in modern streams of engineering. Institutions that concentrate on modern streams have to note this and rethink their plans and strategies in this regard. As the AICTE (2018) suggested, institutions have to continuously monitor future skill requirements and make accordingly suitable changes in the streams of engineering they offer, and even think of new and emerging areas. Though manpower planning has lost its gleam, it may be useful to have a continuous exercise of manpower analysis, including estimation of requirements of manpower of various levels and types for the short and medium terms. This will be useful for efficient monitoring of the system and to adopt necessary policy changes and new policy initiatives. Third, it appears that employers tend to discriminate against those who come with a burden of educational loans. Some mechanisms have to be thought of in such a way that such discrimination does not take place. A better mechanism is to reduce the reliance of students on loans and to ensure that students instead depend upon scholarships. A publicly subsidised higher education system would reduce the need for loans.

Notes

1 In a pioneering study in India, Blaug et al. (1969) attributed graduate unemployment in India to high private rates of return.
2 While a majority of the institutions invite or allow campus recruitment and some, particularly the private institutions, use the 'placement record' to boast of their quality and popularity in their approach to attract students, some institutions might ban on-campus recruitment, fearing that students would become money-minded and lose interest in studies as they get job offers prior to their completion of their studies. It might also disorient students from pursuing further higher studies. But such institutions are very few in the country. On the whole, placement record has also become an important consideration in national assessment and accreditation and national ranking framework.
3 As mentioned in Chapter 4, the employment status of engineering graduates is as at the time of the survey (in the fourth year of the engineering studies); some more might get employed after completion of the final year of engineering studies or even before. After all, graduates also try for employment through many other methods, particularly after completing the studies. Hence, our estimates of rate of 'employment' may have to be seen as underestimates.
4 Major companies that visited different engineering institutions for campus placement in our survey, as per the statements of the institutions, include: Tata Consultancy Services, Microsoft, Samsung, Infosys, Hindustan Computers Limited, McKinsey, Birlasoft, International Business Machines, Computer Science Corporation, Syntel, Maruti Automobiles, Tata Motors, Bharat Heavy Electrical Limited (BhEL), National Thermal Power Corporation (NTPC) and Defence Research and Development Organisation (DRDO) of the Government of India, Accenture, Convergys, I-Flex, Sapient, Tata Tele Services and a few others.
5 As mentioned in Chapter 4, 'native' students refer to the students who are studying in an institution located in the state of which they are the natives. 'Non-natives' are those who went from home state to another state for studies.
6 In the study on Delhi, which was based on sub-sample of the database of this study, Choudhury (2015) however found that women are offered salaries which are about 54 per cent less than that of men.
7 In addition to Chapter 3 and also Chapter 8 in this study, see Rao (2007) and Biswas et al (2010) for details on quality-related aspects of technical education in India. See also Loyalka et al. (2014) on the quality-related aspects in BRIC countries.
8 While no extensive evidence is available on how the performance in secondary board examination is related to the performance of students in their studies in engineering education, the limited available evidence indicates positive correlation between the two. For example, students who scored above 85 per cent in board examination secured 54 per cent in marks in AICTE assessment of engineering students in 2022 and those who scored 40–55 per cent secured only 41 per cent. See Barman (2022).
9 In a preliminary exercise, it has been found that gender (male), type of institution (public), entrance score, mother with higher education, log family income and type of school attended are statistically significantly (at 99 per cent level) related to the log earnings. The estimated equation is:
lnEARNINGS = 0.375 −0.0603 ENGG_INST_TYPE −0.074 GENDER + 0.0047 MOTHER_HIGHER + 0.035 lnHHY −0.154 SEC_SCH_TYPE + 0.013 ENT_SCORE; R-square: 0.079; N: 2854

Part III

10 Summary, Conclusions and Policy Challenges

Objectives and Scope of the Study

India has registered a very impressive growth in its higher education during the post-independence period and more impressively during the last three to four decades. Within higher education, there is a distinct pecking order, at the top of which are medicine and engineering. Engineering education has experienced an enormous expansion, beyond experts' anticipations; and the expansion has been phenomenal in the private sector. With the entry of private sector, engineering education in the country has undergone a sea change over the last three decades. The growth has its own effects on economic growth and the development of engineering education, some of which need serious attention. The main objective of the study is to analyse a few major dimensions relating to the growth of engineering education in India using secondary and primary data and reflect on their implications for public policy.

First, based essentially on secondary data drawn from published and unpublished (available on their websites) records of AICTE, UGC, MHRD, NSSO, reports of official committees and commissions and others, an attempt has been made in the study to understand the changing face of engineering education in India during the last 70 years. Five major dimensions are analysed in the study:

i   Changing trends and patterns of the growth of engineering education.
ii Inequalities in growth in engineering education by gender, caste, region/state, and imbalances in the growth between different branches of engineering education.
iii Quality of engineering education reflected in the performance of the institutions in global and national rankings and employability of graduates.
iv Financing of engineering education by the government and households.
v   Changing labour market conditions that influence the demand for engineering education. An analytical descriptive method has been adopted in this regard.

This forms Part I of the study that focused on macro level picture.

Second, based on primary data collected from about 7,000 students in 48 public and private engineering institutions in four major states – National Capital Region of Delhi, Maharashtra, Karnataka and Tamil Nadu – in India, some of the above-mentioned important aspects are probed further in six chapters in Part II. The survey, conducted in the context of a wider study of higher education in BRIC (Brazil, Russia, India and China) countries also includes interviews and discussions with some students, institutional heads/deans/faculty, management and a few employers and visits to classrooms and laboratories for observation. Institutions included in the sample cover a variety, comprising IITs, NITs, public and private universities, government, government-aided and private colleges. The survey yielded rich information on a variety of aspects of engineering education – the socio-economic and educational background of the students and their parents/households, students' experiences in the engineering institutions, costs of education, quality of education they receive, teaching-learning practices adopted in the institutions, employment prospects, educational aspirations of the students and also views of the faculty/heads and so forth on certain aspects.

The issues investigated, based on the survey that constitutes Part II of the study, include:

i What are the socio-economic characteristics of the students who go to private colleges/universities vis-a-vis public institutions and the reasons.
ii The growing disciplinary imbalance — high demand for some branches of engineering education, and declining or stagnant demand for some others.
iii The unsteady growth in public financing of engineering education and the increasing role of households.
iv Educational loans as a method of financing and the constraining factors the students face in availing the same.
v Quality of engineering education.
vi Changing labour market conditions and the preferences and performance of engineering graduates in the labour markets.

Apart from using descriptive statistics, standard tools of econometrics – probit and ordinary least square regressions are used for this purpose. This primary data-based analysis forms Part II of the study. This complements the macro-level analysis made in Part I; and the findings in Part II confirm some and question some of the major implications derived from the analysis in Part I. Part II also provides a few additional insights derived from the ground level, which are not available at macro level, for example, the students' perceptions on quality of education and a few other dimensions. Together, they also stress the need for a fresh approach and a holistic understanding of the issues involved in engineering education in the country and for bold policy initiatives.

Recap of Key Findings

The extensive macro-level analysis made in the two chapters in Part I highlights the following:

- The expansion of higher education and within higher education, higher engineering education in the country has been very fast. This was necessitated by changing increasing demographic composition in favour of the young, upward pressures with rapid growth in school (secondary and primary) education, high economic growth, particularly in manufacturing and service sectors in India, and increase in employment opportunities within the country and outside and fourth, due to the familiar 'diploma disease'.
- But the expansion in engineering education may not be sustainable, as it has already led to the phenomenon of excess supply over demand. A large number of student places in many institutions remain vacant, necessitating closure of some of the institutions. State income per capita and the number of engineering institutions – total as well as private – seem to be positively related. Interestingly, neither population of the relevant age group (which is the base of demand for higher education) nor public expenditure on education or unemployment rates has any relationship with the spread of institutions in the states. It appears that institutions are opened considering immediate short-term gains, and not based on requirements of the system and long-term considerations of the education system and the society at large.
- Particularly there are too many engineering institutions in the private sector. The growth of private sector in engineering education has reached alarming levels – about 80 per cent of the engineering institutions being in private sector – leaving practically no space for the public sector to grow. Private engineering institutions, mostly being self-financing and almost exclusively relying on study fee, are operating essentially on commercial criteria and less on philanthropic considerations; the students in private institutions also behave as consumers purchasing education, like any other commodity or service. This change in the conception of higher education as a private good as against considering it as a public good or a common good will have detrimental effects on the society's development.
- All this reflects on the unplanned and unregulated growth of engineering education in the country.
- The high level of participation of the private sector, though improved overall access, led to the widening of inequalities in participation in engineering education. There are serious problems with respect to access to engineering education in terms of social groups, geography (region/state), gender and economic conditions of households. Enrolments of Scheduled Castes (SCs) and Scheduled Tribes (STs) have increased considerably over

the years, but still one notices a large gap between scheduled population and non-scheduled population in their participation in engineering education. Inequality by gender has narrowed over the years. Improvement in terms of gender parity is more impressive, with nearly 30 per cent of the students being women as per the latest statistics; however, in general higher education, women constitute a higher proportion – 49 per cent. Regional inequalities are rather high: while some southern states perform better, with a larger numbers of institutions (per one million population), and in terms of proportion of students, many states in eastern, northern and central regions are far behind. However, in terms of geographical concentration, the situation is slowly improving. Of all, inequalities between the poorest groups and the richest strata (measured in terms of monthly per capita consumption expenditure quintiles) in participation in engineering education are the highest.

- Engineering education itself has become more attractive than higher education in arts, humanities, social sciences, natural and physical sciences and so forth. Second, the growth in engineering education in itself has also been skewed, some of the newly emerging streams like electronics engineering, computer science engineering and information technology (IT)-related streams of engineering growing faster at the cost of hitherto popular and standard streams like mechanical, civil and electrical engineering. The large-scale privatisation has also led to disciplinary distortions, as the private providers are largely offering market-friendly and job-oriented programmes in those streams of engineering that help them expand enrolments, generate revenues through student fees, improve financial status and most importantly, increase their profit margin.
- The shift in demand in favour of engineering education may lead to neglect of other branches of higher education in public policy, which may be detrimental to the very growth of a strong balanced higher education system; and so are the disciplinary imbalances within engineering education, which may lead to unsustainable models of development of engineering education.
- The system suffers from a very severe degree of staggering paucity of well-qualified teachers. Teachers with doctoral degrees are very limited in number, and production of PhDs in engineering is also not taking place at the required rate, as very few graduates in engineering education go to post-graduate and doctoral studies. The job market and lack of orientation for further studies and research make postgraduate education and research in engineering a less attractive option for the fresh graduate engineers. There seem to be some welcome trends in recent years. But the problem is not only severe with lack of faculty and poor quality of faculty, but also the system is inflicted with recruitment of 'fake'/'duplicate' teachers and inefficient or corrupt practices in teacher recruitment in private institutions.
- The quality of engineering education has been very unsatisfactory, which pulls down the contribution of engineering education to economic growth and development. The poor quality is reflected at macro level in a handful

of institutions in India figuring high in the global rankings. With respect to global rankings of institutions of engineering education, the situation is marginally, but not much better. But even in the National Institutional Ranking Framework, the performance of many institutions is reported to be far from satisfactory. The poor quality of engineering education is also reflected in low levels of employability of graduates, low productivity, and low earnings.

- Public funding for engineering education has been very inadequate and unsteady, resulting in an increase in the burden on households, and thereby raising issues of affordability of the low- and lower-middle strata of the society. Since nearly four-fifths of engineering education is in the private sector which is dependent on student fees (and other private sources, which are negligible), one can say that four-fifths of engineering education is privately financed! While there has been a modest growth in public expenditure in absolute terms on engineering education over the years, as a proportion of expenditure on technical education, there has been a decline in many states in India. Regional variations are also high in the expenditure on engineering education. In states/union territories like Chandigarh, engineering education accounts for more than three-fourths of expenditure on technical education, while the corresponding proportion forms hardly 1 per cent in Telangana, as per the latest statistics. In the expenditure on technical education, scholarships account for a tiny proportion – below 4 per cent.
- As a corollary to all this, household expenditures have become important in financing engineering education. From the household point of view, education in medical sciences and engineering education are the costliest branches of higher education. Household expenditure per student on these two branches increased faster than in other branches. Expenditure on engineering education forms a sizeable proportion of total household expenditure and of the total expenditure on engineering education, fee accounts for the most.
- Labour market information system on engineering manpower and its utilisation are very limited, resulting in mismatches in supply and demand for engineering education on the one hand and imbalances reflected in gluts and shortages of manpower in the labour market on the other. Available statistics indicate high fluctuations in the rate of hiring of graduate engineers in India. At most, half the students get job offers in the campus recruitment. The low levels of skills and knowledge of the graduates explain the low levels of employability of graduates. Excess supply of engineering education of low quality pushes down the employability of the graduates. The number of colleges in the state and employability seem to be inversely related.
- A good proportion of engineer graduates prefer career in engineering jobs; only a small proportion wishes to take up management and related jobs. While preferences are so, the actual employment pattern may differ. Almost all engineering graduates, whether men or women or graduated in any branch of engineering, expect uniformly equal salaries from their jobs. There is no difference in expectations by gender, surprisingly nor even by

branch of engineering. However, the expectations do differ by the quality of the institution from which one is graduated: those graduating from tier 1 colleges expect higher than those from tier 2, who, in turn, expect higher than those from tier 3 colleges, reflecting inequalities in the quality of the colleges.

All these findings have important policy implications.

The analysis in Part II which is based on primary survey data, gives us a few more detailed insights and valuable conclusions:

- From an analysis of the determinants of the choice of senior secondary school graduates with respect to private versus public institutions for higher education in engineering in India in Chapter 4, we found a few interesting aspects. Engineering education is still male centric; hardly 30 per cent of engineering students are women. A little less than 30 per cent of the students belonged to socially backward sections of the society. A majority of the students (58 per cent) belonged to the lower-income strata. More than one-third of the students go outside their native state for engineering education. A majority of the students come from families with parents having higher education, and also with fathers engaged in professional occupations. As high as 70 per cent to 90 per cent of the students in engineering had their schooling in private institutions in urban areas with English as medium of instruction; and a majority of the students crave to pursue modern streams of engineering like computer science engineering, electronics engineering, telecommunications and IT. A little more than half of all the students did not take pre-coaching as a preparation for competitive entrance examination. Perhaps the emphasis that students lay on coaching is unwarranted.
- The presumption that for many reasons, students belonging to socially backward strata (SCs, STs and other backward castes [OBCs]) are more likely to prefer government institutions and are less likely to enrol in private institutions holds true in this study. This may be because of availability of affirmative practices of reservation policy in public institutions. Similarly, from a gender point of view, female students are more likely to attend private institutions than male students, may be because of the proximity of private institutions. Public institutions are very few.
- The presence of a larger number of siblings in the family reduces the probability of attending private institutions as against government institutions. Private institutions are obviously more expensive. The other two household factors influencing students' choice for institutions are the parents' occupation and state of domicile of the students. Surprisingly, income of the family is found to be statistically not significant. While mother's education has a positive influence in the student's preference towards government institutions, the father's education has no statistically significant effect (i.e. higher-educated mothers prefer sending their children to government institutions).

- As one can expect, a student graduated from a secondary school which is under a central (government) board, which is perceived to be of relatively high quality, is more likely to enrol in public institutions of engineering education than a student graduated from a school managed by a state board.
- Students who completed their secondary education in English medium are more likely to go to private institutions, while those who score high marks in the school end examinations are less likely to enrol in private institutions. Obviously, students with better academic background (marks) compete for better quality institutions, which are in the state sector. This is not the case with students with English medium. English medium may not necessarily represent high quality.
- Students' choice of an institution is significantly determined by the employment prospects, or more specifically, employment assurance that can be indirectly derived from the performance of the institution in terms of record of campus recruitment and offers of placement in jobs made to the students. Offer of employment of students through on-campus recruitment is considered as a positive indicator of employment-providing capacity of the institutions. As the government institutions are able to offer better opportunities for employment through on-campus recruitment by reputed companies, they become a more preferred choice of the students seeking admission than private institutions. Obviously, due to the reputation or brand name of the government institutions, graduates will be able to secure good employment easily than of those graduating from private institutions.
- The other factors determining the students' choice for institutions include the availability of scholarships, cost of engineering education and the streams of engineering that the students intend to choose. Students who could secure scholarships do not prefer private institutions, as scholarships may not be so easily available in private institutions. Students in private institutions afford higher costs (of private institutions) and spend more than those in government institutions. Last, students interested in modern (IT-related) branches of engineering seem to be going more to private institutions than to government institutions. This is because government institutions focus more on offering traditional streams, though they also offer modern streams of engineering sciences to a lesser extent, while private institutions, responding to the market demand, tend to offer more admissions in IT-related and other modern branches and less or almost nil in other traditional but important programmes.
- Among the statistically significant factors that explain the choice of public versus private institutions, after caste, the most important ones that explain the choice for admission in private institutions are preference for modern streams of engineering, secondary schooling in non-English medium schools and the high cost of education. The next three important factors are secondary schooling in a school affiliated to state board, the location of the school (in rural areas) and mother's education. While mother's education has a negative effect on the probability of student

preferring a private institution, all others among the above variables positively influence the choice in favour of a private institution. Some of them require in-depth probing, which is not attempted here.

Within engineering, the demand for branches like electronics engineering, computer science engineering and IT-related engineering has been on the rise. Computer engineering is still the most demanded stream. From the examination of the factors that influence students in their decision-making relating to choice of main streams in engineering education – traditional (civil, mechanical and electrical engineering) or modern (electronics engineering, computer science engineering, and IT-related engineering education) at undergraduate level – made in Chapter 5, a few key signals are clear.

- The probability of seeking admission in modern/IT-related departments is significantly higher among the students belonging to general category than the students belonging to SCs and STs. Surprisingly, belonging to the group of OBCs increases the probability of enrolling in IT-related streams as compared to general category students. Perhaps OBCs are as good as the general category, if not better, with respect to their socio-economic background. Similarly, the other individual characteristics that determine the probability of attending IT-related courses include gender. Compared to male students, female students are more likely to choose IT-related subjects, though gender differences are not very marked.
- Native place of the students is found to be statistically significant in explaining the students' choice. Students migrate, may be temporarily, to other states to take admission in modern areas of engineering, while a majority of those who do not migrate get enrolled in traditional streams.
- In the case of academic background of students, performance in the higher secondary examination turns out to be a statistically significant factor in the students' choice of streams. Higher the percentage of marks scored in higher secondary examination, higher is the probability of one opting for admission in IT-related departments than in traditional branches of engineering. This confirms the general belief that meritorious students score high percentage of marks in their senior secondary examination and also perform better in the competitive common entrance examination; and then they finally opt for IT-related branches. Similarly, students graduated from schools affiliated to state (provincial) board are less likely to enrol in IT-related branches as against traditional streams.
- There is a strong positive relationship between enrolment in modern branches of engineering and enrolment in private institutions. After all, many private engineering institutions offer admissions more in IT-related departments than in traditional areas, while many government institutions concentrate relatively more on traditional departments. Note that traditional disciplines require higher investment in relatively more expensive laboratories and instruments, which many private institutions may be unwilling to make.

- As expected, employment potential and enrolment in disciplines are also related. Students taking admission in IT-related disciplines visualise higher chances of getting better or faster employment in the labour market than the students enrolled in other areas.

Almost everyone prefers to choose modern streams as against traditional areas of engineering. Indian economy is already experiencing a situation of a glut in the labour market with IT engineers. The quality of these IT graduates is also on the decline. Their labour market returns are experiencing a downward trend. But more importantly, the engineering education scene is getting imbalanced with more and more low quality private institutions that too concentrating on modern streams at the cost of standard traditional disciplines. Due to asymmetry of information, students' preference for engineering education is still high, and more specifically the demand in favour of IT-related disciplines is growing. But traditional subject streams are also important for the rapidly growing economy. Low turnout of graduates from traditional departments in years to come may pose a serious bottleneck in the rapidly industrialising and fast modernising economy. Public attention may require on how to boost demand for standard disciplines of engineering in order to have a balanced development of all disciplines of engineering and how to check the growth and functioning of low-quality private institutions which are actually fragmenting engineering education by focusing on some disciplines at the cost of some basic and standard areas.

Thus the first two chapters in Part II have provided empirical evidence, unravelling some of the issues involved in the students' choices. After all, in the context of educational planning and also institutional planning in education, it is very important to know how students/parents decide on their options in higher education.

Analysis of patterns and determinants of family expenditure on higher education provides valuable insights that would be useful for decision-making at household level as well as for public policy making regarding funding higher education. Some of the findings that we arrived at in Chapter 6 conform and a few contrast to the earlier research evidence on the pattern of family expenditure on higher education in India and in other countries.

- Families spend considerably high amounts on engineering education of their children. On average, family spending per student constitutes nearly half of the average income of the family.
- Of the total expenditure on engineering education, fee alone accounts for nearly one-third. As one expects, the higher the rank of the student in the entrance examination, the lower could be the fees, as high-ranking students get admitted in to public institutions or at subsided fee rates in public or private institutions. If one belongs to the disadvantaged sections of students – SCs, STs and OBCs – then the fee she/he has to pay would be lower. These students get either fee waivers or are charged reduced rates. Fee is lower if one is a female. As it is understood, if one goes to a public institution, she/he has to pay lower levels of fees than those who go to private institutions.

- Expenditure on fee levels differ between government and private institutions. It is important to note that there are variations in tuition fee levels among public institutions as well as private institutions even within a state. This reflects the functioning of the fee regulatory committees constituted in the states, particularly in the case of private institutions.
- Expenditure of students enrolled in private institutions is much higher than those enrolled in government institutions. Given that a large part of engineering education is in the private sector, majority of students spend a lot on engineering education.
- There exists a small degree of pro-male bias in family investment on engineering education. There are also wide variations in household spending by social (caste and religion) and economic characteristics of households. Scheduled tribes incur much less expenditure than others. The expenditure is also much higher in the case of students in IT-related branches than students enrolled in traditional branches.
- Household economic conditions measured in terms of owning a house or not, nativity of the students, educational – board of secondary education, social factors – gender, caste and type of institution exercise considerable influence on the levels of household expenditures on engineering education in India. Owning an asset like a house speaks about economic conditions of the household; nativity influences the costs of travel and expenditure on hostels; board of secondary education reflects the quality of schooling; and so on.

Student loans and other financial assistance being received by students in engineering education reduces the financial burden on the families to some extent. But in Chapter 7, we find that:

- All the students, not even all the 'needy' students do not necessarily get financial assistance, or free waivers, or loans. Loans which should be accessible to all, could not be secured by many, even if they are eligible to get loans as per the criteria set by the banks or the government. While educational loans are considered as an important means of financing engineering education in India, according to our survey, only a very small fraction of students gets it; 10 per cent of students – in engineering education received scholarships, fee waivers and other kinds of financial assistance.
- Students, particularly those who are not able to get any kind of financial assistance, take part-time work on the campus to partly finance their education. Their number is also very small. In the case of both the corresponding numbers, they are smaller in private institutions. Opportunities for paid work on campus are not widely available in India unlike in western countries.
- Relatively a higher number of students enrolled in private institutions get loans than the students in government institutions. Of the total, a higher proportion of male students got loans compared to women. Similarly, a higher percentage of students enrolled in conventional/traditional streams of engineering study get loans compared to those enrolled in IT-related

modern streams of engineering education. Note that all students do not necessarily seek financial assistance or apply for education loans.
- Among the factors that explain the probability of getting loans, social category, family income, ownership of assets (house), parents' occupation and costs of education (that students have to incur) are significant.
- Family income of the students is found to be a significant factor in determining the student's probability to get a loan. A student belonging to a rich family is less likely to get loan than a student from a poor family. But students from high-income groups are found to receive higher amounts of loans compared to others.
- Other thing being constant, socially backward (SC) students, who may actually require more, are less likely to get educational loan than other students. The amount of loan provided to these students is also less. Perhaps banks are more willing to give loans to the students belonging to higher social category. All this stresses the need for strengthening the mechanism of state financing of higher education of the disadvantaged sections.

According to the perspectives of some stakeholders in engineering education such as the employers, policy makers, academia, the quality of engineering education in India is far from satisfactory. Chapter 8 presents students' perspectives on the quality of undergraduate engineering education on nearly a dozen key aspects.

- Of all, most strikingly, in contrast to predominant experts' views, engineering students who were interviewed in a wide range of institutions, including many private ones, appear quite satisfied with their education and with their choice of engineering and the institution. This is largely the case whether they are in prestigious IITs or in less notable private institutions. As far as these students are concerned, the higher engineering education system has done 'right' for them. However, this does not seem to be a summative assessment of the quality of education by the students.
- Majority of students reported not to have participated in internships programmes, or got any exposure to industry, or got any opportunities to participate in research projects, or in leadership programmes and so on.
- Students have also reported that they did not develop technical designs or participate in projects with firms. Classroom lecture is the most relied method of teaching and semester/course end examination the main tool of evaluation. Students are aware of some of these problems, but have reconciled to the prevailing situation to the extent of viewing the systems as satisfactory or good or even very good.
- No strong evidence could be found from the survey to say that a majority of students acquire essential attributes of engineers for the twenty-first century that include strong analytical skills, practical ingenuity, creativity, mastery of business and management – awareness of interdependence between technology and the social and economic foundations of the society.

- Yet many students feel that they have acquired "technical abilities" and are "well prepared" for careers, including for careers in other countries. Their overall satisfaction might be constrained by their knowledge of the system, the changing labour market conditions, and overconfidence among themselves. They might also be constrained to admit the weaknesses in the system.

The perspectives of not only the employers but also the students and institutions are important and they need to be taken into consideration. The students' perspectives on quality of education that we reported here may compel researchers to widen their approach to study quality-related problems and administrators and policy makers to rethink their perspectives and policy initiatives. But as quality improvement requires multiple interventions, an understanding of multiple perspectives is also important.

Employability and employment of engineering graduates are reflective of the potential contribution of engineering education to growth and development, in addition to being reflective of the quality of education. Considering the job offers and the starting salaries offered in the on-campus recruitment as employment and earnings of the graduates, probabilities of employment and the determinants of earnings are estimated with the help of logistics and OLS regression equations in Chapter 9.

- Academic performance and related educational variables are the most important predictors of graduate employment, and similar variables and employer/job-related characteristics together account for most of the variance in earnings of engineering graduates.
- Educational characteristics of graduates and their fathers' education are the most important predictors of graduate employment; and second, education characteristics explain the variance in earnings.
- Interestingly, factors such as caste and gender or even family characteristics like father's occupation have no significant role in employment, caste and parental occupation has no significant influence on earnings. This indicates that labour market conditions are not constrained by traditional structural rigidities and are evolving 'progressively'.
- Graduates in modern streams of engineering like electronics and computer science, if employed, are likely to earn more than those who graduated in traditional streams of engineering; but they are at a disadvantage in employment market compared to the graduates in traditional streams. Traditional areas of engineering are probably less subject to market vagaries.

The problems of employability, employment and earnings partly reflect the glut in the labour market. There is overproduction of graduates in modern streams of engineering. Institutions that concentrate on modern streams have to note this and rethink their plans and strategies in this regard. Private institutions became more responsive to market interests in (a) opening new engineering colleges in a short time and (b) offering programmes that are immediately market relevant, but not necessarily qualitatively rich. Since markets are imperfect in a country like India, the market signals are not necessarily perfect and they are of short term value, which private investors did not seem to have realised. This also happened more in those private institutions which are not philanthropy-based and are severely dependent on student fees. Responding to market interests, many institutions tend to overlook their very mission of education and long term implications of their short-term responses to market signals.

Limitations of the Study

The study is subject to a few major limitations.

Singling out different factors that explain students' choice in Chapters 4 and 5, or in household expenditure or in the case of employment and earnings in other chapters is important, but is indeed difficult. The results also indicate the strong interplay of several factors, making explanation difficult. We find here that a multitude of factors explain why students choose public or private institutions, or modern or traditional branches of engineering education in India. We may note that quite a few considerations limit generalisation of these conclusions. The imperfect education market in a developing country like India, characterised by large-scale growth of private education and diminution of public sector, asymmetry of information – there are no strict regulations requiring institutions to share basic information that empowers students to make more informed choices, typical market failures, the limited supply of engineering education facilities of quality, the admission procedures and uneven economic abilities of the households – does not mean existence of a genuine free choice in a typical market framework for the parents or students in selecting a type of engineering institution or a stream of study. These factors do not allow genuine free choice principle to operate. Thus, an important limitation of the study is that we assume the existence of free choice for the students to select institutions or the streams of study of their liking. But this is not the case. So it is important to note that we have used the choice function in this study in a restricted sense. Like the myth of consumer sovereignty, real student choice is also perhaps a myth. So all studies on student choice need to be looked at with some degree of caution.

Second, there may be several important factors that we could not consider in our quantitative analysis in many chapters in Part II, constrained essentially by the survey data that formed the basis of this study. Many important related aspects could not be captured in the survey. For example, dowry, an important feature in Indian society, may have a very dominating effect on the students' choice of streams in engineering. Engineering graduates carry higher dowry, and engineering graduates in IT-related areas may carry further higher dowry. Women also tend to prefer such graduates for marriage. Further, scope for emigration to the western world for higher studies or for employment also does influence students' choices. We also could not consider any supply-side factors. There may be several other quantifiable or intangible factors that could not be brought into this quantitative exercise here. So the results need to be interpreted with some degree of caution.

Third, with respect to definition and measurement of some of the variables, for example, in the case of household expenditure on education, it would have been more appropriate to take in our analysis the *net* household expenditure, that is, the total household expenditure on engineering education minus the amount of scholarship or stipend or any other financial assistance received. However, we do not have the required details on the amount of scholarship or financial assistance received by students during their programme of study. The rank secured in the competitive entrance examination is the most determining factor that influences students' several choices. But the ranks secured in examinations conducted by different boards need to be standardised, and as it is complicated, no attempt has been made and we have not used the data on rank orders much in the study. We also do not have the data on actual employment status or the actual earnings of the graduates, in the absence of which we relied on job offers secured in the campus recruitment in colleges.

Fourth, the data available for the analysis does not allow us to thoroughly compare and contrast students' perspectives on the quality of education they received with data from institutions or the perspectives of the policy makers. As a result, only some partial explanation could be provided for the differences in the perspectives on quality of different stakeholders.

Implications for Public Policy

Despite some of the above-mentioned limitations, this study makes an important contribution, providing valuable insights into the challenges that engineering education in India faces. With trends towards massification of higher education, India is on the verge of building a knowledge society. India's development goals include high and sustainable economic growth, production of globally competitive high-quality manpower and to become an economically advanced country, going beyond being a powerful Asian tiger economy. Realisation of these and related goals require a high level of human capital, both in quality and quantity. It has been realised that higher professional and technical education – especially engineering and technology education – has a vital role in boosting economic growth of the nation.

Many other countries share these development goals. Further, the trends observed here in the case of engineering education in India, dominated by market forces, are not unique. Many other countries are experiencing similar trends. Higher education, particularly engineering/technical education, is growing very fast in many developing and advanced countries like China, Brazil and Russia, to mention a few. Quite a few countries are also experiencing unbalanced growth of several disciplines in engineering education of the kind noted here, and they are also experiencing frequent labour market imbalances. Hence the analysis attempted and the results arrived at here could be of policy relevance for many other countries.

Hence the policy implications of the study are quite significant for India and many other countries. The study may help in making sound and informed public policy with respect to several issues such as the desired nature, levels and directions of growth of engineering education, the effects of rapid growth of private education, improving equitable access to engineering education, enchaining quality and relevance of education, public financing of education, including fees, scholarships and loans and many other related issues in higher education in India.

Some of the important implications for further research and policy making relating to engineering education in India can be outlined as follows:

The study suggests that there is a need for a major restructuring of the engineering education sector, specifically with a better understanding of emerging market dynamics at national and global levels and with a long-term vision for the development of engineering education and higher education as a whole for the development of the nation. Leaving the market to operate freely in engineering education (as has been allowed so far for the last three decades) may lead to a great distortion in the sector, which has started with the devaluation of the engineering degree. Therefore, there is an urgent need to have a strong understanding of the changing aspirations of parents for engineering education, revisit the role of the private sector, search for new strategies to cope up with the declining demand and above all, make an effective intervention by the state to regulate and restructure the engineering education sector. The massive expansion of engineering education emphasises the need to ensure that the system and institutions are effectively and efficiently governed and managed to meet the needs of industry and society. We are conscious that this study has left out many important issues like faculty recruitment policy or nuanced understanding of the students' experiences in and outside the classroom that have serious policy implications. Lack of data is one of the important reasons for not addressing several of these concerns, and therefore we argue for building a strong comprehensive database that covers historical as well as current data on a large set of dimensions of engineering education that would contribute to quality research, informed and effective policy making and planning of technical higher education in the country. This certainly calls for some urgent action.

Besides setting up an institutional structure that would build such a robust and comprehensive database, the study highlights a few more important policy implications. First, there is a need to effectively regulate the growth of engineering education in the country. Mushrooming of a large number of low-quality private institutions of engineering education may improve access, but will not help employment or economic growth or even higher education in the long run. The growth of such institutions needs to be curtailed. Permissions and approvals to open new institutions – public or private – and to offer new programmes need to be based on reliable, transparent and scientific data on the need for such institutions and programmes rather than being influenced by political and economic considerations or short term market considerations. As we have already seen, leaving this to market forces results in different kinds of imbalances and chaos. No new college may be allowed to start. Permissions may be deferred for opening of new colleges for a few years. In the meanwhile, the government may have to take up on a large scale weeding out the substandard institutions and consolidation of the engineering education system, adopting a scientifically determined closures and mergers of institutions. It is not only those where enrolments are less than intake that they need to be closed, but also the institutions in those states where the intake is less than the national average. As it is mandatory that all institutions and all the programmes they offer need to be subject to a national assessment, the mechanisms of assessment and accreditation need to be made robust, scientific and transparent, leaving no chance for manipulation.

Second, a clear focus has to be laid on improving the quality and standards in higher education. Besides consolidating existing institutions and regulating the future growth, special attention has to be given to the recruitment of quality faculty and the provision of a good learning environment that includes good infrastructure consisting of libraries, classrooms, laboratories and modern equipment, which will be conducive for good teaching and learning and also for research. The overall research environment needs massive improvement in a majority of the institutions, with an aim to facilitate the creation of new knowledge and its dissemination. The need for major curricular reforms needs no emphasis. The curricula may have to include knowledge and skills in the core domain, but it also needs to add many other individual traits and social, cultural and human values. While introducing curricular reforms, there is a need to align with market needs, but that needs to be made with caution. The aim in all this should be not just to improve the employability of the graduates, but also to produce holistic personalities who will be able to serve society better. Vertical linkages between high-quality institutions like IITs on the one end and the undergraduate institutions on the other and horizontal linkages between several institutions of the same level may go a long way in enhancing the standards of education in the system as a whole.

Interestingly, though most private institutions in India are found to be offering very poor quality education, probability of getting employment is higher for graduates of private institutions, but they get very low starting salaries compared to those who graduate from public institutions. It is possible that many engineering graduates from low-quality institutions end up in non-engineering jobs and/or low-paying jobs, or immediate short term employment, which reflects yet another form of wastage of resources.

Third, private investors find investment in setting up engineering and technical education institutions yielding high and quick returns, as the existing fee regulatory mechanisms are weak, and there is scope for making money out of fee reimbursement systems floated by some state governments, in addition to many other avenues of making money. These mechanisms which are actually meant to help students seem to help the private management more. Both need to be re-examined and made efficient in such a way that they do not become sources of profit-making. Philanthropy needs to be insisted as an essential major component of the activities of private investors in education.

Fourth, higher education, including technical education, has to be necessarily inclusive in nature. Major initiatives are necessary to ensure that no academically deserving student is prevented from entering engineering institutions for lack of economic resources. Along with general subsidies, specific public subsidies targeted to help the disadvantaged sections have to be strengthened in the form of scholarships and other financial assistance. The limitations, in fact, the ill effects of the cost recovery measures like student fees and loans need to be addressed in making public policies on financing higher education.

High level of household expenditure on higher education will have negative effect on access to higher education, and second, wide variations in household expenditures reflect high levels of inequalities in access to higher education. Societies that would like to expand higher education and aim at providing equitable access to higher education have to think of public subsidisation policies that reduce the need for high household expenditures in general and of marginalised sections in particular.

The analysis of factors influencing receipt of educational loans underline valuable policy implications for modifying or redesigning the educational loan programme in India, besides stressing the need to expand other kinds of financial assistance to improve access to higher education. It appears that employers tend to discriminate against those who come with a burden of educational loans. Some mechanisms have to be thought of in such a way that such discrimination and other forms of discrimination against the really needy students do not take place.

A reliable comprehensive information system on a variety of dimensions of engineering education institutions, including their quality, faculty, programmes, accreditation and assessment on the one hand and information on labour market – short-, medium- and long-term forecasts of manpower, including teaching manpower – requirements and the skills and quality of manpower required on the other will help (a) the state in better planning and policy making, (b) the institutions in their plans for development and (c) equally importantly, the students and their parents in making wise choices about the institutions, the branches of study and about their future education and employment careers.

Above all, a long-term futuristic plan for the development of higher education, and within higher education, various branches like engineering education needs to be developed, which will reflect a long-term vision of the development of the nation from a variety of angles.

As the *National Education Policy 2020* resolved, all, including all engineering education institutions, may be required to transform into holistic and multidisciplinary higher education institutions, offering more subjects outside the core discipline, like arts, liberal arts, humanities and social sciences, emphasising core content values as well as human traits like human values in addition to a variety of skills. These institutions will also have to provide not only undergraduate, graduate and research programmes, but also offer integrated programmes covering undergraduate and graduate studies, focusing at the same time on all the three functions of higher education, namely teaching, research and community engagement. Some of these proposals may promote students' interests in studies at master's level and research programmes, which would result in better knowledge production and dissemination, besides increasing the supply of qualified faculty.

Scope for Further Research

While this study helps to bring a new understanding on a variety of complex issues in engineering education contributing to richer discussions in academic as well as policy fora, it also highlights scope for further research. First, our analysis focuses on the issues and challenges of engineering education at the national level, and we see great value in similar studies at the state/regional levels. This would help to address some region-/state-specific issues in engineering education which are not covered in this study. For instance, why do the patterns in the growth of engineering education in southern states differ from northern states? Is it linked with the state-specific policies on engineering and technical education? As rapid developments are taking place in the labour market, technology and public policies, the study suggests the need for such studies at regular intervals. Second, this study discusses the issues in engineering education exclusively, that too at the undergraduate level only. We have not examined issues relating to postgraduate and PhD levels of education in the field of engineering, except making a few occasional references, which needs a separate study. Third, this study is limited to engineering education only; similar attempts covering other disciplines of higher and professional/technical education in India may be equally useful, for example, medicine and management. What is happening to arts, humanities and social sciences is also important to analyse. This would also help to provide a comparative picture of engineering education with other branches of study in higher education.

Fourth, in the changing nature of the labour market, it is important to take stock of the production of professional graduates in different disciplines and comparing that with their demand in the job market. Manpower analyses are important, as they throw light on a variety of dimensions that will have implications for educational planning as well as economic planning, including for market interventions. Such analyses would help in reducing mismatches, even though manpower planning *per se* lost its charm over the years in the rapidly changing world.

Last, further research is required on the cost recovery measures such as student fee and student loans (both of which have become very popular methods) adopted by the state to fund costly disciplines such as engineering education and their effects on the growth of higher education and their implications for labour market and the society at large.

***

Appendix A
(to Part I)

Table A1 Indicators on Science and Technology (2010–18)

	Researchers	Technicians	R&D Expenditure Percentage GDP
	in R&D Departments (Per One Million Population)		
India	253	73	0.65
Korea	7,980	1,311	4.81
Japan	5,331	524	3.26
Germany	5,212	2,007	3.09
USA	4,412	...	2.84
France	4,715	1,806	2.20
China	1,307	...	2.19
Singapore	6,803	377	1.94
Australia	4,352	–	1.87
UK	4,603	1,305	1.72
Canada	4,326	1,268	1.57
Malaysia	2,937	263	1.44
Brazil	888	978	1.26
Thailand	1,350	297	1.00
Russian Federation	2,784	438	0.99
South Africa	538	130	0.83
Mexico	315	140	0.31
Hong Kong	4,026	316	–

Source: World Development Indicators: Science and Technology http://wdi.worldbank.org/table/5.13

Table A2 Growth of Engineering Institutions in India

	Degree Level	Diploma Level	Total	Percentage Distribution	
				Degree	Diploma
1951	53	89	142	37.3	62.7
1961	111	209	320	34.7	65.3
1971	134	301	435	30.8	69.2
1981	171	363	534	32.0	68.0
1991	351	910	1,261	27.8	72.2
2000–01	680	1,155	1,835	37.1	62.9
2009–10	2,894	1,914	4,808	60.2	39.8
2018–19	3,124	3,440	6,564	47.6	52.4
2019–20	3,168	3,708	6,876	46.1	53.9
2020–21	3,092	3,662	6,754	45.8	54.2
2021–22	3,010	3,591	6,601	45.6	54.4
Growth rate (percentage)	5.8	5.3	5.5		

Source: Statistics of Higher & Technical Education (various years).

Table A3 AICTE Approved Institutions Offering Engineering Education 2020 (Degree and above Level)

	2020	2022–23
Central universities	13	22
Deemed universities – government	9	14
Deemed universities – private	69	79
(State) Government universities/institutions	346	363
Government-aided universities/institutions	64	55
State Private Universities	51	49
Private-aided colleges	6	--
Unaided colleges	2,540	2,294
University managed institutions – government	77	--
University managed institutions – private	44	--
All	3,168	2,969

Source: AICTE Dashboard.

Table A4 Enrolment as a Percentage of Intakes in Engineering Education in States (2012–13 and 2018–19)

State/Union Territory	2012–13			2018–19		
	Intake	Enrolment	Percentage of Enrolment in Intake	Intake	Enrolment	Percentage of Enrolment in Intake
Andhra Pradesh	177,805	93,004	52.31	156,166	88,451	56.64
Assam	4,275	3,190	74.62	5,085	2,605	51.23
Bihar	7,790	4,732	60.75	11,020	5,783	52.48
Chandigarh	915	856	93.55	1,645	1,479	89.91
Chhattisgarh	24,880	13,356	53.68	18,982	6,460	34.03
Delhi	7,532	7,252	96.28	9,098	6,972	76.63
Goa	1,260	1,214	96.35	1,320	1,103	83.56
Gujarat	54,349	45,998	84.63	61,556	28,213	45.83
Haryana	66,050	29,254	44.29	41,873	13,621	32.53
Himachal Pradesh	8,190	3,253	39.72	5,193	1,466	28.23
Jammu & Kashmir	2,485	2,086	83.94	3,945	2,478	62.81
Jharkhand	5,870	4,311	73.44	6,521	3,611	55.38
Karnataka	94,770	74,085	78.17	102,899	68,637	66.70
Kerala	55,850	40,664	72.81	55,845	27,227	48.76
Madhya Pradesh	99,671	66,865	67.09	78,913	38,012	48.17
Maharashtra	156,243	112,424	71.96	144,061	85,747	59.52
Odisha	44,478	22,937	51.57	40,445	17,391	43.00
Puducherry	6,720	4,682	69.67	7,920	3,087	38.98
Punjab	43,869	22,184	50.57	35,914	14,552	40.52
Rajasthan	62,340	34,756	55.75	45,793	15,429	33.69
Tamil Nadu	257,252	178,493	69.38	297,500	143,165	48.12
Telangana	1,73,285	86,746	50.06	1,18,693	69,708	58.73
Uttar Pradesh	145,912	81,553	55.89	103,945	46,686	44.91
Uttarakhand	14,385	6,834	47.51	10,515	4,333	41.21
West Bengal	34,053	25,625	75.25	36,713	19,906	54.22
All States and Union Territories	1,855	1,475	79.52	3,260	1,495	45.86
All India	1,552,084	967,829	62.36	1,404,820	717,617	51.08

Source: AICTE Database.

Table A5 Distribution of Engineering Institutions and Population (Age Group 18–23) 2012–13 and 2018–19

State	2012–13				2018–19			
	Engineering Institutions	Percentage	Population (Lakhs)	Percentage	Engineering Institutions	Percentage	Population (Lakhs)	Percentage
Andhra Pradesh	357	10.590	57.62	4.10	305	9.763	54.42	3.83
Assam	14	0.415	36.47	2.59	19	0.608	37.45	2.64
Bihar	22	0.653	106.18	7.55	38	1.216	118.14	8.32
Chandigarh	3	0.089	1.52	0.11	4	0.128	1.96	0.14
Chhattisgarh	50	1.483	30.19	2.15	46	1.472	31.49	2.22
Delhi	18	0.534	21.48	1.53	17	0.544	23.28	1.64
Goa	5	0.148	1.59	0.11	5	0.160	1.81	0.13
Gujarat	110	3.263	71.33	5.08	126	4.033	72.32	5.09
Haryana	159	4.717	31.85	2.27	130	4.161	31.84	2.24
Himachal Pradesh	21	0.623	7.72	0.55	17	0.544	7.18	0.51
Jammu & Kashmir	8	0.237	14.07	1.00	11	0.352	12.77	0.90
Jharkhand	14	0.415	36.34	2.59	20	0.640	38.70	2.72
Karnataka	192	5.696	73.32	5.22	193	6.178	69.13	4.87
Kerala	153	4.539	31.40	2.23	160	5.122	29.63	2.09
Madhya Pradesh	226	6.704	86.08	6.12	186	5.954	89.64	6.31
Maharashtra	369	10.946	134.40	9.56	363	11.620	132.32	9.31
Odisha	98	2.907	47.00	3.34	94	3.009	46.07	3.24
Puducherry	14	0.415	1.35	0.10	17	0.544	1.67	0.12
Punjab	103	3.055	33.78	2.40	97	3.105	31.21	2.20
Rajasthan	137	4.064	83.76	5.96	117	3.745	90.43	6.36
Tamil Nadu	513	15.218	76.48	5.44	533	17.061	69.63	4.90
Telangana	341	10.116	41.73	2.97	239	7.650	39.41	2.77
Uttar Pradesh	320	9.493	239.15	17.01	253	8.099	250.94	17.66
Uttarakhand	35	1.038	12.41	0.88	29	0.928	11.96	0.84
West Bengal	83	2.462	109.57	7.80	93	2.977	108.53	7.64
Other States and Union territories	6	0.178	18.77	1.34	12	0.384	18.85	1.33
All India	3,371	100	1,405.59	100	3,124	100	1,420.79	100

Source: Based on All India Survey of Higher Education and Census of India.

Appendix A 297

Table A6 Government and Private Engineering Institutions and Intake: Distribution across States (%) 2018–19

	2012–13						2018–19					
	Institutions			Intake			Institutions			Intake		
	Government	Private	Total	Government	Private	Total	Government	Private	Total	Government	Private	Total
Andhra Pradesh	3.50	11.25	10.59	3.29	12.06	11.46	3.87	10.66	9.76	4.92	12.14	11.12
Assam	2.45	0.23	0.42	1.81	0.16	0.28	2.66	0.30	0.61	1.21	0.22	0.36
Bihar	2.80	0.45	0.65	2.80	0.33	0.50	4.84	0.66	1.22	2.51	0.50	0.78
Chandigarh	1.05	0.00	0.09	0.86	0.00	0.06	0.97	0.00	0.13	0.83	0.00	0.12
Chhattisgarh	2.10	1.43	1.48	1.92	1.58	1.60	1.69	1.44	1.47	0.97	1.41	1.35
Delhi	3.50	0.26	0.53	2.72	0.32	0.49	2.18	0.30	0.54	1.98	0.43	0.65
Goa	0.35	0.13	0.15	0.39	0.06	0.08	0.24	0.15	0.16	0.21	0.07	0.09
Gujarat	7.69	2.85	3.26	11.43	2.91	3.50	4.84	3.91	4.03	5.69	4.17	4.38
Haryana	2.80	4.89	4.72	2.27	4.40	4.26	4.36	4.13	4.16	3.11	2.96	2.98
Himachal Pradesh	0.70	0.62	0.62	0.28	0.55	0.53	0.97	0.48	0.54	0.45	0.36	0.37
Jammu & Kashmir	1.40	0.13	0.24	0.87	0.11	0.16	1.45	0.18	0.35	0.90	0.18	0.28
Jharkhand	1.05	0.36	0.42	1.34	0.31	0.38	1.94	0.44	0.64	1.38	0.31	0.46
Karnataka	8.39	5.45	5.70	11.86	5.68	6.11	5.81	6.23	6.18	7.40	7.31	7.32
Kerala	14.69	3.60	4.54	13.13	2.89	3.60	11.14	4.21	5.12	7.60	3.38	3.98
Madhya Pradesh	5.59	6.81	6.70	6.09	6.45	6.42	3.63	6.31	5.95	3.17	6.02	5.62
Maharashtra	7.69	11.25	10.95	6.78	10.31	10.07	7.26	12.28	11.62	4.78	11.16	10.25
Odisha	2.80	2.92	2.91	2.43	2.90	2.87	2.42	3.10	3.01	3.44	2.79	2.88
Puducherry	0.70	0.39	0.42	0.65	0.42	0.43	0.73	0.52	0.54	0.63	0.55	0.56
Punjab	2.45	3.11	3.06	3.27	2.79	2.83	2.42	3.21	3.10	3.10	2.47	2.56

(Continued)

Table A6 (Continued)

	2012–13						2018–19					
	Institutions			Intake			Institutions			Intake		
	Government	Private	Total	Government	Private	Total	Government	Private	Total	Government	Private	Total
Rajasthan	4.90	3.99	4.06	5.22	3.93	4.02	4.60	3.61	3.75	3.97	3.14	3.26
Tamil Nadu	6.29	16.05	15.22	7.16	17.27	16.57	13.56	17.59	17.06	29.65	19.78	21.18
Telangana	1.75	10.89	10.12	1.28	11.90	11.16	3.15	8.34	7.65	1.95	9.52	8.45
Uttar Pradesh	5.94	9.82	9.49	4.85	9.74	9.40	6.78	8.30	8.10	5.00	7.79	7.40
Uttarakhand	1.75	0.97	1.04	1.70	0.87	0.93	1.94	0.77	0.93	1.72	0.59	0.75
West Bengal	5.94	2.14	2.46	4.32	2.04	2.19	4.60	2.73	2.98	2.61	2.61	2.61
All States and Union Territories	1.75	0.03	0.18	1.29	0.03	0.12	1.94	0.15	0.38	0.82	0.13	0.23
All India	100.00	100.00	100.00	100.00	100.00	100.00	100.00	100.00	100.00	100.00	100.00	100.00

Source: AICTE Database.

Table A7 Enrolment in the First Year of Engineering in 2018–19 by Social Category (%)

State and UTs	SC	ST	OBC	Open	Minorities	Total
Andhra Pradesh	12.27	2.15	36.36	45.03	4.19	100
Assam	7.98	15.82	23.19	43.53	9.48	100
Bihar	14.46	1.42	44.37	31.89	7.87	100
Chandigarh	15.89	3.45	1.76	78.90	0.00	100
Chhattisgarh	10.51	10.23	36.16	41.64	1.46	100
Delhi	10.76	1.41	11.06	70.18	6.60	100
Goa	0.82	6.17	19.76	53.13	20.13	100
Gujarat	4.85	5.28	22.68	63.91	3.28	100
Haryana	10.66	0.42	15.40	68.01	5.51	100
Himachal Pradesh	20.40	5.87	11.32	60.10	2.32	100
Jammu & Kashmir	2.54	4.12	5.00	62.31	26.03	100
Jharkhand	10.91	15.09	25.20	43.98	4.82	100
Karnataka	7.79	2.48	34.54	46.60	8.60	100
Kerala	4.01	0.46	35.17	32.96	27.38	100
Madhya Pradesh	9.66	4.91	31.42	48.02	5.99	100
Maharashtra	9.94	1.51	33.68	48.53	6.34	100
Odisha	19.49	12.04	14.20	52.11	2.16	100
Puducherry	8.07	0.36	67.70	18.33	5.54	100
Punjab	16.00	0.93	10.06	64.70	8.31	100
Rajasthan	9.58	6.09	22.69	56.54	5.11	100
Tamil Nadu	16.57	0.74	52.75	22.06	7.89	100
Telangana	9.84	5.15	40.74	35.81	8.46	100
Uttar Pradesh	17.42	0.63	28.46	46.60	6.89	100
Uttarakhand	9.00	1.94	16.82	69.91	2.33	100
West Bengal	8.45	1.08	9.47	75.45	5.55	100
All States and Union Territories	5.15	19.53	16.39	49.36	9.57	100
All India	11.72	2.68	35.12	43.08	7.40	100

Source: Based on AICTE Database.

Table A8 Regional Distribution of Institutions, Intake and Enrolment in Engineering Education, 2018–19 (%)

	Institutions	Intake	Enrolment
Southern	46.32	52.61	55.78
Northern	10.24	8.93	7.92
Eastern	7.23	6.55	6.27
Western	11.78	10.35	12.10
Central	11.46	11.35	10.13
North West	12.58	10.21	7.80

Source: AICTE Database.

Table A9 Distribution of Enrolments in Higher Education across Various Branches by Gender (2018–19)

	Enrolment (in thousands)			Distribution by Gender (%)		
	Male	Female	Total	Male	Female	Total
Arts/Social Science	4,831	5,422	1,0251	32.93	38.95	35.86
Science	2,309	2,404	4,713	15.74	17.26	16.48
Commerce/Management	2,470	2,212	4,681	16.83	15.88	16.37
Engineering/Technology	2,740	1,112	3,852	18.67	7.99	13.47
Medicine	471	726	1,197	3.21	5.21	4.18
Others	1,850	2,048	3,899	12.61	14.71	13.63
Total	14,671	13,926	28,597	100.00	100.00	100.00

Source: All India Survey of Higher Education 2018–19.

Table A10 Growth in Enrolments in Major Categories of Streams of Engineering

	2010–11	2011–12	2012–13	2013–14	2014–15	2015–16	2016–17	2017–18	2018–19
All									
Traditional	34.57	40.89	42.23	45.43	48.31	49.63	48.63	47.17	44.48
IT-Related	52.68	46.12	46.34	43.97	41.15	39.86	40.23	41.73	44.12
Other	12.75	12.99	11.43	10.60	10.54	10.51	11.15	11.10	11.40
Total	100.00	100.00	100.00	100.00	100.00	100.00	100.00	100.00	100.00
Male									
Traditional	41.20	48.75	51.37	55.11	58.32	59.62	58.15	56.26	52.86
IT-Related	45.99	38.54	37.40	34.67	31.61	30.37	31.24	33.23	36.37
Other	12.82	12.71	11.22	10.21	10.07	10.01	10.61	10.50	10.76
Total	100.00	100.00	100.00	100.00	100.00	100.00	100.00	100.00	100.00
Female									
Traditional	18.48	21.20	19.61	21.01	22.68	23.85	24.57	24.47	23.84
IT-Related	68.95	65.13	68.46	67.42	65.59	64.35	62.93	62.94	63.20
Other	12.57	13.68	11.93	11.57	11.74	11.80	12.51	12.59	12.96
Total	100.00	100.00	100.00	100.00	100.00	100.00	100.00	100.00	100.00

Source: AICTE database.

Table A11 Trends in Enrolments in Major Disciplines in Higher Education

	1975–76	1980–81	1985–86	1990–91	1995–96	2000–01	2005–06	2010–11	2015–16	2016–17	2017–18	2018–19
Numbers in Lakhs												
Arts	11.57	11.86	15.49	18.89	27.41	35.57	51.38	67.48	113.57	115.31	125.62	126.60
Science	4.64	5.34	7.01	8.69	12.60	15.74	22.55	31.27	54.17	49.66	55.08	53.53
Commerce/ Management	4.15	5.54	7.82	9.70	14.10	16.55	19.86	29.05	46.37	48.91	57.15	57.85
Engineering and Technology	0.96	1.29	1.77	2.17	3.16	5.29	7.95	28.62	48.85	47.82	42.51	40.76
Medicine	1.05	1.10	1.23	1.50	2.20	2.61	3.48	6.53	11.18	11.83	12.52	13.64
Others	1.89	2.40	2.73	3.30	4.79	4.24	5.05	6.80	10.69	20.74	34.08	35.34
Total	24.26	27.52	36.05	44.25	64.26	80.01	110.28	169.75	284.85	294.27	326.96	327.72
Distribution (Percentage)												
Arts	47.67	43.08	42.97	42.69	42.65	44.46	46.59	39.75	39.87	39.19	38.42	38.63
Science	19.12	19.40	19.44	19.64	19.61	19.67	20.45	18.42	19.02	16.88	16.84	16.33
Commerce/ Management	17.10	20.14	21.69	21.92	21.95	20.68	18.01	17.11	16.28	16.62	17.48	17.65
Engineering and Technology	3.96	4.68	4.90	4.90	4.91	6.62	7.21	16.86	17.15	16.25	13.00	12.44
Medicine	4.33	4.00	3.41	3.40	3.42	3.26	3.16	3.84	3.93	4.02	3.83	4.16
Others	7.81	8.71	7.58	7.45	7.46	5.30	4.58	4.01	3.75	7.05	10.42	10.78
Total	100.00	100.00	100.00	100.00	100.00	100.00	100.00	100.00	100.00	100.00	100.00	100.00

Source: Selected Educational Statistics, All India Survey of Higher Education and UGC Annual Reports

Table A12 Number of Vacant/Unfilled Student Places in Engineering/Technology Institutions

	Total Vacant Seats	Percentage to Total Intake (All Institutions)	Percentage to Total Intake (Private Institutions)
2012–13	584,255	37.64	39.66
2013–14	689,908	42.21	44.33
2014–15	830,203	48.68	51.21
2015–16	776,527	47.60	50.06
2016–17	771,556	49.55	52.40
2017–18	726,108	49.18	51.95
2018–19	687,203	48.92	52.12

Source: AICTE Database

Table A13 Enrolment as a Percentage of Intake in Major Categories of Engineering Streams

	2012–13	2013–14	2014–15	2015–16	2016–17
Traditional	69.25	65.46	55.27	51.97	45.31
IT-Related	55.48	48.94	45.86	49.00	53.12
Other	72.37	69.38	63.40	62.47	59.68

Source: Based on AICTE database.

Table A14 Faculty Vacancies in IITs, 2019

	Sanctioned Strength	Teachers in Position	No. Vacant	Vacancy Percentage
IIT Bombay	1,091	677	414	37.9
IIT Delhi	776	663	113	14.6
IIT Kanpur	743	438	305	41.0
IIT Kharagpur	1,203	722	481	40.0
IIT Madras	1,000	595	405	40.5
IIT Guwahati	630	410	220	34.9
IIT Roorkee	800	432	368	46.0
IIT Hyderabad	284	206	78	27.5
IIT Jodhpur	140	112	28	20.0
IIT BHU Benaras	215	146	69	32.1
IIT Gandhinagar	160	101	59	36.9
IIT Patna	182	117	65	35.7
IIT Indore	188	145	43	22.9
IIT Mandi	159	128	31	19.5
IIT (ISM) Dhanbad	781	304	477	61.1
IIT Tirupati	93	88	5	5.4
IIT Palakkad	93	81	12	12.9
IIT Jammu	93	57	36	38.7
IIT Bhilai	93	47	46	49.5
IIT Dharwad	93	43	50	53.8
IIT Goa	93	44	49	52.7
Total (23 IITs)	9,718	6,009	3,709	38.2

Source: Kalra (2019) in *Indian Express*.

Table A15 Faculty in Engineering/Technology Institutions

	Faculty	Student-Faculty Ratio
2012–13	215,385	15.5
2013–14	301,841	12.2
2014–15	389,711	11.1
2015–16	403,786	10.5
2016–17	406,980	10.2
2017–18	406,927	9.9
2018–19	338,193	11.4

Source: AICTE Database.

Table A16 Rate of Growth Rate in the Number of PhDs Awarded and Enrolment in Undergraduate Courses in Engineering and Technology (%)

Period	PhDs Awarded	Enrolment at Undergraduate Level
1975–76 to 1990–91	4.41	9.69
1991–92 to 2010–11	9.52	14.18
2011–12 to 2018–19	18.57	2.41
1975–76 to 2018–19	9.66	10.15

Source: All India Survey of Higher Education (various years).

Table A17 Number of PhDs Awarded in Engineering/Technology as a Proportion of Outturn of Undergraduate Programs (%)

Year	No. of PhDs Relative to Undergraduate Outturn
2011–12	0.396
2012–13	0.333
2013–14	0.324
2014–15	0.531
2015–16	0.562
2016–17	0.376
2017–18	0.562
2018–19	0.861

Source: All India Survey of Higher Education (various years).

Table A18 Number of Doctorate Degrees Produced in Universities

Years	No. of PhDs in Engineering and Technology	No. PhDs in Higher Education	Percentage of Engineering and Technology PhDs in PhDs in All Subjects	Years	No. of PhDs in Engineering and Technology	No. of PhDs in Higher Education	Percentage of Engineering and Technology PhDs in PhDs in All Subjects
1950–51	10	180	5.56	1997–98	696	11,107	6.27
1955–56	24	416	5.77	1998–99	682	11,067	6.16
1960–61	16	796	2.01	1999–00	723	11,296	6.40
1963–64	19	975	1.95	2000–01	778	11,534	6.75
1973–74	95	3,056	3.11	2001–02	734	11,974	6.13
1980–81	139	6,080	2.29	2002–03	833	15,328	5.43
1981–82	190	6,404	2.97	2003–04	882	17,853	4.94
1982–83	160	6,597	2.43	2004–05	968	17,898	5.41
1983–84	192	6,934	2.77	2005–06	1,058	18,730	5.65
1984–85	210	7,139	2.94	2006–07	844	12,773	6.61
1985–86	194	7,346	2.64	2007–08	427	13,237	10.78
1986–87	224	7,219	3.10	2008–09	1,245	13,768	9.04
1987–88	225	7,934	2.84	2009–10	1,449	14,477	10.01
1988–89	238	8,238	2.89	2010–11	1,682	16,093	10.45
1989–90	252	8,052	3.13	2011–12	2,173	19,861	10.94
1990–91	262	8,016	3.27	2012–13	2,119	20,275	10.45
1991–92	299	8,743	3.42	2013–14	2,533	22,849	11.09
1992–93	277	10,136	2.73	2014–15	4,340	27,327	15.88
1993–94	329	9,923	3.32	2015–16	4,772	27,671	17.25
1994–95	337	9,851	3.42	2017	4,907	34,400	14.26
1995–96	374	10,397	3.60	2018	7,160	40,813	17.54
1996–97	298	10,408	2.86	2020	4,556	25,550	17.83
				Rate of growth*	9.14	7.37	

* Compound rate of growth per Annum (%).
Source: UGC Annual Reports and All India Survey of Higher Education (various years).

Table A19 Expenditure on Technical Education as a Share of Total Expenditure on Education (%)

Years	Percentage to Total Expenditure on Education	Year	Percentage to Total Expenditure on Education
1990–91	2.90	2006–07	3.44
1991–92	4.33	2007–08	3.71
1992–93	4.35	2008–09	4.75
1993–94	4.37	2009–10	4.91
1994–95	4.09	2010–11	4.57
1995–96	3.99	2011–12	5.06
1996–97	3.95	2012–13	5.08
1997–98	4.05	2013–14	5.06
1998–99	4.01	2014–15	5.07
1999–2000	4.04	2015–16	4.86
2000–01	3.95	2016–17	5.80
2001–02	4.11	2017–18	5.80
2002–03	4.11	2018–19	4.75
2003–04	3.88	2019–20(RE)	4.84
2004–05	3.87	2020–21(BE)	4.80
2005–06	3.87		

RE: Revised estimates; BE: Budget estimates.
Source: Analysis of Budget Expenditure on Education (various years).

Table A20 Public Expenditure on Engineering Education as a Percentage of Total Expenditure on Technical Education (States and Union Territories)

Year	%	Year	%
1991–92	21.9	2008–09	18.8
1992–93	21.8	2007–08	19.1
1993–94	17.6	2008–09	18.8
1994–95	18.6	2009–10	15.3
1995–96	18.5	2010–11	15.6
1996–97	18.5	2011–12	15.0
1997–98	19.8	2012–13	15.9
1998–99	17.6	2013–14	16.5
1999–2000	17.4	2014–15	14.6
2000–01	19.4	2015–16	19.1
2001–02	20.5	2016–17	15.4
2002–03	20.1	2017–18	15.4
2003–04	19.3	2018–19	16.5
2004–05	20.1	2019–20(RE)	16.0
2005–06	20.9	2020–21(BE)	16.0
2006–07	20.2		
2007–08	19.1	Average	18.1

Source: Analysis of Budget Expenditure on Education (various years).

Table A21 India: Estimated Stock of Engineers, 1971–2003

Year	Degree Holders	Diploma Holders	Total
1971	1,745	2,304	4,049
1981	3,049	4,258	7,307
1986	3,908	6,014	9,922
1990	4,922	7,978	12,900
1991	5,196	8,593	13,789
1992	5,558	9,111	14,669
1993	5,977	9,701	15,678
1994	6,449	10,260	16,709
1995	6,981	10,978	17,959
1996	7,533	11,731	19,264
1997	8,065	12,422	20,487
1998	8,591	13,123	21,714
1999	9,137	13,795	22,932
2000	9,695	14,560	24,255
2001	10,244	15,317	25,561
2002	10,783	16,067	26,850
2003	11,832	17,205	29,037

Note: Stock is taken at the beginning of the year and in the working age group.
Source: IAMR Year Book, 2007.

Appendix B (to Part II)

Table B1 Definition and Notation of the Variables Used in the Statistical Analysis (in Chapters 4–8)

Variable	Notation	Description and Measurement
Individual Characteristics		
Gender of the student	GENDER	= 1 if female = 0 otherwise
CASTE of the student	SC	= 1 if SC, 0 otherwise
	ST	= 1 if ST, 0 otherwise
	OBC	= 1, if belonging to other backward classes = 0 otherwise
	GENERAL	= 1, if general (non-reserved) category = 0 otherwise (reference category)
Religion of the student	HINDU	= 1, if Hindu, 0 otherwise
	MUSLIM	= 1, if Muslim, 0 otherwise
	OTHERS (Sikh, Jain, Buddhist, Christian)	= 1, if belongs to other religions, 0 otherwise
Household Factors		
Parents' Occupation		
Father's occupation	FATHOCP_PROF	= 1, if professional/technical worker, 0 otherwise
	FATHOCP_BUS	= 1, if businessman, 0 otherwise
	FATHOCP_OTHERS	= 1, if belonging to other occupations, 0 otherwise
Mother's occupation	MOTHOCP_PROF	= 1, if professional/technical worker, 0 otherwise
	MOTHOCP_BUS	= 1, if businessman, 0 otherwise
	MOTHOCP_OTHERS	= 1, if belonging to other occupations, 0 otherwise
Parents' education	FATHER_ED	= Actual years of schooling of father
	MOTHER_ED	= Actual years of schooling of mother
	FATHER_HRED	= 1, if father is higher educated, 0 otherwise
	FATHER_HR_GEN	= 1, if father is higher educated (general), 0 otherwise
	FATHER_HR_PROFL	= 1, if father is higher educated in professional subjects, 0 otherwise

(*Continued*)

Table B1 (Continued)

Variable	Notation	Description and Measurement
	MOTHER_HRED	= 1, if mother is higher educated, 0 otherwise
	MOTHER_HR_GEN	= 1, if mother is higher educated (general), 0 otherwise
	MOTHER_HR_PROFL	= 1, if mother is higher educated in professional subjects, 0 otherwise
Household size	SIBLINGS	Number of siblings in the family

Household's Economic Conditions

Variable	Notation	Description and Measurement
Household income	HHY	Annual income of the household (in ₹)
Ownership of a house	OWN_HOUSE	= 1, if the student's family owns a house = 0, otherwise Parents' occupation
Ownership of a land	OWN_LAND	= 1, if the student's family owns land = 0, otherwise

Student's Academic Background (at School Level)

Variable	Notation	Description and Measurement
Education board (board under which secondary school studies were completed)	SEC_BOARD	= 1, if the student has studied under state board = 0, otherwise
Type of school	SEC_SCH_TYPE	= 1, if the student completed secondary schooling from a private school = 0, otherwise, that is, if the student completed secondary schooling from a government school
Location of the school	SEC_SCH_LOCATION	= 1, if located in rural areas = 0 otherwise
Medium of instruction at school	SEC_MEDIUM	= 1, if English, = 0 otherwise
Academic performance	SEC_MARKS	= % of marks secured in the board (school-end) examination
Preparatory coaching	PRE_COACHING	= 1, if the student has attended any coaching classes in preparation for the entrance examination (for admission into Engineering studies) = 0, otherwise, that is, if the student has not attended coaching classes
Rank in the entrance examination	ENTRANCE_RANK	Rank in the entrance examination
High rank	ENT_RANK_HIGH	=1, if the students have scored 'top/high' rank in the entrance examination = 0 otherwise
Good (medium) rank	ENT_RANK_MED	=1, if the students have scored 'good' rank in the entrance examination = 0 otherwise

(*Continued*)

Table B1 (Continued)

Variable	Notation	Description and Measurement
Low or 'average' rank	ENT_RANK_LOW	=1, if the students have scored 'average' rank in the entrance examination = 0 otherwise
Student's Current Education		
Domicile status	NATIVITY	= 1, if the student belongs to the state where the engineering institution is located = 0 otherwise, (if the student has come from other states)
Score in entrance examination	ENT_SCORE	Not standardised (used in a preliminary exercise)
Type of institution the student is currently studying	ENGG_INST_TYPE	= 1, if the student is enrolled in a private institution = 0 otherwise, that is, if the student is enrolled in a government institution
Stream/branch of engineering	STREAM_STUDY	= 1, if enrolled in modern/IT-related courses = 0 otherwise
Household expenditure on education	HHEXPR	Total household expenditure on engineering education of the student for tor the current academic year (₹)
Scholarship	SCHOLARSHIP	= 1, if received any scholarship = 0 otherwise
Education loan (from a commercial bank)	LOAN	= 1, if taken any education loan = 0 otherwise
Amount of educational loan	LOAN_AMOUNT	Amount of educational loan taken (₹)
Part-time work	PART_TIME	= 1, if the student has done any part-time job during the programme of study = 0 otherwise
Employment		
Employment status	EMPLOYMENT	= 1, if the student has not got any offer of employment in the on-campus recruitment = 0 otherwise, that is, if the student has got any offer of employment
Field of employment	FIELD_EMPLOYMENT	= 1, if the job offered is in engineering sector = 0 otherwise
Type of enterprise where job is offered	TYPE_DOMESTIC	= 1, if domestic = 0 otherwise
	TYPE_FOREIGN	= 1, if foreign = 0 otherwise
	TYPE_JOINT	= 1, if it is a joint venture = 0 otherwise

(*Continued*)

Table B1 (Continued)

Variable	Notation	Description and Measurement
Earnings Offered	lnEARNNGS	Annual salary/wages (₹) offered at the time of campus recruitment (logarithmic form)
Educational aspirations of the student	ED_ASP	= 1, if the student intends to go for further studies = 0 otherwise

Table B2 Explanation on Some Terms/Variables

Terms/Variable	Nomenclature used	Explanation
Type of institution/school	Government Private	Government Government-aided private Private (unaided/self-financing)
Groups of disciplines/streams/branches of engineering	Traditional/conventional Modern/IT-related	Civil, Electrical Engineering, Mechanical, Engineering, Mechanical & Automation Engineering Electronics Engineering, Electronics and Communications Engineering, Electrical and Electronics Engineering, Computer Science Engineering, and Information Technology Related Areas of Engineering
Parents' occupation	Professional Business Others	Junior and senior professional and technical workers like doctors, professors, lawyers, architects, engineers, nurses, teachers, editors, photographers and bank employees Own business, including agriculture (not employed) Clerical and related workers, service workers, farmers, fishermen and related workers, skilled workers (foreman, craftsman etc.), unskilled workers (ordinary labourer), retired, and workers not classified by occupation (athlete, actor, musician, unemployed, partially unemployed), housewives (homemakers)
Household income	Low-income group Lower middle-income group Upper middle income group High income	< ₹1 lakh (mid-value: 50,000) ₹1 lakh to ₹5 lakhs (mid-value: 300,000) ₹5 lakh to ₹10 lakhs (mid value: 750,000) above ₹10 lakhs (mid-value: 1,500,000)
Education board	Central State	Central Board of School Education (CBSE), Council for the Indian School Certificate Examination (ICSE) – both at all India level State (government) boards

Table B3 Summary Statistics of the Variables Used in the Probit Analysis

Variables	Number	Mean	Standard Deviation	Minimum Value	Maximum Value
Individual Characteristics					
GENDER	6,623	0.2861	0.4520	0	1
SC	6,623	0.0738	0.2615	0	1
ST	6,623	0.0187	0.1356	0	1
OBC	6,623	0.1940	0.3954	0	1
GENERAL	6,623	0.7134	0.4521	0	1
RELIGION					
HINDU	6,461	0.8804	0.3246	0	1
MUSLIM	6,461	0.0350	0.1837	0	1
OTHERS	6,461	0.0834	0.2765	0	1
Household Factors					
lnHHY	6,076	12.3298	0.9623	10.82	14.04
OWN-HOUSE	4,899	0.0896	0.2856	0	1
FATHOCP_PROF	6,121	0.20	0.40	0	1
FATHOCP_BUS	6,121	0.2036	0.4027	0	1
FATHOCP_OTHERS	6,121	0.60	0.49	0	1
MOTHOCP_PROF	4,948	0.15	0.36	0	1
MOTHOCP_BUS	4,948	0.08	0.28	0	1
MOTHOCP_OTHERS	4,948	0.76	0.43	0	1
FATHER_ED	6,550	14.5684	3.9130	0	17
MOTHER_ED	6,516	12.9449	4.7369	0	17
SIBLINGS	6,518	1.4641	0.9446	0	6
NATIVITY	6,033	0.6295	0.4830	0	1
Student's Academic Background					
SEC_MARKS	6,141	78.8938	11.1914	30.29	100
SEC_MEDIUM	6,079	0.1477	0.3548	0	1
SEC_BOARD	6,306	0.6562	0.4750	0	1
SEC_SCH_TYPE	6,014	0.7203	0.4489	0	1
SEC_SCH_LOCATION	4,746	0.1140	0.3178	0	1
PRE_COACHING	5,212	0.5259	0.4993	0	1
ENT_RANK Rank	3,986	5,931.198	15,587.96	0	700,000
ENT_RANK_H	3,986	0.5970	0.4905	0	1
ENT_RANK_M	3,986	0.2398	0.4270	0	1
ENT_RANK_L	3,986	0.1630	0.3694	0	1
Student's Current Education					
ENGG_INST_TYPE	6,623	0.6599	0.4738	0	1
STREAM_STUDY	6,623	0.6986	0.4627	0	1
lnHHEXPR	5,900	4.1473	0.9054	1.60941	7.0121
SCHOLARSHIP	6,581	0.1834	0.3870	0	1

(*Continued*)

Table B3 (Continued)

Variables	Number	Mean	Standard Deviation	Minimum Value	Maximum Value
LOAN	6,033	0.1034	0.3045	0	1
PART_TIME	6,294	0.1005	0.3008	0	1
Employment Status					
EMPLOYMENT	6,438	0.7426	0.4377	0	1
Earnings					
Ln EARNINGS	1,532	1.2405	0.4592	1.6094	3.912
Type of Employment					
FIELD_ EMPLOYMENT	1,657	0.1069	0.3091	0	1
TYPE_JOINT	1,657	0.3947	0.4888	0	1
TYPE_DOM	1,657	0.2703	0.4442	0	1
TYPE_FOREIGN	1,532	0.3825	0.4862	0	1
Educational Aspirations					
ED_ASP	4,017	0.5937	0.4912	0	1

References

Abramovitz, M. (1989): *Thinking About Growth*. Cambridge: Cambridge University Press.
Acar, E.Ö., Günlap, B. & Cilasum, S.M. (2016): An Empirical Analysis of Household Education Expenditures in Turkey, *International Journal of Educational Development 51* (November): 23–35.
Acerenza, S. & Gandelman, N. (2019): Household Education Spending in Latin America and the Caribbean: Evidence from Income and Expenditure Surveys, *Education Finance and Policy 14*(1) (Winter): 61–87.
Acevedo, G.L. & Salinas, A. (2000): Marginal Willingness to Pay for Education and the Determinants of Enrolment in Mexico. Policy Research Working Paper No.2405. Washington, DC: World Bank.
Adams, R.D., Evangelou, D., English, L., deFigueiredo, A.D., Mousoulides, N., Pawley, A.L. & Schifellite, C. (2011): Multiple Perspectives on Engaging Future Engineers, *Journal of Engineering Education 100*(1): 48–88.
Agrey, L. & Lampadan, N. (2014): Determinant Factors Contributing to Student Choice in Selecting a University, *Journal of Education and Human Development 3*(2): 391–404.
AICTE: All India Council of Technical Education (1994): *Report of the High-Power Committee for Mobilisation of Additional Resources for Technical Education*. [Chairman: Dr. D. Swaminadhan]. New Delhi: AICTE.
AICTE (1999): *Technical Education in India in Independent India: 1947–1997. A Compendium to Commemorate the 50th Anniversary of Independence*. New Delhi: AICTE.
AICTE (2003): *Revitalising Technical Education: Report of the Review Committee on AICTE* [Chairman: U.R. Rao]. New Delhi: AICTE.
AICTE (2015): *Technical Education in India: A Futuristic Scenario (Report of the AICTE Review Committee, 2015)* [Chairperson: M.K. Kaw]. New Delhi: AICTE.
AICTE (2018): *Engineering Education in India: Short- and Medium-Term Perspectives* [Chairperson: B.V. Mohan Reddy]. New Delhi: AICTE.
AICTE (2019): *All-India Council for Technical Education*. https://facilities.aicte-india.org/dashboard/pages/dashboardaicte.php.
Aldrich, J.H. & Nelson, F.D. (1984): *Linear Probability, Logit, and Probit Models*. Sage
Allen, D.O. (1854): The State and Prospects of the English Language in India, *Journal of the American Oriental Society 4*: 263–75. https://www.jstor.org/stable/592279?seq=1#metadata_info_tab_contents

Altbach, P.G. & Levy, D.C. (2005): *Private Higher Education: A Global Revolution*. Rotterdam, Netherlands: Sense.

Altonji, J. G., Arcidiacono, P. & Maurel, A. (2016): Analysis of Field Choice in College and Graduate School: Determinants and Wage Effects. In: *Handbook of the Economics of Education* (Eds.: Hanushek, E.A., Machin, S. & Woessmann, L.) (Vol. 5, pp. 305–96). Amsterdam: Elsevier.

Anandkrishnan, M. (2014): *Technical Education: Trends, Polices and Prospects*. New Delhi: Bloomsbury.

Ananthasayanam, M.R. (2009): State of Present Day Engineering Education in India, *Current Science* 97(7) (10 October): 979.

Andreou, S.N. (2012): Analysis of Household Expenditure on Education in Cyprus, *Cyprus Economic Policy Review* 6(2): 17–38.

Arneson, R.J. (1989): Equality and Equal Opportunities for Welfare, *Philosophical Studies* 56(1): 77–93.

Arneson, R.J. (1990): Liberalism, Distributive Subjectivism, and Equal Opportunity for Welfare, *Philosophy & Public Affairs* 19(2): 158–94.

Arneson, R.J. (2000): Luck Egalitarianism and Prioritarianism, *Ethics* 110(2) (January): 339–49.

Arrow, K.J. (1973): Higher Education as a Filter, *Journal of Public Economics* 2(3) (July): 193–216.

Asadi, G. (2020): Parents' Investments in the Quality of Education: The Case of Ghana, *Education Economics* 28(6): 621–46.

Asankha, P. & Ajantha, S.K. (2020): Spending Privately for Education Despite having a Free Public Education Policy: Evidence from Sri Lankan Household Surveys, *International Journal of Social Economics* 47(5): 561–80.

Aslam, M. & Kingdon, G.G. (2008): Gender and Household Education Expenditure in Pakistan, *Applied Economics* 40(19–21): 2573–91.

Aspiring Minds (various years): *National Employability Report: Engineers* (Various Years). Gurugram: Aspiring Minds Pvt Ltd.

AspiringMinds (2019): *National Employability Report 2019: Engineers - Annual Report 2019*. Bengaluru. https://www.aspiringminds.com/research-reports/national-employability-report-for-engineers-2019/

Aspiring Minds Team (2019): *Employability of Engineers: State Wise* (16 April). https://www.aspiringminds.com/blog/research-articles/employability-of-engineers-state-wise/

Atkinson, H. & Pennington, M. (2012): Unemployment of Engineering Graduates: The Key Issues. Engineering Education, *Journal of the Higher Education Academy* 7(2): 7–15.

Avery, C. & Turner, S. (2012): Student Loans: Do College Students Borrow Too Much--or Not Enough? *Journal of Economic Perspectives* 26(1): 165–92.

Aydin, O.T. (2015): University Choice Process: A Literature Review on Models and Factors Affecting the Process, *Yükseköğretim Dergisi/Journal of Higher Education* 5(2): 103–11.

Azad, J.L. (1991): *Graduate Unemployment in India*. New Delhi: Association of Indian Universities.

Azam, M., Chin, A. & Prakash, N. (2013): Returns to English-Language Skills in India, *Economic Development and Cultural Change* 61(2) (January): 335–67.

Azam, M. & Kingdon, G.G. (2013): Are Girls the Fairer Sex in India? Revisiting Intra-household Allocation of Education Expenditure, *World Development* 42(1): 143–64.

Badran, I. (2007): Enhancing Creativity and Innovation in Engineering Education, *European Journal of Engineering Education* 32(5): 573–85.
Bairagya, I. (2015): Socio-Economic Determinants of Educated Unemployment in India. Working Paper No.343. Bengaluru: Institute for Social and Economic Change.
Banerjee, R. & Muley, V.P. (2009): *Engineering Education in India*. Mumbai: Observer Research Foundation/Indian Institute of Technology.
Barman, S.R. (2022): Average Math Score of First-Year Engineering Students Below 40%: AICTE, *Indian Express* (14 June 2022). https://indianexpress.com/article/education/average-maths-score-first-year-engineering-students-below-40-pc-aicte-7968111/
Basant, R. & Sen, G. (2013): Who Participates in Higher Education in India? Rethinking the Role of Affirmative Action. In: *Higher Education in India: In Search of Equality, Quality and Quantity* (Ed.: Tilak, J.B.G.) (pp. 110–31). New Delhi: Orient BlackSwan.
Bayar, A.A. & Bengi, Y.I. (2016): Determinants of Household Education Expenditures: Do Poor Spend Less on Education? *Topics in Middle Eastern and North African Economies* (electronic journal) 18(1) (May): 83–111 http://www.luc.edu/orgs/meea/
Becker, G.S. (1975): *Human Capital*. New York: Columbia University Press [2nd edition].
Beg, M.N. & Bhat, G.M. (2021): Gender and Household's Spending on Education: An Empirical Evidence, *Asian Journal of Economics, Business and Accounting* 21(2): 1–13.
Begum, L., Grossman, P.J. & Islam, A. (2014): Parental Attitude and Investment in Children's Education and Health in Developing Countries. Discussion Paper 30/14. Melbourne: Monash University, Department of Economics.
Behrman, J.R., Pollak, R.A. & Taubman, P. (1982): Parental Preferences and Provision for Progeny, *Journal of Political Economy* 90(1) (February): 52–73.
Bhargava, R.N. (2001): Present Engineering Education in India—An Emerging Economy—And a Glimpse of the Scenario in the 21st Century. In: *Educating the Engineer for the 21st Century* (Eds.: Weichert, D., Rauhut, B. & Schmidt, R.) (pp. 77–80). Dordrecht: Springer.
Bhatt, S. (2010): Growth and Development of Engineering Education: An Overview of Indian Scenario, *University News* 48(10): 8–14.
Bhatty, K. (1998): Educational Deprivation in India: A Survey of Field Investigations, *Economic and Political Weekly* 33(27) (4–10 July): 1731–40.
Bifulco, R., Ladd, H.F. & Ross, S.L. (2009): The Effects of Public School Choice on Those Left Behind: Evidence from Durham, North Carolina, *Peabody Journal of Education* 84(2): 130–49.
Birdsall, Nancy. (1996): Public Spending on Higher Education in Developing Countries: Too Much or Too Little? *Economics of Education Review* 15(4) (October): 407–19.
Biswas, G., Chopra, K.L., Jha, C.S. & Singh, D.V. (2010): *Profile of Engineering Education in India: Status, Concerns and Recommendations*. New Delhi: Norosa Publishing.
Blake, J. (1989): *Family Size and Achievement*. Berkeley and Los Angeles, CA: University of California Press.
Blau, P.M. & Duncan, O.D. (1967): *The American Occupational Structure*. New York: John Wiley & Sons.
Blaug, M., Layard, R. & Woodhall, M. (1969): *The Causes of Graduate Unemployment in India*. London: Allen Lane, Penguin.

Blom, A. & Cheong, J. (2010): Governance of Technical Education in India: Key Issues, Principles, and Case Studies. Working Paper No.190. Washington DC: World Bank.

Blom, A. & Saeki, H. (2011): Employability and Skill Set of Newly Graduated Engineers in India. Policy Research Working Paper 5640. Washington DC: World Bank. [Documents of TEQIP II. New Delhi: All-India Council for Technical Education. https://www.teqip.in/docs/t2/B-Employbility%20and%20Skill%20set%20of%20newly%20graduated%20engineers%20in%20India.pdf

Boatman, A., Evans, B.J. & Soliz, A. (2017): Understanding Loan Aversion in Education: Evidence from High School Seniors, Community College Students, and Adults, *AERA Open* 3(1): 1–16.

Boissiere, M., Knight, J.B. & Sabot, R.H. (1985): Earnings, Schooling, Ability, and Cognitive Skills, *American Economic Review* 75(5): 1016–30.

Borah, D., Malik, K. & Massini, S. (2019): Are Engineering Graduates Ready for R&D Jobs in Emerging Countries? *Research Policy* 48(9) (November): 1–15 [10387].

Bose, P.K., Sanyal, B.C. & Mukherjee, S.P. (1983): *Graduate Employment and Higher Education in West Bengal*. Paris: UNESCO-IIEP and Kolkata: University of Kolkata.

Briggs, S. (2007): An Exploratory Study of the Factors Influencing Undergraduate Student Choice: The Case of Higher Education in Scotland, *Studies in Higher Education* 31(6): 705–22.

Britton, J., Dearden, L., Shephard, N. & Vignoles, A. (2016): How English Domiciled Graduate Earnings Vary with Gender, Institution Attended, Subject and Socioeconomic Background. Working Paper W16/06. London: Institute for Fiscal Studies.

Brown, P.H. (2006): Parental Education and Investment in Children's Human Capital in Rural China, *Economic Development and Cultural Change* 54(4) (July): 759–89.

Buckner, E. (2017): The Worldwide Growth of Private Higher Education: Cross-National Patterns of Higher Education Institution Foundings by Sector, *Sociology of Education* 90(4): 296–314.

Callender, C. & Mason, G. (2017): Does Student Loan Debt Deter Higher Education Participation? New Evidence from England, *ANNALS of the American Academy of Political and Social Science* 671(1): 20–48.

Carnoy, M., Dossani, R. & Tilak, J.B.G. (2010): Understanding the Expansion and Quality of Engineering Education in India (draft). Working Paper 23174 (date 05–2010). Stanford: Walter H. Shorenstein Asia-Pacific Research Center, Columbia International Affairs (CIAO) Online. http://ciaonet.org/record/23174?search=1CII:

Carnoy, M., Loyalka, P., Androushchak, G. & Proudnikova, A. (2012): The Economic Returns to Higher Education in the BRIC Countries and their Implications for Higher Education Expansion. Working Papers WP BRP 02/EDU/2012. Moscow: National Research University Higher School of Economics. https://publications.hse.ru/mirror/pubs/share/folder/1m4bvfmg12/direct/59041919.pdf

Carnoy, M., Loyalka, P., Dobryakova, M., Dossani, R., Froumin, I., Kuhns, K., Tilak, J.B.G. & Wang, R. (2013): *University Expansion in a Changing Global Economy: Triumph of the BRICS?* Stanford: Stanford University Press.

Carsten, S., Spieß, C.K. & Storck, J. (2015): Private Spending on Children's Education: Low-Income Families Pay Relatively More, *DIW Economic Bulletin* 8: 113–23. https://www.diw.de/documents/publikationen/73/diw_01.c.497272.de/diw_econ_bull_2015-08-3.pdf

Chakrabarti, A. (2009): Determinants of Participation in Higher Education and Choice of Disciplines: Evidence from Urban and Rural Indian Youth, *South Asia Economic Journal* 10(2) (July/December): 371–402.

Chakravarty, S. & Somanathan, E. (2008): Discrimination in an Elite Labour Market? Job Placements at IIM-Ahmadabad, *Economic and Political Weekly* 43(44): 45–50.

Chandrasekhar, C.P. & Ghosh, J. (2020): Unaffordable Education in the New India, *International Economics Development Associates* (1 December). https://www.networkideas.org/featured-articles/2020/12/unaffordable-education-in-the-new-india/

Chandrasekhar, S., Rani, P.G. & Sahoo, S. (2019): What Do We Know and What Do Recent Data Have to Say? Household Expenditure on Higher Education, *Economic and Political Weekly* 54(20) (18 May): 52–60.

Chaudhuri, K. & Roy, S. (2006): Do Parents Spread Educational Expenditure Evenly Across the Two Genders? Evidence from Two North Indian States, *Economic and Political Weekly* 41(51): 5276–82.

Cheechi, D. & Jappelli, T. (2005): School Choice and Quality. Discussion Paper. No. 4748. London: Centre for Economic Policy Research.

Chevalier, A. (2011): Subject Choice and Earnings of UK Graduates, *Economics of Education Review* 30(6) (December): 1187–201.

Chia, G. & Miller, P.W. (2008): Tertiary Performance, Field of Study and Graduate Starting Salaries, *Australian Economic Review* 41(1): 15–31.

Chopra, R. (2018): BTech (Fail): Empty Seats, Ghost Campuses, Unskilled Graduates; Part of an Express Investigation: Why an Undergraduate Engineering Degree in India Is Rapidly Losing Value — and Currency, *Indian Express* (29 January). https://indianexpress.com/article/education/btech-fail-empty-seats-ghost-campuses-unskilled-graduates-devalued-degree-4977240/

Choudhury, P.K. (2012): An Economic Analysis of Demand for Higher Education in India: A Study of Engineering Education in Delhi. Unpublished PhD Thesis. New Delhi: National University of Educational Planning and Administration.

Choudhury, P.K. (2013): Determinants of Employment Probabilities and Expected Earnings of Engineering Graduates: An Empirical Study in Delhi, India, *Journal of Income and Wealth* 35(2) (July-December): 131–46.

Choudhury, P.K. (2015): Explaining Gender Discrimination in the Employment and Earnings of Engineering Graduates in India, *Journal of Educational Planning and Administration* 29(3) (July): 225–46.

Choudhury, P.K. (2016): Growth of Engineering Education in India: Status, Issues and Challenges, *Higher Education for the Future* 3(1): 93–107.

Choudhury, P.K. (2019a): Student Assessment of Quality of Engineering Education in India: Evidence from a Field Survey, *Quality Assurance in Education* 27(1):103–26.

Choudhury, P.K. (2019b): Pattern and Determinants of Household Expenditure on Higher Education: Evidence from Rural Odisha. In: *The Future of Higher Education in India* (Ed. Bhushan, S.) (pp. 165–80). Singapore: Springer.

Choudhury, P.K. & Kumar, A.K. (2021): An Empirical Analysis of Household Expenditure on Engineering Education in Odisha, *Millennial Asia: An International Journal of Asian Studies* 13(3): 442–69. https://journals.sagepub.com/doi/full/10.1177/0976399620969892

Chowdry, H., Crawford, C., Dearden, L., Goodman, A. & Vignoles, A. (2008): *Widening Participation in Higher Education: Analysis Using Linked Administrative Data*. London: Economic and Social Research Council.

CII (2018): *AICTE-CII Survey of Industry-linked Technical Institutes 2018.* New Delhi: Confederation of Indian Industry and AICTE.

Clotfelter, C.T. & Rothschild, M. (Eds.) (1993): *Studies of Supply and Demand in Higher Education.* Chicago: Chicago University Press.

Cohen, G.A. (1989): On the Currency of Egalitarian Justice, *Ethics* 99(4) (July): 906–44.

Cohn, E. & Morgan, J.M. (1977–1978): Demand for Higher Education: A Survey of Recent Studies. *Review of Higher Education* 1(2) (Winter): 18–30.

Crawford, C. & Vignoles, A. (2014): Heterogeneity in Graduate Earnings by Socio-economic Background. IFS Working Paper W14/30. London: Institute of Fiscal Studies

Dang, H.A. (2007): The Determinants and Impact of Private Tutoring Classes in Vietnam, *Economics of Education Review* 26(6): 684–99.

Datta, S. & Kingdon, G.G. (2019): *Gender Bias in Intra-Household Allocation of Education in India: Has It Fallen over Time?* IZA DP No.12671. Bonn: Institute of Labour Economics.

Daymont, T.N. & Andrisani, P.J. (1984): Job Preferences, College Major and the Gender Gap in Earnings, *Journal of Human Resources* 19(3): 408–28.

de Gayardon, A., Callender, C. & Green, F. (2019): The Determinants of Student Loan Take-up in England, *Higher Education* 78(6): 965–83; 985–90.

Delors Commission (1996): *Learning: The Treasure Within: Report to UNESCO of the International Commission on Education for the Twenty-first Century.* Paris: UNESCO.

Demiroglari, S. & Gürler, Ö.K. (2020): Determinants of Household Education Expenditures by Education Level: The Case of Turkey, *International Journal of Contemporary Economics and Administrative Sciences* 10(1): 235–58.

Dhaliwal, M.S., Mittal, A., Aggarwal, A. & Chand, P.K. (2019): Determining the Factors Affecting the Selection of Private Universities and Colleges in Indian Context: A Structural Equation Modeling Approach, *Journal of Advanced Research in Dynamical & Control Systems,* 11(8): 2579–89.

Dolton, P.J. & Makepeace, G.H. (1990): The Earnings of Economics Graduates, *Economic Journal* 100 (March): 237–50.

Donkoh, S. & Amikuzuno, J. (2011): Determinants of Household Education Expenditure in Ghana, *Educational Research Review* 6(8): 570–79.

Dore, Ronald. (1976): *The Diploma Disease: Education, Qualifications and Development.* London: George Allen & Unwin.

Dossani, R. & Patibandla, M.M. (2012): Preparing India's Workforce for the Knowledge Economy. In: *Knowledge Perspectives of New Product Development: Innovation, Technology, and Knowledge Management* (Eds.: Assimakopoulos, D., Carayannis, E. & Dossani, R. (pp. 223–51). New York: Springer.

Downey, D.B. (1995): When Bigger is Not Better: Family Size, Parental Resources, and Children's Educational Performance, *American Sociological Review* 60(5) (October): 746–61.

Drèze, J. & Kingdon, G.G. (2001): School Participation in Rural India, *Review of Development Economics* 5(1) (February): 1–24.

Dubey, A., Mehndiratta, A., Sagar, M. & Kashiramka, S. (2019): Reforms in Technical Education Sector: Evidence from World Bank-assisted Technical Education Quality Improvement Programme in India, *Higher Education* 78(2): 273–99.

Dunga, S.H. (2014): Determinants of Employment Status and Its Relationship to Poverty in Bophelong Township, *Mediterranean Journal of Social Sciences* 5(21) (September): 215–20.

Duraisamy, M. & Duraisamy, P. (1999): Women in the Professional and Technical Labour Market in India: Gender Discrimination in Education, Employment and Earnings, *Indian Journal of Labour Economics* 42(4): 599–612.

Duraisamy, P. & Duraisamy, M. (1993): Returns to Scientific and Technical Education in India, *Margin* 25(4) (July–September): 396–406.

Duraisamy, P. & Duraisamy, M. (2016): Contemporary Issues in Indian Higher Education: Privatization, Public and Household Expenditures and Student Loan, *Higher Education for the Future* 3(2): 144–63.

Dworkin, R.M. (1981): What is Equality? Part 2. Equality of Resources, *Philosophy & Public Affairs* 10(4): 283–345.

Dworkin, R.M. (2002): Sovereign Virtue Revisited, *Ethics* 113(1) (October): 106–43.

Dworkin, R.M. (2003): Equality, Luck and Hierarchy, *Philosophy & Public Affairs* 31(2) (Spring): 190–98.

Education (Kothari) Commission (1966): *Education and National Development: Report of the Education Commission 1964–66*. New Delhi: Ministry of Education [reprint NCRT 1972]

Elchardus, M. & Bram S. (2009): The Culture of Academic Disciplines and the Sociopolitical Attitudes of Students: A Test of Selection and Socialization Effects, *Social Science Quarterly* 90(2) (June): 446–60.

Emerson, P. M. & Souza, A. P. (2007): Child Labor, School Attendance, and Intrahousehold Gender Bias in Brazil, *World Bank Economic Review* 21(2): 301–16.

Ermisch, J. & Francesconi, M. (2001): Family Matters: Impacts of Family Background on Educational Attainments, *Economica* 68(270) (May): 137–56.

Ernst & Young (2017): *Future of Jobs in India – A 2022 Perspective*. Kolkata.

Fernandes, L. (2006): *India's New Middle Class: Democratic Politics in an Era of Economic Reform*. Minneapolis, MN: University of Minnesota Press.

Frenette, M. & Rank, K. (2016): Earnings of Postsecondary Graduates by Detailed Field of Study, *Economic Insights (Canada)* No 056 (March). Statistics Canada, Catalogue no.11–62E6-X

Gangopadhyay, K. & Sarkar, A. (2014): Private Investment in Education: Evidence across Castes and Religion from West Bengal, *Economic and Political Weekly* 49(13) (March 29): 44–52.

Ganpule, D. (2018): A Study of Household Expenditure on Higher Education in Mumbai. Unpublished PhD Thesis. Mumbai: S.N.D.T. University.

Gaurav, J.G. (2020): *Skill Gap Analysis of Civil Engineering Sector In India: Skills Needed to Succeed in Job Market*. California, CA: Notion Press.

Ghuman, R.S., Singh, S. & Brar, J.S. (2009): *Professional Education in Punjab: Exclusion of Rural Students*. Patiala: Punjabi University.

Gill, H.S. & Malhotra, P. (2019): An Exploratory Study of Factors Influencing the Choice of Management Institutes, *Journal of Gujarat Research Society* 21(4): 83–94.

Glocker, D. (2011): The Effect of Student Aid on the Duration of Study, *Economics of Education Review* 30(1): 177–90.

Goel, S. (2007): Women Engineering in India, *International Journal Inter Disciplinary Sciences* 1(6): 49–56

Gokuladas, V.K. (2010): Technical and Non-Technical Education and the Employability of Engineering Graduates: An Indian Case Study, *International Journal of Training and Development* 14(2): 130–43

Gokuladas, V.K. (2011): Predictors of Employability of Engineering Graduates in Campus Recruitment Drives of Indian Software Services Companies, *International Journal of Selection and Assessment* 19(3): 313–19.

Gong, X., Van Soest, A. & Zhang, P. (2005): The Effects of the Gender of Children on Expenditure Patterns in Rural China: A Semiparametric Analysis, *Journal of Applied Econometrics,* 20(4): 509–27.

Gosavi, V.P (2013): Threat of Vacant Seats in Engineering Colleges: Reasons and Remedies, *American International Journal of Research in Humanities, Arts and Social Science* 2(1) (March–May): 75–80.

Government of India (1945): *Report of the Committee Appointed to Consider the Development of Higher Technical Institutions in India* (Sarkar Committee Report). New Delhi: Department of Education, Health and Agriculture. https://www.iitsystem.ac.in/sites/default/files/reviewreports/N.R.Sarkar.pdf

Government of India (1949): *Report of the University Education Commission (December 1948–August 1949)* [Chairman: S. Radhakrishnan]. New Delhi.

Government of India (1986): *National Policy on Education.* New Delhi.

Government of India (1991): *Selected Educational Statistics.* New Delhi: Ministry of Human Resources Development.

Government of India (2004): *Report of the Committee to Review Working of the Indian Institutes of Technology* (Rao Committee Report). New Delhi: MHRD.

Government of India (2009a): *National Knowledge Commission: Report to the Nation 2007.* New Delhi.

Government of India (2009b): *Report of 'The Committee to Advise on Renovation and Rejuvenation of Higher Education'.* New Delhi: MHRD [Chairperson: Yashpal]. http://mhrd.gov.in/sites/upload_files/mhrd/files/document-reports/YPC-Report.pdf

Government of India (2011): *Statistics of Higher and Technical Education 2009–10.* New Delhi: MHRD.

Government of India (2019): *Draft National Education Policy 2019.* [Report of the Committee chaired by Dr K Kasturirangan]. New Delhi.

Government of India (2020): *National Education Policy 2020.* New Delhi: Ministry of Education.

Goyette, K. A. & Mullen, A.L. (2006): Who Studies the Arts and Sciences? Social Background and the Choice and Consequences of Undergraduate Field of Study, *Journal of Higher Education* 77(3): 497–538.

Gross, R.N. (2018): *Public vs. Private: The Early History of School Choice in America.* Oxford: Oxford University Press.

Gujarati, D.N. (1985, 2003): *Basic Econometrics.* New York: McGraw Hill [4th edition].

Gupta, N. (2010): Doctoral Research in an Indian Institute of Higher Learning in Science and Technology, *Science, Technology and Society* 15(1): 113–33.

Hashimoto, K. & Heath, J.A. (1995): Income Elasticities of Educational Expenditure by Income Class: The Case of Japanese Households, *Economics of Education Review* 14(1) (March): 53–71.

Himaz, R. (2009): Is there a Boy Bias in Household Education Expenditure? The Case of Andhra Pradesh in India Based on Young Lives Data. Working Paper No.46. Young Lives, Department of International Development, University of Oxford.

Himaz R. (2010): Intrahousehold Allocation of Education Expenditure: The Case of Sri Lanka, *Economic Development and Cultural Change,* 58(2): 231–258.

Hodgman, M.R. (2018): Understanding For-Profit Higher Education in the United States through History, Criticism, and Public Policy: A Brief Sector Landscape Synopsis, *Journal of Educational Issues* 4(2) (July): 1–14.

Hofstein, A., Ben-Zvi, R., Samuel, D. & Kempa, R.F. (1977): Some Correlates of the Choice of Educational Streams in Israeli High Schools, *Journal of Research in Science Teaching* 14(3) (May): 241–47.

Hopcroft, R.L. & Martin, D.O. (2016): Parental Investments and Educational Outcomes: Trivers–Willard in the U.S., *Frontiers in Sociology* 1(3) (31 March): 1–12.

Hossler, D. & Gallagher, K. (1987): Studying Student College Choice: A Three-phase Model and the Implications for the Policymakers, *College and University* 2(3) (Spring): 207–21.

Hoxby, C.M. (1998): How Much Does School Spending Depend on Family Income? The Historical Origins of the Current School Finance Dilemma, *American Economic Review* 88(2) (May): 309–14.

Hu, S. & Hossler, D. (2000): Willingness to Pay and Preference for Private Institutions, *Research in Higher Education* 41(6) (December): 685–701.

Huebler, F. & Lega, E. (2017): The World's Families: Hidden Funders of Education, *Global Partnership for Education* (5 June 2017). http://uis.unesco.org/en/blog/worlds-families-hidden-funders-education

Iddrisu, A.M., Danquah, M., Quartey, P. & Ohemeng, W. (2018): Gender Bias in Households' Educational Expenditure: Does the Stage of Schooling Matter, *World Development Perspectives* 10–12 (June–Dec.): 15–23.

Interesting Engineering (2016): Top 10 Countries That Produce The Most Engineers, *Interesting Engineering* (22 February). https://interestingengineering.com/top-10-countries-with-the-most-engineering-graduates

Jackson, G.A. (1982): Public Efficiency and Private Choice in Higher Education, *Educational Evaluation and Policy Analysis* 4(2): 237–47.

Jadhav, N. (2020): *Future of the Indian Education System: How Relevant is the National Education Policy 2020?* New Delhi: Konark Publishers.

James, E. (1987): The Political Economy of Private Education in Developed and Developing Countries. Education & Training Series Report No.EDT71. Washington DC: World Bank.

James, E. (1993): Why Do Different Countries Choose a Different Public-Private Mix of Educational Services? *Journal of Human Resources* 28(3) (Summer): 571–92.

James, E., Alsalam, N., Conaty, J. C. & To, D. L. (1989): College Quality and Future Earnings: Where should You send Your Child to College? *American Economic Review* 79(2): 247–52.

Jenkins, G.P., Anyabolu, H.A. & Bahramian, P. (2019): Family Decision-making for Educational Expenditure: New Evidence from Survey Data for Nigeria, *Applied Economics* 51(52): 5663–673.

Jha, C.S. (2005): Global Issues in Engineering Education, *University News* 43(39): 13–19

Johnes, G. (1994): Determinants of Student Loan Take-up in the United Kingdom, *Applied Economics* 26(10): 999–1005.

Jones, E.B. & Jackson, J.D. (1990): College Grades and Labor Market Rewards, *Journal of Human Resources* 25(2) (Spring): 253–66.

Jorgenson, D.W. & Griliches, Z. (1967): The Explanation of Productivity Change, *Review of Economic Studies* 34(3) (July): 249–83.

Kalra, S. (2019): High Student Intake, Lack of Quality Teachers Lead to Staff Shortage at IITs, *Indian Express* (December 18) https://indianexpress.com/article/education/high-student-intake-lack-of-quality-teachers-lead-to-staff-shortage-at-iits-6169827/

Kambhampati, U.S. (2008): Does Household Expenditure on Education in India Depend Upon the Returns to Education? Discussion Paper em-dp2008–60. Henley-on-Thames, Greenlands: School of Economics, Henley Business School, University of Reading.

Kanellopoulos, C.N. & Psacharopoulos, G. (1997): Private Education Expenditure in a 'Free Education' Country: the Case of Greece, *International Journal of Educational Development 17*: 73–81.

Kapur, D. & Mehta, P.B. (2004): Indian Higher Education Reform: From Half-baked Socialism to Half-baked Capitalism. Working Paper 103. Cambridge, MA: Center for International Development at Harvard University.

Karnataka Knowledge Commission (2012): *Report on Higher Education Vision 2020*. Bangalore: Government of Karnataka, Mission Group on Higher Education.

Kasturirangan, K. (2004): Technical Education and National Development. In: *Academics and Beyond: Tryst with Engineering & Technical Education* (Eds.: Pani, A. & Rehman, F.) (pp.70–76). New Delhi: Association of Indian Universities [reprint 2016].

Kaul, T. (2018): Intra-Household Allocation of Educational Expenses: Gender Discrimination and Investing in the Future, *World Development 104*(C) (April): 336–43.

Kenayathulla, H.B. (2016): Gender Differences in Intra-household Educational Expenditures in Malaysia, *International Journal of Educational Development 46*(C): 59–73.

Khare, M. & Arora, S. (2023): Jobless Growth in India: Employment–Unemployment of Educated Youth. In: *Higher Education, Employment, and Economic Development in India Problems, Prospects, and Policies* (Eds.: Mishra, R.K., Kujur, S.K., &. Trivikram, K.) (pp. 152–65). New Delhi: Routledge India.

Kingdon, G.G. (1996): Quality and Efficiency of Private and Public Education: A Case-Study of Urban India, *Oxford Bulletin of Economics & Statistics 58*(1) (February): 57–82.

Kingdon, G.G. (2005): Where has All the Bias Gone? Detecting Gender Bias in the Intra Household Allocation of Educational Expenditure, *Economic Development and Cultural Change 53*(2): 409–51.

Kingdon, G.G. (2017): Private Schooling Phenomenon in India: A Review. IZA Discussion Paper No.10612. Bonn: Institute of Labour Economics.

Kinser, K. & Levy, D.C. (2007): For-Profit Higher Education: U.S. Tendencies, International Echoes. In: *International Handbook of Higher Education* (Eds.: Forest, J.F. & Altbach, P.G.) (pp. 107–19). Netherlands: Springer.

Kirkeboen, L.J., Leuven, E. & Mogstad, M. (2016): Field of Study, Earnings, and Self Selection, *Quarterly Journal of Economics 131*(3) (August): 1057–111.

Kirp, D.L. (2003): *Shakespeare, Einstein, and the Bottom Line: The Marketing of Higher Education*. Cambridge, MA: Harvard University Press.

Kong, Jun. (2011): Factors Affecting Employment, Unemployment, and Graduate Study for University Graduates in Beijing. In: *Advances in Applied Economics, Business and Development*. (Ed.: Zhou, Q.). ISAEBD 2011. Communications in Computer and Information Science (Vol. 209, pp. 353–61). Berlin, Heidelberg: Springer. https://link.springer.com/chapter/10.1007/978-3-642-23020-2_52

Korfmann, F., Müller, S., Ehlert, S. & Haase, K. (2021): Students' Perceptions, Academic Departments' Image, and Major-Choice in Business Administration Studies—The Example of Hamburg Business School, *Higher Education Quarterly* 75(1) (January): 51–76.

Kothari, V.N. (1986): Private Unaided Engineering and Medical Colleges: Consequences of Misguided Policy, *Economic and Political Weekly* 21(14) (April 5): 593–96.

Kripal, Prem. (1990): The Educationist. In: *India's Maulana*. (Ed.: Hameed, S.S.). Abul Kalam Azad Centenary Volume 1. New Delhi: Indian Council of Cultural Relations and Vikas Publishing House

Krishna, A. (2014): Examining the Structure of Opportunity and Social Mobility in India: Who Becomes an Engineer? *Development and Change* 45(1) (January): 1–28.

Kulkarni, N.G. (2017): Improving Employability of Engineering Graduates: A Study of Colleges based in North Karnataka. Unpublished PhD Thesis. Dharwad: Karnatak University.

Kumar, A. (2017): Household Expenditure on Higher Education in India: Evidence from NSSO Data. Unpublished MPhil Dissertation. New Delhi: Jawaharlal Nehru University.

Kumar, D. & Choudhury, P.K. (2021): Determinants of Private School Choice in India: All about the Family Backgrounds? *Journal of School Choice* 15(4): 576–602.

Kuvat, Ö. & Ayvaz K.Ö. (2020): An Analysis of Out of Pocket Education Expenditures in Turkey: Logit and Tobit Models, *Ege Academic Review* 20(3): 231–44. Doi: 10.21121/eab.795986

Lakshmanasamy, T. (2017): Demand for Private Tuition – A Quantile Regression Analysis of Household Expenditure on Private Coaching in India, *Journal of Educational Planning and Administration* 31(2) (April): 115–39.

Lancaster, G., Maitra, P. & Ray, R. (2008): Household Expenditure Patterns and Gender Bias: Evidence from Selected Indian States, *Oxford Development Studies* 36(2): 133–57.

Layan, P.J.S. (2013): Dynamics of Household Expenditure on Education: A Comparative Study on Rural and Urban Areas of Kerala. Unpublished PhD Thesis. Kottayam, Kerala: Mahatma Gandhi University.

Levy, D.C. (2006): The Unanticipated Explosion: Private Higher Education's Global Surge, *Comparative Education Review* 50(2): 218–40.

Lewbel, A. & Houthakker, H.S. (2008): Engel Curve. In: *The New Palgrave Dictionary of Economics* (Eds.: Durlauf, S.N. & Blume, L.E.). London: Palgrave Macmillan. https://doi.org/10.1057/978-1-349-95121-5_525-2

Li, D., & Tsang, M. C. (2003). Household Decisions and Gender Inequality in Education in Rural China, *China: An International Journal* 1(02): 224–48.

Liao, T.F. (1994): *Interpreting Probability Models: Logit, Probit, and Other Generalized Linear Models*. 101, Quantitative Applications in the Social Sciences. Thousand Oaks, CA: Sage.

Lin, Xiaoshan. (2019): "Purchasing Hope": Consumption of Children's Education in Urban China, *Journal of Chinese Sociology* 6(8): 1–26.

Loyalka, P., Martin C., Froumin, I., Dossani, R., Tilak, J.B.G. & Yang, P. (2014): Factors Affecting the Quality of Engineering Education in the Four Largest Emerging Economies, *Higher Education* 68(6) (December): 977–1004.

Loyalka, P., Liu, O.L., Li, G., Chirikov, I., Kardanova, E., Gu, L., Ling, L., Yu, N., Guo, F., Ma, L., Hu, S., Johnson, A.S., Bhuradia, A., Khanna, S., Froumin, I., Shi,

J., Choudhury, P.K., Beteille, T., Marmolejo, F. & Tognatta, N. (2019): Computer Science Skills Across China, India, Russia, and the United States. *Proceedings of the National Academy of Sciences 116*(14): 6732–36.

Loyalka, P., Liu, L., Li, G., Kardanova, E., Chirikov, I., Hu, S., Yu, N., Ma, L., Guo, F., Beteille, T., Tognatta, N., Gu, L., Ling, G., Federiakin, D., Wang, H., Khanna, S., Bhuradia, A., Shi, Z. & Li, Y. (2021): Skill Levels and Gains in College STEM Education in China, India, Russia, and the United States. *Nature Human Behaviour 5*(7): 892–904.

Loyalka, P., Shi, Z., Li, G., Kardanova, E., Chirikov, I., Yu, N., Hu, S., Wang, H., Ma, L., Guo, F., Liu, O.Y., Bhuradia, A., Khanna, S., Li, Y. & Murray, A. (2022): The Effect of Faculty Research on Student Learning in College, *Educational Researcher 51*(4): 265–73.

Lunn, A. & Kornrich, S. (2018): Family Investments in Education during Periods of Economic Uncertainty: Evidence from the Great Recession, *Sociological Perspectives 61*(1): 145–63.

Luo, T. & Holden, R.J. (2014a): Investment in Higher Education by Race and Ethnicity, *Monthly Labor Review* (March). https://www.bls.gov/opub/mlr/2014/article/investment-in-higher-education-by-race-and-ethnicity.htm. https://doi.org/10.21916/mlr.2014.9

Luo, T. & Holden, R.J. (2014b): Do Different Groups Invest differently in Higher Education? *Beyond the Numbers: Special Studies & Research 3*(13) (U.S. Bureau of Labor Statistics). https://www.bls.gov/opub/btn/volume-3/do-different-groups-invest-differently-in-higher-education.htm

Machlup, F. (1962): *Production and Distribution of Knowledge in the United States.* Princeton, NJ: Princeton University Press.

Macmillan, L., Tyler, C. & Vignoles, A. (2015): Who gets the Top Jobs? The Role of Family Background and Networks in Recent Graduates' Access to High Status Professions, *Journal of Social Policy 44*(3): 487–515.

Macy, A., & Terry, N. (2007): Determinants of Student College Debt, *South Western Economic Review, 34:* 15–26.

Maddala, G.S. (1977): *Econometrics*. Tokyo: McGraw-Hill.

Madheswaran, S. & Shroff, S. (2000): Education, Employment and Earnings for Scientific and Technical Workforce in India: Gender Issues, *Indian Journal of Labour Economics 43*(1): 121–37.

Madheswari, S.P. & Mageswari, S.D.U. (2020): Changing Paradigms of Engineering Education - An Indian Perspective, *Procedia Computer Science 172*: 215–24.

Majumdar, T. (1983): *Investment in Education and Social Choice*. Cambridge: Cambridge University Press.

Mahmood, T., Ahmad, A.S. & Ahmad, A.S. (1992): Does Education of Head of the Household Affect Intra-Household Education Level and the Living Style? *Pakistan Economic and Social Review 30*(1) (Summer): 19–32.

Malish, C.M. & Ilavarasan, P.V. (2016): Higher Education, Reservation and Scheduled Castes: Exploring Institutional Habitus of Professional Engineering Colleges in Kerala, *Higher Education 72*(5): 603–17.

Mani, S. & Arun, M. (2012): Liberalisation of Technical Education in Kerala: Has Higher Enrollment Led to a Larger Supply of Engineers, *Economic and Political Weekly 47*(21) (26 May): 63–73.

Manski, C.F. & Wise, D.A. (1983): *College Choice in America*. Cambridge, MA: Harvard University Press.

Marginson, S. (2016): World-Wide Trend to High Participation Higher Education: Dynamics of Social Stratification in Inclusive Systems, *Higher Education* 72(4): 413–34.

Maringe, F. (2006): University and Course Choice: Implications for Positioning, Recruitment and Marketing, *International Journal of Educational Management* 20(6): 466–79.

Martin, M. & Godonoga, A. (2020): SDG 4- Policies for Flexible Learning Pathways in Higher Education: Taking Stock of Good Practices Internationally. IIEP-UNESCO Working Papers. Paris: International Institute for Educational Planning.

Masterson, T. (2012): An Empirical Analysis of Gender Bias in Education Spending in Paraguay, *World Development* 40(3): 583–93.

Mathew, A. (2016): Reforms in Higher Education in India: A Review of Recommendations of Commissions and Committees on Education. CPHRE Research Paper No.2. New Delhi: National University of Educational Planning and Administration.

Mathur, A. (1987): Why Growth Rates Differ within India: An Alternative Approach, *Journal of Development Studies* 23(2) (January): 167–99.

McMahon, W.W. (1974): *Investment in Higher Education*. MA: Lexington: DC Heath & Co.

McMahon, W.W. (1984): Why Families Invest in Education? In: *The Collection and Analysis of Economic and Consumer Behaviour Data* (Eds: Sudman, S. & Spaeth, M.) (pp. 75–89). Urbana-Champaign: University of Illinois.

McMahon, W.W. (2018): Total Return to Higher Education: Is There Underinvestment for Economic Growth and Development? *Quarterly Review of Economics and Finance* 70(C): 90–111.

Mehrotra, S. (Ed.) (2005): *Economics of Elementary Education: The Challenge of Public Finance, Private Provision and Household Costs*. New Delhi: Sage.

Mehrotra, S. (2020): Employability of Tertiary-Level Graduates in India. In: *Education, Democracy and Development: Equity and Inclusion* (Eds.: Varghese, N.V. & Bandyopadhyay, M.) (pp. 130–48). New Delhi: Shipra Publications.

Mercer Survey (2017): *Inside Employees' Minds Financial Wellness*. New York: Mercer/Marsh and McLennan Companies. https://www.mercer.com/content/dam/mercer/attachments/global/inside-employees-minds/gl-2017-inside-employees-minds-financial-wellness.pdf

Mincer, J.A. (1974): *Schooling, Experience and Earnings*. New York: National Bureau of Economic Research.

Minello, A. & Blossfeld, H-P. (2017): From Parents to Children: The Impact of Mothers' and Fathers' Educational Attainments on Those of Their Sons and Daughters in West Germany, *British Journal of Sociology of Education* 38(5): 686–704.

MHRD: Ministry of Human Resource Development (2003): *Revitalizing Technical Education. Report of the Review Committee on AICTE* [Chairman: U.R. Rao]. New Delhi: Government of India.

MHRD (2005): *Report of the CABE Committee on Financing of Higher and Technical Education*. New Delhi: Central Advisory Board of Education, Ministry of Human Resource Development, Government of India (June). [Chairperson: B. Mungekar] Member-Secretary/author: Jandhyala Tilak]. http://mhrd.gov.in/sites/upload_files/mhrd/files/document-reports/Report%20CABE%20Committee%20on%20Financing%20Higher%20and%20Technical%20EducationL.pdf

MHRD/MOE (2011a, 2017, 2018a, 2019, 2020, 2022): *All India Survey on Higher Education 2011-11, 2016–17, 2017–18, 2018–19 2019–20* [and] *2020–21* (and various earlier years). New Delhi: Ministry of Human Resource Development

(Education), Government of India. https://www.education.gov.in/en/statistics-new?shs_term_node_tid_depth=384

MHRD (2011b): *Report of the Working Group on Technical Education for the XII Five Year Plan*. New Delhi: Department of Higher Education, Government of India.

MHRD (2011c): *Taking IITs to Excellence and Greater Relevance. Report of Dr Anil Kakodkar Committee*. Mumbai: Indian Institute of Technology.

MHRD (2015): *Technical Education in India: A Futuristic Scenario. Report of the AICTE Review Committee 2015*. (Chairman: M.K. Kaw). New Delhi: Government of India.

MHRD (2018b): *Analysis of Budgeted Expenditure on Education* (Various Years). New Delhi: Government of India. https://www.education.gov.in/en/statistics-new?shs_term_node_tid_depth=387

Mishra, A. (2011): INDIA: Degrees Replace Dowries for Educated Classes, *University World News* (27 November). https://www.universityworldnews.com/post.php?story=20111125211736183

Mitra, A. & Sarkar, N. (2019): Factors Influencing Household Expenditure on Private Tutoring in Higher Education. In: *Future of Higher Education in India* (Ed. Bhushan, S.) (pp. 195–212). Singapore: Springer.

Monks, J. (2009): Impact of Merit-based Financial Aid on College Enrolment: A Field Experiment, *Economics of Education Review* 28(1): 99–106.

Moore, R.L., Studenmund, A.H. & Slobko, T. (1991): Effect of the Financial Aid Package on the Choice of a Selective College, *Economics of Education Review* 10(4): 311-21.

Motkuri, V. & Revathi, E. (2020): Private and Public Expenditure on Education in India: Trend over last Seven Decades, CESS-RSEPPG Research Brief 2. Hyderabad: Centre for Economic and Social Studies.

Muniswamy, S., Jaafar, N.I.M. & Nagarat, S. (2014): Does Reputation Matter? Case Study of Undergraduate Choice at a Premier University, *Asia-Pacific Education Researcher* 23(3): 451–62.

Murnane, R., Willett, J. & Levy, F. (1995): Growing Importance of Cognitive Skills in Wage Determination, *Review of Economics and Statistics* 77: 251–66.

Nahm, J. & Hong, W-H. (2009): Spending on Private Education: Semiparametric Estimation Approach, *Journal of the Korean Economy* 10(3) (December): 307–39.

Naik, J.P. (1971): *Education of Scheduled Castes*. ICSSR Monograph. New Delhi: Indian Council of Social Science Research.

Nair, N.G. (2004): Household Cost of School Education. Discussion Paper No.64. Thiruvananthapuram: Centre for Development Studies.

Nalla-Gounden, A.M. (1994): Financing Education (for All). Paper presented in the National Seminar on Financing Education for All. New Delhi: National Institute of Educational Planning and Administration. (Draft/mimeo)

Narayana, M.R. (2005): Student Loan by Commercial Banks: A Way to Reduce State Government Financial Support to Higher Education in India, *Journal of Developing Areas* 38(2): 171–87.

Narayana, M.R. (2019): Scholarship Schemes for Student Financing. In: *India Higher Education Report 2018: Financing of Higher Education* (Eds.: Varghese, N.V. & Panigrahi, J.) (pp. 213–66). New Delhi: Sage.

NASSCOM-McKinsey (2005): *Extending India's Leadership of the Global IT and BPO Industries: NASSCOM-McKinsey Report, 2005*. New Delhi: National Association of Software and Service Companies and McKinsey and Company.

National Science Board (NSF) (2018): *Science and Engineering Indicators 2018*. Alexandria VA.

NCERT (2018): *National Achievement Survey 2018 – Class X*. New Delhi: National Council of Educational Research and Training. https://ncert.nic.in/SRCX.php

Nguyen, A.N. & Taylor, J. (2003): Post-high School Choices: New Evidence from a Multinomial Logit Model, *Journal of Population Economics* 16(2): 287–306.

Nigam, N. (2020): Rise and Fall of the Indian Engineering Degree, *Indian Express* (15 January). https://indianexpress.com/article/education/how-the-indian-engineering-degree-lost-its-sheen-this-decade-6182675/

NSSO: National Sample Survey Organisation (1991): India - Survey on Participation in Education July-June 1986–87, NSS 42nd Round, *Sarvekshana* 14(3) Issue no.46 (January-March).

NSSO (1998): *Attending an Educational Institution in India: Its Level, Nature and Cost (NSS 52nd Round 1996–97)* [Report No.439]. New Delhi: National Statistical Organisation, Ministry of Statistics and Programme Implementation, Government of India.

NSSO (2008): *Education in India: Participation and Expenditure. The 64th Round: July 2007-June 2008)*. New Delhi: Government of India.

NSSO (2014): *Education in India: Social Consumption: Education and Health: The 71st Round: (January–July 2014)*. New Delhi: Government of India.

NSSO (2016): *Education in India* (NSS 71st Round January–June 2014). New Delhi: Government of India.

NSSO (2018): *Household Social Consumption on Education in India: the 75th Round* (June 2017–July 2018). New Delhi: Government of India.

OECD: Organisation for Economic Co-operation and Development (2006): *Evolution of Student Interest in Science and Technology Studies—Policy Report*. Paris: Global Science Forum. http://www.oecd.org/science/inno/36645825.pdf

OCED (2016): *OECD Science, Technology and Innovation Outlook 2016*. Paris.

OECD (2020a): *Education at a Glance: OECD Indicators*. Paris.

OCED (2020b): How has Public and Private Expenditure on Tertiary Education Evolved in Recent Years? *OECD Education and Skills Today* (24 January). https://oecdedutoday.com/expenditure-on-education-evolved/

Omori, M. (2010): Household Expenditures on Children, 2007–08, *Monthly Labor Review 133*(9) (September): 3–16.

Panchamukhi, P.R. (1987): Graduates and Job Markets: A Quantitative Study of Two Universities in India. IIEP Occasional Paper No.74. Paris: UNESCO-International Institute for Educational Planning.

Panchamukhi, P.R. (1990): Private Expenditure on Education in India: An Empirical Study. Pune: Indian Institute of Education. Unpublished Report. New Delhi: Planning Commission.

Panda, G. (2006): *Women in Higher Education: A Study of Engineering Colleges in Orissa*. New Delhi: Jawaharlal Nehru University (unpublished MPhil Dissertation).

Pandey, M. & Pandey, P. (2014): Better English for Better Employment Opportunities, *International Journal of Multidisciplinary Approach* 1(4) (August): 93–100.

Parikh, P.P. & Sukhatme, S.P. (2004): Women Engineers in India, *Economic and Political Weekly* 39(2): 193–201.

Park, C.K. (2015): Student Factors on Employment of Engineering Graduates: A Korean University Case, *Asian Journal of Innovation and Policy* 4(3): 288–306.

Patel, P.J. (2016): Research Culture in Indian Universities, *Social Change* 46(2): 238–59.
Perali, F. & Barzi, F. (2011): Equity and Access to Tertiary Education: Demand for Student Loans in Italy, *SSRN Electronic Journal* (July). https://papers.ssrn.com/sol3/papers.cfm?abstract_id=1713989 [and] https://papers.ssrn.com/sol3/papers.cfm?abstract_id=1713989
Prabhu, B.V. & Kudva, A.S. (2016): Success of Student Internship in Engineering Industry: A Faculty Perspective, *Higher Education for the Future* 3(2): 1–19.
Psacharopoulos, G. & Mattson, R. (2000): Family Size, Education Expenditure and Attainment in a Poor Country, *Journal of Educational Planning and Administration* 12(3) (July): 169–86.
Psacharopoulos, G. & Papakonstantinou, G. (2005): The Real University Cost in a 'Free' Higher Education Country, *Economics of Education Review* 24(1):103–08.
Psacharopoulos, G. & Tilak, J.B.G. (1992): Education and Wage Earnings. In: *Encyclopaedia of Educational Research* (Editor-in-Chief: M.C. Alkin) (pp. 419–23). New York: Macmillan/American Educational Research Association.
Psacharopoulos, G. & Woodhall, M. (1985): *Education for Development: An Analysis of Investment Choices*. New York: Oxford University Press/World Bank.
QEPEF (2016): *Recognising and Understanding Engineering*. London: Queen Elizabeth Prize for Engineering Foundation. https://qeprize.org/news/recognising-engineering
Qian, J.X. & Smyth, R. (2011): Educational Expenditure in Urban China: Income Effects, Family Characteristics and the Demand for Domestic and Overseas Education, *Applied Economics* 43(24): 3379–94.
Quang, V. (2012): Determinants of Educational Expenditure in Vietnam, *International Journal of Applied Economics* 9(1): 59–72.
Ramsey, A. (2008): *Graduate Earnings: An Econometric Analysis of Returns, Inequality and Deprivation Across the UK: Main Report*. London: Department of Employment and Learning, Government of UK. https://dera.ioe.ac.uk/9751/1/graduate_earnings__main_report.pdf
Rani, P.G. (2010): Changing Landscape of Higher Education in India: The Case of Engineering Education in Tamil Nadu. Occasional Paper No.36. New Delhi: National University of Educational Planning and Administration.
Rani, P.G. (2014): Education Loans and Financing Higher Education in India: Addressing Equity, *Higher Education for the Future* 1(2): 183–210.
Rao, R. (2019): Engineering Education Needs Serious Rethinking, *Business Line* (17 February). https://www.thehindubusinessline.com/opinion/columns/rajkamal-rao/engineering-education-needs-serious-rethinking/article26297580.ece
Rao, S.S. (2006): Engineering and Technology Education in India: Uneven Spread, Quality and Social Coverage, *Journal of Educational Planning and Administration* 20(2) (April): 205–25.
Rao, S.S. (2007): Neglected Terrain in the Quest for Equality: Women in Elite Engineering and Technology Education. In: *Women's Education and Development* (Ed.: Tilak, J.B.G.) (pp. 187–212). New Delhi: Gyan Publishing.
Rao, V.K.R.V. (1961): *University Education and Employment: A Case Study of Delhi Graduates*. Delhi: Institute of Economic Growth and Bombay: Asia Publishing House.
Raposo, M. & Alves, H. (2007): A Model of University Choice: An Exploratory Approach. MPRA Paper No.5523. Munich Personal RePEc Archive. http://mpra.ub.uni-muenchen.de/5523/

RBI: Reserve Bank of India (2014): *Handbook of Statistics on Indian Economy 2013–14.* Mumbai.
RBI (2020a): *Reserve Bank of India Bulletin 2020.* Mumbai.
RBI. (2020b): *Handbook of Statistics on Indian Economy 2019–20.* Mumbai.
Reddy, B.S. & Reddy, K.A. (2019): Public Financing of Private Education: A Case Study of Fee Reimbursement Scheme (FRS) in Andhra Pradesh. In: *India Higher Education Report 2018: Financing of Higher Education* (Eds.: Varghese, N.V. & Panigrahi, J.) (pp. 308–35). New Delhi: Sage.
Rimfeld, K., Ayorech, Z., Dale, P.S., Kovas, Y. & Plomin, R. (2016): Genetics affects Choice of Academic Subjects as well as Achievement, *Scientific Reports*, 6, [26373]. DOI: 10.1038/srep26373 http://research.gold.ac.uk/20652/1/Rimfeld%20 2016%20Sc%20Reports%20Choice.pdf
Rizk, R. & Owusu-Afriyie, J. (2014): Determinants of Household Expenditure on Children's Education in Egypt, *International Journal of Education Economics and Development* 5(4): 332–49.
Rochat, D. & Demeulemeester, Jean-Luc. (2001): Rational Choice Under Unequal Constraints: The Example of Belgian Higher Education, *Economics of Education Review* 20(1): 15–26.
Rukmini, S. (2015): Names of Over 50,000 Teachers Figure on Rolls of More Than One Institution, *The Hindu* (11 May 2015). https://www.thehindu.com/news/national/faculty-names-fraud-across-engineering-colleges-in-india/article719 0827.ece
Russo, C.J. & Ranieri, N. (2017): School Choice: An Overview of Selected International Perspectives. In: *Wiley Handbook of School Choice* (Eds: Fox, R.A. & Buchanan, N.K.) (pp. 46–55). New Jersey, NJ: John Wiley & Sons.
Sá, C., Tavares, D.A., Justino, E. & Amaral, A. (2011): Higher Education (related) Choices in Portugal: Joint Decision on Institution Type and Leaving Home, *Studies in Higher Education* 3(6) (September): 689–703.
Saha, A. (2013): An Assessment of Gender Discrimination in Household Expenditure on Education in India, *Oxford Development Studies* 41(2): 220–38.
Sahin, M. (2010): Impact of Problem-Based Learning on Engineering Students' Beliefs about Physics and Conceptual Understanding of Energy and Momentum, *European Journal of Engineering Education* 35(5): 519–37.
Salim, A.A. (1994): Cost of Higher Education in Kerala: A Case Study, *Journal of Educational Planning and Administration* 8(4): 417–30.
Salim, A.A. (2008): Opportunities for Higher Education: An Enquiry into Entry Barriers. In: *Higher Education in Kerala: Micro Level Perspective* (Eds.: Nair, K.N. & Nair, P.R.G.) (pp. 49–88). Delhi: Danish Books.
Sandy, J. (1989): Choice of Public or Private School. *Social Science Journal* 26(4): 415–31.
Sanyal, B.C. (1987a): *Higher Education and Employment: An International Comparative Analysis.* Philadelphia, PA: Falmer.
Sanyal, B.C. (1987b): Graduate Unemployment and Education. In: *Economics of Education: Research and Studies* (Ed.: Psacharopoulos, G.) (pp. 172–79). Oxford: Pergamon.
Sarkar, N. (2017a): Linkage between Household and Government Expenditure on Higher Education: Examining the Indian Case, *Journal Community Positive Practices* 17(3): 14–24.

Sarkar, N. (2017b): Determinants of Household Expenditure on Higher Education in India, *International Education and Research Journal* 3(6): 12–14.

Sarkar, S. (2019): Employability of Engineering Graduates in India: A Challenge Needs to Address, *BWEducation* (1 June). http://bweducation.businessworld.in/article/Employability-Of-Engineering-Graduates-In-India-A-Challenge-Needs-To-Address/01-06-2019-171291/

Schofer, E. & Meyer, J.W. (2005): World-wide Expansion of Higher Education in the Twentieth Century, *American Sociological Review* 70 (December): 898–920.

Schultz, T.W. (1981): *Investing in People*. Berkeley, CA: University of California Press.

Schultz, T.W. (1988): On Investing in Specialized Human Capital to Attain Increasing Returns. In: *State of Development Economics: Progress and Perspectives* (Eds.: Ranis, G. & Schultz, T.P.) (pp. 339–52). Oxford: Basil Blackwell.

Schwartz, J.B. (1985): Student Financial Aid and the College Enrollment Decision: The Effects of Public and Private Grants and Interest Subsidies, *Economics of Education Review* 4(2) (April): 129–44.

Sengupta, A (2017): Mismatch between Skills and Jobs in Indian Labour Market during the Post-Reform Era: Estimates with Unit Level Data. IARIW-ICIER Conference on Experiences and Challenges in Measuring Income, Inequality and Poverty in South Asia. New Delhi (November 23–25). http://www.iariw.org/India/sengupta.pdf

Sengupta, A. (2020): Rapid Growth of Private Universities: Transformation of the University Space. *Economic and Political Weekly* 55(22) (May 30): 45–52.

Sengupta, A., Kannan, K.P. & Raveendran, G. (2008): India's Common People: Who are They, How Many are They and How do They Live? *Economic and Political Weekly* 43(11) (March 15): 49–63.

Sengupta, D. (2011): College Admissions: Story of the Tightly-Knit Group of Middlemen Who 'Fix' Admissions, *Economic Times* (25 December). https://economictimes.indiatimes.com/industry/services/education/college-admissions-story-of-the-tightly-knit-group-of-middlemen-who-fix-admissions/articleshow/11234507.cms?from=mdr

Senthilkumar, N. & Arulraj, A. (2011): SQM-HEI – Determination of Service Quality Measurement of Higher Education in India, *Journal of Modelling in Management* 6(1): 60–78.

Shafiq, M. N. (2011): What Criteria Should Policy-Makers Use for Assisting Households with Educational Expenditure? The Case of Urban Bangladesh, *South Asia Economic Journal* 12(1) (March 3): 25–37.

Sharan, R. (2004): Engineering Education in India: A Critical Look, *IASSI Quarterly* 23(1): 63–79.

Sharma, K. (2018): IITs, IIMs, NITs have Just 3% of Total Students But Get 50% of Government Funds, *The Print* (30 July). https://theprint.in/india/governance/iits-iims-nits-have-just-3-of-total-students-but-get-50-of-government-funds/89976/

Sheppard, S.D., Macatangay, K., Colby, A. & Sullivan, W.M. (2009): *Educating Engineers: Designing for the Future of the Field*. Stanford, CA: Jossey-Bass.

Simões, C. & Soares, A.M. (2010): Applying to Higher Education: Information Sources and Choice Factors, *Studies in Higher Education* 35(4): 371–89.

Sindhwani, P. (2019): Indians are Spending Enormously on Education Even with Few Jobs in Sight, *Business Insider* (November 29). https://www.businessinsider.in/education/news/average-education-expenditure-in-india-increases-fourfold-to-8331-per-student/articleshow/72282009.cms

Singh, A. (2016): Integrated Marketing Communication (IMC) Tools and Demand for Private Engineering Institutions in Delhi NCR. Unpublished PhD Thesis. Delhi: Delhi Technological University.

Singh, A. & Singh, S. (2014): Private Engineering Education in India: Past, Present and Future, *International Journal of Management and Social Sciences Research* 3(11) (November): 39–46.

Singh, A. & Singh, S. (2015): Marketing Practices Adopted by Private Players: A Study of Private Engineering Institutions in Delhi NCR. In: *Frontiers of Infrastructure Finance* (Ed.: Pradhan, R.P.) (pp. 53–66). New Delhi: Bloomsbury.

Singh, G. (1993): Fees and Economic Background of Students: A Study of University of Delhi, *Journal of Educational Planning and Administration* 7(4) (October): 427–51.

Singh, R. (2016): A Regression Study of Salary Determinants in Indian Job Markets for Entry Level Engineering Graduates. Masters Dissertation. Dublin: Technological University https://arrow.tudublin.ie/scschcomdis/90/

Sivasankaran, J. & Babu, S. (2008): Wastage in Engineering Education in Kerala. In: *Higher Education in Kerala: Macro Level Perspectives* (Eds.: Nair, K.N. & Nair, P.R.G.) (pp.89–110). New Delhi: Danish Books.

Solow, R.M. (1960): Investment in Technical Progress. In: *Mathematical Models in the Social Sciences* (Eds.: Arrow, K.J., Karlin, S. & Suppes, P.) (pp.89–104). Stanford: Stanford University Press.

Spence, M.J. (1973): Job-Market Signalling, *Quarterly Journal of Economics* 87(3) (August): 355–74.

Statista Research Department (2020): *Reports*. https://www.statista.com/statistics/1043283/india-hiring-rate-engineers/

Steelman, L.C. & Powell, B. (1991): Sponsoring the Next Generation: Parental Willingness to Pay for Higher Education, *American Journal of Sociology* 96(6) (May): 1505–29.

Subbarao, E.C. (2013): India's Higher Engineering Education: Opportunities and Tough Choices, *Current Science* 104(1) (10 January): 55–66.

Subramanian, A. (2019): *Caste of Merit: Engineering Education in India*. Cambridge, MA: Harvard University Press.

Subramanian, B. (2015): Engineering Education in India: A Comprehensive Overview. In: *International Perspectives on Engineering Education: Philosophy of Engineering and Technology* (Eds.: Christensen, S., Didier, C., Jamison, A., Meganck, M., Mitcham, C. & Newberry, B.) (Vol.20, pp. 105–23). Cham: Springer.

Subramanian, S. & Deaton, A. (1991): Gender Effects in Indian Consumption Patterns, *Sarvekshana* 14(4) (April–June): 1–12.

Swaminathan, P. (2014): *Wasted in Engineering: Story of India's Youth*. Chennai: Notion Press.

Tan, J.P. (1985): Private Direct Cost of Secondary Schooling in Tanzania, *International Journal of Educational Development* 5(1) (January): 1–10.

Tansel, A. & Bircan, F. (2006): Demand for Education in Turkey: A Tobit Analysis of Private Tutoring Expenditure, *Economics of Education Review* 25(3): 303–13.

TEQIP (2002): Technical Education Quality Improvement Programme of Government of India. Document No.3. Working Document for Institutions and States. Noida: National Project Implementation Unit, EdCIL House. https://www.teqip.in/docs/t1/TEQIP-WD.pdf

Thurow, L.G. (1975): *Generating Inequality*. New York: Basic Books.

Tilak, J.B.G. (1980): An Economic Analysis of Structure of Personal Earnings: A Case Study, *Margin* 12(4) (July): 74–86.

Tilak, J.B.G. (1985): Educational Finances in India. Occasional Paper No.12. New Delhi: National Institute of Educational Planning and Administration.

Tilak, J.B.G. (1987): *Economics of Inequality in Education*. New Delhi: Sage.

Tilak, J.B.G. (1991): Family and Government Investments in Education, *International Journal of Educational Development* 11(2): 91–106.

Tilak, J.B.G. (1992a): Student Loans in Financing Higher Education in India, *Higher Education* 23(4): 389–404.

Tilak, J.B.G. (1992b): Public and Private Sectors in Education in India. In: *Emergent Issues in Education: Comparative Perspectives* (Eds.: Arnove, R.F., Altbach, P.G. & Kelly, G.P.) (pp. 173–85; 331–34). Albany, NY: State University of New York Press.

Tilak, J.B.G. (1993): Financing Higher Education in India: Principles, Practice and Policy Issues, *Higher Education* 26(1) (July): 43–67.

Tilak, J.B.G. (1994): South Asian Perspectives (on Alternative Policies for the Finance, Control, and Delivery of Basic Education), *International Journal of Educational Research* 21(8): 791–98.

Tilak, J.B.G. (1995): Has Manpower Planning any Future in Educational Planning in a 'Marketised' Economy? In: *Impact of New Economic Policy on Manpower and Employment in India* (Eds.: Raghavan, K., Sharma, H. & Sekhar, L.) (pp. 252–70). New Delhi: Agricole/Institute of Applied Manpower Research.

Tilak, J.B.G. (1996): How Free Is 'Free' Primary Education in India? *Economic and Political Weekly* 31(5–6) (3 & 10 February): 275–82; 355–66.

Tilak, J.B.G. (1997): Lessons from Cost Recovery in Education. In: *Marektising Education and Health in Developing Countries: Miracle or Mirage?* (Ed.: Colclough, C.) (pp. 63–89). Oxford: Clarendon.

Tilak, J.B.G. (1999): Financing Technical Higher Education in India. In: *Institutional Building: An International Perspective on Management Education* (Eds.: Misra, S. & Chand, P.G.V.S.) (pp. 101–31). New Delhi: McMillan.

Tilak, J.B.G. (2000): *Household Expenditure on Education in India: A Preliminary Examination of the 52nd Round of the National Sample Survey*. New Delhi: National Institute of Educational Planning and Administration (July) monograph.

Tilak, J.B.G. (2002a): Determinants of Household Expenditure on Education in Rural India. Working Paper No.88. New Delhi: National Council of Applied Economic Research.

Tilak, J.B.G. (2002b): Elasticity of Household Expenditure on Education in Rural India, *South Asia Economic Journal* 3(2) (September): 217–26.

Tilak, J.B.G. (2002c): Determinants of Household Expenditure on Education in India, *International Journal of Development Planning Literature* 17(3&4) (July–October): 165–82.

Tilak, J.B.G. (2003a): Higher Education and Development. In: *Handbook on Educational Research in the Asia Pacific Region* (Eds.: Kleeves, J.P. & Watanabe, R.) (pp. 809–26). Dordrecht: Kluwer Academic.

Tilak, J.B.G. (2003b): State, Households and Markets in Education: Government's Unwillingness and Households' Compulsion to Pay for Education vis-à-vis the Exploitative Markets, *Review of Development and Change* 8(2) (July–December): 115–44.

Tilak, J.B.G. (2004): Public Subsidies in the Education Sector in India, *Economic and Political Weekly* 39(4): 343–59.

Tilak, J.B.G. (2005): Financing Higher Education in India under Structural Adjustment. In: *Financing Higher Education in a Global Market* (Eds.: Michael, S.O. & Kretovics, M.A.) (pp. 257–99). New York: Algora Publishing.

Tilak, J.B.G. (2009a): Private Sector in Higher Education: A Few Stylized Facts, *Social Change* 39(1) (March): 1–28.

Tilak, J.B.G. (2009b): Student Loans and Financing of Higher Education in India. In: *Students Loan Schemes: Experiences of New Zealand, Australia, India and Thailand and Way Forward for Malaysia* (Eds.: Yunus, A.S.M., Bakar, R. & Rahman, S.A.) (pp. 64–94). Pulau Pinang, Malaysia: IPPTN and Penerbit Universiti Sains Malaysia Press.

Tilak, J.B.G. (2010a): A Weak Attempt to Curb Unfair Practices in Higher Education, *Economic and Political Weekly* 45(38) (18 September): 19–21.

Tilak, J.B.G. (2010b): Policy Crisis in Higher Education: Reform or Deform? *Social Scientist* 38(9–12) (September–December): 61–90.

Tilak, J.B.G. (2012): Higher Education Policy in India in Transition, *Economic and Political Weekly* 47(13) (31 March): 36–40.

Tilak, J.B.G. (2014): Private Higher Education in India, *Economic and Political Weekly* 49(40) (4 October): 32–38.

Tilak, J.B.G. (2015): How Inclusive Is Higher Education in India? *Social Change* 45(2) (June): 185–223.

Tilak, J.B.G. (2016a): Global Rankings, World-Class Universities and Dilemmas in Higher Education Policy in India, *Higher Education for the Future* 3(2) (July): 1–18.

Tilak, J.B.G. (2016b): A Decade of Ups and Downs in Public Expenditure on Higher Education. In: *India: Higher Education Report* (Eds.: Varghese, N.V. & Malik, G.) (pp. 307–32). London: Routledge.

Tilak, J.B.G. (2023): Education, Skills and Employment in India: Some Stylized and Not-So-Stylized Facts, *Artha Beekshan: Journal of the Bengal Economic Association* 32(1–2): 98–134.

Tilak, J.B.G. & Choudhury, P.K. (2019): Inequality in Access to Higher Education in India between the Poor and the Rich. In: *India: Social Development Report 2018: Rising Inequalities in India* (Eds.: Haque, T. & Reddy, D.N.) (pp. 187–202). New Delhi: Oxford University Press.

Tilak, J.B.G. & Nalla-Gounden, A.M. (2005): Private Costs and Public Financing of Elementary Education in a High-Achiever State: Tamil Nadu. In: *Economics of Elementary Education: The Challenge of Public Finance, Private Provision and Household Costs* (Ed.: Mehrotra, S.) (pp. 285–323). New Delhi: Sage.

Tilak, J.B.G. & Sudarshan, R. (2001): Private Schooling in Rural India. Working Paper No.76. New Delhi: National Council of Applied Economic Research.

TOI (2019): Education Loans in India Shrink 25% in 4 yrs, *Times of India*. https://timesofindia.indiatimes.com/business/india-business/edu-loans-in-india-shrink-25-in-4-yrs/articleshow/69490291.cms

Trivers, R.L. (1972): Parental Investment and Sexual Selection. In: *Sexual Selection and the Descent of Man, 1871–1971* (Ed.: Campbell, B.) (pp. 136–79). Aldine: Chicago University Press.

Trivers, R.L. & Willard, D.E. (1973): Natural Selection of Parental Ability to vary the Sex Ratio of Offspring, *Science* 179(4068) (5 January): 90–92. Doi:10.1126/science.179.4068.90

Trow, M. (2007): Reflections on the Transition from Elite to Mass to Universal Access: Forms and Phases of Higher Education in Modern Societies since WWII. In: *International Handbook of Higher Education* (Eds.: Forest, J.J.F. & Altbach, P.G.) (pp. 243–80). Dordrecht, Netherlands: Springer.

Tymon, A. (2011): The Student Perspective of Employability, *Studies in Higher Education* 38(6): 1–16.

UGC: University Grants Commission (1973): *Examination Reform: A Plan of Action*. New Delhi: University Grants Commission.

UGC (various years): *Annual Report (Various Years; 1975–76, 1985–86, 1990–91, 2014–15, 2017–18)*. New Delhi: University Grants Commission.

UIS: United Institute of Statistics (2020): *Education Statistics*. Vancouver. www.UIS.Uneco.org

UIS (2022): *UNESCO World on Higher Education Conference 2022*. http://uis.unesco.org/sites/default/files/documents/f_unesco1015_brochure_web_en.pdf.

UNESCO (2010): *Engineering: Issues, Challenges and Opportunities for Development*. Paris: United Nations Educational, Scientific and Cultural Organization.

Upadhyay, C. (2014): Engineering Mobility? The 'IT Craze', Transnational Migration, and the Commercialisation of Education in Coastal Andhra. ProGlo Working Paper No.7. Bangalore: National Institute of Advanced Studies & Amsterdam Institute for Social Science Research.

Uplaonkar, A.T. (1983): Occupational Aspirations of College Students, *Social Change* 13(2) (June): 16–26.

Urwick, J. (2002): Determinants of the Private Costs of Primary and Early Childhood Education: Findings from Plateau State, Nigeria, *International Journal of Educational Development* 22(2) (March): 131–44.

Varghese, N.V. (2015): Challenges of Massification of Higher Education in India. CPRHE Research Paper 1, Centre for Policy Research in Higher Education. New Delhi: National University of Educational Planning and Administration.

Varghese, N.V., Panigrahi, J. & Rohtagi, A. (2018): Concentration of Higher Education Institutions in India: A Regional Analysis. CPRHE Research Paper 11. New Delhi: National Institute of Educational Planning and Administration.

Varma, R. & Kapur, D. (2010): Access, Satisfaction, and Future: Undergraduate Education at the Indian Institutes of Technology, *Higher Education* 59(6): 703–17.

VIF: Vivekananda International Foundation (2019): *Towards More Effective Education: Emergence of STEM Education in India*. VIF Taskforce Report [Chairperson: Aggarwal, K.K.]. New Delhi.

Vijay, A. (2013): Appraisal of Student Rating as A Measure to Manage the Quality of Higher Education in India: An Institutional Study Using Six Sigma Model Approach, *International Journal for Quality Research* 7(3): 3–14.

Voigt, K. (2007): Individual Choices and Unequal Participation in Higher Education, *Theory and Research in Education* 5(1) (March): 87–112.

WENR (2007): *Engineering Education in India: A Story of Contrasts*, *World Education News and Reviews*, New York: World Education Services.

Weisbrod, B.A. (1977): *Voluntary NonProfit Sector*. Lexington, MA: Lexington Books.

Weisbrod, B.A. & Karpoff, P. (1968): Monetary Returns to College Education, Students Ability, and College Quality, *Review of Economics and Statistics* 50: 491–97.

Wheebox (2020 and 2022): *India Skills Report 2020: Reimaging India's Talent and Landscape for a $5T Economy* [and] *India Skills Report 2022*. Gurugram, Haryana, India. https://wheebox.com/assets/pdf/

Willis, R.J. (2016): Wage Determinants: A Survey and Reinterpretation of Human Capital Earnings Functions. In: *Handbook of Labour Economics* (Eds.: Ashenfelter, O.C. & R. Layard, R.) (Vol. 1, pp. 525–602). North-Holland: Elsevier, Science Direct.

Williams, R.A. (1983): Interaction Between Government and Private Outlays. Discussion Paper No. 79. Canberra: Australian National University, Centre for Economic Policy and Research.

Winberg, C., Bramhall, M., Greenfield, D., Johnson, P., Rowlett, P., Lewis, O., Waldock, J. & Wolff, K. (2020): Developing Employability in Engineering Education: A Systematic Review of the Literature, *European Journal of Engineering Education* 45(2): 165–80.

Wiswall, M. & Zafar, B. (2015): Determinants of College Major Choice: Identification using an Information Experiment, *Review of Economic Studies* 82(2): 791–824.

Wolf, F. & Zohlnhöfer, R. (2009): Investing in Human Capital? The Determinants of Private Education Expenditure in 26 OECD Countries, *Journal of European Social Policy* 19(3) (July): 230–44.

Wongmonta, S. & Glewwe, P. (2016): An Analysis of Gender Differences in Household Education Expenditure: The Case of Thailand, *Education Economics* 25(2): 183–204.

Working, H. (1943): Statistical Laws of Family Expenditure, *Journal of the American Statistical Association* 33(221): 43–56.

World Bank (1986): *Financing Education in Developing Countries: An Exploration of Policy Options*. Washington DC.

World Bank (2013): *International Comparative Study: Engineering Education in India*. Report No.57. South Asia Human Development Sector. Washington DC.

World Economic Forum (2020): *Global Competitiveness Report 2017–18: Insight Report*. Geneva: World Economic Forum. http://www3.weforum.org/docs/GCR2017-2018/05FullReport/TheGlobalCompetitivenessReport2017%E2%80%932018.pdf

Yadav, V.G. & Yadav, G.D. (2010): Fuelling the Indian Economic Engine by Retooling Indian Technical Education, *Current Science* 98(11) (10 June): 1442–57.

Yueh, L. (2006): Parental Investment in Children's Human Capital in Urban China, *Applied Economics* 38(18): 2089–111.

Zhang, Y. & Zhou, X. (2017): Can Higher Household Education Expenditure Improve the National College Entrance Exam Performance? Empirical Evidence from Jinan, China, *Current Issues in Comparative Education* 19(2) (Spring): 8–32.

Ziderman, A. (2020): Experience with Student Loans, Higher Education. In: *Encyclopaedia of International Higher Education Systems and Institutions* (Eds.: Teixeira, P. & Shin, J.) (pp. 413–20). Dordrecht: Springer.

Zimmermann, L. (2012): Reconsidering Gender Bias in Intrahousehold Allocation in India, *Journal of Development Studies* 48(1): 151–63.

Index

ability to pay 173, 177
academic (educational); background 5, 124, 127, 135, 153, 159, 163, 165, 170, 192, 194, 208, 210, 260, 281, performance 261, 270, 133, 152, 192, 261; record 133, 147; success 169
accountability 63, 79, 134
admission 69, 105, 117, 121, 135, 143, 153, 164, 281; procedures 70, 143, 287
affordability 17, 79, 106, 179, 200, 279
agriculture 30, 57
AICTE (All India Council for Technical Education) 4, 20, 37, 59, 65, 76, 96, 112, 149, 175
Altbach, P.G. 17
Anandkrishnan, M. 18, 217
Andhra Pradesh 8, 28, 44, 70, 88, 110
Arrow, K.J. 260
artificial intelligence 16, 25, 100, 271
assessment 19, 109, 221, 223, 235, 239, 285, 290
asymmetry of information 120, 143, 148, 171, 240, 283, 287
Atkinson, H. 260
Australia 178, 266

baby-sitting 74
Banerjee, R. 18, 55, 78, 217
Bangladesh 181, 183
Becker, G.S. 176, 191, 192
Behrman, J.R. 191
Biswas, G. 18, 25, 217
Blau, P.M. 192
Blaug, M. 260
Blom, A. 25, 100
Board(s) (of education or examinations) 124, 135, 136, 145, 165, 210, 288

branch(es) of engineering 5, 9, 26, 56, 137, 147, 157, 162, 171, 181, 218, 264, 279, 280, 281, 288
BRIC 5, 9, 276
brute luck 153–54
budget expenditure 7, 20, 21, 80

campus recruitment 9, 64, 140, 162, 252, 256, 270, 288
campus work 161, 202, 203
Carnoy, M. 5, 9, 24, 28, 67, 177, 241, 249, 285
caste 6, 20, 50, 93, 108, 127, 143, 156, 189, 208, 280, 270, 275, 284–86
centrally funded 70, 82
Chakrabarti, A. 118, 154
China 16, 76, 172, 180, 260, 276, 288
Choudhury, P.K. 15, 67, 118, 134, 185, 260
civil engineering 23, 54, 57, 103, 137, 148, 163, 254
classrooms 9, 110, 134, 159, 227, 258, 290
Clotfelter, C.T. 118
cloud computing 101, 271
coaching 89, 121, 142, 151, 159, 241, 280
cognitive factors 148
Cohn, E. 118
collaboration 78, 100, 221, 271
commercialisation 3, 8, 89, 112, 217
communication skills 100, 156, 185, 194, 220, 228, 263
communications engineering 94, 258
companies 98, 105, 143, 252, 257, 281; domestic 257, 259, 269; foreign 257, 259; venture 257, 269
computer sciences 6, 9, 225
computer sciences engineering 9, 58, 121, 137, 147, 167, 227, 265, 280

Constitution of India 62
constitutionally 262
consumer sovereignty 287
consumption expenditure 22, 53, 90, 94, 174, 185, 278
corrupt(ion) 70, 78, 278
cost of education 132, 138, 143, 160, 210, 281
cost recovery 4, 79, 111, 176, 200, 214, 291
course structure 226, 227, 228
creamy layer 62
credit market 177, 208
curricular reforms 107, 110, 290
curriculum 11, 63, 93, 102, 135, 165, 218, 226, 260

Deaton, A. 180
debt 201, 264, 265; aversion 206
decision-making 61, 101, 141, 154, 170, 191, 210, 282
deemed universities (institutions deemed to be universities) 2, 3, 28, 64
Delhi 8, 23, 32, 98, 184, 218, 233, 260, 276
Delors Commission 111
demand-supply (demand and supply) 64, 102, 105, 107
democratic 106, 108
demographic 16, 43, 60, 178, 192, 277; burden 127, 132, 192
differentiated demand 28, 117, 134
disadvantaged 50, 86, 110, 129, 138, 200, 262, 283, 291
disciplinary imbalance 18, 54–58, 276, 278
discrimination 129, 181, 190, 212, 253, 261, 266, 291
disguised unemployment 97, 249
Doctorate(s) (also PhDs) 6, 72, 113, 169, 237–39, 278
Dore, R.M. 74
dowry 171, 181, 193, 287; negative 193, 207
Dréze, J. 135
Duraisamy, P. 2, 177, 253, 266.

earnings (also wages) 177, 196, 203, 249, 253, 257, 258, 265–69, 270, 288; *see also* salaries
economic: class(es) 53, 145, 189, 201, 266; growth 1, 10, 15, 17, 24, 106, 259, 270, 275, 288;
reform(s) 18, 19, 21, 108; status 26, 91, 127, 144, 149, 157, 181, 193, 212, 262
educated unemployment 260; *see also* graduate employment
education loans 7, 139, 161, 168, 200–11, 285
educational aspects 127, 140, 141, 162, 169
educational aspirations 127, 140–41, 156, 162, 169, 183, 192
efficiency 6, 134, 173, 201
egalitarian 199
egalitarianism 153, 172
electrical engineering 6, 54, 103, 147, 170, 237, 278
electronics engineering 3, 9, 41, 54, 121, 125, 137, 153, 163, 189, 266, 282
employability 4, 61, 67, 95, 107, 240, 249, 268, 270, 286
employment: assurance 141, 142, 281; market 260, 263, 271, 286; probability(ies) 169, 252, 260, 261, 265; prospects 100, 140, 156, 162, 169, 210, 276, 281
Engel/Engel function 178, 191
engineering knowledge 100, 101, 114, 271
engineering skills 25, 100, 114
entrance examination 32, 42, 69, 121, 128, 131, 136, 144, 159, 282, 288
equitable access 11, 16, 79, 87, 199, 201, 289, 291
ethnicity 182, 206, 266
evaluation 145, 218, 234–37, 240
examinations 120, 125, 135, 142, 166, 180, 192, 236, 240, 281
excellence 64, 68, 80, 106, 110
excess demand 4, 28, 117, 121, 136
excess supply 6, 70, 76–77, 249, 277
expenditure function 191, 197
externalities 1, 15, 29, 200

faculty: duplicate 6, 75, 278; shortage 6, 70–71, 72
family: background 9, 118, 260, 267; enterprises 68; expenditure 89–94, 173–99; income 90, 118, 129, 186, 190, 205, 215, 262, 285; investment(s) 176, 183, 189, 192, 284; model 191; size

145, 209 (see also sibship); see also household
fee: levels 79, 93, 114, 197, 198, 284; reimbursement 8, 26, 88, 110, 290; waivers 54, 197, 201, 214, 283
field work 236, 247
financial assistance 138, 145, 161, 186, 200–16, 284
financing 4, 79–89; see also funding
forecast(s) 98, 101, 291
foreign companies 257, 259
free choice 144, 148, 171, 287
funding 4, 6, 8, 11, 43, 63, 79, 80–89, 198, 200–16, 218, 279, 283; see also financing

GDP deflators 114
gender 64, 109, 125, 156; bias 92, 154, 180, 181, 182, 190; differences 149, 170, 175, 189, 253, 282
general higher education 27, 87, 89, 117, 137, 175, 185, 205, 249, 278
geographic(al) 8, 43, 44, 145, 181, 278
geographic concentration 43
Germany 180
global: economic slowdown 21, 38, 41; economy 1, 18, 231, 233, 245–46; markets 21, 25, 64, 221, 232; university rankings 6, 63, 68, 217
globalisation 2, 5, 21, 26, 102
governance 8, 17, 28, 42, 107, 218, 219
government failure 134
government-aided (private) 1, 8, 64, 68, 93, 134, 159, 166, 176, 218, 223, 238
graduate employment 259, 261–64, 270, 286; see also graduate unemployment
graduate unemployment 4, 35, 97, 259, 272
Greece 178, 179
Griliches, Z. 1
gross domestic product 81, 183, 261; see also national income
group work 228, 236, 247
Gujarati, D.N. 126, 199

heteroscedasticity 199
hidden funder 174, 198
Higher Education Council of India 112

Hopcroft, H.L. 182
hostel(s) 117, 128, 186, 258, 284
household: characteristics 127, 129, 164; cost 137–38, 160, 168, 210; expenditure 89, 104; (expenditure) quintiles 22, 53, 180, 94, 278; income 125, 157, 164, 177, 178, 182, 191, 244, 260, 267; see also family
Houthakker, H.S. 178
human capital 1, 4, 10, 15, 105, 118, 173, 176, 192, 265, 288; specialised 1, 4, 16, 105; specific 94
human resources 15, 102, 256, 271
humanities 18, 30, 49, 89, 90, 111, 154, 161, 172, 227, 278, 291, 292

income elasticity 174, 178, 179, 180, 185
Indian Institute of Technology 19, 65, 114, 227, 239; see also IIT
individual attributes/characteristics 127, 128, 156, 163
industrial production 33, 35, 36
inequality 18, 43, 53, 62, 92, 103, 137, 200, 278; by caste 50; by gender 48, 61, 278
information technology (IT) 4, 17, 24, 64, 125, 202, 225, 254, 278
infrastructure 24, 65, 108, 135, 177, 217, 240, 254, 258, 290
instructional practice(s) 235
intake 19, 23, 32–34, 36, 44, 47, 58, 76, 85, 109, 195, 290
interdisciplinary 229
IT coolies 97
IT craze 55, 57

James, E. 28, 117, 265
Japan 76, 113, 178
job: market 72, 103, 105, 134, 141, 147, 155, 169, 184, 252, 261, 263, 268, 292; offer(s) 10, 140, 146, 162, 169, 252, 256, 257, 272, 288; prospects 119, 162, 184
joint entrance examination (JEE) 31, 41
Jorgenson, D.W. 1

Kapur, D. 28, 51, 75
Karnataka 9, 36, 43, 44, 62, 84, 98, 181, 241
Kasturirangan, K. 25, 60

Kerala 28, 36, 52, 84, 180
Kingdon, G.G. 92, 134, 180
Kirp, D.L. 29
knowledge: development 59, 231; economy 15, 17, 24, 25, 67, 98, 249; market(s) 25; production 15, 111, 292; society 4, 10, 16, 88, 237, 288
Kothari, V.N. 4

laboratories 2, 9, 107, 137, 140, 168, 227, 235, 258, 282
labour market 5, 9, 26, 42, 64, 76, 94, 100, 103, 120, 140, 158, 171, 283, 286; imbalance 172, 289; information 76, 105, 106, 279
learning environment 110, 119, 290
loanees 206, 211
location of the school 124, 135, 143, 166, 210
logit 119, 185, 201, 208, 214, 260
low income 129, 157, 160, 177, 184, 202, 211
Loyalka, P. 26, 68, 74, 217, 229
luxury good 184

Machlup, F. 1
Maharashtra 7, 28, 43, 84, 98, 181, 233, 276
making money 28, 110, 290
mal employment 249, 256
Majumdar, T. 173
manpower 2, 20, 41, 76, 95, 105, 113, 253, 271, 279, 292; analysis 271; planning 105, 113, 271, 292; survey 105
manufacturing 60, 97, 156, 277
Marginson, S. 29
market: demand 143, 281; failure 200, 287; imperfections 148, 171, 205; relevance 109, 134, 218; signals 32, 97, 135, 287
marketing 42, 69, 102, 221, 231, 256
markets 64, 94, 108, 120, 221, 231
marriage 26, 171, 193, 241, 287
McMahon, W.W. 15, 183, 191
mechanical engineering 41, 54, 98, 103, 137, 237, 254, 266
medicine 30, 48, 60, 89, 155, 185, 275, 292
medium of instruction 121, 127, 133, 134, 142, 159, 166, 192, 210, 261, 268
Mehrotra, S. 70, 181
meritocratic 51

middle class 18, 26, 50, 108; new 18, 26, 108
middlemen 42, 69
migration 47, 132
Mincerian 2, 250, 265, 267
minorities 52
mismatches 6, 18, 64, 95, 113, 279, 292
mother's education 131, 142, 143, 158, 165, 183, 197, 280
multidisciplinary 111, 291

Nalla Gounden, A.M. 2, 180, 181
national assessment 109, 223, 290
National Board of Accreditation 63, 67, 109, 217; see also NBA
National Education Policy 11, 16, 60, 78, 111, 291
national income 80, 88; see also gross domestic product
National Institute of Ranking Framework (NIRF) 6, 63, 69, 217, 279
National Institute of Technology (NIT(s)) 19, 66, 70, 80, 96, 113, 120, 136, 197, 231, 276
National Research Foundation (NRF) 112
nativity 158, 165, 284; see also residential status
negative dowry 193, 207
new middle class 18, 26, 108
non-engineering 96, 102, 158, 256, 267, 290
normal good 180
not-for-profit institutions 3

occupancy rate 36, 58
OECD 113, 154, 173, 199
on-campus recruitment see campus recruitment
opportunity cost 138, 161, 169
Other Backward Classes (OBCs) 52, 121, 149, 190, 262, 208, 280

paid work 233, 284
Panchamukhi, P.R. 180, 181, 260, 267
parents'(al): aspirations 77; bias 92; education 118, 131, 149, 157, 164, 182, 127, 132, 149, 183, 205; investment 176, 183; occupation 131, 144, 157, 174, 192, 208, 260, 267, 286; preferences 144, 185; pressures 144

participation 3, 22, 31, 49, 53, 61, 86, 128, 156, 219, 240, 277
part-time: faculty 239; job (work) 127, 138, 139, 160, 162, 169, 192, 203, 214, 284
pedagogy(ical) 78, 99, 107, 140, 235, 270
philanthropy(ic) 3, 28, 110, 277, 287, 290
placement 64, 95, 105, 150, 162, 254; record 253, 254, 272
polytechnics 2, 20, 21, 78, 80
postgraduate 20, 40, 59, 78, 112, 175, 184, 217, 225, 239, 278
preferences 6, 102, 144, 181, 259, 268, 276; families' 185, 198, 205; students' 102
preferential treatment 159, 207
prestige 148, 264; *see also* reputation
private: colleges 2, 11, 44, 75, 89, 98, 117, 125, 148, 202, 271, 276; expenditure 22, 174, 199; schooling 184; universities 3, 8, 64, 117, 253, 254, 267, 276
probit 10, 118, 126, 141, 155, 185, 276
professional: education 1, 15, 36, 49, 132, 137, 184, 200, 205; knowledge 240; skills 100, 102, 271
profit-making 3, 100, 110, 290
progressive closure 38, 62, 77
pro-male bias 180, 181, 198, 284
Psacharopoulos, G. 178, 179, 182, 200, 265
public: administration 256; expenditure 20, 63, 80, 84, 107, 178, 277; finance(ing) 4, 11, 80, 201, 276, 289; good 29, 173, 200, 277; institutions (of higher education) 38, 47, 69, 82, 92, 111, 114, 117, 142, 258, 281; policy 2, 79, 87, 106, 176, 198, 201, 252, 270, 278, 283, 288–92; sector 3, 28, 61, 143, 260, 277, 287; subsidies 79, 110, 290, 291; subsidization 199, 291; universities 61, 239, 253

QS rankings 65, 68, 69
quality of education 5, 63, 64, 70, 85, 92, 106, 166, 219, 223, 241, 261, 285

race 118, 154, 178, 182
Radhakrishnan Commission 233

Rao, U.R. 44, 96, 109
Rao, V.K.R.V. 11
rate of return (returns to education) 2, 4, 24, 177, 192, 249, 266
recruitment policy 108, 289
regional: concentration ratio 44, 46, 47, 48, 62; imbalance 6, 19, 36, 43, 44; language 134, 263
regulation 28, 63, 78, 88, 111, 112
religion 10, 18, 61, 178, 184, 190, 284
reputation 25, 119, 141, 205, 264, 268, 281
research: degree(s) 71, 72, 237, 239; and development 25, 59, 67, 114; environment 74, 78, 110; evidence 176, 182, 198, 283; institutions 65, 78; orientation 237
reservation(s) (policy) 21, 53, 62, 128, 129, 262, 280
residential status 127, 132, 194
rich-poor gap 94
rural schools 135, 166
rural-urban (geographic or regional) disparities 22, 43, 61, 92, 134, 166, 178
Russia 5, 172, 229, 276, 288

salaries 10, 20, 72, 103, 105, 251, 258, 259, 266, 269, 279, 290; *see also* earnings; wages
sanctioned intake (strength) 20, 36, 58, 70–71, 76
Sanyal, B.C. 259
Scheduled Castes (SCs) 50, 149, 208, 262, 277
Scheduled Tribes (STs) 50, 121, 129, 149, 262, 277, 284
scholarships 11, 54, 85–88, 111, 138–39, 160, 168, 187, 196, 202–203, 289, 291
school choice 118, 141
Schultz, T.W. 1, 15, 178
science and technology 2, 16, 68, 113, 154, 229
secondary schooling 2, 16, 68, 113, 154, 229
self-employed 212
self-financing (colleges) 2, 8, 28, 41, 68, 74, 108, 114, 202, 238, 277
self-regulation 79
semester 21, 140, 227, 240, 252, 285; -end examinations 2, 36–37
service sector(s) 24, 25, 61, 277
shortage of faculty 70–71

siblings 32, 127, 142, 183, 209, 280
sibship 183
size of the household 132, 183, 192
skilled workers 95, 131, 144
social: capital 131, 144, 262; category 128, 156, 193, 208, 215, 285; skills 101, 102; status 21, 148, 156, 197, 241; stratification 29, 199
socialisation 154
socioeconomic 21, 91, 182, 186
software 22, 55, 102
Solow, R.M. 1
Spence, M.J. 260
state government(s) 20, 28, 82, 88, 108, 109, 110, 117, 120, 166, 290
state-aided (private-aided) 11, 64, 79, 93, 110, 126, 134, 159, 166, 175, 218, 238, 276; see also government-aided
stratification 29, 129, 199
student loans see education loans
student-faculty ratio 72
students' perceptions 10, 217–48, 276
sub-disciplines 54
Subramanian, A. 51, 102, 180

Tamil Nadu 8, 28, 36, 45, 84, 98, 181, 233, 276
teachers 20, 59, 70, 74, 93, 106, 136, 166, 218, 235, 237, 240, 278
teaching: methods 218, 236, 247; practices 234–35; strategies 235
technical: knowledge 101, 235, 264; progress 1
techno coolies 97
technology: modern 94, 194
TEQIP (Technical Education Quality Improvement Project) 76, 83, 110
textbooks 91, 138, 161, 185
Thurow, L.G. 260
time use 233, 234

total factor productivity 1
Training 23, 68, 78, 94, 100, 107, 218, 262; on the job 100, 101
transport 91, 138, 161, 185, 189, 233
Trow, M. 16
tuition fees 89, 93, 185, 189, 197, 204, 211
Tymon, A. 240
type of school (institution) 134, 160, 166, 192, 210

UK (also England) 76, 154, 205, 206, 260, 266
undergraduate education
UNESCO 15, 16, 24, 259
University Grants Commission (UGC) 7, 16, 22, 235, 241, 275
union government 64, 80, 81, 82, 88, 106
unskilled (work/ers) 131, 144, 208
'upper caste institutions' 51
urban schools 135, 166
USA 206, 227

vacancy 70, 71
Varghese, N.V. 68
Voigt, K. 144
voluntary unemployment 253

wages 17, 20, 60, 64, 97, 101, 148, 157, 258, 266
welfare state 173, 175
well-being 15, 173
Weisbrod, B.A. 28
widening 61, 77, 175, 190, 277; access 16; inequalities 81
Winberg, C. 94
Wolf, F. 173
Working, H. 178
World Bank 25, 31, 70, 110, 200

Ziderman, A. 200
Zimmermann, I. 180